Land

of the

Eagle

a novel by

Harry F. Casey

A *Scribe* Book

LAND OF THE EAGLE

A *Scribe* Book

Published by
Scribe Publishing
PO Box 913, King City, CA 93930

ISBN 0-9659184-0-8

Library of Congress Catalog Number 97-92254

For Peggy, my wife, best friend
and partner in all things,
most particularly in creating this story

The following verses by an anonymous author may be heard to this day
wherever Irish music is played and rebel songs are sung.

DEAR OLD SKIBBEREEN

Oh, father dear, I oft' times hear you speak of Erin's Isle,
Her lofty scenes and valleys green, her mountains rude and wide,
They say it is a lovely land, wherein a prince might dwell,
And why did you abandon it? The reason to me tell.

My son, I loved my native land
with energy and pride,
'Till the blight came over all my
crops—my sheep and cattle died.
The rent and taxes were to pay, I could
not them redeem,
And that's the cruel reason that I left
old Skibbereen.

Your mother, too, God rest her soul,
fell on the snowy ground.
She fainted in her anguish seeing the
desolation 'round.
She never rose, but passed away from
life to mortal dream,
And found a quiet grave, my boy, in
the Abby near Skibbereen.

Oh, well do I remember the bleak December day
The landlord and the sheriff came to drive us all away.
They set my roof on fire with their cursed English spleen,
And that's another reason why I left old Skibbereen.

And you were only two years old and feeble was your frame,
I could not leave you with my friends, you bore your father's name.
I wrapped you in my cota mor, at the dead of night unseen,
I heaved a sigh and said goodbye to dear old Skibbereen.

It's well I do remember the year of forty-eight
When I arose with Erin's boys to battle against my fate.
I was hunted through the mountains, a traitor to the queen,
And that's another reason why I left old Skibbereen.

Oh, father dear, the day will come when vengeance loud will call,
And we will rise with Erin's boys and rally one and all.
I'll be the man to lead the van beneath the flag of green,
And loud and high, we'll raise the cry, Revenge for Skibbereen

What a legacy! Such a tragedy!
Thousands are saying goodbye
The Land of the Eagle is calling
as they bid the green island goodbye

Chorus from *The Green Island*

ACKNOWLEDGMENTS

This is fiction in a historical setting and the main characters are the product of the author's imagination, but there are some names of persons who actually lived in the times sprinkled around, like salt and pepper, to flavor the story.

For encouragement and advice, I am grateful to my friend, Otis Carney, best-selling author. And for a boost along the way, I am indebted to Richard Wheeler and Dale Walker, award-winning western novelists, and to my exacting editor, Ann Fisher.

For the scenes in Ireland, I received guidance from Pat Cleary, historian of Skibbereen, County Cork, Ireland, where I visited to check on my own Irish roots. I also thank Tom Carey, librarian at the Irish Cultural Center in San Francisco, for directing me to a plethora of books on Irish history. For information on the potato famine, in which a million and a half Irish people starved to death, I relied on *The Great Hunger*, the definitive work of Cecil Woodham Smith, and on *This Great Calamity*, which details the famine years of 1845 to 1852, by Christine Kinealy. I also studied diaries and first person accounts of famine times and the "coffin ships," and the special publications of Skibbereen's newspaper, *The Southern Star*.

My knowledge of the history of Southern Monterey County has firm grounding in the history of my own ancestors, in the area from 1857, and in my half century as a reporter and then editor and publisher of *The King City Rustler*. Diaries, such as that of Francis Sylvester, postmaster at Jolon in 1861, and various biographies, particularly of pioneers of San Juan Bautista from 1850 through 1880, were of great help. I am indebted to Robert Johnson, former history professor at Hartnell, who compiled a history of Monterey County prior to 1881, to Mary Beth Orser for her history of Soledad, and to South County Newspapers for continued access to the files of *The King*

City Rustler, Soledad Bee and *Gonzales Tribune*. I delved into stacks of research papers of my mother, the late Tid Casey, who had an avid interest in California history, and I studied histories of Bancroft and Caughey.

I am particularly grateful to Elmer Eade of King City, whose memory of early-day farming techniques was invaluable. And I thank the following for assistance in many ways: Liz Cecchi-Ewing and the staff at King City library, Martin Weybret, Fred Weybret, Fran Petersen, Al Oliveira, Ed Fischer, Dan Hayes, Carol Bunte Brown, K.L Eade, Michael Barbree, John Eade, Ernest Gnesa, Patricia Stephens, Margaret Jacobson, Gerri Bolles and Ruth Ann Sonniksen of Monterey County Supervisor Tom Perkin's office, Meg Weldon and Joy Hey of Monterey County's Agricultural and Rural Life Museum in King City, Donna Hansen, Jeff Schmidt, Bill O'Keefe, Richard Nample, Vic Butt, Romona Bender, Keith Brown, Bobby Miller, R.M. Hall, Chuck Hoonan, Dr. Robert Hostetter, Dr. Duane Hyde, my daughters-in-law, Sharon Jane Casey and Holly Casey, my daughters, Sharon Ruth Casey and Patty Griffin, and my sons, Richard and Bill Casey.

– Harry F. Casey

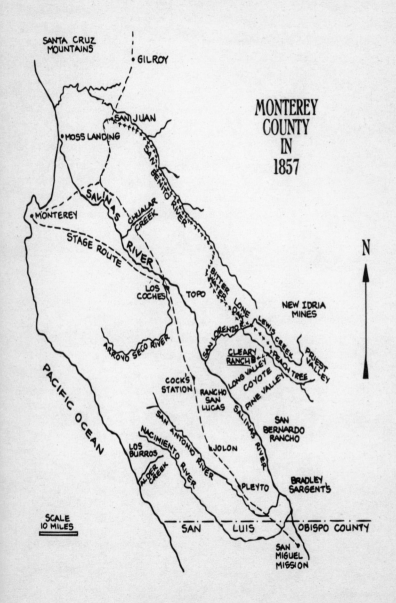

SANTA CRUZ
MOUNTAINS

• GILROY

SAN JUAN

• MOSS LANDING

SAN
BENITO RIVER

SALINAS

• MONTEREY

CHUALAR
CREEK

STAGE ROUTE

RIVER

MONTEREY
COUNTY
IN
1857

N

LOS
COCHES

TOPO

BITTER
WATER

LONE
OAK

NEW IDRIA
MINES

ARROYO SECO RIVER

SAN LORENZO

LEWIS CREEK

CLEARY
RANCH

PEACH TREE

PRIEST
VALLEY

COCK'S
STATION

RANCHO
SAN
LUCAS

LONG VALLEY

COYOTE

PINE VALLEY

SALINAS RIVER

SAN
BERNARDO
RANCHO

PACIFIC OCEAN

SAN ANTONIO RIVER

NACIMIENTO RIVER

LOS
BURROS

ALDER CREEK

JOLON

PLEYTO

BRADLEY
SARGENT'S

SCALE
10 MILES

SAN   LUIS   OBISPO COUNTY

SAN
MIGUEL
MISSION

CHAPTER ONE

"**H**AVE A CARE THERE, DAMN YOU! Those are children, not chickens!"

Jeremiah Cleary's voice rang out above the angry mutterings of the crowd of people watching two red-coated soldiers chase four crying children from the tiny cottage.

"Hurry up about it," an officer on horseback shouted.

"Damn you,- Bradshaw. She's widowed but a month," Jeremiah yelled to the landlord's agent. "Have you no pity?" He was frustrated in the face of British guns.

"The rent is overdue." Bradshaw answered, looking around for the speaker from atop his horse in the center of the yard. "The law is the law."

"British law, not Irish." Jeremiah muttered through gritted teeth.

Jeremiah Cleary, his brother Matthew, their friends, John and James Hurley, and most of the neighbors had gathered when the landlord sent the law that October day of 1847 to evict the Widow Leary from her tiny cottage near Skibbereen in County Cork, Ireland. But they all stood by helplessly with clenched fists, faces red with anger, shouting impotent threats as two soldiers lifted the struggling woman through the doorway and threw her to the hard ground and another carried a squirming, screaming child under each arm and dumped them in the yard atop their wailing mother.

Other soldiers threw the family's pitiful possessions into a heap by the cottage door—a table, two broken chairs, a mattress spilling shuck, some tattered blankets and cracked crockery. Still others placed a ladder against the thatch and carried an axe up to the center pole.

The pole splintered and gave way with a loud "crack," like a shot from a gun.

As it dropped, all eyes were on the falling roof. At that moment John Hurley broke away from his friends, threw off restraining hands and made a dash toward Bradshaw. With an animal-like roar of rage, Hurley grabbed the huge man by the leg and twisted. The frightened horse neighed, lunged sideways and reared. As the rider fought for control of the animal, Hurley gave a savage pull and Bradshaw tumbled to the ground, his head hitting the hard-packed earth with a thud as loud as the cracking center pole.

The landlord's agent lay still.

For a few seconds there was no sound. All stood still, mouths agape. The soldiers were shocked that there would be any resistance. And the others, the starving, defeated people, were surprised by such violent action by one of their own. They all looked at Bradshaw, his body crumpled, twisted, so still on the ground beneath the hooves of his snorting horse.

Hurley looked there, too, then started to bend over to see to the injured agent. "My God, is he dead?" Hurley cried.

"Run, John, run," Jeremiah yelled. Others joined in, "Run, man, run for your life."

Hurley sprang into action, his legs pumping as he cleared the yard, sprinted for the rock wall by the road and disappeared into the tangle of trees and furze bushes.

The yard became a mass of confusion as the British officer roared, "Get him! After him, men!" The foot soldiers leaped the wall, crashing through the hedges in confusion. The officer whipped his horse to make him take the wall, but the horse balked and the rider was flung over into the stickery furze. He rose cursing, untangling himself as Jeremiah grabbed the horse's reins and pulled each time the man attempted to mount. "Damn you, you fool! Let go," the officer cried.

"Just trying to help, your honour," Jeremiah said, tugging at his forelock, but stepping in front of the prancing horse.

It took long moments for the other horsemen to get themselves sorted out from the crowd and savagely sawing on the reins, pull their horses around. They left the roadside in a clatter of shod hooves on the cobbles. When the sound died out in the distance, all was silent again. Even the widow woman had stopped wailing and sat in the dirt with her children until neighbors took them away. Bradshaw still lay in an inert heap on the ground, but no one went near him.

The crowd of people quietly slipped away.

Jeremiah and Matthew Cleary climbed Knockauneen Hill toward their own home in Coolnagurrane, a townland of Skibbereen. The path took them by several small cottages, some roofless, deserted—"knocked" in evictions the same as the one they'd just witnessed. On every side the small fields and gardens showed the ravages of the potato blight.

Jeremiah Cleary was twenty-one years old and Matthew had just turned nineteen. The brothers were six feet tall, but so emaciated that their ragged coats of gray frieze cloth hung loosely on their big, bony frames. Their lank legs were covered to the knee by britches, but they wore no stockings and their feet were bare. Their hats, the crowns crushed, the brims hanging limply, covered heads of unruly, thick black hair.

Matthew's blue eyes sparkled with a touch of humor, although the skin of his face was stretched tightly and shone with the pallor of near-starvation. Jeremiah's eyes were brown and serious, often brooding, but there were crinkles at the corners, and his mouth hinted he might smile, someday, if there'd be anything in his life to smile about.

The brothers stopped to catch their breath. Their starved bodies tired easily. Matthew slumped down on a rock and asked, "Was Bradshaw dead?"

"Won't matter," Jeremiah answered. "They'll hang John if they catch him, the bastards. Just for daring to lift a hand." God, how he hated the British. Jeremiah had been a hedgemaster, teaching children in the Cleary cottage because their parents mistrusted the new Protestant-run national schools. Once such schools had been held in secret, in the woods, in cow sheds, under the hedges, when it was unlawful to educate Irish children. Jeremiah himself was a product of such a school. He knew of the former glories of Ireland, but he suffered the life of her people's debasement from centuries of British oppression. It galled him, grated on his soul.

"You'd better watch yourself, too, Jerry," Matthew advised. "That officer didn't care much for your help with his horse. He'll be remembering you."

"Aye," Jeremiah agreed. He'd been thinking that same thing. He knew of people thrown in British jails for doing far less. Perhaps he should go away somewhere. Canada, as so many others did? No, that was still British. America? The thought wasn't a new one. Jeremiah rose to his feet and gave a hand up to Matthew. They trudged on up the path.

With each step the path led them around ruined potato beds and Jeremiah could almost smell again that awful, foul, disgusting stench that had risen from the plantings and covered their world like a fog. He and his brothers had rushed to the fields with their father and frantically dug with their spades. Bed after bed had turned up mushy, repulsive, rotten potatoes. The day before the air had been pure and clean, the potatoes growing lush and full in their plots.

It had been a happy time because soon the *pratie* barrel would be filled and that meant full bellies again after nearly three years of famine. They'd eat large firm *praties*, boiled and peeled and dipped in warm salt water and drink cold buttermilk from the crock. There'd be company in the cottage again and laughter, a fiddle player and some dancing.

Instead there was that terrible smell. And Da and the rest of the family, the neighbors in every field, stood in silent despair, the anguish on their faces a pitiable thing. They were stunned. Unable to believe this terrible disaster had happened again. At first there was that impossible quiet. Then through the fog-like smell voices were heard.

"What happened?"

"Did God bring the blight again to punish us?"

"What will we do?"

"Oh, my God, have mercy. We'll starve."

Jeremiah stopped walking, squeezed his eyes shut and willed the memory to leave him. He looked back down the hill toward Skibbereen, the Ilen River in the distance rolling sweetly toward the sea, and the green hills beyond. How could a land so beautiful be so cruel, he wondered. And then the idea returned. He'd leave. He had to. There was nothing for him here except danger and starvation. With each faltering step up the path, Jeremiah's resolve hardened. It was a terrible thought to leave his mother and father, his brothers, his friends and all he loved. But he'd do it. Perhaps with a job in America he could earn enough money to send some home to save the family.

Already death had struck the Cleary household. Jeremiah and Matthew had helped their older brother, Little Liam, build a coffin large enough to hold three children. The image of his dying brother, Timothy, floated into Jeremiah's mind. He saw the pitiful two-year old boy, too hungry and sick to even cry, just big, staring eyes sunken back into their sockets. And he saw both his little sisters, Nora and Mary, too weak to fight the fever, one dying in their mother's arms, the other in his.

While their father, Liam, simply sat and watched and their mother, Ellen, was too anguished even to keen, the neighbors gathered and their keening was more than Jeremiah could stand. "The devil take that screeching," he complained to Little Liam. "It's bad enough to be bearing the loss without them wailing like *banshees*."

"It's their way, Jerry. You know that. They share our grief. It may be helping mother."

"Aye," he said, blessing himself. "*Ta said ar shli ha firnne.* They are gone to their eternal reward."

5

They had carried the coffin to Abbystrewery, where Father Brendan Hayes said the prayers over the grave. He couldn't keep up with the funeral masses as death was finding its way into so many cottages. These thoughts kept pace with Jeremiah's progress up Knockauneen Hill as he and Matthew stopped often to rest. He was so quiet that Matthew asked, "What's troubling you, Jerry?"

But Jeremiah just frowned and shook his head, trying to form in his mind the words he'd use to tell his parents he was leaving for America.

The brothers arrived home to find their mother and father in the middle of an ominous discussion. "I'll not be giving up this farm," Liam said adamantly. "My grandfather farmed this holding and his before him. Our life is in this earth." He set his jaw in the first show of spirit his wife had seen since the children died. "We'll not be going to the workhouse. And I'll not put my family on the road."

A soup kitchen had been established in Skibbereen at the steam mill, but it was only for the destitute. Those who had property, even year-to-year-leases such as the Clearys, were not eligible for free soup.

"But what will we do? This is the last of the meal," Ellen said as she placed two meager cakes on the pan over the peat fire. "And the rent is soon due again, Liam. How will that be paid?"

Liam sank onto a stool at the table, head in his hands, the momentary spark gone from him. He'd once mustered the courage to ask Gort, the landlord's agent, for a delay until there was enough sun for the wheat crop to ripen, or until the sow farrowed again, or the cow dropped a calf. But "No!" was the brusque answer. "If you don't want the place, Cleary, there's others that do." Liam knew he hadn't the courage to ask again. To pay the rent they'd sold the last of their milk cows.

The Clearys had watched with their neighbors, their mouths set in bitter lines, as the sacks of wheat, the pigs and calves and sheep were taken off toward Cork to the ships loading for

England, the procession protected by red-coated soldiers as it passed down lanes lined with pleading, famished people, along roads clogged by the homeless ones.

Liam looked up helplessly and Ellen came to him and placed her hand on his shoulder. "Take the spinning wheel," she said. "It will bring good money. I'll not be needing it, Liam, the sheep gone these two years now."

Jeremiah and Matthew stood in the doorway, looking from one parent to another. Jeremiah broke the silence, "It grieves me mightily, but I must be leaving. I'll be off to America."

Ellen's hand flew to her mouth and she gasped. "Oh, Jerry, you can't be meaning it."

Liam slowly took his head from his hands and looked up at his son. "Emigrate, will you?"

"It's the only way," Jeremiah said. "I can earn money in America and send it home so you can buy food and pay the rents to save — "

"And I'll go, too," Matthew interrupted. "Two of us with jobs can send home twice as much."

"Oh, no, not two of my boys," Ellen cried. Liam rose from the table and put his arm around his wife.

"Two less mouths to feed, Da," Matthew insisted. "You'll still have Little Liam to help you and there's not that much left to do here now."

The thought of taking Matthew hadn't occurred to Jeremiah. Sometimes he worried about his younger brother, the scamp whom everybody loved, who'd rather take a drink, sing a song or do a dance than entertain a serious thought. Matthew would be a responsibility, but perhaps it made sense. Two of them could earn twice as much money to send home.

Jeremiah agreed. "It's for the best, Da." He crossed the tiny room to embrace his mother. "When will you go," she asked, sobbing against his chest. She clung to him as he turned back to his father to explain what had just happened at the eviction of Widow Leary.

7

"I'd best be gone right away," he said. "That officer will be asking around and there'll be some informer who'll tell who I am. In a few days he'll be up here asking questions."

Liam bowed his head and finally gave his blessing, but Ellen was grief stricken. After losing her three youngest to the fever she couldn't bear even the thought of saying goodbye forever to two sons. Despite her pleading, they all knew this was the only course and they helped Jeremiah and Matthew load their meager possessions into the donkey cart. "We've no need for it now and nothing left to feed the little brute," Liam said. "Its sale will help buy your passage."

They put in Jeremiah's five precious books and the butter churn, which their mother offered. "With the cow gone, I have no need of it."

That night as word spread from cottage to cottage that the Cleary boys would be leaving for Cork in the morning, neighbors gathered to say farewell. They tried to wake Jeremiah and Matthew off in grand style. It was part of the ritual of leaving, just as if the boys had actually died. But without food, with no tobacco for the short pipes, even with Pat McGurk to wet the waking with a generous contribution from his dwindling hoard of *poteen,* the illegal home-made whiskey that had the kick of an ox, it was a spiritless affair. Noelle O'Shea tried to liven things up with his fiddle, but others were too weak and weary to do the steps.

Among the company were Declan Hurley, his wife, Annie, their son, James and daughters, Catherine and Molly. "Do you think John got away?" Declan Hurley asked Jeremiah.

"If anyone could, it would be John," Jeremiah answered with more confidence than he really had.

"It's best you're leaving, lad," Hurley said. "They'd be making trouble for you because of what you did for John. James told me about the horse and we're thanking you."

Jeremiah nodded to the Hurley family sitting on the hob by the fireplace. He let the talk swirl around him, everyone had an opinion on "Amerikay" or advice on what the Cleary boys should do. But Jeremiah's eyes kept straying back to Molly Hurley, whom he remembered as one of the brightest students of his hedge school, but all arms and legs and freckles. Now she was nearly sixteen and blooming, despite her hunger. Her thick, curly black hair and sparkling blue eyes drew his approving attention. His eyes locked onto hers and she smiled. The thought occurred to Jeremiah that he wished he would still be around when she became a woman. But the smile she gave him was a wan, sad one, something in it said she, too, was sorry he was leaving.

Jeremiah's thoughts went back to days before the famine on a St. Patrick's night when the Cleary house, larger than most, was packed with friends just like this night, but it was, oh, so different. The talk, encouraged by the *poteen*, the laughter and the singing and dancing to lively fiddle tunes filled it to bursting. When they called for the *shanachie*, the story teller, Jeremiah had obliged with the legend of St. Brendan of Kerry, the first to discover America with his boatload of Irish monks. They all took this with a grain of salt, Jeremiah included, but it was a good tale and just might be true.

Would it ever be like that here again?

His eyes returned to Molly Hurley. Aye, if he stayed on perhaps one day he'd court her and he saw in her eyes just a hint that she'd let him. But it wasn't to be. He was leaving at dawn.

It was McGurk's wife, Sheila, who brought him back to reality as she started to *caoine* in her high voice. "Fine boys, they are," she wailed. "Them that's the wonder of their mother's eyes. So strong, they are, and helping their father in the fields, and so kind to their mother." Her voice rose to a higher pitch. "And now they'll be leaving and no more will they gladden this cottage. No more will their family be seeing them, no more will they be a joy to their parents and to their many friends."

Now other voices joined in, the women keening in unison, "Oh, they'll be missed. Gone forever, they'll be. God protect them in a foreign land. God grant them health. God give them strength. God console their grieving parents. Bless them, oh

Lord, these wonderful boys who go so far away and will never again see their homes — ”

As the sun came up over Coolnagurrane, Jeremiah and Matthew shook hands with all the men, embraced the women, received pats on the back and words of encouragement. *"Fod sol agot,"* they said. "Long life to you, Jerry." "Good luck, God bless you, Matt." *"Go n-eiri an bothar teat,"* they said. "Have a safe trip."

Little Liam embraced each of his brothers, but couldn't speak. Their father put both his hands on their shoulders, each in turn, and gave them a long look. He shook hands with Jeremiah, stern in his attempt to control himself. "Be caring for your brother, now," he said. "Matt will need looking after." Jeremiah nodded and the elder Cleary turned away.

But their mother desperately clutched each of them. She couldn't let go. She hugged them, kissed them and cried as if her very soul was being wrenched from her breast. "My boys, my boys," she sobbed. "And I'll never be seeing you again."

Jeremiah and Matthew embraced their mother one last time, choking back their own tears. Then, with breaking hearts, they prodded the donkey and walked away without once looking back.

CHAPTER TWO

"**D**AMN YOUR SOULS!" Jeremiah shook his fist at the rapidly departing coach. "You cruel-hearted bastards. *Mullacht De Ort*," he shouted, "the curse of God on you!"

The coach and four had nearly run them down. The pounding hoofs of the horses and the rolling wheels of the elegant coach splattered muddy water from the morning rains over them and the other wretched, pitiful travelers who lined the road to Cork City. Well-fed, well-dressed passengers peered out, curious but unconcerned, at the miserable scene.

"Save your breath, Brother. Better to use it on this damn ass. *Diabhal geann*," Matthew exploded, trying to goad the reluctant donkey back onto the road.

"Calling on the devil won't be helping, either, Matt," Jeremiah said. "The little brute has the hunger in him as we do. He can't be going faster."

Their slow pace matched that of other tattered travelers making their way to Cork City, many hunched over with sacks on their shoulders or children in their arms. A few led ponies or donkeys, which were also pulling carts. And some had hitched themselves to the carts or pulled slidecars, once used to haul peat from the bogs, which slid on metal runners across the mud. They trudged along with a purpose, to reach Cork and find passage to America, to escape the famine ravaging Ireland.

"We'll never get to Cork at this pace," Matthew complained. He'd had no sleep and his head throbbed from the effects of McGurk's *poteen*.

"We'll get there, Matt. And a sound ship we'll find to take us out of this," Jeremiah said, waving his hand toward the skeletal forms of a starving family sitting in front of a ruined hut at the entrance to Bandon town.

"A scrap for my baby," the mother implored. "Save my baby." But the baby in her arms was already dead.

"Just look at those people!" Jeremiah raised his eyes to the heavens and cried, "God, how do you allow this?"

When darkness came the brothers rolled up together in their one thin blanket in the shelter of a ruined, roofless cottage. The donkey, tethered to the cart, cropped what grass was left by the side of the road and complained because there wasn't more.

"Hush up, you miserable *bosthoon*," Matthew yelled. "At least you have something for your belly. We have nothing in our guts but the growling."

About midday they reached Cork and joined a river of humanity flowing along the narrow streets toward the docks, the sick and starving mingling with the well-fed. Prosperous businessmen and merchants, hurrying to their stores, jostled the ragged travelers. Hawkers shouted their wares, the virtues of the grog shops, lodging places, goods for sale, services to perform.

"My God, Matt, look at that." Jeremiah pointed toward the harbor, a forest of masts, ships tied to the docks and anchored in the river, their bare spars gleaming like bones in the sunlight. "How will we be finding the right ship in this mess?" They were standing in awe at Merchants Quay when a ship's agent approached them.

"Two pounds ten for passage on the Sir Willard Pottinger! You'll be safe and sound. Fresh water all the way. You'll be fed well and there's ample space for all. She's a good clean ship, or my name isn't Michael Maloney."

Jeremiah asked, "And where is it headed, this Sir Pottinger ship?"

"Why Boston, my lad, the jewel of cities in Amerikay, where you'll be finding gold in the streets bigger than the *praties*. Jobs there are for all."

The Cleary brothers conferred. The price was as cheap as any they'd heard about and the ship would leave right off.

"You'll never regret it, lads." Maloney said as his greasy fingers counted the money. "In six weeks time you'll be hale and hearty in the land of opportunity. Good luck to you."

We'll need it, Jeremiah thought. The brothers now had barely enough money to buy food for their long journey. Everything they'd sold, the old donkey and cart, Jeremiah's books and the butter churn, had brought them only ten pounds. They'd need a cook pan, some meal for cakes, tea perhaps, some bacon or salt pork, if it could be had, or salted fish. With less than two hours to shop, Jeremiah and Matthew made their way to Patrick Street where they found more hawkers and street vendors competing with the shops.

"Tea! Tea here! The finest variety, steeped but once and that in the parlors of the gentry. You'll not be finding better tea at the price to be taking a good solid hold on your water." The Clearys paid two shillings for a sack of second-hand tea and more of their few remaining coins for two shuck-filled mattresses.

"Vegetables, get your fresh vegetables and *praties*, the last in Ireland!" A hawker grabbed Matthew's arm. "Ward off the scurvy, my lads, be sure you carry vegetables."

But Matthew, shaking him off, turned to a grog shop. "Just a bit to wet our tongues on the trip will discourage the scurvy, sure Jerry," he insisted. But his brother's grip on his shoulder kept him moving along Patrick Street.

"This lot will have to do," Jeremiah said sternly. "Beside, there's a ration given out by the ship. That agent said so."

Carrying their mattresses, with their supplies in sacks clutched over their shoulders, Jeremiah and Matthew produced their precious tickets at the gangway and were permitted to board the *Sir Willard Pottinger*. Soon the deck was

13

crowded amidships with passengers while the authorities searched for stowaways. Then Jeremiah and Matthew, hunched over, found their way below, blinking in the gloom of the steerage. "What is it, these places are made for the likes of the wee people?" Matthew complained as they jostled against others who were trying to squeeze their belongings and their whole families into the six-by-six foot berths, bare wood bordered by slats.

"Room for all he said," Jeremiah grumbled. He looked around, appalled at how many people were trying to cram themselves into steerage. "And I suppose we're to be taking turns to breathe?"

Matthew had an eye for the *colleens,* particularly the buxom one with the saucy smile in the very next berth, and gave her a grin and a wink. "Be watching yourself there," Jeremiah warned.

Matthew frowned at his brother and shrugged his shoulders to the girl, who laughed as if to say, "another time."

"What about privies?" Jeremiah whispered. "Or are they thinking we're not having need for them?"

"I dare say, old boy." Matthew grinned and replied in his best English accent. "How crude of you. The bloody Brits don't do that sort of thing themselves, don't you know? And even if they did, it would never stink, of course."

They located the privies on the forward deck, two makeshift structures for more than four hundred men and women. The Clearys heard the shocked expressions of the females, particularly the young girls, when they realized they'd have to attend to private matters within sight of everyone, including the ribald sailors.

They found a group of passengers gathered around a tiny fire pit on the foredeck. "How can we all be fitting our pots and pans on that little thing?" they asked each other.

"Don't be worrying. Just fill your belly with this tasty morsel," a man said with a bitter laugh, as he plucked weevils from the hard ship's biscuit. "I'm not knowing if it's a bug or one of my teeth."

"Is that what they feed us?" a mother of four asked, a frown of dismay on her care-worn face.

"Oh, aye, it is. But there's wonderful variety," was the answer. "One day you'll be getting biscuit so hard you have to stomp it to crack the crust and the next day this generous English captain gives us a whole pound of meal. Moldy, of course."

Jeremiah and Matthew, shaking their heads over the agent's lies, went to the crowded railing for a last look at Ireland. Jeremiah's thoughts were of home, his family and Molly Hurley's wan smile. In the dusk the ship was sailing down the River Lee off Cobh, and by nightfall was in the open sea.

* * * * *

The ship rose high on the crest of the wave and plunged into the trough with a crash. The wind shrieked and whistled through the bare spars and the ship's timbers creaked and groaned. Rain pelted the ship and thunder roared. Lightening flashes slashed the black sky, showing the decks awash with foam. The ship pitched and rolled, twisted and churned, buffeted by the fierce Atlantic storm.

"Mercy, Lord. Have mercy." "My God, we'll all drown!" "Holy Mary, Mother of God, save us. Save us!" "Let us out, damn you! Let us out."

But the crescendo of screams and prayers from deep within the belly of the vessel were feeble against the roar of the gale. Wave after wave broke over the bow and poured water into the steerage berths through the locked hatch grills, which kept the passengers captive below decks.

Three weeks out of Cork, at first sign of the storm, the frightened passengers had been herded from the open decks and forced below. "Get down there, go below. Quickly now," the

15

bosun mates ordered. "It's for your own safety." And they'd been locked down there for three days and nights with no food, no water, and no word about the storm that raged above.

It was sopping wet and pitch dark as they prayed and clung to each other, holding tightly to keep from being thrown out of their bunks. A heavy chest broke loose and careened down an aisle, smashing into a woman who'd fallen to the deck. "Stay in your bunks," Jeremiah shouted as he and Matthew threw themselves on the chest to halt its slide and fought to secure it in the dark. They located the injured woman by her screams and as gently as they could, lifted her into a bunk. But there was nothing they could do for her crushed leg.

After four days entombed in the bowls of the Sir Willard Pottinger, the storm abated and the miserable immigrants were allowed back on deck. Jeremiah and Matthew helped carry the dead up the ladder and they were slipped into the ocean with brief ceremony. But little could be done for the many injured as no medical treatment was available. The worst news came as they dried off in the welcome sun. They learned that the ship had been blown off course and to beat her way back would take days. The voyage was extended by at least two weeks.

When it finally reached land, the Sir Willard Pottinger had buried ninety-six passengers at sea, and one hundred twelve were deemed by health authorities too sick with fever, cholera and an assortment of other diseases to land in Boston. The passenger list had recorded four hundred and ten men, women and children in spaces intended for three hundred people.

The Cleary brothers, as emaciated as they were, their clothing in shreds, their eyes sunken into their sockets, were in better condition than most who survived the crossing. When it came their turn for inspection, they straightened their backs and looked fearlessly into the eyes of the officious little doctor with the stick, who pointed it this way or that to settle the fate of each person. One direction meant Boston, the other the dreaded Deer Island.

Jeremiah and Matthew stood on the dock and glowered back at the ship, their ears ringing with the shrieks and anguished cries of parents being separated from their screaming children, and the piteous pleas of wives clutching their husbands. "Have mercy," they cried as the ill were roughly carried off to the immigrant hospital on Deer Island.

The bare bowls of the stinking, foul, storm-shattered privies gleaming on deck were their last sight of the British hell ship. The Cleary brothers turned away and stepped into the chaos of Boston's Commercial Street.

It was crammed with wagons, carriages, horses and people, jostling, pushing, shoving for the advantage of being the first to greet the immigrants with their goods and services. The cries of hawkers, sometimes in Irish with the accent of home, competed with the curses of teamsters and coachmen guiding their vehicles through the crowds.

Each proclaimed the virtues of their various accommodations, one calling out, "I'll find you gentlemen the finest rooms or my name ain't Seamus O'Grady. God preserve your honours, you'll think yourself in heaven after the Sir Willard Pottinger!"

"That wouldn't be hard to do," Jeremiah muttered as they pushed their way through the clamoring throng.

"It's worse even than Cork!" Matthew exclaimed.

"But they do look better fed," Jeremiah noted.

It was getting dark when the Cleary boys finally settled down for the night in one small room of a three-story building, without furniture or light in Paddytown on Broad Street. Some straw on the floor was the extent of the accommodation. The overflowing privies were in the small courtyard below, but few third floor dwellers climbed down and back in the night, which was attested to by the foul mess in the hallways. And there was no light because the windows were boarded shut against the stench. But having breathed the air of the passenger spaces of the Sir Willard Pottinger for two months, neither Matthew nor Jeremiah complained to the landlady.

17

"Ten dollars a month and you'll be paying on time or it's out you go," she shrilled at them. The brothers looked at each other and shook their heads. Matthew tiredly waved his hand.

"We've got to have faith there's more to it than this." Jeremiah, exhausted himself, tried to reassure his brother. "Let's see what the morrow brings."

They sat on the filthy floor, but felt it moving, rocking beneath them with the same motion as the ship. They unwrapped the last of their worm-riddled biscuits. It took concentration to methodically chew and keep from retching. But it was the only way to ease the gnawing in their shrunken, gaseous stomachs. They were so tired, so very bone weary, and sad, not even the sensation of the swaying tenement building could keep them from falling into an exhausted stupor.

Every morning, the Cleary brothers went down to the wharves along Atlantic Avenue and Commercial Street to make themselves available for unloading ships or whatever odd job came their way. At a dollar a day, the wages seemed rich. But the first ten dollars went to pay the rent. As squalid as their accommodations were, they'd not be evicted. A bit of bread, a cheese, the occasional meat pie, sometimes a pint at the end of a hard day, and the money was gone.

And their clothing, what was left of the frieze coats and the knee britches were objects of scorn and ridicule in Boston. "These rags are worn out anyway," Jeremiah said. "There'll be no respect for us if we don't dress respectable."

They parted with two dollars for secondhand, but clean, trousers, shirts and vests, and another dollar each for brogans, which pinched their toes, but were a necessity. Only their battered hats remained as they looked at each other in their new finery.

"And aren't we the grand ones?" Matthew said with a chuckle and a quick dance step that made him grimace with the pinch of his new shoes. Jeremiah nodded and laughed. But whether they spent the day fruitlessly searching for work, or were successful down at the docks, the brothers dreaded returning to their squalid room on Broad Street—and the continual cacophony of people coming and going, the shouts, the fights, children yelling, and the wailing and keening when someone died of the fever or cholera or tuberculosis. Jeremiah kept telling his brother, "There has to be something better than this."

CHAPTER THREE

ONE EARLY MORNING as Jeremiah was waiting at dockside with a group of stevedores, hoping for an unloading job, he was startled by a snorting horse as a freight wagon pulled to a halt just behind him. Jeremiah jumped and whirled around.

A loud voice demanded, "Two men here! Be quick about it."

Jeremiah almost fell between the wagon wheels as he waved his hand and answered before any of the others could speak up. "Me, sir, and my brother."

"Your name?" the man asked, peering down at him.

Jeremiah looked up at the man on the high seat beside the driver. In a dark suit, his derby hat perched above a ruddy, round face framed by white whiskers, he was obviously someone of importance.

"It's Jeremiah Cleary, your honour. I'm strong and a willing worker and so is my brother."

"All right, Jeremiah," the man said with a laugh. "If you'll untangle yourself from my wheels and stop scaring my horses, you're hired." He looked around. "And where's this brother?"

"I'll get him, sir." Jeremiah sprinted to the neighboring wharf where Matthew was still waiting to find any kind of day work. Jeremiah grabbed him by the arm and propelled Matthew down the street. "Matt, we've got a real job!" he exclaimed breathlessly. They ran up to the waiting wagon,

19

which had a sign on the side proclaiming it to be the property of Atlantic Drayage Co.

"This is Matthew Cleary, sir, and we can do anything you'll be needing," Jeremiah said with smiling confidence.

"Jerry and Matt, are you? All right. I'm Mister Charlton. I'll pay one dollar per day. You'll work from can see to can't see. Now climb on and we'll be off."

The brothers jumped into the wagon and turned to grin at each other with satisfaction. At last, a real job.

Each morning at dawn they arrived at the warehouse on Atlantic Street to find the freighter hitched up, the big horses snorting steam, their hooves anxiously stomping, signaling their readiness. The driver gathered the lines in his ham-like hands as Matthew and Jeremiah leaped into the wagon bed and then they'd be off, trotting through the emptiness of the early morning streets on their way to pick up a cargo for the docks. It was hard work, lifting and hauling, stacking boxes, loading and unloading. And when they'd see the end of one cargo stowed, there'd be a mad dash to pick up another, and then another. The sweat poured off of them, but the better food in their bellies gave them new strength. "At last your putting some meat on that skinny carcass," Matthew kidded his brother.

"You've been good workers," Charlton observed as he paid them off at week's end. "Come back Monday morning and we'll see if there might be something a bit more regular around here, if you don't mind mucking the stables."

Jeremiah and Matthew found themselves on the regular payroll of The Atlantic Drayage Company. They shoveled out the stables and barns, and were soon caring for the thirty dray horses, feeding, watering, brushing, and currying. Jeremiah began caring for the harness, cleaning and polishing, and fixing the team bells so they'd give the proper ring when Atlantic Drayage rounded a corner of State Street or pulled up in Haymarket Square. The horses were huge, but gentle brutes, willing and kind. Jeremiah's confidence in handling them grew with each day. He'd lift their big feet, brush the day's street muck from their feathers and scrape their hooves clean. They'd nicker a welcome as he came into each stall with their grain. He had a way with horses and it was noticed by Charlton.

"I can't give you more money, Cleary," Charlton explained. "The owners won't allow it. But I can give you a decent place to stay. You and Matt can put your things into that spare space off the main tack room. You can use the stove to cook your meals. Be careful. We can't suffer a fire here, you know. Anyhow, you can act as night watchmen, too."

But Matthew didn't have his brother's way with horses. He'd handle them all wrong and they'd know it, which made matters worse. Charlton suggested that Matthew assist the blacksmith, working the bellows, fetching tools, and pouring water on the tempering iron, when he wasn't mucking the manure, which was most of the time. He hated it.

"Jerry, it's this I've ciphered," Matthew said, who hadn't ever ciphered a sum in his life. He was sitting on a keg of nails, sipping from a small brown bottle, and had that same mischievous look in his eye that Jeremiah hadn't seen since they'd shared a mug of *poteen* back home.

"The average horse shits a half ton each month," Matthew said, "and we have thirty horses here so it's fifteen tons I shovel each month. We've been here these ten months so I've mucked out one hundred and fifty tons of horse shit." Matthew grinned at his brother. "So there, you're the scholar, Jerry. Am I right?"

"That you are, Brother." Jeremiah laughed. "But all that horse shit has given you a full belly and something to shit yourself, I'm thinking."

Matthew passed the small jug to Jeremiah, who lifted it and offered a toast, "*An Sciobairin!*"

Matthew echoed his brother, "To Skibbereen!"

But Jeremiah felt a wave of uneasiness sweep over him when he thought of home. How were they faring? Should he have stayed? Weren't they the better for his leaving, him and

21

Matthew sending the money orders to Skibbereen for the rent and a bit of meal? And they did have Little Liam to help with the work. But when he thought of himself and Matthew, sitting here with full bellies, with jobs to do and hard money for it, he felt sad, helpless that he couldn't do more.

He wanted to write but when he dipped the pen into the ink the words wouldn't come. How could he write his own cheerful news when all he heard from the latest wave of Irish immigrants was how much more terrible things were in Ireland. How much worse could they get, he wondered. Stories spread as each ship came to rest at the dock and then spewed out its cargo of pitiful refugees. Jeremiah put down his pen. He'd write the letter later. The gloomy tales he'd heard this day were too depressing.

The potato crop had failed again. *"Tha shein ukrosh,* the hunger, is in every house," reported the new arrivals and the dead cart drivers, who were paid by the load, had become so indifferent to their grisly task that they'd sometimes pick up a body before the person had actually died. Jeremiah listened in horror as one immigrant told about a young man dumped into the famine pit at Abbeystrewery.

"His leg was broken by the spade that was covering him with dirt, and so he cried out, you see. And didn't the lad live? And isn't he walking the streets of Skibbereen this very moment with a limp? Sure and cursing the dead cart driver each time he passes by."

This story put Jeremiah in a black mood the whole day. That night after he and Matthew fixed their evening meal by lamplight, Matthew, who wasn't one to brood, tried to make light of the story.

"Ah, sure now, that was probably only old Dooly with a skinfull," he said, laughing. "You'll remember they claimed he had a hollow leg to hold all the porter he guzzled. No wonder he walked with a limp."

Matthew reached for his jug, took a hefty swig, and hobbled across the room in a parody of old Dooly. Jeremiah had to smile at his brother's imitation, but the smile turned to a frown when he saw Matthew take yet another gulp of whiskey.

"You're not having a hollow leg, Matt. Shouldn't you be going easy with that?" Jeremiah was remembering how he'd seen strong drink take hold of so many and addle their wits.

"Easy, is it? Easy, you say. I'll be doing my drinking as I'm wanting," Matthew retorted. "I'll be thanking you to keep your nose in those books of yours and out of my business! It's myself that can be taking care of myself."

"Oh, you can, can you?" Jeremiah could feel an angry heat rising in his neck. "And hasn't it been myself that has been watching over you every breathing minute since we left Coolnagurane?"

Matthew's eyes widened with growing resentment and anger. "Watching, is it? Sure and you've been on my back like ugly on a hump. I'm not even to say hello to the girl on the ship. You're dragging me off to this dump to shovel shit. You're saving my money for me. The only thing you let me do for myself is go to the privy!" Matthew reached for his bottle and tilted his head to take a defiant drink. "You may be my brother, but my keeper you're not!" His eyes brimmed with hot tears.

Jeremiah reached across the table to snatch the bottle away, but struck a lamp. He made a stab with his hand to catch the lamp and overturned the table. The lamp hit the floor and the glass shattered, the flame leaping out and running along the wooden floor.

"Fire!" Jeremiah exclaimed. The brothers stared in shock for a moment at the spreading blaze, as the fire started to lick at the straw on the stable floor. "Quick! Throw your blanket on it," Jeremiah shouted.

Matthew grabbed up his bedclothes to smother the flames. Jeremiah took down a water bucket, dipped it into a horse trough and splashed it on the fire. The flames hissed and died out.

It was over.

The brothers stood there, breathing hard, looking from the charred blanket to the black smudge on the floor and the broken glass of the lantern chimney. Each avoided the other's eyes. They both moved at the same time to right the table and silently replaced the remnants of their meal. When they bumped into each as they were cleaning up, they each said, "Sorry" in unison. But their eyes remained averted.

CHAPTER FOUR

JEREMIAH WALKED AROUND his four-horse team, checking the harness and talking to the big, black Percherons. "Dooly, there, now don't you be shirking your job today, you *sthronsuch*," he spoke to one of the wheelers. "Lazy thing, if you're not after pulling your load, it's Foley that'll be biting you and you'll not relish that, now will you?"

Jeremiah stopped to loosen the britchen on one of the leaders. He had named him O'Farrell, after his own hedgemaster in Ireland. "That's better, eh? Won't be pinching your arse later today, old fellow." He gave a pat to O'Farrell's huge rump and climbed into the wagon seat.

The horses turned their heads to see around their blinkers and acknowledged the morning greeting with soft sounds of their own. "Don't be giving me that *malarkey* now. We've work to do," Jeremiah scolded them. Now that he was a teamster, Jeremiah made three dollars a day and even with the twenty dollar postal order going to Skibbereen each month, he and Matthew were saving money.

He let off the brake and shook out his lines. He spoke to his team in Irish and the wagon rolled out of the shed. The clip-clop of their shod hooves marked out an early morning rhythm on the cobblestones and echoed through the quiet streets. As Jeremiah turned into Hanover Street on his way to load the first cargo of the day at Quincy Market, he thought about his good fortune. There weren't many jobs for Irishmen in Boston. The signs on the windows of businesses seeking help usually read: "No Irish Need Apply."

Jeremiah maneuvered his team around an open ditch where laborers were installing a new sewer line. Jeremiah nodded a greeting to the men as he passed and suddenly realized he was looking down into a familiar face. "John Hurley!" he shouted. "Is it yourself?"

Hurley's sturdy body, stripped to the waist, immediately straightened up. He brushed a shock of black hair from his forehead. "That it is and can I be believing my very own eyes? Is it Jerry Cleary sitting up there all high and mighty?" Hurley shook his head, grinning, wiping the sweat from his brow with the back of his hand.

Jeremiah stomped on the brake, wrapped the lines around the handle and jumped to the ground. "And I thought you a dead man, or in a British gaol," he cried as he and Hurley hugged and pounded each other on the back.

"Hey, you there! You, the driver of that wagon," the foreman yelled. "Get out of my ditch and be leaving my workmen to their job."

Jeremiah climbed back up on his wagon, shouting to his childhood friend, "John, when the work is finished for today, find me at Atlantic Drayage." Hurley nodded and waved. The foreman glared after Jeremiah as he pulled away.

The Cleary brothers were waiting for John Hurley when he came around at dusk. The three men sat in the little tack room off the stable and Matthew offered his jug of E.C. Booze's Old Cabin Whiskey. John took a swig and passed it back. Jeremiah waved it away. He was too anxious to hear the news.

"How did you do it?" he asked. "How did you keep away from them? The last I saw of you was your tail going over the rocks by the side of the lane. And them chasing you on their horses, jumping the fences and shouting the halloos like one of their fox hunts."

John took another swallow and launched into his story. "I ran and ran and my breath was gone. I went through so many hedges and jumped so many rock fences, they couldn't follow me on their horses. I laid out in the woods all night and never moved the next day. I kept working my way north. Got in with some others on the run in Galway and we hid out in Derry until we could get across and find passage from Liverpool. But what about Bradshaw. Dead, is he not?"

"We don't know," Jeremiah answered. "We left soon after you."

"Well, I made it. I'll be getting my papers one day so I can be an American and vote," Hurley stated with pride. He took another pull on the bottle and wiped his mouth with the back of his hand. "I'm to be in the Democratic Party and I'll be having a job with the city. It's Dan Hennessy himself who says so. You'll see. I'll not always be a laboring man."

Jeremiah was anxious for news of Hurley's sister, the younger one, Molly, with the black hair and snapping blue eyes. "Your family, John? Have you heard from home?" Jeremiah inquired.

"Well enough," John replied. "I had a letter from my brother, James, thanking me for the money I've been sending. That's all that's keeping body and soul together there, I'm thinking."

"Aye, that's the way of it," Jeremiah sadly agreed. He sat quietly for a moment, but finally he asked it. "And your sisters? How do they fare?"

"Still well enough by James' letter," John responded. "But you remember Tom Kelleher, don't you now? Catherine was promised to him, you know. But he died on the Relief Works, still trying to earn those few pence even after the fever was in him. And my poor sister suffers for it."

The Cleary brothers offered their sympathy and again Jeremiah sat silently for a moment. He'd been filling his *dhudeen,* tamping tobacco into the short pipe. He brought out a match, but didn't strike it. He hadn't yet heard what he most wanted to know. "And your younger sister, Molly? Married is she?"

"No," John answered.

Jeremiah struck the match and held it to his pipe, puffing until it glowed. He sat smoking, lost in his own thoughts. John turned to Matthew, smiling. "And how do you get along here in Boston, Matt?" he asked. "Sure, and it's a good job you have and a tidy, warm place for your living."

Matthew snorted. "Hah! A grand job it is. And do I like shoveling shit after these horses day after day? And pumping those bellows." He indicated the forge through the open door. "And it's himself there," Matthew jerked a thumb at Jeremiah, "sitting up there behind those four horses, prancing around Boston, hardly lifting a thumb all day. Lovely. Just lovely."

John laughed. "Well now, and what is it you're after wanting to do?"

"Me?" Matthew moved a thumb to stab himself in the chest. "Me, is it? I'd be in Californy digging out all that gold. John lad, do you know that they're taking up nuggets as big as this fist?" He shook his fist to show Hurley the size of the nuggets, but he was really shaking it at Jeremiah, who sat listening, not saying a word.

"And what is it you'd be doing with all that gold, Matt?"

"I'll strike it so rich I'll go back to Skibbereen first class all the way. And won't I just be owning the boat? And when I get there I'll lay all those sacks of gold in front of that bastard Becher, him that owns everything, and buy up all his land." Matthew cocked his head to the side as if he were enjoying the vision of his return to Skibbereen as a wealthy man. "And won't I be firing that agent, evicting him right on the spot, and forgiving all the rents? And won't they'll all be crying out, 'Matt Cleary, it's a grand man you are?'"

"Go on with you," Jeremiah scoffed. "You're a *blatherskite*, Matt Cleary. It's the liquor talking."

"Is it now? And just what does this say?" Matthew became indignant. Since the night of the fire in their room, the relationship of Matthew and Jeremiah had noticeably changed. Matthew's defiance and sarcasm were never far from the surface. He pulled a newspaper from his pocket and thrust it at his brother. "Sure and aren't you the scholar now, Jerry? A fellow left his newspaper here. Said it was all about the gold rush to Californy. Read it for yourself."

Jeremiah smoothed out the clipping and read aloud. *No capital is required to obtain this gold, as the laboring man wants nothing but his pick and shovel and a tin pan with which to dig and wash the gravel and more frequently, pick gold out of the crevices or rocks with their butcher knives in pieces from one to six ounces.*

Matthew grinned triumphantly at John. "Right! And I'm for heading to Californy and all that gold. But himself there, he's for staying here to earn it penny by penny."

Jeremiah raised a hand. "Wait now. Here's another item." *Beware of hasty money making, beware of seeking to become rich by extraordinary means. Be assured that all the gold in the world will not make you happy.*

"Maybe not," Matthew declared. "But isn't Matt Cleary just the lad to be giving it a try?"

Jeremiah had to laugh, but then his face sobered as he scanned an editorial in the Boston paper. "John," he said. "Be listening to this. This is what they think of us here."

Hurley listened attentively as Jeremiah read aloud: *Children of the bigoted Catholic Ireland, like frogs that were sent out as a plague against the Pharaohs, have come into our homes, our bed chambers and eating places. Unlike the Germans, the Swedes, the Scots, and the English, these Irish, when they arrived among us, too idle and vicious to clear and cultivate land, and so earn comfortable homes, dumped themselves down in our large villages and towns, crowding the meaner sort of tenements, and filling them with wretchedness and disease. From a political point of view, what are they but marketable cattle?*

"Marketable cattle, are we?" Hurley growled. "We'll be showing them!" He pounded the table with a clinched fist. "We'll be getting the vote one day and they'll see those cattle come to market. Dan Hennessy is leading the way."

Matthew and Jeremiah joined John Hurley the next evening out on Hanover Street, where John lived a bit removed from the slums of Paddytown. He had passed the word among his friends, "We'll be having a bit of a *hooley* to celebrate this reunion with the Cleary boys."

Matthew brought along a bottle. Jeremiah noticed that no matter how broke they were, Matthew always had money for liquor. But this was an occasion.

"And what is it you have there?" Hurley joked when Matthew presented his gift.

"This is singing whiskey," Matthew explained. "There's three kinds, you know. Fighting whiskey to get you a broken nose, loving whiskey to get you a broken heart, but singing whiskey will only get you a cracked voice. I'll be sticking with singing whiskey."

"Grand, just grand," John said, grinning at the logic. "Let's be singing."

A fiddler struck up a tune and a young man played his tin whistle. Some one produced a *bodhran,* the Irish drum, and others just banged on the table or clapped their hands. They started with the sad songs of Ireland and the immigrants' laments, but the music soon turned to lively jigs and polkas.

The room filled as the *colleens* arrived from down the street. Matthew was singing when he noticed the red-haired girl in the crowd. He stopped suddenly as if he was struck, smitten, and slid to his knees, hand over his heart, looking up at her. "And who might you be, *colleen dhas*? And aren't you the pretty thing?"

She laughed as he stood up, giving him a playful slap. "Go along with you now. You've no need to be knowing my name."

But Matthew pulled her to her feet and she came willingly. He held her at arm's length and appraised her. Tall, willowy, a trim little waist tucked under an appealing bosom, green eyes, long, wavy red hair. She met his gaze and laughed again, this time appraising him. And when the tall, handsome, laughing charmer motioned for them to dance, she nodded. Soon she was step dancing with him. Around and around they went, hands at their sides, elbows stiff, feet flashing the intricate steps. Eyes locked together, first one and then the other beat out the tattoo on the floor. People gathered around, clapping to the rhythm. The music played faster and faster until they both collapsed to the cheers of the crowd.

Matthew left her gasping as he grabbed for the bottle. He threw his head back and shouted, "*Beimedth a gole*, let's be drinking!" He passed the bottle and the fiddler struck up another tune.

Jeremiah sat alone in a corner, taking it all in, enjoying just being there, but staying apart from the whirling, dancing, singing fun of the party. Even when John Hurley or someone else engaged him in conversation, Jeremiah's eyes were on Matthew. He saw his brother dancing with the redhead again, this time keeping his arm around her when the dance was over. Matthew took another drink and offered the bottle to the girl. She pushed it away, but he whispered into her ear and she giggled. Matthew took her hand and led her to the door.

Jeremiah's eyes narrowed as he saw them leaving. He got up quickly and headed after them. At the door he looked down the hall and watched the two shadowy figures come together. It was more than an embrace; they melted into one another. Jeremiah was about to walk over to them when he felt a hand on his shoulder. It was John Hurley.

"It's all right, Jerry. I'm knowing the girl. She can be taking care of herself. And Matt now, he's a grown man. He'll be finding his own way."

"A grown man, is he? And just when did this happen?" Jeremiah grumbled. "You're not knowing the half of it, John. He's not grown up at all, he's not. He needs looking after just as my old da said."

Reluctantly Jeremiah let Hurley lead him back into the room. He knew he wasn't considered as much fun to be with as Matthew. And why not? he asked himself. *Sure and he leaves all the worries to me and doesn't have a care in the world. It's as if I'm the father, not the brother.*

Jeremiah tamped more tobacco into his *dhudeen*, lit up, and sat there puffing. Gradually his thoughts drifted away from his brother and turned to his dream—the dream he rarely spoke of, certainly not to Matthew, who would just make a joke of it. Jeremiah kept it safe, hidden inside in his head where no one could touch it. He cherished it, fondled it in his mind, warmed himself with it, kept it always in front of him.

One day he'd have his own land, a home, a *colleen* for a wife, and children.

* * * * *

"There must be two hundred thousand tons of manure piled up around Boston every year," Charlton had told Jeremiah. "It's your contract if you want to haul it."

Jeremiah offered to take in his brother as a partner, but Matthew declined with a laugh. "Isn't it bad enough to share the room with you, Brother, after those shit hauls? I'd not want to be stinking like that myself, would I now? I'll be sticking to my forge until we go to California."

So Jeremiah took the contract to rid Boston of manure, dumping it in Belmont, Lexington and Arlington for farm fertilizer. "And isn't hauling shit an Irish monopoly?" he asked his big wheel horses. "Manure and garbage. No one else wants to do it." But the gold coins clinked into the money sack.

And there was that little bit he added from teaching, especially those from the west of Ireland who mostly spoke Irish and had to learn to read and write in English, know some American history and principles of democracy, and do simple sums if they were to get ahead, become citizens and vote. But schooling wasn't for Matthew.

"I won't be needing reading and writing to find those big gold nuggets," he bragged.

John Hurley, who had attended the same hedge school back home as Jeremiah, told him, "That's enough learning for the likes of me. It's all I'll be needing here to help Dan Hennessy."

There's enough saved to make the trip, Jeremiah decided, nothing really to hold them here. "*Bedad,* Dooly, you old *sthronsuch,* I'll miss your lazy arse," he said and meant it.

Steam from their heated hides, as well as from their wide-open nostrils, rose into the chilly air as the horses pulled into the Atlantic yard that night. Jeremiah was eager to tell his brother the decision to head for California. But he was greeted by a very anxious Matthew who clutched a letter in his hand.

"It's from the priest, Jerry," Matthew said, nervously handing the letter to Jeremiah. "I can't make it out."

Jeremiah took Father Hayes' letter, but had to wait a moment before he could bring himself to read it. When he did finally look at it, the words swam before his eyes distant and unreal.

I am sorry to be the one to bring you sad tidings, but your brother Liam has asked me to tell you. Both your parents have been called by God. Liam was gone from the home for two days seeking work. When he left Coolnagurrane they were in health, but when he returned the fever was on them. He did what he could, but there was no stopping its course. God rest their souls. Liam built coffins and they were buried in the Abby cemetery. Crosses were placed and Liam claims one day there will be gravestones. I, myself, said the prayers over them. May the good Lord bring you comfort in your sorrow. Yours in Christ, Fr. Brendan Hayes.

Jeremiah had read the letter aloud, his voice breaking. He and Matthew sat in stony silence, their heads bowed as darkness came down around them.

It was black dark in the barn when Jeremiah lit a lantern and went to unharness the team.

CHAPTER FIVE

J EREMIAH SLIPPED IN THE MUD, cursed and grabbed a dangling vine to pull himself up. But he could hardly make out the trail, could hardly see it through the water cascading off the brim of his battered hat. Rain spilled from the skies, from the trees all about them. He looked down at Matthew, fighting through the steamy jungle just below him.

"Hold up, Jerry. Let's rest a bit," Matthew called as he climbed up and flopped down beside his brother in the muck. The two sat, breathing hard, as the rain squall passed and the hot sun shining down through a gap in the jungle cover steamed their wet clothing. Matthew took a deep breath, but then, with an oath, spit and coughed out a mouthful of mosquitoes, which had suddenly risen in clouds from the marshes. They were in their beards, their noses, their ears, biting through their clothing. After a while, it was a futile waste of energy to even slap at them.

The Cleary brothers were crossing the Isthmus of Panama toward Panama City. There was barely a path to follow; snarled trees and hanging vines impeded their way, snakes slithered ahead of them. Strange birds shrieked down at them from branches of the tropical trees.

From where they sat resting, they could see the river rolling toward the Atlantic. Dugout canoes, poled by natives, their sing-song chanting echoing over the water, made their way up the Changres River carrying passengers in a steady procession.

"Look at that lot down there," Matthew gasped. "That's the way to be traveling. Sitting back, taking it easy and letting the

33

natives do the work." Matthew took out his tobacco and passed it. Jeremiah had long since given up keeping his pipe lit in the frequent downpours. He cut off a plug with his pocket knife and began chewing. Matthew had his quart bottle and, after a healthy gulp of the raw whiskey, he smacked his lips and offered it to his brother. Jeremiah took a drink, shuddered and wiped the back of his hand across his mouth. He handed it back to Matthew, who finished it off and tossed the bottle into the jungle.

They'd arrived three days before at the mouth of the Changres River after a voyage of three weeks from New York in the sidewheel steamer, Ohio, operated by the Atlantic Mail Steamship Co. with calls at Savannah, New Orleans and Havana. Although most passengers disembarked to savor the taste of those exotic cities, the Cleary brothers stayed on board, appreciating the vastly improved accommodations of the Ohio to those of the infamous Sir Willard Pottinger. It had been almost two years since that nightmare voyage, but they'd not forget it for the rest of their lives.

On being put ashore at Changres, the passengers were swarmed over by boatmen with offers to carry them up the river to the trails that led down to Panama City. The Clearys refused the offers, choosing instead to save their money. They'd brought nothing on their trip but the clothes on their backs, having left their few possessions with John Hurley back in Boston. Each brother had his carefully-hoarded funds in a money belt bound around his waist inside his trousers.

"That lot down there," Matthew said pointing to the river passengers, "will be getting to Panama long before we will."

"That they will," Jeremiah agreed, "if we sit here all day." He rose to his feet and faced the jungle. What at first looked to be an easy trek across a tiny piece of land had now taken three days and no end in sight. They'd had little sleep, laying on the wet ground at night with vines for pillows, roots sticking into their backs, animals and birds screeching all around them.

Jeremiah stretched his aching limbs, sighed, pushed away some tangled vines, and started climbing.

Their first view of Panama City was a complete surprise. It lay below them on a tiny peninsula, an age-old Spanish city jutting into the calm, bright blue waters of the bay. Its two-story houses of *adobe* or stone had wrought-iron balconies overlooking narrow streets and crooked alleys. Bright red tile adorned the roofs and the bell towers, from which sounded notes in varying harmony as the hours were struck. Along the tree-lined, shady streets, beneath the verandas, moved a bizarre mixture of people. There were the natives, some in brightly-hued garments, some in white pantaloons; the Africans, their near nakedness gleaming as they moved from shade to sun; the Spanish men in colorful, silver-ornamented *caballero* costumes topped by broad-brimmed Panama hats, the women in colorful dresses, heads covered by *mantillas*.

And walking up and down the narrow streets were the American travelers, the California bound, going in and out of the cantinas, the cafes and dance halls, the gambling casinos, lounging in groups in shady alcoves, passing the time as they waited for the ships that would carry them on the next leg of their journey.

The Clearys joined the group in front of the shipping office and learned they'd be embarking on the Oregon, which wasn't due in from San Francisco until the next day, and would lay over for two. Jeremiah decided local accommodations were too expensive so they bought canvas for shade, and two blankets for beds and found an isolated spot on the beach where they stretched their weary bodies under their canopy. Despite the sultry heat, the two exhausted young men fell quickly to sleep.

It was dark when they awoke and made their way toward the lights and noise of Panama City. A raucous din hung over the city like a cloud—rhythmic music, loud laughter, shouts, and the stomp of dancing feet poured through every window and door. Matthew felt the excitement and quickly made his choice of cantinas.

"Let's give this one a try," he urged his brother. "We'll be having a *deorin*, just a small drop, and then go on."

"I'd rather eat first," Jeremiah responded. "We haven't been doing much of that these past days. My belly thinks it's still in Ireland," But he let Matthew pull him into the *cantina* where the spicy food, so foreign to his palate, forced him to order a whiskey to wash it down. Jeremiah sat at a table sipping his drink, watching the boisterous mob swirling dizzily around him. At one end of the room musicians were playing guitars, violins and mandolins, creating music for the dancers who could barely hear it over the roar of the other patrons. These lined the long bar, sat at tables in groups, or gathered around the gambling tables, shouting to each other and laughing as they placed their bets, cheering when they won, and loudly bewailing their poor fortune when they lost.

Here and there throughout the barroom were the women. Jeremiah watched them and his lip curled in distaste. No Irish *colleen* would do the things they did for money, no matter how dire her circumstances. Some were very attractive, though, he admitted to himself, and they moved about the room in seductive ways, enticing the men to further drink, to gamble and to go upstairs.

Matthew was right in the middle of it. He had a glass of whiskey in one hand and a woman in the other, whirling around the dance floor with Irish steps the likes of which this girl had never seen before. He was laughing as the whiskey spilled. He banged down the glass and roared for another, fumbling at his money belt for a gold piece to slap on the bar.

Jeremiah narrowed his eyes as he saw the woman push herself up against his brother and run her hands through his hair. She had large breasts that threatened to fall out of her low-cut bodice and Matthew's eyes were focused on them as he tossed off his whiskey.

"You like me, *querido*?" she whispered, sticking her tongue in his ear, and rubbing her breasts against him.

36

"Sure now and all you *señoritas* look good, especially you, darlin' lass," Matthew slurred.

"Perhaps you would like me more if you got to know me better?" she asked. "You would like to go upstairs with me, no? But first, you would buy a bottle and we may continue our party in my room?"

Jeremiah watched as his brother dug at his money belt to pay for the bottle, all the time grinning lecherously at the lusty woman. Too late to stop him now. He'd have to just sit here and wait until Matthew had his fun and then get him back to the beach. Jeremiah was still nursing his original drink and the other patrons, even the girls, left him alone—his brooding and distant look didn't invite company.

Matthew followed the woman up the stairs, his eyes having trouble focusing on her rump as it undulated from side to side just above him. He stumbled and she reached out to help him. Jeremiah waited. It seemed like a long time, too long. Matthew didn't appear.

But the girl did, at the head of the stairs, and she was signaling to a man in the crowd, a sinister-looking figure, who detached himself from the gamblers and hurried up the steps. The hair rose on the back of Jeremiah's head. Adrenaline pumped through him. He jumped up from the table, took the stairs two at a time and ran into a long hallway leading to the back of the building. He caught a glimpse of a door closing and hurried to it. He put his ear against the door and could barely make out a couple of low voices.

"Hurry. Roll him over so I can reach the belt."

"He's dead weight. Help me, he's out cold."

"See, I told you—this belt is heavy with gold pieces."

Jeremiah quietly and carefully pushed open the door and silently entered the room. He saw his brother sprawled across the bed, hanging face down, fully clothed, an empty glass still clutched in one hand. The man with his back to the door was trying to turn the unconscious Matthew as the woman unstrapped his money belt. Neither saw Jeremiah step up, grab a chair, and crash it down on the robber's head with all his furious strength. The chair shattered as the man dropped to the bed. Jeremiah still had a chair leg in his hand, which he swung again and again, pounding the man's skull, smashing his nose, striking his shoulders, cracking his collarbone, breaking his arm. The woman was too frightened to scream. She watched this madman and feared for her life. Jeremiah waved his stick at her and she cowered against the bedstead. He pointed to her unconscious, bleeding accomplice.

"Care for this filth, you slut," Jeremiah said with a rage that made his eyes bulge. "He may live, but he won't be robbing anyone else for a while."

He lifted the limp body of his brother, draped him over a shoulder with one arm and dragged him from the room, through the hall and down the stairs. He carried Matthew through the crowd and into the street. Hardly anyone noticed.

He had to stop on his way to the beach for Matthew to be sick. "Good," Jeremiah said. "It's a lesson you'll learn from this, God willing." He dunked Matthew's head in the waters of the bay, brought him up gasping and slung him into their shelter. Matthew passed out again. Jeremiah felt sick himself. He was shaken. He hadn't known he was capable of such a fierce rage. As a boy he had done the usual wrestling about on the ground with the other children. And he'd used his fists a few times in those free-for-alls, but that was sport. This time he might have killed that man. He'd have to be keeping his temper in check.

CHAPTER SIX

"AND ISN'T THAT A BEAUTIFUL SIGHT NOW!" Matthew exclaimed. "California, it is. Gold, here comes Matt Cleary." He did a little jig step on the deck and Jeremiah couldn't help smiling.

The Cleary brothers stood on deck watching as the Oregon entered the narrow channel known as the Golden Gate. A cold, wispy fog shrouded the city clinging to the hills by the bay, but they could make out a dim outline. "I'll be finding some miners as soon as we land and find out about the gold fields," Matthew said, his eyes shining with excitement.

But Jeremiah's eyes were on the mountains, the morning sun glinting off their peaks as they broke out of the fog. "Look there, Matt," he said. "It looks like fine fertile land." He wondered if his future was in those hills.

Jeremiah and Matthew were ready the moment the Oregon tied up near the Pacific Steamship office and a surge of anticipation hurried them down the gangway and into the traffic and commotion of Liedsdorf Street. They headed uptown, enthralled by the sights and sounds of San Francisco.

"Look at those fellows there," Matthew said, pointing to three roughly dressed, bearded men walking across the street. "I wonder if they're miners. I'll ask them."

But Jeremiah held him back. "Let's find lodging first," he insisted. They took a room at Mrs. King's U.S. Hotel on Kearny Street, and then set out to see the city and find a meal. Matthew had hardly eaten a bite before he spotted the same three men at a table across the room. He jumped up and eagerly approached them. Jeremiah watched him in animated conversation, dreading what he knew was coming. Matthew returned to his side, his eyes bright.

"They're miners, Jerry, just as I figured." Matthew went at his steak and potatoes with gusto. "They have good paying claims and they'll be returning to the Sierras and I can be going with them!"

"So you'll be going with them, you will? And when will you be leaving?" Jeremiah asked.

"We'll be taking a boat across the bay in the morning and heading up the Sacramento River. I can be working for them on shares or go out on my own to find gold," Matthew explained. "They say there's still plenty to be found."

Jeremiah sighed, a deep, regretful sigh. He didn't like the idea of Matthew going out on his own. But it had to come sometime. He'd be missing him something terrible. He nodded, paid for the meal, and headed back to the hotel as Matthew hurried off to get outfitted.

In the morning, as Matthew was waiting to meet his new friends, they watched a tall, thin man putting a handwritten poster on the notice board in the lobby. Obviously a rancher, the man was cursing the paper, the board, the hotel and life in general. Jeremiah edged over to read the notice. It said: *Teamster wanted. Must handle six horses and freight wagon. See Weeb Jefferson at U.S. Hotel.*

Jeremiah called after the retreating man. "Mister Jefferson — ! I could be driving your team. That's my line of work."

Weeb Jefferson stopped and turned around in surprise. "Oh, yeah? You say you're a teamster, do you. What's your name."

"Cleary, your honour, Jeremiah Cleary."

He gave Jeremiah a quick once-over and nodded as if to say, "You'll do."

"Well, Cleary, you go over to the livery stable on California Street and tell them Weeb Jefferson sent you. If you can hitch up my team and drive the wagon over here, I'll pay you ten dollars and keep to take me to San Juan Bautista. Three days. If you can do that we'll talk about a steady job."

"Yes, sir," Jeremiah said as he hurried off. He returned shortly in command of a six-horse hitch and a huge, loaded freight wagon. Weeb Jefferson was waiting. So were Matthew and his miner friends, ready to leave for the docks and their boat.

Jeremiah jumped down from the wagon seat and clasped Matthew's hand. "You be taking care of yourself now, Brother. Ease off on the drink a bit." He saw Matthew's mouth tighten. "You'll do just grand and find a mountain of gold." Jeremiah tried to work up a smile, but saying goodbye was harder than he thought it would be.

Matthew reached out, took his brother by the shoulders and looked into his eyes. He saw the love and concern there. "Don't you be worrying about me now," he said. "It's yourself you better be caring for." He gave Jeremiah's shoulders a squeeze. "And, Jerry, it's sorry I am for causing you the trouble."

Tears welled in both their eyes, but Jefferson was climbing onto the wagon. "Move out," he ordered. The horses were anxiously stomping their feet, rattling their harness, team bells ringing. There was no more time for good-byes.

"I'll be at some place called San Juan Bautista," Jeremiah called down to Matthew. "When you get back, be looking for me there."

Jeremiah gathered the lines, spoke to the team, and the horses leaned into the collars. He looked at Matthew one last time and the two men waved at each other. Then the Jefferson wagon was off at a trot down California Street heading south.

Jeremiah had no idea where San Juan Bautista was located, but he soon learned it was a settlement built around the old Franciscan mission on the San Benito River about eighty miles to the south, the only town, except for Monterey, in that part of California.

He learned that and much more from the garrulous Jefferson. "That damn teamster I had picked a helluva time to get drunk and head for the gold fields. Should be driving this damn team myself, dammit," he muttered. "Hate driving horses. Rather ride them any day. Reason I sold out in Illinois, damn farming, getting the damn harness tangled up all the time. Reason I bought me a cattle ranch. Got me eight thousand prime acres of good grazing near San Juan and near a thousand cows. That's the life for a man, raising cattle. Not the

41

damn farming. Hate the damn work horses and farming. You know how to plow?"

Jeremiah had let Jefferson's words swirl around in him without disturbing his concentration on the six-horse hitch, nor his concern for his brother. But the question startled him. Plow? He thought it better not to admit that he'd never run a plow, so instead he just grunted.

Jefferson went right on. "Yep, Emily likes it there. Comfortable old *adobe* house. And she relishes the life around San Juan, regular damn metropolis now. North-south stages stop, right on the main line. King's Highway, they call it. Not much more than damn wheel tracks in the dirt. Four general stores, livery stable, couple of blacksmith shops, hotel, even a damn French restaurant. Would you believe that?" He looked across at Jeremiah, who felt himself being appraised.

A heavy, black beard hid his face, but Jeremiah's clear, brown eyes were steady on Jefferson's and he responded in his best English, though he knew his thick brogue was hard for his new employer to understand. "Sure and it must be a lovely town, just lovely," he said.

After four days on the road and three nights in wayside inns, Jeremiah heard all about the ranch, the hired hands, the town, and Weeb Jefferson's personal likes and dislikes. It was dusk when he guided the team into the yard at the ranch.

"The boys will show you where to put up the damn team, Cleary, and make yourself comfortable in the bunkhouse over there," Jefferson said as he disappeared into the huge *adobe* house.

Jeremiah was greeted by shy smiles and the friendly voices of the *vaqueros* as he stepped into the bunkhouse. "*Como està, señor?*" "*Buenas noches, señor*," "*Como le va?*"

He didn't understand Spanish, but he knew these were welcoming words, so he nodded politely and sat down on the rawhide bed. He watched and listened as the men spoke, laughed, and playfully slapped each other on the back. At first the four young *vaqueros* all looked alike to Jeremiah—brown skin, black hair, lean bodies—and one older man, gray-haired, slightly bent, who observed the younger ones with an indulgent grin crinkling his weathered face. Jeremiah watched as one brought a bucket of water from the well and filled the wash basins. He got the idea as they all washed up, still laughing, splashing, and joking together, so he joined them at the basins, washing his face and hands, too, and drying off on the common towel.

Dusk was falling, but Jeremiah could still see the ranch buildings, sheltered by a stand of huge oak trees. They were cradled against the foothills, which fell away before him into farming fields and pasture land, reaching toward the mission and the town in the distance across the river. Behind him he could make out the trail to the mountains, winding among the oaks and pines of the high country. It was peaceful and beautiful. But he felt so strange, so alone. How would he ever understand, how would he fit in here? Before, Jeremiah had always had Matthew to share experiences with him in this alien land. But now he had only himself.

He followed the cowboys outside and was surprised to see them heading for the main house. They entered around at the rear, and Jeremiah realized that the talking and joking had abruptly ended. The *vaqueros* took off their big *sombreros* and hung them on wall hooks. They quietly took their places on benches around the large table, which ran the length of the room.

"Well, now, Cleary, are these boys treating you all right?" Weeb Jefferson asked as he entered the room and took a seat. Jeremiah was surprised. The boss himself ate with the hired hands? The gentry sitting down with the workers? This was certainly much different than in Ireland, or Boston, for that matter.

"Yes, sir," responded Jeremiah and the *vaqueros* grinned. But no one spoke. They sat politely, looking expectantly at the kitchen door, which swung open and surprised Jeremiah again. Out of the kitchen came a large, red-faced woman, an

43

apron covering her ample girth, a wide smile on her face, and laughing eyes under a mop of gray hair. In each hand she held a steaming bowl, which she placed before the cowboys.

"Here you are, boys, eat hearty." She was back a moment later with a platter piled high with meat.

This must be the ranch cook, Jeremiah thought. He turned his attention to filling his plate with beans, they were calling them *frijoles*, summer vegetables, and *carne*, beef steak. Jeremiah had never seen so much food being passed around.

"Ramòn, you head up to the Cienega and check those damn cattle, make sure they still have water." Jefferson was giving orders for the next day's work.

"Agapito, you and Jorge ride to the San Justo. Bring back that damn bull. He's a mean one. Think you two can handle him?"

"Rogelio, you'll go with me to drive those damn dry cows up into the hills for pasture, and Celestino, I guess you'll be working with the colts, huh?"

To all these orders, the cowboys were nodding politely and agreeing. There was a chorus of "*Si, señor.*"

These *vaqueros* seemed to understand more English than they let on, Jeremiah mused. He was startled when Jefferson suddenly addressed him. "Cleary, we'll get you lined out in the morning. Celestino can show you where the damn — "

The kitchen door burst open and the stout woman again entered the room, took off her apron, and sat down at the table. "Weeb, you quit giving orders and let these poor, tired boys eat their supper," she admonished with a shake of her finger. "And stop saying damn."

"Yes, Emily," Jefferson agreed with a sly wink at Jeremiah as if to say, "You see how it is around here."

Jeremiah was beginning to. Now this was even more than a bit strange, he thought. This man's wife, it is, doing the cooking and them eating right here just as if they are the same as the help. He'd have to be getting used to this.

That night, although it was a warm, summer evening, Jeremiah knew he'd be cold in the *adobe* bunkhouse without a blanket or extra clothes. As he was looking around the bunkhouse for a blanket, Celestino, the old man, came up to him. *"Por favor, señor,"* he said, offering Jeremiah a tattered patchwork quilt. "Please use this to keep you warm, *Señor* Cleary."

"Well, thank you," Jeremiah said. And then decided to put it into one of the few Spanish words he'd learned. *"Gracias,"* he added, or thought that's what he'd said. He wondered because they all laughed, then blew out the lamps, and settled down for the night.

Here he was on a California cattle ranch near a place called San Juan Bautista, Jeremiah marveled, and Matthew was somewhere on his way to seek gold, the saints preserve him. It had all happened so fast. Jeremiah pulled off his brogans, settled himself against the rawhide bedstrings, pulled his quilt over him and shut his eyes.

But he didn't sleep. His mind was too full of his strange surroundings and an acute awareness that he was starting a new life. The thought flickered for a moment that he'd write home and tell his mother and father where he was and describe this new life. Wouldn't they be amazed? But they were dead and he'd no one to write to except his brother Little Liam, and like Matthew, Liam couldn't read. But maybe one day he'd write it all to Liam, who'd have a scholar read it to him. Composing such a letter in his mind, Jeremiah finally fell asleep.

CHAPTER SEVEN

"Señor Cleary, this *estièrcol*, these shit piles. It must be removed, *por favor*."

Celestino was showing Jeremiah around the ranch the next morning. The main corrals, as well as the barn, with its stalls and mangers, were made of *adobe or* sun-dried mud. Further out were the horse corrals of peeled pine, and still further Jeremiah could see the brush piled up against posts to form barriers for the cattle. Here and there were piles of manure. It was to these that Celestino pointed.

Jeremiah looked at them in dismay. For this he came from Boston? Was he back to loading manure again? Is this what they thought of an Irishman's worth? Jeremiah was about to rebel and ask for his pay, but, then he remembered last night at supper time. The boss sat down with the working men and the wife cooked the meal. They didn't look down on the cowboys nor on the newest ranch hand—Mexican or Irish. The Jeffersons seemed to believe that their employees were as good as themselves. Strange!

Cleary, he told himself, you better be putting your Irish pride behind you and see what happens. If the boss wanted him to haul shit for two dollars a day plus room and board, he could do it. He'd done it before and it hadn't hurt him any. But he was glad Matthew wasn't around. He'd be splitting his sides laughing.

Jeremiah hitched two horses to the wooden scraper and went to work. Well before the sun was high, he found himself outside the *adobe* wall behind which Celestino was working a colt. He stopped to watch and was soon fascinated. A two-year-old gelding was loose across the corral and Celestino stood with a coiled hair rope and *bozal* over his arm. In one hand he had a handful of small pebbles. With the other he was tossing the little rocks at the horse. Jeremiah was astounded. Throwing rocks at a horse? What way was this to train an animal?

The sorrel colt stood with his rump to Celestino and each time a pebble would strike, he'd jump and run across the back of the corral. With each toss the old *vaquero* would call out, "*Ven aquì. Ven aquì.*" Finally the colt turned and faced him. The *vaquero* stepped backwards and softly encouraged the horse. "*Bueno, hombre, bueno.*"

Each time the colt turned away and presented his rump, Celestino pelted it with a little rock and called, "Come here." Each time the horse faced him, Celestino retreated and encouraged the colt with his quiet, "Good, good." After more than a half hour of this, the colt stopped its nervous running. It stepped gingerly up to Celestino and stood facing him. It was patted on the neck, rubbed all over the ears, chest, withers, touched on the nose. Then Celestino turned and walked away, ignoring the animal. The colt looked after him, nickered, stamped its foot, hesitated a second, and then followed the old cowboy.

At the fence Celestino stopped, turned back to the colt and worked his arm around the horse's neck, pulled the *bozal* up over its nose, and ran the headstall around the ears. He led the young animal to a post, tied him, and approached the watching Irishman. Jeremiah shook his head in amazement.

"Celestino, how did you do that? How were you getting him to come to you like that?"

"Well, *Señor* Cleary, what you see was not the first day I do this with this colt. Many mornings we do this and she finally works. Sometimes it happens faster, sometimes more slowly. This young horse, *señor*, she gets so tired of me pestering him, she figures it out, that I will stop if he comes up to me."

Celestino explained that this colt had been handled, and halter broken soon after birth, and then turned out for a year. Now he'd be broken to be easily caught, to face the cowboy head-on instead presenting his rear, the kicking end. He'd be saddled and bridled and let loose in the corral for hours at a time. Then he'd be turned out again until he was a four-year

47

old before he'd be caught up and expected to learn his job as a ranch horse working cattle.

"Once upon a time, *señor*, I myself could ride the wildest horse in the *remuda*. I broke horses the way all the rest. I would ride him until she no longer wished to buck with me. But then, *Señor* Cleary," Celestino sighed as he explained, "the stiffness came upon me and I could no longer ride as a youth. I learned that there is an easier way to train a horse, a way that makes a better horse, and no broken bones for the *vaquero viejo*. All this she take time, time and patience. *Señor* Jefferson gives me the time. God gives me the patience."

Over the next few weeks Jeremiah was a frequent visitor to the corral to watch Celestino working with the colts. The *vaquero* lifted newborns into his arms, hugged them, petted them, scratched them, ran his hands all over their bodies, showing them that "*las manos*" don't hurt, that hands can be gentle. He placed soft ropes around their bellies and ran loops over their rumps to tug by so the colts couldn't be harmed. He pulled the colts this way and that until they learned to lead.

"Celestino, one day when we both have time, would you be teaching me these things with the colts?" Jeremiah asked.

"Si, senior," was the answer. "I think you would be a good man with the horses. I watch you with the big *hombres* and you work them well. These babies will trust you, too."

But that had to wait. Jeremiah was kept busy with the everyday chores of his new life. There were his special duties — driving Mrs. Jefferson into San Juan for an occasional shopping trip or a visit with friends, taking the six-horse hitch and freight wagon to Alviso for a shipment of supplies, or to the mill in Pescadero Canyon in the Santa Cruz Mountains for a load of redwood.

When the rains came, Weeb Jefferson told Jeremiah one evening, over supper, "Those forty acres will need plowing for the wheat."

Jeremiah nodded through a mouthful of *tortilla* packed with *chili verde* and tried not to show how worried he was. He'd passed over the plowing question and the fact that he'd never done it. But he'd seen others plow fields back in County Cork, farming with horses for the gentry on large estates. Could he be doing it? Well, he'd just have to figure out how.

The single-share plow was in the shed waiting for him. For weeks now he'd been studying the plow every time he passed it by, and the plow, silent and cold, just sat there, a challenge. Which way does the damn thing go? he wondered.

It was mid-November when the ground was right, and Jeremiah hitched two horses to the plow and entered the field. He made sure no one was watching as he called to the team and felt the plow share take hold. It dug in and started to turn up the moist earth as the horses leaned into their work. Well now, there's nothing to this, he told himself. Just hold these arms, these handles here, steady it is, and follow along around and around the field. But he learned that to turn left, it wasn't enough to turn the team, he had to turn the plow. That was a trick. He soon realized that when he lifted the right handle, the plow swung left. If he lifted the left handle, it went to the right. Handling the lines, holding on to the plow handles, keeping the horses straight, walking all day behind the plow, was hard work, but he was proud to be mastering a new skill.

And yet he was relieved and grateful to hear the Angelus bell ring out each evening from Mission San Juan, it's echoing chimes signaling the end of another work day. It was six o'clock and the bells never failed to sound on time, rung by the padres on solar time, taken from a big sun dial standing in the mission garden.

But there was no question that Jeremiah's favorite respite from farming was when he hitched a horse to the surrey and took Mrs. Weeb Jefferson for a fast trot into town. San Juan stood on a rise of ground commanding all of the valley, flat in places and gently rolling in others, through which flowed the San Benito River. Oak trees of all sizes dotted the landscape, some whose girth and leafy breadth testified to their ancient presence.

They arrived in town amid a flurry of activity. Horsemen reined their mounts in and out among pedestrians and vehicles. The crowded streets were a swirl of color and confusion. The freight wagon for the quicksilver mines at New Idria was loading from Harris' store for the sixty-mile haul back to the mines. Another wagon had just arrived from Alviso with supplies off the San Francisco steamer for James McMahan's general store. Rigs of all kinds, from elegantly-appointed carriages and traps behind spirited horses to squeaking *carretas* pulled by plodding oxen, were coming and going as ranchers and travelers, the drummers and cattle buyers, went about their business in this bustling commercial center.

Jeremiah helped Mrs. Jefferson step down from the surrey. "I'm going over to McMahan's," she said brightly. "I think he's got in some new bolts of cloth."

"Yes, ma'am," Jeremiah nodded. "I'll be going over to Twitchel's forge to pick up those plow shares if he's got them sharpened yet."

That's when Jeremiah first saw the girl.

She came out of Harris', her arms filled with packages and lightly bumped him. "Excuse me, *señor*," she said with a light laugh. He stepped aside to let her pass and politely touched his hat. The lithe manner of her walk, her trim body, which seemed to float along inside her red cotton dress, were a pleasant sight to follow up the street. Jeremiah was disappointed when she turned to enter McMahan's store. But just before she disappeared inside she stopped for a moment, turned and looked back at him. Jeremiah felt his heart quicken as she caught his eye.

He picked up his sharpened plowshares at Twitchel's, placed them in the surrey and joined the men watching the horse-shoeing. He listened to the talk about rainfall, crops, the price of liquor and the good and bad points of the horse being shod. Watching the sparks fly from the forge, and hearing the clang of hammer on metal, reminded Jeremiah of Matthew at work in Boston. Where was that brother of his now? Off somewhere in the Sierras. Had he found his cursed gold? Was he safe?

As he walked back to McMahan's he looked for the girl in the red cotton dress, but she was nowhere to be seen. When he entered the store he heard the familiar brogue of Tommy Lannigan, the traveling tinker, who'd come in on the south-bound stage, reporting the good news of Ireland. He'd heard from a lad just off the Pacific Steamer that the potato crop had been lush and healthy, and that there was no longer hunger in every cottage. "And he was telling me," Lannigan said, "that they couldn't keep his poor old mother in her bed, her getting up in the middle of the night and wandering like a daft one, walking the lanes and peering into the gardens in the light of the moon, just to look at the vines to be making sure of them, bless the old dear."

Jeremiah smiled. He'd heard the same from his brother, Liam, who had the priest write a letter for him about the good potato crop and that the holding was saved, thanks to the money Jeremiah sent home.

He followed Emily Jefferson out of the store, placed her packages in the surrey and gave her a hand up. As she settled herself, he climbed up beside her and took the lines. She was in a chatty mood, as usual, this time fussing about Weeb.

"I do worry about him, Jerry. His arthritis is acting up so. And he won't do a thing for it. He won't even go see Doc McDougal. When he's horseback all day, it pains him the whole night through. Land sakes, I don't know what to do. He insisted on riding off with the boys to the high country."

"Yes, ma'am," Jeremiah replied. He knew she didn't expect a real answer and he'd heard it all before anyway. He'd been working on the ranch nearly three years now and had an ever-growing affection for this aging couple. They depended upon him more and more. In response to Jefferson's insistence, Jeremiah now felt comfortable calling him "Weeb." But he just had not been able to bring himself to call her "Emily." Yet she seemed offended if he said "Missus Jefferson," so he settled for "ma'am." He'd grown accustomed to the easy informality of life in the West.

In Ireland I'd be lifting my hat and bending my knee to the owners. Jeremiah grimaced. Even the landlords' agents put on airs and expected subservience from the tenants. "If it please your honour," and "Yes, your honour," and "No, your honour." Here a man could stand on his own two feet and be respected as a fellow human being. There was a sense of equality, not the arrogance of class consciousness.

"What do you plan to do, Jerry?" Emily Jefferson's question jolted Jeremiah.

"Plan to do, ma'am? I plan to drive on home, put up the horse and do my chores."

"No, Jerry, no. You know that's not what I mean. What do you plan to do with your life? Weeb and I were wondering about that just the other day."

Jeremiah kept all his attention on the horse as he thought about how to answer her. He could shrug and say he didn't know. But he did know. And Mrs. Jefferson deserved a better answer. Still, he'd never shared his dream with anyone but his brother, and with him very little. Matthew was too fond of making jokes about it. So he'd held his dream closely, of land and all that went with it.

Emily Jefferson had hardly slowed for a breath. "Weeb and I were saying how you seem to be a young man of ambition. And you obviously have more education than most of your country-men. You have a job here with us as long as you want, of course. We never had children, you know, Weeb and I. Forgive us for being silly old fools, but sometimes we think of you as the son we never had. But is that what you truly want?"

Jeremiah glanced sideways at this kind, matronly woman. If she thought of him that way, Jeremiah knew Emily Jefferson would understand. Suddenly, he felt a real need to tell her. Emily untied her bonnet strings and slipped the hat from her head. She gave her full attention to Jeremiah.

"It's land. I'm wanting land, Emily. My own land. Someday I'll have a farm, some cattle and raise horses to sell, horses I'll train with my own hand. And it's a house I'll have that no one will take from me."

Jeremiah couldn't keep the emotion from his voice and didn't even realize he'd called her Emily. She looked into his eyes for a moment and his sincerity brought tears to her own. "I'm sure you will one day, Jerry." She reached over and patted his hand where it rested on the reins.

They rode in silence and then another thought occurred to her. "Jerry, don't you think you'll return to your home in Ireland someday?"

"No, I'll not," he answered. He said it simply and emphatically.

She studied him, waiting for him to explain. She felt as if she was probing too deeply, but she couldn't help herself. "Why not, Jerry?" she finally asked.

"Between the landlords and the British there's nothing for a man but to exist, if they'll even let him do that."

"Don't you have folks there?"

"Dead, they are, my mother and father and the younger children. Of the hunger and fever," Jeremiah's voice broke. "They starved."

He took a deep breath to control himself and continued. "My brother Matthew, who came with me, is off hunting gold, and my brother Liam has the lease on the farm now. But he can't own it. They'll not let you own your land there, only rent it. And should he improve it, they raise the rent." Jeremiah shook his head and sighed. "I'll not be a part of it, Emily. The British crown sits too heavy on Ireland. My future is here. I'll be an American. I'll be going soon to Monterey to put in my papers for citizenship. This is my country now!"

Emily sat in silence for a while as they rode. Then finally she said, "Well, Jerry, when you get your land, you'll need a wife to share it with. You never seem to be interested in the San Juan girls. Is there somebody?"

"No. I don't have time yet to think of girls. When I find my land and make my home will be time enough to be thinking of a wife."

But that wasn't exactly the truth. He did think of girls, at least one girl. The girl he'd seen in the red dress.

CHAPTER EIGHT

"*ANDELE, PRONTO*," Rogelio yelled as he spurred his horse along a ridge to head off a bunch of wild cows making a break for a deep, brush-choked ravine.

The young *vaquero* and Jeremiah were gathering cattle from the high country and driving them down to Weeb Jefferson's lower pastures. Jeremiah was bouncing along on his horse, trailing Rogelio and marveling at the way the cowboy sat so tall, so straight in his saddle, his long legs hardly bent as he reacted to the horse's every move, riding his stirrups, his seat, his body one with the saddle. Rogelio appeared at ease, even at a gallop, moving in rhythm, as if he were a part of the animal beneath him. Jeremiah wondered if he'd ever ride like that himself.

But his preoccupation with keeping his seat every time the saddle rose up to whack him didn't keep his mind from wandering to that girl. Over the last two weeks, every time he'd gone into San Juan, she was there. Somewhere. Walking down the street. In one of the stores. And she'd look at him with snapping black eyes, tilt her head, and open red lips to let her white teeth flash behind a saucy smile. If he walked into a store, she'd be there. If he turned a street corner, he'd nearly bump into her.

Jeremiah tried hard not to think about her and to concentrate on riding the horse. After a day such as this he was black and bruised, sore all over. At supper time that night Jeremiah found a soft pillow waiting for him at his place on the bench and a bottle of horse liniment before him on the table. Jeremiah tried to grin as he sat down very gently on the pillow. The *vaqueros* smiled at him with amusement.

"Perhaps, you would prefer to ride Viejo. The old one's pace might be more to your liking, Cleary," Rogelio said. The others tried not to laugh, but Jeremiah didn't mind their good-natured teasing half as much as Emily Jefferson did.

"You leave Jerry alone," she scolded. "He'll be riding just like the rest of you one day. You'll see." Rogelio gave her a slightly apologetic nod.

That night when Jeremiah went to bed, as soon as he fell asleep, he dreamt of the girl. She was walking ahead of him, her hips undulating. He imagined her thighs rubbing together inside the cotton dress. She turned and laughed, a light teasing laugh. He was just about to touch her when he awoke in a sweat. And he didn't even know her name.

The next morning, Jeremiah had to drag himself out of bed so stiff and sore he could hardly move without wincing, hurry out and saddle up. The cattle, which had been running on open range since fall, were wild and hard to drive. They were mixed with those of the San Justo, and other ranchos, and all had to be herded to a central spot in the valley. There they had to be separated by ownership and each calf mothered up according to the brand on the cow.

Weeb sat tall on his horse amid all the swirling dust, loping horses, bawling calves and angry cows, and calmly recorded his tally. He and the other ranch owners kept track of every pair, how many heifer calves there were, how many castrated bulls, adding up the total for each brand. There was rarely a dispute here among friends and neighbors. When branding was complete, the cattle were driven in separate herds to their home range.

A few days later, Jeremiah's soreness had eased some and he stood with Celestino leaning on the pole corral watching Agapito and Ramon saddle an unbroken gelding from the *remuda*. This was obviously not a horse which had known Celestino's hand. He fought the rope, pulled back, and nearly threw himself as they snubbed him to a post in the center of the corral.

"Watch now, *señor*," Celestino said. "Ramòn will ride that big, black *cabron*. This will be something to see."

Agapito choked down the straining animal and eared it, while Ramòn slipped the *jàquima* over the horse's head and pulled down the blinds. They didn't bother with a blanket and had the saddle up in seconds. The *làtigo* was pulled through the cinch ring and tied off. Ramòn tugged at his *sombrero*, setting it tightly on his head. Then *mecate* and a fistful of mane in one hand, saddle horn in the other, he stepped into the stirrup and swung up. "*Pronto —* " he called, leaning over to lift the blinds, and Agapito released the horse.

With a squeal of rage, the black lowered his head, put his nose between his two front feet, and then shot into the air, pawing at the sky. He plunged back to land on four rigid legs to jolt his rider, but Ramòn stayed tightly in the saddle. The horse reared and twisted his body, landed on his front feet and kicked viciously with his hind legs. He bucked in a circle and then reversed. With each jump he kicked out with a powerful, jolting twist. Ramòn stuck. Around and around they went, the big black doing everything to unseat his rider. Celestino and Agapito were calling encouragement to Ramòn, who soon had the winded animal trotting around the corral.

"*Viva, Ramòn. Viva!*"

"I'd like to be trying that." The words just blurted out of Jeremiah.

The astounded *vaqueros* looked at each other. Let this *irlandès* ride a bucking bronco? What if he gets hurt? *Caramba*, what if he gets killed? What would the *patròn* say about that? More important, what would the *señora* do? Ramòn and Agapito considered it. On the other hand, Ramòn had just taken the buck out of the black for today. Or most of it. Maybe? Perhaps!

Agapito shrugged. "*Si, lo quieres, es tu muerte.*" Ramòn agreed. "If you wish it, it's your death."

"*Cuidado,*" Celestino cautioned. "Watch out. Be careful."

But all Jeremiah understood was the yes part. He eagerly climbed the fence and was quickly helped into the saddle. He nodded at Agapito when he felt ready and the two *vaqueros* stepped back, releasing the horse. The black humped up and started off with short, crow-like hops. Jeremiah kept his hand tightly clasped around the saddle horn and feet solidly in the stirrups. *I'm riding this bucking horse. Me, it is, Jeremiah Cleary, up here staying with this wild horse.*

Then suddenly the black climbed skyward on his hind legs and came down with a stiff jolt on two front feet, his head bowed out of sight. Jeremiah lost his grip on the saddle horn, his feet slipped out of both stirrups, and his seat left the saddle. He flew in a loop right over the horse's ears and landed with a sickening thud. The wind was crushed out of him like a collapsed bellows. He lay crumpled and still as the two *vaqueros* rushed to his side. Celestino hurried to the gate and stepped through, caught and tied the horse.

"How is he?" Celestino called.

"*No se,*" Ramòn answered.

"I don't know, either," Agapito agreed. Jeremiah moaned and started to sit up.

"*Gracias a Diòs,*" Celestino murmured, blessing himself. "*Como esta?*"

Jeremiah was gasping for breath, his head ached, blood poured from his nose, his chest pained. His eyes slowly began to focus. And a vision floated into his dazed view. Bending over him, a sympathetic pout to her red lips, and a frown of concern above those black eyes, was the girl in the red dress. But now it was a white cotton dress and the red was in the comb holding her jet black hair. Was this an angel?

Jeremiah shook his head to rid himself of the vision. But she was real and she was worried about him. "*Pobrecito,*" she murmured.

Jeremiah was as embarrassed as he was hurt. Pride goeth before a fall, he thought as his head cleared. He struggled to his feet.

Celestino asked again, "How are you, Jerry?"

"Just grand," Jeremiah said. "Just grand." And he limped from the corral.

That night at supper, his ribs pained him so he could hardly breathe. He managed to muster a surprised smile when the girl appeared, helping to serve the meal. He nodded when she was introduced by Emily.

"This is Guadalupe Morales, Rogelio's sister. Weeb insists she help me for a few days until my back is better," Emily said. "We call her Lupe."

"How do you do, ma'am," Jeremiah said politely. At last he had a name.

Lupe nodded back, but said nothing.

She continued serving, but kept her eyes cast down and didn't even glance his way while Ramòn told the story of the bucking bronc. He did it with many hand motions, the last illustrating Jeremiah's cartwheel over the head of the horse. Everyone was laughing, including Weeb, but Emily felt sorry for her Irish cowboy. "Ah, poor Jerry," she said. "Where did you land?"

"All over," Jeremiah replied. "Everywhere."

Throughout supper, he couldn't stop glancing over at Lupe Morales. When she passed him a plate, her touch was hot. He didn't know much about girls, but he realized that Lupe would welcome his advances. But what would follow if he were to take her off alone?

His thoughts roamed over her. He imagined his hands on her body, cupping those enticing mounds beneath the loose dress, pressing himself against her soft roundness. He could lose himself in those eyes and kiss the pout from those crimson lips, as red as the dress she wore the first time he saw her. When his thoughts ran like this he felt himself swell up and was ashamed.

CHAPTER NINE

THROWING THE FINAL FORKFUL of hay to the horses, Jeremiah stretched, walked to the barn door, and looked out into the yard. It was November and darkening dusk came early. The air was crisp and he took deep breaths as he started back into the barn. Then something caught his eye. Somebody had entered the yard and he couldn't make out who it was. A tall man, not one of the *vaqueros*, was coming toward him.

Matthew!

Jeremiah dropped his pitchfork and ran toward his brother with arms wide open. Matthew came into them and they held each other tightly.

"How are you, my brother?" Jeremiah cried. "Are you in health? Did you find gold? How did you get here?"

Matthew laughed and tried one of his skipping dance steps. "How am I? Just grand, Brother, fine, lovely. And as to how I got here, the answer to that will be telling you the answer to your other question. I walked. From San Francisco."

Even in the gathering dark, Jeremiah could see that Matthew's brogans were falling apart, his clothes were tattered. But the sunken cheeks and the hollow look of his eyes were what chilled Jeremiah. His brother showed the effects of a hard three years. "Ah, Matthew, Matthew, it's just happy I am to be having you back," Jeremiah enthused. "You're just in time for supper."

He took his brother's arm and moved him toward the house, but Matthew pulled back. "I can't be doing that," he protested. "They'd not be expecting me. It wouldn't be fitting. I'll wait out here for you."

It took a while for Jeremiah to convince his brother that California *rancheros* didn't need advance notice to offer hospitality, that he'd be welcomed. Finally, Matthew set aside his pride, squared his shoulders, and entered the room where the ranch hands were seated in their usual places at the big table with the Jeffersons. Conversation abruptly stopped and all eyes were on the Cleary boys as they came through the doorway.

"This is my brother," Jeremiah announced. "He just arrived from the gold mines."

Matthew nodded and met the gaze of each in turn. But if they were aware of his shabby appearance they were too polite to stare. There were mumbled greetings from the men and then Emily Jefferson, the surprise worn off, sprang from her seat and made a place for Matthew. "I'll get another plate," she said, hurrying off to the kitchen.

"Welcome," Weeb boomed. "Jerry's been wondering how you were doing, dammit. It's damn good you're back here. Sit down and have some supper."

Matthew tried not to let his hunger show and no one asked him about the gold mines—it was obvious he hadn't found the Mother Lode. He was eating steadily, head down when Lupe Morales leaned over him to place another plate of stew on the table.

Startled, Matthew glanced up at the girl, partially hidden by black hair falling across her face to her shoulder. But when he saw her sparkling eyes and red lips, and the low cut blouse, he quickly looked away.

When supper was over, Weeb gave the men their instructions for the next day's work. Then he added, "And, Jerry, take your brother to the bunkhouse. He's a welcome guest."

Jeremiah puffed on his pipe and Matthew pulled a small flask from his otherwise empty pockets. They sat on the bunkhouse steps, quietly at first, just pleased to be together again. Then Matthew asked if there'd been any news from home.

"Well, there was a letter from John Hurley in Boston. He'd had it from James that all is well with Liam. He's married, by the way. More evictions about the countryside. John mostly wrote about politics in Ireland and Boston. The usual."

"Grand," Matthew said, raising his bottle. "Let's be drinking to that, a rising."

Jeremiah waved off the bottle and snorted in derision. "It's all talk. They'll not be doing anything but form organizations and make speeches. If they do anything else the British will just make more martyrs for them to sing about," Jeremiah said with disgust. "Now be telling me about yourself."

Matthew stared into the darkness for a moment. "Well now, there's not all that much to tell," he said uncomfortably. "As you can see, I'm back with nothing. Others struck it rich all about me. Jerry, I saw nuggets as big as my fist. I heard it said about the luck of the Irish, but none stuck to me. Not yet." Matthew took a pull on his flask and gave his brother a defiant glare. "This was all that kept me going." Jeremiah shook his head, but said nothing. "I'll be heading back," Matthew continued, "soon as I make myself another stake. I'll be striking it one day and I'll ride back here in style, in a grand carriage. Maybe I'll buy this rancho."

Jeremiah shook his head and raised an eyebrow, but held his tongue.

"We went to Sonora," Matthew continued, "but the claims were all taken and I worked for others. Every bit of dust I was paid went to buy my food and lodging. I went on to Jamestown, and filed my own claim on Wood Creek, and worked it for four months. I found a trace of gold there. Enough to raise up my hopes, but it failed to pay."

Matthew finished off his bottle and set it on the steps beside him. "I joined a group of men headed for Grass Valley and we washed for gold with a Long Tom. We should have built a sluice like the others were doing. Our amount of gold was pitiful. We gave it up and I worked for wages at the sawmill there until I had enough to head back here."

Jeremiah tried to think of some consoling words, but they didn't come. "And how was it you found me?" he asked.

"Finding you was the easy part. In San Francisco I asked for San Juan Bautista and they pointed south. When I arrived I

61

asked for you. They told me McMahan, at his store, knew every Irishman around here and sure enough he knew you."

"What will you do now?" Jeremiah asked.

"It's a job I'm after and then I'm back for the gold country. Placerville, it will be, as soon as I've earned a bit to get me there and keep me until I strike it."

"I could be speaking to Weeb Jefferson. He might want another hand around the place," Jeremiah offered.

"You'll not. I'll get my own job. It's no man's charity I'll be taking," Matthew declared. "I saw a forge in town. I'll ask if there's a helper wanted."

They sat in silence for a moment and then Matthew asked, "That girl in there, who is she?"

"Be watching yourself. That's Rogelio's sister."

"All I was asking was her name."

"Guadalupe Morales," Jeremiah told him. "You be leaving her alone."

"Are you having her staked out for your own then?"

"Don't you be dirtying her with your black tongue. She's a good girl."

"Aye."

In the morning Matthew was gone. But Jeremiah soon received word from his brother that he'd taken a job at Twitchel's forge at the corner of Franklin and Third in San Juan. Busy from dawn 'til dark repairing wagon wheels, shoeing horses, forging tools, the blacksmith was glad to have some experienced help. Matthew's skills soon returned and his Irish charm attracted customers.

Guadalupe Morales, no longer needed at the ranch since Emily's back had stopped paining her, was once again living in town. Jeremiah was thinking about her when next he walked up Third Street. Suddenly, there she was before him, wearing a yellow dress this time, a yellow rose in her dark hair. Standing on the corner, one hip thrust out to rest a package, her bare arm around it. She appraised him as he approached, her head tilted in that appealing way she had, her eyebrows raised. He started to turn away. Lupe stepped out in front of him, laughing. "What is the matter, *Señor* Cleary? You do not like me, perhaps?"

"No, ma'am," he answered. But that wasn't what he meant. "Yes, ma'am," he amended. The devil take this girl, she had him all mixed up.

"Perhaps you would help me, no?" The eyebrows shot up in a delightful curve to punctuate the question. "This package, it is heavy."

Jeremiah nodded politely and took the package from her. Her warm, bare arm caught in his and she gently untangled herself. The contact sent a rush of blood to his head and again she laughed. The package wasn't a bit heavy, he realized, as he followed her down the street. But he willingly played the charade in exchange for the view she gave him, her lush, supple body moving in front of him, the dress molding and caressing the curves of her legs and buttocks. She led him to a small *adobe* only two blocks away and opened the door. Jeremiah handed her the package and held the door open for her. She brushed against him as she went inside, the contact of her body sent a shiver through his entire being.

"Thank you," Lupe said and with a quizzical smile she held the door open.

For a moment Jeremiah stood still in indecision. And then the moment was gone. She realized his unwillingness to enter her house and so she gently shut the door. Jeremiah walked off, his thoughts in turmoil. But he knew that had he gone inside, there would be meaning to the act. Maybe he'd have met her parents. Or, what if her parents weren't home? What then would have happened?

Jeremiah Cleary, he told himself, as he strode off to find his horse and surrey, you have a good job with the Jeffersons and you could court this woman. Now you want her. But could you love her? Could you stay right here and make a home? If you go through that door, it means marriage. That's Rogelio's sister, he reminded himself. She's a good Catholic girl, no different than those *colleens* who flirted and teased in Ireland.

Not that they'd ever had much time for such a serious one as me, always with an eye for the books. I don't know much about girls. But if I go through that door what happens to my dream of my own land? Would I ever go off to find it? Would I leave a wife and maybe some babies? And what of my dream of having a real Irish colleen for my wife? Is that a dream worth keeping? I have no land and I have no Irish girl waiting for me. Could it ever happen, or am I just the one to believe in the fairy folks? And here's a flesh and blood creature, a beautiful girl, just inviting me to court her. And I can imagine what it would be to hold her, touch her, kiss her, love her.

Aye, it's daft you are, Jerry Cleary, he told himself.

Before he left for the ranch, Jeremiah tied up at the rail in front of the post office. He waited while the postmaster rifled through his stack.

"Ah, here you are, Cleary. It's from Boston."

It was from John Hurley and Jeremiah hurriedly scanned it for news of Ireland. Near the end he found what he was looking for. *Catherine and Molly are at home with my brother and father. Your brother Liam is married now to Eileen Coughlan from Drimoleague and is on your family holding.*

Molly at home, Jeremiah thought. That means she's not married. Catherine must still be in mourning for her dead betrothed. But Molly not married! She'd be a grown woman by now.

Jeremiah slowly read the first part of John's letter: *Dear Jerry and Matt, I hope this finds you in good health and prospering in California. I write to advise you that I am now a married man. My wife's name is Rose and we will have a child soon. I am foreman of a street crew now and a member of the Democratic party in Dan Hennessy's ward. We are doing well. James writes that the harvest in Ireland was good and no hunger this year, but new land laws make it even easier for landlords to evict and some are clearing out their land to graze sheep. Knocked houses are everywhere. There is much unrest and agitation in Skibbereen. Here in Boston we have organized to raise money for Ireland. If you can help the cause send a contribution through me.*

Jeremiah snorted. So that was it. An appeal from John for the cause. The cause! Unrest and agitation, is it? Another rising planned? Another failure with men killed and thrown in jail to rot. He'd not be a part of the politics. Leave that to John and Hennessy and the rest in Boston. And to James, too, in Ireland. God help them. Irish politics had no part in his American dream.

He tucked the letter in his pocket and swung into the saddle. Now he had more to chew on as he rode home—the girl in the red cotton dress, Irish politics and Molly Hurley.

CHAPTER TEN

"LAND SAKES," Emily said with a happy smile, "I can smell the meat cooking from here. And just listen to that music. And we're still a mile from town."

"And the rumble of all those damn people," Weeb grumbled. He didn't like crowds, but today was an exception—Sunday, June 24, 1856, the day of the annual fiesta to commemorate the feast of St. John, patròn saint of Mission San Juan Bautista. But it was also the opening of Angelo Zanetta's new Plaza Hotel and people came from all the ranchos to join the townspeople for the festivities.

Jeremiah drove the surrey into the excitement and confusion of the square to let out Weeb and Emily in the midst of all the laughing, talking, shouting people. The veranda of the Plaza Hotel was ablaze with colorfully-dressed women; the *señoritas* among them casting glances from behind their fans at the young, gaudily-attired *caballeros*, who kept their mounts prancing to impress the ladies.

Jeremiah finally found a place on a side street to park the surrey amid all the saddle horses, buggies, wagons and ox carts. He stood with Matthew watching from the shade of the livery stable as a chicken was buried in the center of the square, just the head sticking up. Jeremiah had seen this event before. He didn't care for the brutality, but Jeremiah was always amazed at the riding skill. That was Jorge at the edge of the plaza, his palomino prancing, making ready for the run.

"Andale, pronto!" he shouted and the palomino flew across the plaza, straight for the chicken. Swiftly, Jorge bent over the horse's side, skimming the ground, and deftly plucked the head from the bird. The crowd cheered. Jorge grinned at the applause and rode across the square, bowing to the ladies on the veranda, their fans fluttering, their white handkerchiefs waving.

The brothers watched the vaqueros demonstrate their abilities with the *reata,* and Ramon win the bucking bronco contest. Then Matthew announced that he was going off to meet some friends at Florney's Saloon. Jeremiah decided to go along and keep a quiet eye on his brother.

He puffed his pipe as Matthew amused his friends with jokes and Irish songs and, when he'd had some huge swallows from the jug, an exhibition of some tipsy step dancing.

When the excited sounds from the plaza indicated they were bringing out the bull and the bear, Matthew and his cronies, and a reluctant Jeremiah, headed outside. They pushed through the crowd to find a place in front of the mission and cheered for the bear as the huge animal was goaded from a cage atop a cart and staked to the center of the plaza. Then the crowd cheered equally as loud for the bull. Jeremiah didn't want to watch. He'd seen such a spectacle before and he had no interest in seeing the poor brutes tear each other apart. But Matthew was eager to witness his first bull and bear fight and insisted on staying.

Jeremiah looked away as the bull made a rush and drove a horn into the bear's side. He felt a hand on his shoulder. "I, too, refuse to watch such a cruel thing," a soft, familiar voice said. He quickly turned toward the voice and there, by his shoulder, stood Lupe Morales.

Without thinking, Jeremiah said, "Come. Let's get away from here."

She took his hand and held it under her arm and let him escort her through the crowd into the mission corridor. But the cries of the crowd, now in full blood lust, reached them there, too, so they slipped through an open door into the mission courtyard. Neither spoke as Jeremiah, still clutching her arm, led her to the sundial in the garden. There they stood, all their attention focused on the sundial. She clamped his hand beneath her arm and pressed it to her. He felt the heat of it, the swelling of her breast against the back of his hand. He could hardly breathe. His whole body was on fire.

Slowly she raised her head and looked up at him, her long lashes swept up to open eyes that questioned his. He turned to face her and drew her to him. Looking down, he felt himself melting into those eyes and gently took her chin in his hand. She raised her parted lips and he kissed her. Softly, gently, easily at first. And then demandingly, fiercely, with a hunger he'd never known before. Her arms went around his neck and her fingers wound into his hair. Her body moved against his.

He took her by the shoulders and held her away from him. Neither had spoken. He led her to a bench and they sat, side by side, but facing each other. He wondered at the forces raging inside him. She tilted her head and studied him, a half smile on her face.

"You love me, no?" Lupe asked, her raised eyebrows demanding an answer.

"I don't know," Jeremiah answered. "Maybe."

"What will we do?" She was a little girl seeking an answer and he didn't have one to give. It would be so easy to claim love for her, he thought. And it would be so easy to love her. Then he could have her. He looked at her, drank in the promise of her lush body. Yes, he wanted this woman. He must have her.

It was then he realized the crowd noise from the plaza had died down. People were entering the mission garden. The carnage was over. Jeremiah thought he should find Matthew, get him away before he went back to Florney's and more drinking. He looked again at Lupe, so pretty and vulnerable, sitting with her hands in her lap, gazing up at him, the innocent question still in her eyes.

But Matthew was already back at Florney's Saloon, drinking toasts to the victorious bull, when the talk turned to Charlie Folger's big, sorrel saddle horse, which nobody could shoe.

"I could shoe him," Matthew spoke up.

"You'll have to throw him and tie him to get a shoe nailed on. He's a kicking fool," Folger warned.

"Sure now and isn't it myself that's the best farrier this side of the Mississippi?" Matthew boasted.

Somebody bet five dollars and they led Folger's horse over to the blacksmith shop. The forge wasn't lit, so Matthew would have to put on cold shoes. They'd brought along a bottle and everyone had another shot while Matthew selected the right size shoes.

"You're not even going to tie up a foot?" Folger asked nervously.

"No need for that," Matthew slurred.

Folger clamped down on the twitch and the horse stood still, but snorting, nostrils flared, ears back. Matthew reached down to lift a hind foot.

"Watch out, Matt — !" someone shouted.

Jeremiah was still seated in the garden with Lupe when Charlie Folger found him. He came running over, frantic, gasping for breath. "Hurry, Jerry, come quickly — !"

"What's the matter?" Jeremiah asked, knowing it had to do with Matthew. He looked at Lupe. "I have to go. I'll come to you." She nodded silently and watched the two men race from the garden.

"How bad is he?" Jeremiah asked, his heart pounding.

"Bad," Folger said. "The horse kicked him with both hind feet at once. Got him in the chest and — "

"And where?"

"The head," Folger answered.

Matthew was laid out on a table in Charlie Folger's parlor. His friends, sober now, were gathered around, shamefaced before Jeremiah's stare. He looked at his brother laying there so still and white, his labored breath coming in harsh, short gasps as the doctor stitched up the lacerated scalp, swathed Matthew's head in bandages, and checked his bruised chest for broken ribs.

"How bad is it, doctor?" Jeremiah anxiously looked into the somber eyes of Doc McDougal, who sadly shook his head.

"I don't know. If he lives, he may be demented from a blow like that. Prepare yourself."

Jeremiah looked aside to wiped away his tears as several men helped the doctor move Matthew to a room in Folger's house and lowered him onto the bed. For the rest of the evening, Jeremiah sat by his brother's side, watching his every move, looking for a sign. Weeb and Emily, who'd heard the news from Lupe Morales, hurried over to see how Matthew was doing. Then Weeb drove the surrey home so Jeremiah could spend the night by his brother's bedside.

Jeremiah looked at Matthew's ashen face, his eyes rolled back in his head. *If I hadn't left him, if only I'd stayed with him, kept him away from the drink, this wouldn't have happened. But I was with a girl. That girl.* Thoughts of Lupe mingled with guilt. *God in heaven, I want that woman. But if I had stayed with my brother he'd not be here near death.*

Just after dawn, Matthew moaned and moved. He tried to sit up, but Jeremiah gently pushed him back onto the bed. In the pale glow of the lantern, Jeremiah could see the glint of his eyes.

"Jerry," Matthew whispered. "What happened? What are you doing here? What in the hell was I drinking?"

Jeremiah was so relieved to hear his brother speak, the fear and guilt vanished. And anger replaced them. "The drink was bad enough, you fool," Jeremiah berated him. "You tried to shoe that outlaw horse and got kicked in the head."

"Did I now?" Matthew spoke in a louder voice, more like himself. "And doesn't it only go to prove what I always said?"

"And what is that?" Jeremiah asked sarcastically.

"That those brutes are stupid. Any horse should know that he can't kill an Irishman by kicking him in the head." Matthew lay back on the bed, grinning, while Jeremiah sat there, shaking his head in exasperation.

* * * * *

Each day after his chores were finished, Jeremiah rode into town to visit Matthew. As his health improved the two began talking again about the future. Jeremiah wanted desperately to dissuade Matthew from going back to the mines.

"Come along with me, Matt. We'll find good land and go into ranching together. There's plenty of good government land left, just for the taking. All we have to do is ride out and find it."

"Me? Me, is it, you're asking to spend my days following some horse around a field?" Matthew laughed derisively. "Me, spend my waking hours riding around on the back of one of those brutes? Well now, Jerry, and wouldn't that be a sin against humanity? My humanity, not to mention my sore arse!"

Matthew looked at Jeremiah excitedly. "I've got a better idea, Brother. You come with me. We'll dig up so much gold you can be buying the best ranch in all of California."

But Jeremiah shook his head. "No, Matt. Mining for gold is not for me. My life will be on the land."

"So what will you do, Jerry?"

"I'm going off to find my own land."

"And when will you leave?"

"Soon."

"Will you be going — alone?" Matthew grinned as he waited for his brother's answer.

"And what is it you're meaning by that?"

"Sure, and wasn't it myself that was watching you sneak off at the fiesta with Lupe Morales?"

"That's my business," Jeremiah retorted, glowering at Matthew. "You'd best be leaving Lupe out of this."

"Oh. And now why is that? If you're not wanting her, I just may go calling myself."

"You be leaving her alone." Jeremiah felt his anger rising. "She's a good, decent girl."

"But not good enough for you, is it? Right, Jerry?"

"You'll not be talking that way about her, Matt. I'm warning you."

Matthew raised his head and for a moment the two brothers glared at each other. Then Matthew shrugged and laughed.

On his ride home that night, Jeremiah pushed the argument over Lupe out of his mind. He'd sort that out later. He felt a surge of excitement thinking about finding his own land. First he'd try the hills toward the coast, the Jolon country he'd heard about, where there was plenty of water and good grass deep in the canyons, but not much open flat land left for farming. His second choice would be on the east side of the Salinas Plain, one of those little valleys. That country was mostly unsurveyed, free government land for the taking by preemption.

But then images of Lupe Morales overrode all his dreams and future plans. *I told her I'd come to her. But I haven't yet. When I said it, I fully meant it, but if I do go, that means marriage. Do I really love her? Or is it that she just sets my blood to boil? Is she the one I want beside me always? Or is this just me, who's never had a woman, wanting to rut like some animal?*

All night he lay awake, grappling with desire and conscience. In the morning he gave notice to Weeb Jefferson and began packing his things, making arrangements for his hors-

71

es, two big, stout, white, work mares that Emily Jefferson had named Maud and Nellie when Jeremiah had found them running wild with their colts in a herd of mustangs in the San Joaquin Valley. "Every work mare I ever heard of back in Illinois was named Maud or Nellie," she said. "I'm sure that's what they called those two before they ran off from some immigrant wagon train." Jefferson would pasture them along with Jeremiah's two brood mares while he was on his land search. And yes, Jefferson would sell him cattle when he was ready for them.

But Weeb Jefferson wasn't happy about it. "I'm sure going to miss that damn Irishman," he told Emily. "Why's he want to up and leave, dammit?"

"Weeb, you stop that swearing and grumbling." Emily's response was automatic. "You know that boy has always wanted a place of his own."

"I'm not grumbling, dammit. I just wish he'd stay. He might not be much of a talker, but he's one helluva worker and he's practically been running this place."

"Jerry has to leave, Weeb. It's time he got on with his life. He broods about that brother of his too much. Blames himself because Matthew drinks. Thinks it was his fault Matt got hurt. Tries to find a way to stop him from going off to the gold mines again."

"Dammit, Emily. There isn't a solitary thing Jerry can do to stop his brother's drinking. Or keep him from going off to hunt gold. He can't be living his damn brother's life for him." Emily knew her husband was right and the conversation ended there. She also had to admit that, as happy as she was for Jeremiah to be heading out on his own, she, too, would miss him something fierce.

Jeremiah rode to town on his gray gelding, the colt he'd broken himself and called Bouchal, to say goodbye to Matthew, who was getting ready to head off to the mines again. "You can always find me when you come back," he told his brother. "McMahan or Weeb will know where I am."

They clasped hands and Matthew said, "I wish you well, Brother. Find your land and be happy on it. I'll come looking for you with bags of gold."

The two men gave each other one final hug and pat on the shoulder and then Jeremiah led his horse around to the side street. He tied Bouchal to the hitching rail, and knocked on the door of the little *adobe*. Lupe opened the door and gave a glad cry when she saw him standing there. She held out her hands to take his. But Jeremiah resisted their pull. He stood in the doorway just looking at her for a long moment. Slowly, the smile faded from her face.

"I've come to tell you goodbye. I'm leaving San Juan," Jeremiah said.

"But I thought — ?" Lupe bit her lip and looked at him, searching his face. "You are leaving me, too," she whispered, tears welling up in her eyes.

He nodded, turned away from her, walked to his horse and mounted. As he rode past the door he saw her, still standing there, stiff and proud. And beautiful. But the tears in those big, black eyes haunted him.

CHAPTER ELEVEN

J EREMIAH RODE HUNCHED over with the strong north wind at his back. He'd pulled the collar of his heavy sheepskin coat up over his ears and tied his sombrero tightly with a string under his chin, not because it was cold, but because of the force of the blowing sand, which entered into every crevice of his clothing.

The windswept Salinas Plain into which Jeremiah rode in the spring of 1857 was a long, narrow valley, nearly one hundred miles from the headwaters of the Salinas River to where it emptied into Monterey Bay. In the summer it was a sad sight, just a ribbon of dry sand amid willow trees and fields of tall mustard waving in the wind. On each side of the river, stretching to the foothills east and west, it was empty and wild. Some maps called it the Great Salinas Desert and settlers on the valley floor were few.

In the winter the river came frightfully alive as water tumbled out of the tributaries, churning and roiling, rushing toward the sea and carrying all in its way, soil from the banks, scrub brush and even large trees. But in the spring it was a beautiful sight, flowing deeply and peacefully, murmuring amid the wildflowers.

In May it was too wide to cross where Jeremiah hit it above the mouth. And he'd heard the warnings about quicksand. So he led Bouchal onto the ferry and paid out the Mexican silver piece for the crossing. He was heading for the hills to the west of the river, which stood green and dark, promising lush valleys and meadows, streams and springs with abundant water. That's where most of the large ranchos were, but the land agent had said there was still open land to be had. Those hills to the west, the Lucias, had more the green look of Ireland, and were in sharp contrast to the hills to the east of the Salinas Plain, the Gabilans.

Jeremiah could see those just across the valley, low and rolling, sort of gentle, but with hardly a tree. How could such land, which didn't grow a tree, be fertile? And was there enough water for stock? Or for a house? Perhaps, he thought, that was why there was so much unsurveyed government land for the taking in those Gabilans.

Sleeping out at night, Jeremiah let the hobbled Bouchal graze nearby. He avoided people. Not that there were that many—a lonely cabin here or there, the ruins of Mission Soledad, and Rancho Los Coches, a wayside inn.

He forded the Arroyo Seco River, still high from spring runoff and nearly up to Bouchal's withers. Jeremiah and the horse dried out in the midday sun as he took the old ruts of the ox cart trail up a canyon, which he'd been told would lead him to Mission San Antonio, and on to the settlement of Jolon. He camped on a small creek above the mission and rode into the tiny town next morning. He tied Bouchal in the shade behind a large inn of *adobe* brick, eased the cinch, and hung the bridle over the saddle horn. The morning sun was already high, chasing the shadows and warming the veranda as Jeremiah stepped up.

He walked into the cool gloom inside and looked around. It was an elegant place with its thick walls and huge, beamed ceiling. A wide fireplace of rock filled one end of the room and the bar ran practically its length. A listless game of poker occupied four men at a corner table and two *vaqueros* lounged against the bar talking horses.

The bartender came over. "What'll you have?"

"Just information, please, if you're not minding," Jeremiah replied.

The bartender recognized Jeremiah's thick brogue. "Sure, Paddy, I've got a lot of information and advice — "

"My name isn't Paddy," Jeremiah interrupted. "It's Jeremiah Cleary. I was told that there'd be free government land in this valley. Would you be kind enough to tell me where I'll find it?"

The bartender shook his head. "My advice to you, Mister Cleary, is to look somewhere else. This valley is mostly owned by the big ranchos. Oh, there may be some government land left in the canyons here and there, but it's not worth much."

"Hey, Paddy"—one of the card players entered the conversation—-"I thought you were one of the greasers by that hat you're wearing." He pointed to Jeremiah's *sombrero*. "You might even be an American, or close enough to it. At least you're a white man. We can direct you."

Jeremiah eyed the man. He didn't like what he saw. His jaw was swollen with tobacco and the stains of it streaked his droopy mustache. He was a big man, but had gone soft in his middle.

Jeremiah stepped over to the table. "My name is not Paddy," he said politely. "It's Jeremiah Cleary and I'll thank you to call me so. If you can tell me about free land, I'll thank you for that, as well."

"Sure, sure, Paddy, don't be getting on your high horse," the big man said. "We just moved into this country ourselves. We're camped down the valley with our families and there's land there enough for all."

"Watch out, Mister Cleary," the bartender warned. "That's not government land down there. Those people are squatters. They're trying to steal land from Don Rios."

"Who you calling a squatter?" the big man cried out. His hard eyes bored into the bartender. "God dammit, we're American citizens and we've come all the way from Missouri to take up free land. The government promised. Right, boys?"

"Yeah, that's right," chorused the other three at the poker table. They pushed back their chairs and stood up. One of them said, "There's more land around here than these Mexes will ever need. We're entitled to it! And nobody can stop us."

"These greasers don't even own the land," the big man insisted. "They just think they do. We won the damn war. This country is part of the good old U.S.A. now, ain't it boys? The land is for Americans —"

"I'm not knowing about that," Jeremiah interrupted. He looked toward the bartender. "What's a squatter?"

"These people here." The bartender jerked his thumb in the direction of the foursome who stood glowering by their table. "They take possession of somebody else's land and make it their own. The trouble is some of these old Spanish and Mexican land titles are clouded up so sometimes they get away with it. They're no better than thieves."

"Nobody calls me a thief," the big squatter yelled, "I'm going to break your neck, you sonofabitch! And that goes for you, too, you greaser mick, as soon as I finish with this bastard!" He started over the bar for the bartender

Jeremiah wanted no part of this. He'd not lose his temper as he had in Panama. On the other hand, the bartender had been helpful to him and he didn't want to see him hurt.

As the big man started to climb the bar, Jeremiah moved quickly. He grabbed the man by the hair and jerked. The big man's head was twisted backward and down at the same time as Jeremiah swung his knee up to the man's face. The squatter slumped as his nose cracked and blood gushed out. Jeremiah drove a sharp, hard right into the man's midsection, his fist sinking deep into the flabby gut. The big squatter went limp, sliding against the bar as the air whooshed out of him. He dropped slowly over on his side and lay still.

"*Bedad*, I want no other man's land," Jeremiah stated, his steady gaze watching the other three men. "Will you be after taking his part?" They hurriedly backed away.

Jeremiah glared as the three squatters picked up the big man and set him in a chair. He slumped, still out cold. But his friends obviously wanted no more to do with the Irishman. Jeremiah waved off the thanks of the bartender and backed out onto the veranda, and into a commotion in front of the inn.

There were shouts and a sudden flurry of activity as the hostlers brought around a team of four fresh stage horses. And up the road, rounding into view, came the stage from Cock's Station, the horses at a trot. They came to a stop in front of the inn and the driver called out, "Here's your mail sack for San Antonio, Mister Sylvester." The sack was slung onto the veranda for the postmaster, who was hurrying across the dusty street.

Two men stepped down from the stagecoach and picked up their baggage as the hostlers were changing teams. Jeremiah noticed one wore a star on his vest and the other, in a suit and bowler hat, seemed to be giving orders. The pair entered the inn. In response to a question, one of the other spectators explained, "That's Appleby from San Francisco, agent for the Atchinson Land Company, and the other's Sheriff John Keating from Monterey. They've come to evict the squatters from the Hidalgo place."

"That's good," Jeremiah said.

"Not really," the man explained. "Those people been on that land up there for years, mostly Indians and Mexes. They thought it was theirs for generations. Now this land company claims to own it. Looks like he's got the law on his side today. There'll be a lot of families on the road by nightfall."

Jeremiah shook his head. This could be Ireland. Evictions and the law. Poor people put out on the road. But good squatters and bad squatters? Now that took some understanding. He walked around back, bridled Bouchal, pulled up the cinch and stepped on. He took the stage road toward Cocks' Station and out of the Jolon country. He didn't understand it. Too much conflict.

Jeremiah was muttering to himself as he rode. "Greaser mick, is it? Paddy this and Paddy that, like I'm still in Boston."

Getting further on down the road, Jeremiah continued complaining to the horse. "American citizens, they were. Saying it like they're better than me. And what am I now, I ask you, Boy-0? Sure, and isn't it an American citizen I am myself these past six months?" He slapped his saddle bag where the important paper was tucked away. "I'd not be getting my own land without this, I'm thinking."

Jeremiah thought of the proud day he'd been to the court-house in Monterey, stood up before the county clerk and raised his right hand to swear. He swore to defend the United States of America against all enemies and renounced allegiance to the kingdom of Great Britain.

"And wasn't that a good one now, Bouchal?" He slapped his leg and laughed aloud. Bouchal jumped at the unusual sound from his rider. Renounce allegiance to Great Britain? Jeremiah scoffed. What allegiance? The cruel monsters. God may have blighted the potato, but England starved the Irish.

At Cocks' Station, Jeremiah was greeted by the owner, Henry Cocks. "You'll find a stall in that barn over there. Fodder for both you and your horse, and a bed for you, one fifty for the night," Cocks said.

Jeremiah unsaddled Bouchal and rubbed the big, gray geld-ing down with straw and led him to the water trough. Jeremiah filled the manger with sweet barley hay and turned Bouchal into the stall. "Enjoy this," he told the horse in Irish. "It'll be another long time again before we both feast."

In the morning he crossed the Salinas River, took a long, open ridge to the east and found himself on a wide plateau dot-ted with grazing cattle. The land looked good to him as he tra-versed a gradual slope leading to the valley below. The hills around were carpeted in bright colors, the green of the grass broken in patterns of gold and blue, red, purple and white, a profusion of wild flowers just opening to the morning sun. They competed for space with wild oats, filaree and burr clover, and Jeremiah breathed in their fragrance. He reached the valley floor and skirted the small lake he'd been told about called Bitter Water.

He found a little creek breaking down the valley wall from the east and followed it to its junction with another meander-ing in from the south. The two formed a larger stream twisting and winding toward the west. He saw a few more signs of set-tlers, a cabin here and there, a scattering of growing wheat crops, a few cattle on the hillsides. He followed the stream southward. It was near dusk, and both horse and rider were tired as they reached the spot where the beautiful little valley widened out. He saw, on a commanding mound, a lone peach tree growing beside a small *adobe* house overlooking log corrals and the adjacent fields marked by brush fences. He made for the foothills to the west of the valley, and camped for the night beside the stream.

Sitting by his dying camp fire after a meager supper and some coffee, Jeremiah puffed on his pipe. The land he'd ridden through that day had good soil and water. There were oak trees scattered through the valley floor and on the nearby slopes, and pines standing higher up. But others had found it first. Jeremiah wanted more space. He wanted land that would be all his own with no fear that one day it would be taken away from him. The way it might if he were still in Ireland.

Jeremiah studied the starry night sky and voiced out loud to God that one day he'd raise his own children and no fever would kill them, and he'd fill their little bellies with good food so they'd grow strong—sure, and help him in the fields. He managed a smile with that thought and it was still there, gently on his lips as he fell into a peaceful sleep.

At dawn he climbed out of what he now called Peach Tree Valley and found a trail leading up the ridge to the west. He topped out as the sun reached its morning rays into the long valley spread out below him. Jeremiah sat on Bouchal and looked westward. The pine trees ended on the ridge behind him. Some sturdy oak trees led the way into the valley, but they soon were replaced by scrub oak, chaparral and chemise brush. Then even those became sparse and the low hills on each side of the valley were nearly bare.

Jeremiah narrowed his eyes, put a hand up to shade them from the brightness of the day, and intently surveyed the scene. He could see for five or six miles — there was no sign of habitation, no houses, no cattle. The path he was on had seldom been used. This must be empty land.

Empty, but for the tall wild oats and other grasses, which grew in abundance on the valley floor and covered the hillsides. This meant excellent feed for horses and cattle. Sitting on Bouchal, belly deep in the tall grass, Jeremiah exulted. The past winter had been moderately dry, so he knew that this soil would grow bountiful crops if blessed by even a little rainfall. He eased his horse down the trace, which took him into the narrow valley. It was met on his right by a canyon, flat on the bottom and sheltered on each side by hills that were low and gently rounded. This canyon, more than a mile long, opened into the widest, flattest expanse of the main valley.

It was there that Jeremiah stepped down from Bouchal, took off the saddle and bridle, buckled on the hobbles, and turned him loose. The horse moved off, grazing in wild oats as Jeremiah walked across the valley toward some low trees, the only ones in sight. He bent down to feel the earth, scooping up a handful. He squeezed it, rubbed it, broke it into particles, and let it sift through his fingers. He knew it was rich loam, and he found it as deep as he could prod with a broken tree branch.

He straightened up and looked around him. This would grow fine crops, he knew. But where was the water?

He went to Bouchal, saddled up and rode to the base of the hills, searching for a water course, a stream bed. Nothing. No wonder that this land was open for the taking.

Suddenly Bouchal jumped, spooked by a furry animal bounding out from the bank under the horse's feet. It ran into a nearby gulch and Jeremiah saw that they had disturbed a coyote den. "Well now, Bouchal, he needs water just like all God's creatures," Jeremiah spoke aloud to the horse. "Where does he drink? If there's one, there must be many. Where do they all drink?"

Within moments Jeremiah had his answer. Bouchal had stepped into swampy ground, a depression in the field at the edge of the hill. Surrounded by the green of the spring season, it had been undetectable. Now that he'd ridden right up on it,

81

Jeremiah could see a trickle of water seeping up from the ground leading into a narrow course that traversed the south edge of the valley. He quickly stepped from the horse and led him forward. Bouchal sniffed the water while Jeremiah keenly watched, and then the horse lowered his head and began to drink. Jeremiah cupped his hands and brought the cold water up to his own mouth. The taste was strange, alkali and other minerals he couldn't place. But it was fresh and clear. He took up another handful. He didn't savor it, but he could drink it.

Jeremiah drank his fill and splashed his face. Then he noticed the tracks leading down to the water, a trail along the bank, and on it the sign of deer and antelope. Game came here to drink, he realized. Was that little bit enough water for a farm, to keep stock? Surely, a well dug here would provide a supply.

Jeremiah rode Bouchal up the hill to the south and looked around. He could see a good stand of pines close enough to cut timber. As he rode toward it for a better look, he spotted another ravine with a tiny trickle that dripped from a spring. He got down and tasted it. It was bitter, but it could be boxed up to water cattle.

And so it might be possible. But he knew California. The wet green of the spring turned to dry brown in the summer. Many a springtime settler, thinking he was putting his home on the bank of a stream, found himself on a bone dry gulch when July rolled around.

Jeremiah sighed. He suddenly yearned for those emerald green fields of Ireland with water everywhere. But, he reasoned, if enough water could be developed here, wheat could be planted, cattle would fatten on the tall grasses. He could even raise horses. He could have a grand ranch here.

Would Molly like it?

He was at it again, letting his mind get fixed on her. Was it that she'd become a symbol, the name for an illusionary wife he'd have one day after these long, lonely years? Or was she real? Was there a flesh and blood Molly in Skibbereen? And if so, would she remember him?

That night Jeremiah made his camp on a knoll overlooking the valley. He lay on his bed under the open sky, the coyotes' yips and howls echoing around him, and was dazzled by a million stars. The immensity of God's world overwhelmed him so he couldn't close his eyes. He was comforted by the steady sounds of Bouchal cropping grass. He lay there, composing in his mind a letter to Molly Hurley, asking her to come and be his wife. But would she come?

CHAPTER TWELVE

MATTHEW CLEARY, clean shaven, stripped to the waist, his lean, supple muscles rippling as he pumped the bellows, watched the forge fire turn cherry red. He lifted the metal with heavy tongs, placed it on the anvil, whacked it with his hammer, once, twice, and plunged it into the water barrel. The steam hissed and gathered in a cloud. He followed the steam out of the open doorway, wiped the sweat from his face with his red bandanna and surveyed the busy main street of San Juan Bautista.

What was he still doing here? He'd recovered completely from being kicked in the head by Charlie Folger's horse. Fit and healthy, his meager belongings gathered, he should have been on his way long ago to seek gold in the Sierra's. Instead he'd returned to his job with Twitchel, moved into a little room behind the blacksmith shop, and settled in. Matthew wondered at himself. That kick in the head had knocked out his taste for whiskey, too. He hadn't had a drink since.

He looked down the street and saw her coming. She passed by nearly every day—on the other side of the street, never looking his way—carrying her packages. Matthew stood, his hammer and tongs in his hand, marveling at the graceful way she moved, almost as if she was swaying to music.

"*Buenos dias, señorita,*" he called.

But she didn't acknowledge the greeting. She never did. But he didn't stop trying. That's why he'd stayed in San Juan. He admitted it to himself. He was infatuated with Lupe Morales. Not in love with her. Of course, not. Matthew Cleary wasn't about to fall in love. He had adventures planned, gold to find, money to spend. He wasn't intending to shackle himself with a wife and a passel of children.

A few days later his persistence resulted in a nod from Lupe and a few days after that she responded. "Hello, *Señor* Cleary," was all she said but now she walked on his side of the street and finally she surrendered her packages for him to carry.

Matthew gave her his best crooked grin when they reached the door of the little *adobe* house. When she took the bags from his arms he reached for her hand. But she pulled it away and went inside. The door closed.

Matthew stood there a moment looking at his hand. It was hot from her touch. Damn that woman! She was in his mind all day and he dreamed of her at night. She had to know he was trying to court her, but gave no encouragement. Was there somebody else? Matthew never saw her with anyone. Was she still thinking about Jeremiah?

The next time he carried her packages, he invited her for a buggy ride in the evening. Lupe cocked her head to the side and considered the offer. Then she smiled and Matthew's heart jumped in his chest. "*Si, señor.* That would be nice. A picnic perhaps?"

Matthew grinned. He could hardly calm himself to answer. "Yes. A picnic would be grand," he blurted. "What shall I bring?"

"Leave that to me, *Señor* Cleary."

He arranged for a horse and buggy and borrowed a lap robe, his thoughts leaping to dusk by the river, just the two of them, the water softly rippling, the moon rising, and then Lupe in his arms. He could taste the sweetness of her full lips, feel the warmth of her body. His imagination soared. He reveled in anticipation.

She was waiting when he pulled up the rig in front of her house. In one hand she had a picnic hamper covered by a red and white checkered cloth. Her other hand held onto a young boy.

"This is my little brother, Hernando, *Señor* Cleary. He's coming on the picnic with us. Isn't that nice?"

"Oh, grand," Matthew said, barely hiding his disappointment. "Just grand."

But before the summer was over, there were moonlight rides and other picnics without the little brother.

* * * * *

Jeremiah went first to Monterey, where he filed his preemption papers on one hundred sixty acres of land, and on his return to San Juan was surprised to meet Matthew still in town.

"Well, well, Matt. Good to see you." They shook hands, wanting to embrace, but not doing so. "But I'm surprised you're still here. How are you? What happened?"

"Nothing," Matthew said. "I've got a good job here, putting a little aside. The gold can wait."

"I never thought I'd be hearing that from you." Jeremiah said.

Matthew shrugged. "Well, and did you find your land?"

"I did," Jeremiah answered. "It's seventy miles south of here in a little valley that I'll be having all to myself. And now I'm going to be hauling supplies back there and build a house."

Just then he heard the tapping sound of heels on the wooden sidewalk and looked up as Lupe Morales approached. She saw Jeremiah with Matthew, averted her eyes, and quickly turned away.

"Is that why you're still here, Matt?" Jeremiah asked.

"None of your business," his brother replied and went though the shop door, back to his forge.

Jeremiah stood there looking after the retreating girl for a moment and then at Matthew, busily hammering on his anvil. He was relieved to find that the sight of Lupe didn't disturb him as it once had. If Matthew treated her well and she responded, it was no business of his. Right? He sighed and put Matthew and Lupe out of his mind.

He walked over to the post office to finally send that letter to Molly in Ireland. As he handed over the letter, fear started deep in his belly. He'd ridden all the way to San Francisco and purchased the passage tickets. They were in the envelope with a money order for traveling expenses. He'd spent hours agonizing over the wording of the accompanying letter. What if he hadn't worded it properly? What if she refused the tickets? What if she didn't want to come? Good God, what if she was already married? It was too late to change anything now. It was done.

Then he figured it would take at least two and a half months for the letter to go across the Isthmus and the Atlantic and arrive in Skibbereen. It would take the same time for an answer to reach him. Five months, maybe six.

Waiting would be hard, but he had much to do. He shoved down his anxiety and strode into McMahan's store. Jeremiah gave his list to the storekeeper and asked, "James, who do you know to make *adobe* brick? I'll be needing to build a house on my new land."

"Calistro Salazar," McMahan answered. "You should know him. Works for Weeb sometimes. They say he's the best. Where you settling, Jerry?"

"I call it Long Valley," Jeremiah said. "Takes five days to get there in my wagon on the river route. Not much water, good soil, plenty of grass."

"Well, good for you. Better stock up plenty, if it's that far." McMahan advised. "Guess we won't be seeing much of you."

Jeremiah found Calistro Salazar and asked the question in his halting Spanish, *"Quire usted trabejar para me?"*

The Indian looked at Jeremiah, a puzzled frown on his face and politely inquired *"Como?"*

Jeremiah tried again and added, *"Un peso Americano por dia y comida."*

Salazar nodded in sudden understanding and replied, "Oh sure. I'll work for you. A dollar a day, American money, and you'll feed me." He said it with a wide grin and a hint of a brogue.

Jeremiah had to smile.

They hitched up the work horses and loaded the big Studebaker freight wagon, which Jeremiah purchased for seventy-five dollars, with pots and pans, some dishes and cups, food staples, axes, an adz, saws, hammers, a keg of nails, shovels and redwood for building water troughs, shoring up the well they'd dig, and making the table and chairs and the bedstead Jeremiah had in mind.

He and Calistro Salazar left San Juan early that fall, winding along the San Benito on the river route toward Long Valley. It was slow going, the team making twelve miles a day, four nights and five days on the road to reach Peach Tree. Jeremiah and Calistro cut trees and brush, widening the trail for the wagon, and finally rolled down the hill to Jeremiah's land. They made camp and, although it was late in the day, began digging the well.

After several days of hard work, the dropping bucket made a satisfying splash. They knocked together a water trough of redwood, erected a pole corral and cut brush from the hilltops to make drift fences to hold the grazing horses, before they started on the house.

From dawn to dusk they labored, hauling water to make mud, filling the forms for *adobe* bricks and drying them in the sun, cutting pine and dragging the timber from the next valley, the big work horses straining against their collars, sweating and stopping often to blow in the mid-day heat. Hauling rock in the wagon from San Lorenzo Creek to form the fireplace was even harder. But the house began to take shape, two rooms, the larger about twelve by twenty feet with a door in the center, the fireplace at one end and an opening at the other to a small bedroom. Jeremiah hung deer hides to cover the openings. He'd bring doors, window glass and more redwood shakes for the roof from San Juan before the rains.

"I know it's not so grand as the homes in San Juan," he told Calistro. "But it will do." He was comparing it in his mind to the cottages of Ireland. Would Molly like it?

Molly? His mind was on her constantly, especially as he fashioned the bedstead and laced the rawhide springs. Would she like the furniture he'd made? He knew she hadn't even received his letter yet, but anguished over what she'd think. Would she remember him? How would she feel? Would she come?

Sometimes he scoffed at himself for even thinking about a girl he hadn't seen for so long. She'd become part of the vision he'd cherished all this time of his own land and a *colleen* for a wife. He wondered if the young girl still had that quick wit? And the merry smile. The freckles. Was she still as pretty as he remembered?

It would be March or April before he'd have an answer. The waiting had not gotten easier, even with all the work he had to do to distract him. It was like to drive him daft, he thought.

* * * * *

While Jeremiah and Calistro were camped in Long Valley building the house, San Juan was alive with the excitement of the annual fiesta. There were festivities in the plaza and a *gran baille* that evening in the hotel. Lanterns hung from the ceiling, bunting decorated the walls, music filled the room for the swirling dancers. It echoed from the open windows, spilling into the plaza where more dancers in brilliant costumes whirled in a kaleidoscope of color.

Matthew proudly escorted Lupe Morales, radiant in a red dress, her lustrous black hair flowing down her back, caught on one side by a crimson rose, moist lips glistening, and eyes shining in the lamplight. He led her through the intricate steps of the Spanish dances, twirled her, held her close and swung her away again. She threw her head back and laughed for the pure enjoyment of the moment.

When the music stopped, they stood hand in hand, still laughing too hard to catch their breath. And when the music started up again, the beat was just right for Matthew to begin an impromptu exhibition of Irish dancing. The crowd circled the couple and clapped as Lupe tried the steps, tentatively at first, watching Matthew, and then faster and faster, arms at her side, her nimble feet flying on the floor. When the dance and the music were over they ducked out of the circle of applauding people, and walked into the darkness hand in hand.

Matthew stopped and pulled her to him. She was in his arms and he bent to kiss her, his lips crushing hers. Lupe gave a startled, hurt cry and pulled back. She looked at Matthew, searching his face in the moonlight. Then she stepped back into his embrace and looked up at him. She parted her lips and kissed him, gently, and then opened her mouth to him and moaned her hunger for love. He pressed against her, molded her breasts in his hands, stroked her back, her hips, kissed her neck. Lupe moved her body against his hardness, her hands caressing his hair.

They broke apart and with their arms tightly around each other, walked quickly to her house. There Lupe came against him again, softly kissed him, and opened the door. He moved to go inside with her. But she put her hand against his chest to gently stop him and said, "No, Matthew. Only in the marriage bed."

Matthew stood before the closed door, the words ringing in his ear. "Only in the marriage bed, only in the marriage bed."

Later he lay in his little room behind the forge and the words kept repeating in his mind, "Only in the marriage bed." Images of Lupe Morales, her beauty and her happy laugh, the feel of her body against his, the softness of her lips, the musky smell of her hair and the promise in her eyes kept him tossing and turning, awake all night.

When the dawn finally crept through the window of his room, Matthew Cleary thought to himself, it's a good job you've got, there's money coming in and you could be finding a little house and, what's more, you've not touched the drink now for months. Sure and it's time you settled down. He grinned to himself in the darkness as he sat up and threw off the covers.

The marriage bed, is it? And why not?

CHAPTER THIRTEEN

"WELL NOW, getting married, you say? Grand news!" Jeremiah clapped his brother on the shoulder and vigorously pumped his hand. "Lovely lass, that Lupe, just lovely. And when is this grand event to take place?"

"Soon as the banns are read at the mission," Matthew said, his face all smiles at his brother's reaction. "Next month."

"And won't that be a fine day? I'll be wanting to be here for such an event, your wedding day." Jeremiah was worrying about his own time schedule. He had to get back to his house, finish it and return to await his letter.

"Ah, Jerry—there's a bit of a problem, you see. Ah—Lupe, ah—that is—Wasn't I wanting you to stand up with me, my own brother? Sure now and I was, Jerry." Matthew took a deep breath but it was hard for him to look Jeremiah in the eye. "But Lupe, she was insistent. Put her foot down, she did." Matthew hung his head for a moment, almost mumbled the words, "Truth is, she doesn't even want you at our wedding."

Jeremiah stood facing Matthew by the forge and stared, his eyes filled with hurt. He blinked, started to speak, then turned away and walked out of the shop.

He was back in Long Valley when the wedding took place. He finished the roof, hung the doors, glazed the one window, all with an eye on the sky. By the time the wedding date had passed, Jeremiah had sorted it out in his mind. Pleased for his brother, he finally made himself understand Lupe Morales. There'd been nothing between them, not really. But there could have been—if he'd wished it. Was it she'd felt scorned? Well now, wasn't she his sister-in-law? They'd make it up.

The early rains softened the ground so Jeremiah hitched the horses to his plow and began working up the soil to plant his wheat. All the while, round after round, as the single share plow cut into the rich loam, Jeremiah thought about Molly. Would she have the letter by now? How would she answer?

"What do you think, Nellie?" he asked the big white mare as he led her from the water trough and put her with Maud to graze for the night. "Will she come? What will she look like, eh? Not big as you, I'm hoping. We'll be liking her whatever, now won't we, old girl?"

The gentle, work horses stopped munching grass for a moment, turned their big heads toward him, ears cocked forward, as if trying to understand. They'd never seen Jeremiah in such a playful mood.

His crop planted, a tight roof on the cabin, Jeremiah wasn't bothered by the gray, heavily overcast sky as he hitched his team to the empty wagon and started his trek back to San Juan. He slept under the wagon the second night on the river as the storm hit and was soon thoroughly soaked as he pushed Nellie and Maud to beat the rising waters down the San Benito River. He was welcomed at Weeb Jefferson's and settled into the bunkhouse.

When the weather cleared, Jeremiah caught Bouchal, who'd been running free on Jefferson's pasture, and saddled up for a trip to town. He was anxious to visit Matthew and Lupe, offer congratulations, pay his respects. Over dinner with Weeb and Emily, he was given an account of the wedding, which the Jeffersons had attended.

"It was a great occasion, Jerry," Emily said. "Lupe's relatives from San Jose came down and Rogelio stood up with Matthew. He was so handsome. Wearing a new suit and looking so fit and trim. He doesn't drink anymore, Jerry. Not a drop. Did you know that? Not since his accident. And Lupe was beautiful in a white gown. With lace and all. I think it was her mother's. Afterwards there was a big wedding fiesta in the plaza. The boys cooked a bull's head and there was music and dancing. You'd have been very proud of your brother. Too bad you couldn't be there."

Weeb Jefferson nodded in agreement. "Damn good party," he said. "Wanted to dance myself, but Emily wouldn't do it."

"Well, I'm glad Matthew is settling down," Jeremiah said. "Lupe's a grand girl. The responsibility will do him good."

* * * * *

For two months Matthew had been the husband Lupe had dreamed he'd be, attentive, fun to be with, an ardent lover, and a good provider. Then one night the supper she'd prepared had grown cold and Lupe was ready for bed when she heard his voice. He was singing as he came toward the house. " — *we'll drink brown ale and pay the reck'ning on the nail* —" Matthew's usually fine tenor cracked as he roared the words, " — *no man for debt shall go to jail* — ".

Lupe went to the door. "Matt, quiet down," she implored in a hushed voice. "You'll wake the neighborhood."

"Wake the neighborhood, is it? And sure, why not?" Matthew stumbled through the door and clutched at Lupe to steady himself. "Tell them we're going to be rich."

"Oh, Matt, you've been drinking," Lupe said. "You promised you wouldn't."

"Just a couple with the boys. Celebrating." Matthew slurred the words and reached for Lupe. He stumbled and fell heavily onto a chair. "We're going to be rich, my lil' darlin', rich."

Lupe put the coffee pot back on the stove and began warming some *tortillas* and beans. "Some good strong coffee and food are what you need," she told him.

"Not hungry," Matthew mumbled. "Trying to tell you. Going to the gold fields. Find nuggets big as your thumb, my love. Decided. Leaving in the morning."

"Oh, Matthew, you're not making sense. Winter's nearly on us. You can't travel in those mountains in the winter." Lupe poured a cup of steaming coffee and placed the plate of beans and *tortillas* in front of him. "You'll forget that idea in the morning."

"I'll not!" Matthew emphatically exclaimed. Then he noticed the food. "Told you. Not hungry!" Angrily, he pushed the plate away and reached for Lupe, pulling her onto his lap and knocking the cup of hot coffee to the floor. Lupe tried to get up, but Matthew held her. "Told the boys I'm leaving in the morning. So I'm leaving."

Lupe struggled, trying to break from her husband's grasp. Matthew tried to kiss her. "Don't," she cried. "You're drunk. Leave me alone." Lupe squirmed, but Matthew's grip was like a vise and he held her close, his free hand groping her breasts and beneath her skirts.

"Better love your husband, Lupe. Tonight's last chance for a while." Matthew's breathing was becoming harsh, the boozy odor more than Lupe could stand. She fought to get loose, scratching at his face with a free hand. Matthew caught it and lifted her into his arms, carrying her to the bedroom. She beat on him with her fists and cried in protest, but he was too strong for her.

"Marriage bed, you said, my lil' darlin'. Marriage bed it is."

The next morning a silent Lupe, her mouth set in a thin grim line, watched a sheepish Matthew gather his outfit together and prepare to leave. He reached into his pocket and brought out a fistful of banknotes, placing them on the table. "Plenty of money here, Lupe, to hold you until I get back," he said, not looking at her. "You'll do fine."

Slowly he turned around and faced her. "I do love you, Lupe. I'll be back with the gold and make it all up to you. We'll be rich. I promise."

"Rich? Rich?" Lupe's bitter voice spit out the words. "What's rich? I don't need to be rich. I need my husband."

Matthew moved to embrace her, but she flung off his arms and pushed him away. He stood there, uncertain for a moment, then hefted his pack and opened the front door. Lupe watched him walk out, his back to her, striding away. Suddenly, she screamed, "Matt! Matt!" and ran after him. He stopped, turned, put down his pack and gathered her into his arms.

"Please don't go! Not now," she begged. "The snows will be deep in those Sierras." Lupe was sobbing against his chest. "Stay. You can go in the springtime."

"I can't stay," Matthew said, caressing her hair, kissing her forehead. "I told the boys I was going. I have to go."

Matthew gently removed her arms, gave her a lingering kiss, shouldered his pack and strode off. He didn't look back.

CHAPTER FOURTEEN

THE LETTER THAT JEREMIAH had written in his little adobe house in Long Valley on a warm October day finally reached Skibbereen on a cold, gray, drizzling day in January. It now crackled in Molly Hurley's pocket as she climbed up the path along Knockauneen Hill to Coolnagurrane, through the rocks and around the hedges. Her bare feet were muddy, the result of a morning rain, and her dress was more patches than whole. Her hair was a tangle of black curls, which she had to keep brushing from her eyes just to see her way.

Molly Hurley was excited and her shining blue eyes showed it. When she'd climbed to her favorite resting rock overlooking Skibbereen, she sat down and took out the letter, which had just been handed to her. It was posted in San Francisco, a strange place in far off California, and the return address showed it was from Jeremiah Cleary.

Molly opened the envelope, peeked in and saw two tickets and a postal money order. She pulled out the tickets and looked them over. One to cross the ocean to Boston, the other for steamboats to California. Her heart began to pound. Then she lifted out the neatly-folded letter and spelling out each word letter by letter, slowly began to read. And to smile.

Dear Miss Mary Margaret Hurley, I hope you are well and also all in your house. I am the same and live in California near a place called San Juan Bautista. It's south of San Francisco. I have land of my own now and built a house. It isn't a grand house, but someday it will be better. I have a cow, four work horses, a riding horse, and others. I am a farmer and will raise cattle as well. I know it has been many years since you saw me. I was once your teacher and I recall you well. I have enclosed two tickets and money for travel expenses in the hope that you can find it in your heart to leave your home and family. I ask you to join me in California and become my wife.

She said the word aloud to taste it, "Wife." Become my wife, Jeremiah Cleary said. Molly looked again at the ticket for the ship to America. Only a few years ago possession of such a ticket meant survival — an escape from the hunger. It would still be much envied, for it meant opportunity. But these tickets meant much more. They meant marriage to a man she hardly knew at all, and life in a distant, unknown place. If she traveled there, surely she'd never see her family again.

Molly's eyes filled with tears at the thought of leaving her sister, brother and father here in the little cottage in Coolnagurrane. They'd miss her so and she'd miss them. She couldn't go. No! She'd not be the one to emigrate as so many others had. Then again, her brother, John, was in Boston and she could be seeing him, now couldn't she? And he had a wife and children of his own. John Hurley was an important man with the City of Boston. The money orders from John were keeping her family these days.

San Juan Bautista. Such a strange name for a town. Near San Francisco? That couldn't be so far from Boston that I couldn't be visiting there, now could it? And Miss Mary Margaret Hurley he calls me—him, who used to call me Molly when I sat at his feet to learn my letters, or when he came by the house to see my brothers.

But marriage? Now that was another thing. She hadn't thought about it. Well, that wasn't quite true. Molly wrinkled her nose and disturbed a scattering of freckles. The sad fact of it was that there were few young men left because of the famine. So many had died or gone off to America.

The Jerry Cleary she remembered was quiet, a stern teacher. But he was kind, and at his school was always taking the little ones on his knee and telling them stories. Yet so serious.

She recalled his younger brother, Matthew. Now there was the happy one — even when the hunger was on them he'd have a joke, or do a dance, and flirt with the girls. But always the one with the *poteen*, they said, and his brother there with that watchful eye upon him. Aye, Jerry was the responsible one, the schoolmaster. He seemed a man you could trust. Tall and lean, clean shaven, a nice smile if he'd ever be using it. But quiet, sitting in the corner with his pipe like one of the old ones.

*And me but fifteen, all arms and legs, and so skinny with the
hunger, when he left for America. Recalls me, does he? He must-
n't have much of a memory if it's me he wants. He should see me
now. Still thin, I am, and short. Some tell me blue eyes and
black hair are nice, but my bit of comb doesn't even get my curls
untangled. And hardly a stitch of clothes to be covering me.
And now I'm twenty-three and he must be at least thirty by
now. But that's not really so old.*

It would work, she decided, and she'd try so hard to please
him. *If I stay here I'll not have much chance for marrying and
having children of my own.* She blushed at the thought. What
would the getting of them be like? She had an idea, what with
the cottage being small and her parents young once. Jeremiah
would surely be kind and gentle with her. She blushed again,
this time feeling the heat course through her entire body. The
church said it was a duty and all, once a girl was married. But
there were those young married ones who whispered among
themselves, even giggled a bit. It wasn't all duty, Molly had
concluded.

But would Jeremiah love her? And could she love him? She
felt a surge of excitement at the thought of being a wife.

"Become my wife, he asks." Molly spoke aloud. Suddenly she
knew she would. "I will!" she exclaimed. Then she looked
around the little glen. But only the hedges and rocks were her
witnesses. She folded the letter and carefully tucked it into her
pocket, and then ran on up the hill to the Hurley home.

"Cauth, Cauth — !" she called.

Catherine stepped to the doorway of the one-room cottage.
She was stunned as Molly breathlessly blurted out her news.
Of course the older sister remembered Jerry Cleary. But Molly
going to America? The thought of her leaving was almost
unbearable. Catherine had been mother and sister to Molly
since their mother had died. The straw bed in the loft they'd
shared these many years would be so empty without her. And
now Molly was going to that distant place and Catherine
would have a void in her life forever.

She brushed the tears from her eyes and put on a smile. She'd not be the one to dissuade her. "It's a chance for happiness, Molly. You'll be making a life for yourself out there. I want you to do it."

Catherine hid her real pain, borne of the realization that her intended had died in the famine, and at her age, with the young men all gone, she'd never marry herself, never have the husband and children she yearned for.

"And when do you take this wonderful trip, little sister?" Catherine asked. "How soon must I be losing you?"

"Jerry's letter says I am to wait until spring as the crossing will be easier for it, and the tickets are for American ships, and they are known to be so much better than the British, and I have extra money to see me through, and I can stay over in Boston with John, and will you please help me write a letter to Jerry so he'll know I'm coming, and what can I be wearing, my dress so ragged, a disgrace it is, and — "

Catherine laughed at her sister's excitement. She took her by the hand and led her to the old, weathered trunk in the corner of the cottage. It was one of the few pieces of furniture the Hurleys never sold. It dated from a better time in their lives, and once held the family treasures. Lifting the heavy lid, Catherine brought out a dress, the only one remaining, all else having gone years ago to pay back the loans from the *gombeen-man*.

"Oh, Cauth, that was mother's dress," Molly protested. "It's the only decent garment we have. You'll be needing it, and it would fit you, not me."

"Hush, hush, dear, we'll cut it down," Catherine said. "It's you'll be needing it now."

Molly suddenly fell into her sister's arms and burst into tears. "I can't leave. I can't go so far away from you and James and Da."

Catherine held her sister and stroked her hair. "Molly, dear Molly, and won't I be caring just fine for Da and James? Believe me, they wouldn't want you to be missing this chance at life. We'll all be happy for you."

Molly hugged her sister tightly. She'd be off on a great adventure, but Catherine would stay behind, probably never wed, fixed forever in this cottage, in duty to the family. Catherine didn't complain about her lot, but Molly knew.

"Oh, Cauth, how I wish you were going with me."

"Aye, Molly, I know," Catherine said, patting her shoulder. "Now don't you think you should be after answering your letter?"

Molly pulled one of the family's two stools to the tiny table and sat to sharpen a quill. Catherine found a piece of plain white paper in the trunk and placed it in front of her sister with the bottle of ink. Molly dipped her quill in the ink and held it poised over the paper. She looked at her sister. "I don't know how to address him."

"Write Dear Mister Jeremiah Cleary," Catherine said.

"Oh, Cauth, that seems so silly."

"It's the way he addressed you."

Molly considered. "But should I be so formal with him? And won't I be marrying the man as soon as I'm setting eyes upon him again?"

"But it's Miss Hurley he's calling you," Catherine insisted.

Molly smiled mischievously up at her sister. "Sure and he'll not be so formal in bed, will he now?"

"Mary Margaret — !"

Catherine seemed so shocked, Molly couldn't help breaking into laughter. "It's a sin to be talking that way," Catherine said, giving her sister a playful slap on her head. "Stop it now, Mary Margaret. Stop that."

"Oh, Cauth, do ease yourself." Molly's eyes danced with mischief. "I'm not a child."

Catherine sat down at the table, across from this girl-woman who was her sister, and who was going off across the ocean to marry, and she had to fight back the tears that were welling up.

CHAPTER FIFTEEN

"DON'T YOU WORRY, Jerry. Your letter will come." Emily could see the frown of disappointment on Jeremiah's face as he came into the house after putting up his horse. Another trip to the San Juan post office and still no word from Molly Hurley. Jeremiah's anxiety had been mounting each day and led him to confide in Emily. "I wrote to her and asked her to be my wife, but there's been no word and its way past time I should be hearing."

"Jerry, if she's as smart as you say she is, she won't pass up the chance to marry you," Emily consoled. "Now stop worrying and come have some supper."

Jeremiah was staying in the Jefferson bunkhouse, riding out with the *vaqueros*, helping with chores around the ranch, and waiting for Molly's letter. He couldn't go back to Long Valley, because the river was still too high to ford. And he wouldn't think of leaving until he had his answer. But this waiting put his nerves on edge.

Sometimes when he went to the post office, he'd find Lupe Cleary at the counter, asking for mail. She'd nod at Jeremiah, but never stopped to talk. Finally, one time, he asked her, "Any word from Matthew?"

She shook her head and hurried off. He watched her disappear down the boardwalk. *Damn that brother of mine.*

Jeremiah led Bouchal over to the hitching rack in front of McMahan's store and had just tied him up when he was startled by a shrill squealing of pain and fright. He saw a buggy horse rear up across the street as a man beat on the animal with a whip.

"Damn you miserable sonofabitch — !" the man shouted. "I'll teach you to step over the traces." With each word he struck the horse another blow and red gashes were appearing on the glossy bay hide. The horse neighed again in pain and tried to jump away, but it was tied to a post. The whip rose and fell again.

Jeremiah started across the street. "Stop that!" he yelled. "Don't you be treating an animal that way."

But the man ignored him. Cursing the horse, yanking on the bit, he pulled down the rearing animal and reversed the whip, hitting it on the head by the butt. As he raised it to strike again, Jeremiah grabbed his arm. The man whirled and landed the butt end of the whip on Jeremiah's shoulder, knocking him to the ground.

"Mind your own goddamned business!" he shouted at Jeremiah, who was slowly rising from the street, looking at the man through a red haze of mounting anger. Jeremiah came off the street in a rush, his swinging fist catching the man on the side of the head, staggering him. He drove the next blow into his stomach and doubled him over. Then locking both his hands together Jeremiah swung with all his strength, hitting the man flush on the temple. Down he went. But Jeremiah took a handful of his shirt with one hand and, lifting him off the ground, struck him with his fist, breaking his nose.

The horse beater tried to crawl away, blood spilling from his nose, gushing from his mouth, but Jeremiah went after him, again lifting him to his feet and smashing him about the head. The man went limp just as hands reached out to restrain Jeremiah.

"That's enough, Jerry. Easy now." It was James McMahan holding him, pulling him away. Others were helping. A crowd had gathered around and Jeremiah stood in the center of the circle, breathing hard, the red haze gradually clearing from his eyes. He looked down and saw the man unconscious at his feet.

"My God, Mister Cleary, you damn near killed that fellow," someone said.

"How is he?" Jeremiah asked.

"What'd he do to rile you up so, Cleary?" another man asked.

"That fellow hit Cleary with his whip," a voice declared. "I saw it all."

Jeremiah was still catching his breath as the others bent over the man, who was coming to, muttering, whimpering, still bleeding from the nose, his face battered, both eyes turning black and blue. Jeremiah stepped over the huddled man, pushed his way through the circle, and walked up to the horse.

"It's all right, boy. There now, there now," he soothed, rubbing his hands over the horse, quieting down the animal. It stopped shying from his hands, fear leaving its eyes. Jeremiah continued talking to the horse, calming it. But he felt a hand on his shoulder and turned around to face a pistol aimed at his middle. It was held by Charlie Stone, the sheriff of San Juan Bautista.

"You're under arrest for assault, mister."

Jeremiah stood silently, looking at the big Colt forty-four. "No need for the gun, sheriff," he said quietly. "I'm not going anywhere."

But Stone kept the pistol on Jeremiah. "Turn around." He felt Jeremiah's pockets for a weapon. "Come on. You can cool off in jail." He turned to the crowd and pointing to the man on the ground, "Take that man over to Doc McDougal," he ordered.

"He had it coming, you know," Jeremiah tried to explain.

"Excuse me, Sheriff. But that's the truth." James McMahan stepped up to Sheriff Stone. "I heard the ruckus and was watching from the door of my store. That fellow," he pointed to the injured man being carried off, "was beating that horse over there," McMahan indicated the bay gelding hitched to the buggy, "and Cleary here tried to stop him. But the fellow took his whip to Cleary. Looked like self defense to me."

"Well, Mister McMahan, would you testify to that in court?" Sheriff Stone asked.

"Certainly, I would, Sheriff, if it got that far. But I don't see the need to arrest Mister Cleary."

Sheriff Stone still held the pistol aimed at Jeremiah. He seemed uncertain for a moment, looking from McMahan to Cleary and back again. Reluctantly, he lowered the Colt, holstered it and said, "Well, Cleary, if Mister McMahan here is vouching for you, his word is good enough for me. But you'd better not cause any more trouble around San Juan." He turned on his heel and walked off.

"Thank you, James," Jeremiah said. "That sheriff was rubbing me the wrong way. It disturbs me to have a gun held on me."

"It's over, Jerry," McMahan said. "Let's go over to Florney's and relax a bit."

"Well now, and wasn't I going to make the same suggestion," Jeremiah said, attempting a friendly laugh. "Better to be cooling off in the saloon, than in jail. But first somebody better be looking after that horse."

Jeremiah rode back to the Jefferson ranch that evening, vowing to keep his temper in check. He knew he'd have killed that man with his fists if he hadn't been stopped. It was frightening to know he was capable of such violence. But that bastard was abusing the horse.

As he nursed his bruised fist that night, he began thinking Molly wasn't ever going to write to him. And that was probably why he was so irritable lately. So easy to anger. He'd been so lonely for so long. Once he at least had Matthew to share things, but those days were over. He slept fitfully, dreaming of Molly, but the sheriff came between them and he couldn't reach her, and the horse was being beaten and the sheriff's gun was pointed at him and it was all jumbled together in a nightmare of angry frustration. He woke in a sweat, had a lingering feeling of sadness and couldn't go back to sleep.

The next afternoon he rode back to town and entered the post office, his usual optimistic anticipation dulled by the unhappy dreams of the night before. The postmaster greeted him, "Well Cleary, here's a letter for you. Hope it's the one you've been waiting for."

Jeremiah's hand trembled as he took it. He slowly turned it over and saw the postmark, "Skibbereen, Ireland". It was from Molly Hurley.

He stood looking at it. Afraid to open it. Then, putting it securely in his pocket to the disappointment of the curious postmaster, Jeremiah turned and walked outside. He mounted Bouchal and trotted off, out of town. He wanted to be alone to read Molly's letter. Where the road turned off to the Jefferson ranch, Jeremiah stopped Bouchal under the spread of an oak tree and, sitting in the saddle, took out the letter and carefully tore it open. He was shaking so he could hardly pull the paper from the envelope and shut his eyes as he unfolded it. He opened them and willed himself to look at the words.

Dear Mr. Jeremiah Cleary. I hope this finds you in good health and all in our home are well also. Thank you for your generous proposal of marriage and for the tickets and passage money. I do recall you as once my teacher. My family remembers you, also, as a kind and trustworthy man. My father has given me permission to marry you and his blessing is on our union. I shall depart from the Cove of Cork April 11 and arrive a month hence in Boston. There I shall visit my brother John and his family before continuing my trip. I shall write you from Boston to advise you of my intended arrival in San Francisco. I remain, sincerely yours, Mary Margaret Hurley.

A grin had begun to grow on Jeremiah's face as he read the letter. As he slowly read it again, the smile widened. Molly was coming! Molly would marry him!

Jeremiah suddenly stood in his stirrups and let out a tremendous whoop. Spooked, Bouchal leaped ahead, crow hopped, and broke into a full gallop, Jeremiah yelling like an Indian as they raced down the lane into the Jefferson's yard. "She's coming, she's coming," he shouted to the surprised *vaqueros*, who were just putting up their horses. He brought Bouchal to a sliding stop and hit the ground running toward the house.

Jeremiah raced into the kitchen where Emily was preparing supper and grabbed her around the waist. "She's coming, Emily! She's coming!" He swung her off her feet and danced her around the kitchen.

Suddenly, Jeremiah realized the exhibition he was making of himself. He stopped, breathing hard, his face turning crimson under the black beard. He dropped his hands from Emily's waist and looked around to see if anyone else had been watching.

There were five heads wearing *sombreros* framed in the open kitchen door. And on each face was a big grin. *"Bravo*, Jerry. *Bravo!"* they cried.

Embarrassed, Jeremiah looked at the floor, then slowly he raised his eyes to meet Emily Jefferson's. "Emily," he said quietly. "Molly's on her way."

CHAPTER SIXTEEN

Molly Hurley fought to keep her place at the railing. She'd been there since dawn when the ship entered the Golden Gate. There was a lot of good-natured pushing and jostling as the steerage passengers vied for a first look at San Francisco, dimly visible through the morning fog. The Oregon glided toward the Liedsdorf pier, its paddle wheel churning as it reversed to slow the ship. The city loomed suddenly from out of the mist. Molly was so excited she could hardly stand still— was he there, in the mob of people waiting by the Pacific Steamship dock?

As the faceless crowd began to take on shapes and Molly could make out individuals, she anxiously looked among the moving, waving people for a man who might be Jeremiah Cleary. "Please, God," she whispered under her breath, "Let him be a good man and kind and someone I can learn to love." She'd been offering up such prayers since she'd left Ireland. But now she was terribly worried. Had he gotten her letters? Did he know when she was arriving? What if something had happened to him?

Molly straightened her dress, the one Catherine had taken from their mother's chest, cut down and sewed to her size. She'd changed into it early that morning and it barely fit her, she'd gained a few pounds eating all that delicious food at her brother's house in Boston. She'd placed her ragged dress in the bag she carried along with the beautiful new one, the one to be married in, chosen for her by her sister-in-law Rose in Boston. And her shoes!

Dear God, she'd forgotten to put on her shoes. What would he be thinking of her without shoes? She took them out of the bag and quickly hopped about, squeezing her feet into them. Bending over to hastily button them up, Molly smiled at the memory of Rose saying, "Come along now, dear, we'll find you proper clothing to be meeting this Jeremiah of yours."

Molly's eyes had opened wide in astonishment at the wonders of the Boston shops as Rose selected a dress, a nightgown, some undergarments, the shoes, and other accessories she'd need, plus a little bag to keep everything in.

Will he like me? She smoothed back the wayward curls, tucking most of them under her bonnet. As she adjusted her shawl for the hundredth time, Molly continued to scan the crowd. Where was he? The Oregon had tied up in its berth and people were coming aboard. Disembarking passengers were hurrying down the gangplank. Greetings were being called. Couples were embracing. Children were running about. Amidst the pandemonium Molly saw no one who could possibly be Jeremiah Cleary.

A large, brutish-looking man was making his way toward her, pushing through the crowd at the rail. Molly felt a sinking sensation in her stomach and her mouth went dry as the man was waving and grinning right at her, showing gaps from missing teeth. She breathed a sigh of relief when he walked on past her to greet a woman standing nearby. Another man waved to her, a thin, ugly man, and Molly's heart skipped a beat, but thankfully another woman waved back.

Molly was the last one at the rail, looking down on the tall, black-bearded man who now stood out alone from the crowd below. But this lean, strong-looking man couldn't be the hedge-master she remembered. A beard covered the lower half of his face. He wore rough clothing and a wide-brimmed hat. Molly looked past him to see if there was anyone who looked familiar, any other possibility.

Jeremiah stood in the back at the corner of the dock. With each passing moment his apprehension grew. What if she'd missed the boat? What if she'd decided in Boston not to come after all? What if she took one look at the likes of him standing there stiff and uncomfortable in his new work clothes and decided she didn't want him? He'd debated with himself about wasting the money on a bath and a haircut. The half a dollar seemed a great extravagance. But then, he knew a first impression was important so he finally even let the barber trim his beard. He didn't want to be scaring the poor girl off, now did he?

He saw a pretty girl at the rail and wondered if that could be Molly. Now, Jeremiah Cleary, he scolded himself, don't be aiming so high. But his eye came back to that one again, a slight girl, her face bright and eager as she searched the crowd. It could certainly be her. Finally he gathered his courage and stepped forward. He looked up and met her eyes. He was pierced by their clear blue, steady gaze. Her face was enough to make him homesick. Not a raving beauty, perhaps, but for him something far better, a real Irish *colleen* with fresh, fair skin, and black curls creeping from beneath her bonnet.

"Miss Mary Margaret Hurley, is it?" he called up to her.

"Aye, it's Molly Hurley. And would you be Mister Jeremiah Cleary?"

His face broke into that gentle smile that crinkled his eyes and she knew him. As she returned his smile, a great protective tenderness swept over him. Jeremiah came aboard and took her bag, and her elbow, and guided her off the ship. He didn't say a word as he led her to the street where a two-horse

107

team hitched to a wagon stood waiting. Jeremiah helped her up onto the seat. He placed her small satchel with the load in the wagon, and the lightness of it made him realize how little she had. He was reminded of how little he'd had when he first arrived.

Jeremiah called to his horses and set the team to a street that led along the waterfront, but southward, and then away from San Francisco. Still Jeremiah hadn't spoken and Molly was full of questions. Where were they going? Where was this San Juan Bautista place? When would they get there? When would they be married? But he was so silent and seemed so stern, she held her tongue.

Jeremiah didn't speak because he couldn't. He was smitten. Struck dumb. He'd dreamed of this moment for so long, held a vision of Molly in his mind, a spirit—an ideal with no form because he really didn't know her, didn't know how she would truly look or what she'd be like. And here she was! He could barely look at her, but he'd seen enough to know she was short, hardly up to his chest, and with freckles across her nose. He remembered those, all right. But the skinny arms and legs were gone, and in their place, from what he could see, at least, was a roundness that promised much more in other places. Jeremiah could feel the heat of her presence on the wagon seat beside him, even though he dared not look at her. She was real, sure enough.

And he was in love.

"Mister Cleary, please. Where are we going?"

"San Juan," he answered.

"Oh," she said. "And where is that?"

"Down the road, eighty miles or so."

"Oh."

Then Molly realized that if his San Juan is eighty miles down the road, they'd not be getting there tonight. It was already well past midday. "Mister Cleary?"

He concentrated on handling the lines, watching the rumps of Maud and Nellie. Whatever she wanted, he enjoyed the sound of his name on her lips. Her voice was pure music, he thought, and he, who couldn't carry a tune, was singing inside with the joy of it. It trickled and bounced along like a rippling stream. He loved the sound of her words.

"And where is it that we are to be married?"

"San Juan," he replied.

"Oh."

We'll be three nights on the road, she thought. And not married. Surely, he wouldn't —

They'd traveled another five miles in the afternoon sun when Molly tried again. "Mister Cleary. How will we be spending the nights on the road?"

"We'll camp."

"I see," she said.

Camping, is it now? And how would they be doing that? Molly kept her mind on the possibilities as the wagon rolled on through the hot August afternoon. Just before dusk, Jeremiah pulled into a grove of trees and made camp near a spring. He unhitched the team, watered them and staked the horses to graze. He set about building a campfire and Molly tried to help, but not knowing what to do she kept getting in his way and saying, "Sorry."

Soon he had a plate of hot beans before her as she sat cross-legged on the ground, her full skirt wrapped around her. He poured her a steaming cup of coffee and warned, "Careful now. That tin will burn you if you'll not let it cool."

That's the first thing he's said to me all day, Molly thought. She worried that he didn't like her, that maybe he wanted to send her home, but couldn't do it. Or was he always so quiet?

Jeremiah busied himself making room in the wagon, setting sacks and bundles on the ground, and then called to her. "Miss Hurley, it is here you'll be sleeping."

"Oh," she said as she wondered where he'd be sleeping. But she didn't ask. She watched him as he took another blanket out of the wagon and left camp. He walked off into the grove of trees. When he didn't return for some time, Molly also went into the trees, in the opposite direction. When she returned she settled herself in the blankets on the wagon bed. But it wasn't to sleep. She was wide awake. What if he comes to the wagon? Surely, he wouldn't ask anything of her, not until they we're married.

Finally, she heard soft snoring from back in the woods. She smiled. She was really so tired from the long day and excitement. She closed her eyes and was soon fast asleep, and still smiling.

It was late afternoon of the fourth day when Jeremiah turned the team off the main road and down the lane toward the Jefferson ranch. He'd been very quiet, but Molly was beginning to understand. This man who had been an articulate schoolmaster was shy with her now that she was a grown woman. She could feel that he liked her well enough. And his gentleness had put her at ease. Molly began to think that marriage to this man just might be a good thing. Perhaps she would even learn to love him. She watched him managing the team, his hands so firm on the lines, his voice commanding. He was so sure and capable.

If only she could get him to talk to her. She'd tried every way she knew, been a regular chatterbox. She'd given him all the news of home, every bit of information about Skibbereen, the neighbors of Coolnagurrane, about Catherine and James, about her father, and that she'd seen Liam and the messages he'd sent, and Father Hayes and his blessing upon them. She talked endlessly about Boston, how kind Rose was to her, about John and his politics, and their children.

Jeremiah's responses had been "Oh," and "Grand," and an occasional "Well now."

Just once he'd asked a question and she understood it was only because of concern for her. "And the passage, Miss Hurley, was it a hard one?"

That set her off again, chattering about it almost the whole afternoon. "The passage? Sure and didn't I think it would never end, day after day as the ship rocked and I'd be sitting on deck looking up at the sky one moment and then down at water the next? There was a bit of a storm a few weeks out from Cobh, and some people were seasick, but it was not so bad."

Jeremiah still had no comment, so she rattled on, telling him about the other passengers, the funny things that happened, the songs they sang and the story telling to pass the time.

Molly looked at Jeremiah for a reaction but his attention was focused on the lines in his hand guiding the team. Did he even hear her, she wondered. How would she get a reaction from this man? "After the sailing ship, the paddle steamer seemed to go so fast that we were in Panama before we even got settled into our berths." She looked over at him, but he only nodded. *Is it that I'm after boring him? Maybe I should stop chattering. He probably thinks I'm one of those women who can't keep her mouth shut, that talks from morning to night.*

The fact was that Jeremiah was enthralled by her lilting voice, hearing every enchanting word and then wanting more. He'd been stealing glances at her as she spoke and he loved the expressive movements of her face as she emphasized a point or laughed at a memory making her nose crinkle and the freckles jump about.

Now she was talking about crossing the Isthmus of Panama. "It was a grand train and the lovely seats had backs to them to rest against and it went so fast I could hardly see the jungle. It was terrible hot, but the tracks followed along the most beautiful river." *True, the river was beautiful, but the smoke and cinders from the engine and the steamy heat of the jungle floated back into the open windows of the passenger cars and nearly choked me. I thought it would take forever and when the train finally pulled into Panama City I was hot and sticky and filthy and even my teeth felt gritty. But I'd best not mention that or he'll think I'm the kind of woman who complains about every little thing.*

Jeremiah just smiled as he imagined Molly whizzing along through the jungle. Grand, it was, that Molly had enjoyed it, a far better experience, he remembered, than he and Matthew had.

The moment Emily Jefferson saw Jeremiah's wagon swing into the yard, she hurried from her kitchen door, wiping her hands on her apron and rushing up to them with her wide, cheery smile.

"Oh, Jerry, what a nice young woman you have — ! You didn't tell us how pretty she is. How do you do, Miss Hurley. We're so happy to have you."

Weeb appeared, walking up from the corral. He looked approvingly at Molly. "Well, well, Cleary, that looks like a damn fine woman you've got there."

"Weeb, you stop that swearing in front of this young lady," Emily scolded.

Jeremiah handed Molly down from the wagon, as the *vaqueros* began lining up like a reception committee. Jeremiah presented each by name as they formally bowed to Molly. She made an effort to repeat the names, although the Spanish twisted her Irish tongue. But she smiled at each and they were captivated. Jorge and Ramòn, Agapito, Rogelio, and especially the smiling Celestino, who spoke for them all, *"Buenas tardes, señorita. Con mucho gusto,"* he said, grinning from ear to ear.

Emily took charge. With her arm around Molly she guided her into the house. "You poor dear, you must be so tired from such a long trip. Come and rest. I'll have a hot bath for you in no time. Now, Jerry, you go along with the boys. You can see Molly at supper."

When Molly sat down at the long table that night she was radiant. Jeremiah sat across from her and glowed with pride at the *colleen* sitting opposite him. Molly was amazed at the variety of foods being placed on the table. Weeb kept urging her to try this or that, as if he'd prepared it himself.

"Have some more of this beef, Miss Hurley," he said proudly. Raised the damn thing myself. Slaughtered it, aged it, everything right here. Best damn beef in California."

"Weeb, stop it," Emily interrupted. "I won't have that swearing. And Molly doesn't want to hear about you aging your beef."

But Molly did want to hear about beef. To her, who had never tasted such meat, this was a strange, new experience. What did he mean by age it? She'd have to ask Jeremiah, if she could get him to talk to her. Meanwhile, the *vaqueros* kept their eyes on their plates, occasionally stealing a shy glance at Jeremiah's bride-to-be. Her black, curly hair caught at the nape of her neck with a ribbon, her fresh, young, smiling face with the bright blue eyes, her small but very womanly figure, made it impossible for Jeremiah to take his eyes off her.

But despite his preoccupation with Molly, Jeremiah had one other thing on his mind, his brother. He hesitated to ask Rogelio because sometimes he wondered how Rogelio felt about Matthew being married to his sister. But Jeremiah finally overcame his reluctance. "Has there been any news of my brother?"

Rogelio surprised him. He looked up with a big smile and replied, "*Oh, sì, señor.* Much good news. Lupe has heard that her husband has found a place with gold for the taking and he is engaged in washing it from the stream. He will return soon *muy rico.*"

Jeremiah kept his doubts to himself, but Molly was intrigued by this news. She hadn't even thought to ask after Matthew. "Your brother is a gold miner, Mister Cleary? I didn't know he was married. Where is his wife? Do they live here?"

Jeremiah was caught with a mouthful of steak and methodically chewed. The room fell silent as they waited for him to answer. He took his time, swallowed, and looking at his plate, mumbled, "We'll be seeing them after Matt returns from the mines."

Weeb started giving orders for the next day's work and soon they were all pushing away from the table. Weeb insisted the young couple borrow the surrey to run into San Juan. They were to see Padre Mora at the mission, go to confession, and make final arrangements for the wedding which was to take place the next morning. When they arrived, the padre waved them into his study. He took both of Molly's hands in his and warmly smiled. *"Bienvenida, señorita, alla parroquia de San Juan Bautista."*

"He's welcoming you to this parish," Jeremiah explained. Molly smiled her thanks.

The Franciscan shifted to English. "Your wedding *en la mañana,* in the morning," he corrected himself, "it will be at — ah, *como se dice,* how do you say, *son las ocho y media* — ?"

"Yes, Father," Jeremiah agreed. "We'll be married at half eight," he told Molly. Between Jeremiah's meager Spanish with an Irish brogue and the priest's limited English with a Spanish accent, they struggled through the arrangements, with Molly understanding little of what was being agreed to, although she was comforted by the gentle priest with the kind eyes.

They moved into the dark church, with only the glowing light of the sacristy candle to guide them. Padre Mora took his place in the confessional and Molly entered. She was out again in no time and knelt to say her prayers. Her penance was light and her eyes reverently roamed the dim church. It was foreign to her, but she felt the peace and timelessness of it, the holiness. Jeremiah took her place. He knelt facing the priest behind the shrouded opening.

"Bless me, Father, for I have sinned," he commenced the age-old ritual. It had been a long time since his last confession. In fact, he hadn't been to church much since he'd come to California, the blathering in Spanish being more than he could understand even though the Latin words of the Mass were familiar. In Ireland, of course, it had been walking with his family down Knockauneen Hill from Coolnagurrane every Sunday to the church on North Street to hear Father Hayes say Mass. That was long ago and Jeremiah felt it was time to make his peace with God.

When asked by Padre Mora to recount his sins, Jeremiah wondered how he could tell him about Lupe Morales. He hadn't done anything, he knew. But it had been on his mind. So Jeremiah confessed his sinful thoughts. But there were no recriminations. The padre was silent and then murmured encouragement for him to continue.

"The worst problem is my temper, Father. I nearly killed a man in Panama. He was a bad one, and hurting my brother. And I badly beat a man here in San Juan who was abusing his horse, knocked him unconscious. When my temper is lost, I can't control myself, and I'm afraid that I'll do mortal harm."

"Temper is a wicked thing, my son. But this is a hard country and God knows you must protect yourself. God wants you to be kind, to love one another, to turn the other cheek. But He understands if you must protect your own life, or your brother's. He knows what is in your heart. You must stay away from occasions of temptation. Be faithful to your wife. God understands when you are far from church and must miss Mass, but say your prayers faithfully and God will be with you. Now your sins are forgiven. For your penance say the rosary, all five mysteries. Go and sin no more."

Jeremiah only understood half of it, but he felt as if a great weight had been lifted from him. He walked with a light step and as they left the church, he said to Molly, "Well now, and that wasn't so bad, was it, Miss Hurley?"

Molly cocked her head up at him mischievously. "Mine wasn't. I said it in Irish."

As they walked around the plaza together, Molly placed her hand in his. It felt so soft, so small in Jeremiah's big, work-callused hand, but the warmth of it heated his blood and coursed through his veins like a runaway team. It was an innocent, sweet thing, to hold his hand, he knew, but it set his entire being on fire. He looked down at this woman who would soon be his wife and knew he wanted her, desperately.

They looked in the window of the Plaza Hotel where they could see someone lighting the candles in the elegant dining room. Tables were set with white linen, sterling silver and crystal stemware.

"Ooh, how grand," Molly exclaimed, wide-eyed.

"I'll be bringing you here to eat one day."

"But, Mister Cleary, it's much too grand for the likes of us."

"Not in America, Miss Hurley. You'll see. One day. I promise."

Molly looked up at this big man she was about to marry. He was so confident, she felt she could trust him. That night, after Emily Jefferson had fussed over her and ironed her new dress for the morning, Molly lay awake in a big, soft featherbed. She was puzzled. Weeb and Emily were so friendly, so hospitable to them. These had been Jeremiah's employers, hadn't they? They owned this ranch and this big home. They were gentry, weren't they? Yet, they were Jeremiah's friends.

What a strange, wonderful, fascinating place, this America.

CHAPTER SEVENTEEN

"DAMN FINE WEDDING!" Weeb Jefferson proclaimed as soon as Padre Mora had pronounced Jeremiah and Molly husband and wife. Weeb pumped Jeremiah's hand and then heartily kissed the bride.

James McMahan, the storekeeper, and his wife, being Catholic, had been witnesses for the couple and the Jeffersons and all the *vaqueros* were there in church. Everyone was happily congratulating the newlyweds. Jeremiah never seemed more quiet and shy and his new wife was never more ebullient. As he helped her up into the wagon seat, Molly smiled proudly at her tall, strong, black-bearded husband.

The sky was a bright blue and the sun hot as the Clearys rode along the San Benito River, which still held a little water slowly meandering between shallow pools. Jeremiah sat straight and serious beside his young bride, allowing himself an occasional sideways glance to make sure she was really there. She was almost too lovely to look at, the dear little thing. And still, he didn't know what to say to her, how to make conversation.

"What kind of trees are those funny little things?" Molly asked.

"Scrub oaks."

"Are the hills always so brown?"

"No. They're green in the spring."

"Like Ireland?"

"No, not quite!"

"Does your horse have a name?" Molly asked.

"That he does."

"And what might it be?"

"Bouchal," Jeremiah said.

"That's a grand name, and what do you call the cow?"

"You'll be naming her," Jeremiah said, smiling down at this snip of a girl, who once sat at his feet doing her sums and learning her letters. And now she was a grown woman. His wife.

But what was the matter with her? Jeremiah noticed Molly seemed uncomfortable. He saw her reach down to unbutton her new shoes. She glanced shyly at Jeremiah as she slipped them off, wiggled her toes and rubbed her feet. He nodded and gave her a smile of understanding. It was hard to get used to wearing shoes after a lifetime of going barefoot.

The wagon was heavily-loaded and Jeremiah had put his young grays in four-up with their mothers. The two big, white mares, the wheelers, were taking the brunt of the load, and the gray colts were leaders. The cow was tied behind, her calf trotting along at her side. Bouchal, also, was on a lead rope behind the wagon, followed by Jeremiah's brood mare. The only noise to break the peaceful quiet of the day was the incessant clucking of the chickens protesting their presence in the crate stacked atop the wagon.

Suddenly, one of the leaders reared, whinnied with fright and landed against his partner, pulling the other off stride and throwing the wheelers off balance, nearly tipping over the wagon. The grays bolted and the mares couldn't hold them. Jeremiah, hauling in on the lines and shouting at his team, spotted a mother skunk and her three offspring under the wheels of the wagon. He cursed as the wagon rolled over them. But he had more than the stink of it to bother him just now. As he tried to pull up the galloping horses, the wagon struck a boulder in the river and careened on two wheels before righting itself. A terrified Molly hung on with both hands and clenched her teeth to smother a scream. Flour sacks, pots and pans, bundles and packages spilled out, along with the crate of chickens.

"Whoa, there, Nellie — ! Whoa, Maud! Whoa!" Jeremiah sawed on the lines.

He finally brought the team to a halt in the midst of tangled traces and harness. The horses stood blowing. "*Mullacht de ort*," Jeremiah yelled at the retreating skunks. "The curse of God on you. Bad *cess* to you. Dammit to hell. *Keeroge* out of hell."

The cow had broken loose in the melee, but she was quietly grazing on the river bank. The brood mare's halter had snapped and she was trotting away. Bouchal's lead rope had broken, but the big gray was quietly standing ground-tied. The infernal chickens were squawking and fluttering down along the river bed.

Jeremiah cut loose with another spasm of Irish oaths, but when he stopped for a breath he heard Molly laughing so hard she had doubled over and tears were running down her face. Jeremiah turned red and started to sputter.

"Dammit, woman. What the bejesus are you laughing at?" he bellowed. "Can't you see the trouble that damn skunk caused?"

But Molly was so overcome with laughter, she couldn't speak. Jeremiah just got madder. "You could have been killed! The damn wagon could have been smashed and then what would we do? Now I have to saddle Bouchal and catch that damn horse and chase those damn chickens, fix the damn harness and — !" Jeremiah ran out of breath. Damn, he thought, he was sounding just like Weeb Jefferson. He looked over at Molly and started to grin. The grin turned into a chuckle, that turned into a laugh, then into a whoop. He shouted. He hooted and roared. He shook with laughter and nearly fell off the wagon.

Every time he'd stop laughing, he and Molly would look at each other and start laughing all over again. Even as he chased chickens along the river, trying clumsily to catch them, Jeremiah was laughing. Both he and Molly felt the tension of the last few days melting away.

That evening when they'd made camp for the night, the two prepared what Molly considered a virtual feast. She peeled potatoes and set them to boil while Jeremiah cut steaks from the haunch of beef Weeb had carefully wrapped for their trip. Emily had included a loaf of her delicious bread. As they ate, Molly silently wondered what the night would bring. Jeremiah, looking across the campfire at his bride, had the same thoughts. But he'd not rush her, not give her cause for alarm. Perhaps he should again put his blankets in the trees outside of camp.

But he didn't want to do that. He wanted her. Now! Watching Molly in the light of the fire, curly hair tousled, her cheeks flushed, a quizzical smile on her full, red lips, Jeremiah ached to reach out for her and draw that firm little body up against his. Easy now, Cleary, he thought, you're not knowing a woman, you'll not be knowing how to act. You'll be rough, you'll hurt the poor girl. Go easy now.

He set his jaw, went to the wagon and prepared Molly's bed as she watched, still sitting by the fire. She was surprised when he took his blankets, just as he'd done the previous nights, and with a curt, "Good night, Missus Cleary," disappeared into the dark.

Molly was disappointed, she had to admit, and wondering, too, if she'd offended him in some way. She'd been afraid of what she didn't know, but she wanted to find out, to be a wife, to offer herself, to let this man love her, to love him. Why didn't he want her?

Molly lay in her bed on the wagon and looked up at the stars. She blinked back tears. She'd imagined all sorts of things for this night. But not that she'd be alone in her bed. Anger began to mount in her breast. Not good enough for him, was she. Was that what he was thinking? Well, now she'd show him. *No, now wait a bit, Molly Hurley. No, it's not Molly Hurley any more. It's Molly Cleary and being a wife is my duty. I think he's just the shy one. That's what he is. I've been seeing it these past four days. This tall, strong, capable man is afraid of a tiny woman.*

Molly began to smile up at the stars. She said a little prayer, "Please, now, Father in heaven, if this be your will, help me to be a good wife." She took a deep breath and called into the darkness. "Mister Cleary, I'm cold. Would you be so kind as to warm me?" She lay still looking at the stars, not moving.

She heard a rustle by the wagon, and felt it move, and then Jeremiah's face above her blotted out the stars. She raised her arms to welcome him and his beard scratched her face, her neck, her breasts. He was whispering to her in Irish, "*Macushla, macushla*, my darling."

He held her head in his two hands and looked down into her eyes. He stroked her hair, and kissed her eyelids, kissed her mouth, and her neck. His lips found her breasts and suddenly she was on fire, too. She clasped her arms about him and opened herself to him. He was slow and gentle, just as she'd hoped he'd be. The pain was brief and she let herself become one with his rhythm. She gloried in the act. The passion and wonder of it. Joy filled her heart. Afterwards, as they fell asleep in each other's arms, she thought, so this is what it is to be a wife!

Molly was smiling when the sun struck her face in the morning. She sat up to see her husband building the breakfast fire.

"Good morning, Missus Cleary," he said smiling.

"Ah, now, Jerry," she replied with a laugh. "Don't you know me well enough now to be calling me Molly?"

He stopped stoking the fire and came over to her. He looked up to where she was peering over the edge of the wagon bed. "Molly," he said sweetly.

"Thank you," she said and leaned down to give him a soft kiss. "Now be after saying it again," she whispered in his ear. "Be saying my name the way you said it last night."

Jeremiah felt his knees go weak. "Molly, oh, Molly love," he said in a hoarse whisper. He helped her down from the wagon and took her in his arms and they kissed with a passionate intensity. Jeremiah was for climbing back in the wagon and making love again to his wonderful new wife. But Molly finally loosed his hold on her.

"We've got a whole lifetime for that, Jeremiah Cleary," she chided him. "Besides, I'm hungry. And whatever you're cooking over there for our first breakfast as man and wife smells — ah, Jerry, it smells like it's burning."

Jeremiah sniffed the air and grimaced. "Molly. I do believe you made me burn our breakfast."

"All my fault, is it? So that's the way it's going to be?" But Molly was laughing.

CHAPTER EIGHTEEN

"**J**ERRY, THE DARK IS SINGING."

Crickets chirped. Frogs croaked. The river gurgled. The symphony of the night was accented by the hoot of an owl and the yipping of coyotes on the ridge. Just before giving in to the drowsiness, Molly smiled with happiness. It was lovely, delicious, to be so secure in the arms of Jeremiah, lulled by the night sounds. She snuggled against his shoulder and fell sound asleep.

Suddenly, a scream!

It ripped through her dreams. It brought her upright from the bed. Had she imagined it? Jerry pulled her into his arms and soothed her. And then the scream rose again, filling the night. From a nearby hill it came, a tortured, choking sound, an agonizing screech that sent shivers through Molly, that lifted the hair from the nape of her neck.

"It's nothing to be afraid of, Molly love," he said stroking her hair. "It's only a mountain lion, a big cat making that noise. Perhaps he's brought down some game and is proud of himself. Or maybe he's calling to his sweetheart across the mountain. He means no harm to us."

Molly lay back down again, shivering. She was certain she'd just heard the sound of a woman having her throat cut, screaming for her life. Molly's pulse raced. "Jerry, you're after telling me that creature means us no harm?"

"The mountain lion, *macushla*, is a cowardly animal," Jeremiah explained. "He'll not attack a human unless he's cornered, or if he's starving. True, I've heard of them going after colts or calves if they're that hungry. But there's game all about. That one has a full belly and is just telling the world of it."

Molly couldn't go back to sleep. She thought about the lion and about all else she'd learned these past few days about this new country. It was so strange, so different than Ireland. There were so many things to learn. Just this morning Jerry had found that big footprint in the river sand and had called her to it.

"Take a look at this, Molly love. That's a grizzly bear track. And see, there's a bit of water in it which means that bear passed through here just ahead of us. Don't be walking out alone, now, too far from the wagon."

Molly stared at the paw print and tried to imagine an animal so large. When she was a child she'd seen a bear. A comical creature, on a rope in the hands of a gypsy performing in Skibbereen for a few shillings from the people gathered around. The traveling bear had been the talk of the village for weeks. She couldn't equate that funny bear with the huge creature that must have made this track. If it worried Jerry, it must be fearsome indeed. She'd noticed he kept his rifle beside him on the wagon seat.

But he'd not used it on that loathsome snake. She'd nearly stepped on it by the river as it slithered over the rocks. Molly stood transfixed, terrified as the snake coiled and made a rattling noise. "Jerry — !" she screamed.

Jeremiah whirled around from the wagon where he was packing up, startled by the fear in her voice. He sped to her side, lifted a large rock above his head and threw it with such force that it smashed the snake before it could strike.

Jeremiah took out his knife, placed his boot on the snake and cut off the rattles. He offered them to her as a souvenir, but Molly shuddered and turned away. She'd remember to watch where she stepped always.

There were so many dangerous and bothersome things in this wild country. There were black flies to be swatted and mosquito bites that left welts, yellow jackets that would follow a forkful of meat right into her mouth if she didn't watch out, nettles that burned her legs, stickers and burrs that caught in her skirt.

"What's that beautiful bush there?" Molly asked, "The one growing on the bank of the stream there, Jerry, with those lovely leaves of red, yellow and green?

"Poison oak," Jeremiah told her. "Don't even let it brush against you or you'll get a mean, itching rash."

It was high noon of the fifth day and the August sun was blazing hot when Jeremiah pulled up the lathered horses, breathing heavily from the pull out of Peach Tree Valley. But he didn't even think to find shade as he stopped the team to rest. This was the moment he'd been waiting for, to show Molly his land.

"See. There, Molly love," he said, pointing down at the valley. "Down there. You can see our house."

Jeremiah was so proud to be showing it to her at last. Lengthening before them was the long valley. On one side stood the *adobe*, gleaming in the bright sunlight. Nearby could be seen the corrals and brush fences, although they were nearly hidden by the tall, brown grass.

Molly was appalled!

This was her new home? This fiercely hot, nearly treeless valley? This was the end of her long journey? This was where she was to spend her life? The sweat dripped beneath her bonnet. She felt flushed and uncomfortable in her clothing. She was thirsty. She had a headache. The heat had never bothered her so. And she ached with disappointment.

All that beautiful country they'd passed, the broad valleys with their oak trees, the hillsides full of pines, the little lake, the flowing creek. She'd been thinking this long valley place would be like that. But it was not. It was terrible. Nothing but brown grass stretched away before them. There was hardly a tree to break the landscape. And the house—how bleak it looked, shining white in the sun, and so alone, with one scraggly tree on the hill nearby to keep it company.

Molly watched Jeremiah as he waved his hands and spoke so proudly of his valley, presenting his queen with her domain. "So now, Molly love," he asked, "what are you thinking?"

124

She was near to tears, but didn't want him to know, to see her disappointment. She couldn't hurt him, not this man she now loved. She avoided his question with one of her own. "The house, Jerry. Why does it shine so?"

"Limestone, Molly. It's in the mortar used for plaster on the walls. We made the house of mud bricks called *adobe*, then plastered it with the limestone." Jeremiah, shielding his eyes with his hand against the sun, had just started to explain how he'd hired Calistro Salazàr to help him build the house, when Molly interrupted him.

"Oh look, Jerry, that huge bird! It's beautiful!"

Jeremiah looked to where she was pointing and saw an eagle soaring above the valley. "That's an eagle, Molly, just like the bird on the coins. Americans call it the symbol of freedom."

They watched the bird circle and lift higher and higher, floating on the air currents, finally passing out of sight over the hills.

Then Jeremiah turned to Molly and suddenly realized how hot she was there in the sun. He called to his team, rattled the lines, and headed down into the valley. "You'll find it cool inside the house," he promised. Molly nodded and mustered a wan smile.

They drove up to the house and Jeremiah let the team stand while he opened the door. Then he lifted his bride down from the wagon and carried her into the house just as he had dreamed of doing for so long. He was right—it was cool inside. Wonderfully cool. A haven from the burning sun. Molly took off her bonnet and shook out her curls. She loosened her dress and let the cool of the house reach her skin.

"Would you have a drink of water for your thirsty wife, Mister Cleary?"

Jeremiah hurried to the well and drew a full bucket. He placed it on the shelf, found his dipper, and handed the brimming ladle to Molly. She drank heartily, quenching her thirst, scarcely tasting the water. Then she noticed it, an aftertaste, a strangeness on her tongue. Not bitter, but different. A slightly puzzled look wrinkled her brow.

Jeremiah noticed her look. "You'll get used to the drink, Molly. It's alkali and other minerals. You'll learn to relish it."

She set down the dipper by the bucket, thinking even the water in this country is strange, and began looking around her house. It was dim inside, but she could see it was a large room with a fireplace at one end and a door at the other. A single window was covered by a hide of some kind, hanging over thick panes of glass like a curtain. Real glass! What a wonder, she thought. But she wouldn't be having some animal hide covering real glass. She'd make a curtain for that, she decided.

She walked through the door into a smaller room and admired the bed that Jeremiah had made. It was a redwood frame with leather thongs stretched across. That grand feather mattress Emily had given them as a wedding present would fit it just lovely. She smiled and her eyes traveled around the room.

In the corner stood a sturdy chest, covered with cowhide and adorned with big brass studs. "That I found in San Juan," Jeremiah told her. "And wasn't McMahan wanting a fortune for it, and didn't I convince him to sell it for less?" He grinned. "And do you like it?"

She slowly began to realize that this *adobe* house was a vast improvement over the tiny cottage she'd shared with her family in Ireland. She glanced up at her husband, standing there looking so anxious as he followed her around the house, watching her. She knew how much he wanted her to like the place. To like the furniture he'd made, the bed, and that little table with the coal oil lamp, and the table for eating, those chairs. She smiled at him. "Oh, yes, Jerry. And this house. It's a lovely house, just lovely. And there's so much in it. You've done a grand thing."

Jeremiah was so relieved. He took her in his arms and was about to kiss her when she pulled back. Again she looked up at him with that teasing grin. "Just one more thing we'll be needing, Jerry."

"Oh, and what might that be now?"

"Another room to be holding all the children."

Jeremiah felt like getting that feather mattress out of the wagon that minute. Molly seemed willing enough, smiling at him with that sparkle in her eyes. But he couldn't leave the team standing there in the sun without water. And the chickens in the crate were complaining. He set the crate on the ground and loosened the slats. While Molly watched over them, out came the hens, bobbing their heads and looking around with quick, darting, pecking motions, their bright eyes checking out the yard. The rooster flapped his wings and crowed his pleasure.

Jeremiah unhitched and put the horses in the corral with the mare and the cow. The calf came bawling and immediately began to suckle. Jerry started hauling water from the well, pouring it into the big redwood trough. It took some time to soak up, to stop leaking, and the horses were greedy. Molly went to the well to help him, and together they finished watering the horses and the cow. Jeremiah turned the stock into the pasture encircled by the brush fence and they were soon grazing on wild oats nearly as high as their heads.

"Molly, now you see what fine land this is to be growing such wild grasses," Jeremiah exclaimed, still citing the merits of his land. "We'll be having grand crops and one day our cattle will cover these hills." He swept his arms in a circle, explaining his dream. "And one day we'll raise the finest horses in the country—they'll bring good, hard money, as well."

"But our best crop, Jerry, will be your sturdy sons and daughters," Molly said with a teasing smile.

It was cooler now after they'd finished unpacking the wagon and storing the goods in the house. The pots and pans, the big kettle, the huge washtub, the likes of which Molly had never seen. She had dishes, and some forks and spoons now. Grand things such as these she'd never known in Ireland, even before famine times.

"The cost must be very dear," Molly said. "How is it now you're being so rich?"

"I'm not," Jeremiah protested. "I've saved for this for a long time and the money's about gone. What's left will pay Weeb for the cattle I'll be buying." Jeremiah explained that he'd have to ride back to San Juan soon and drive home his ten cows, all bred to Weeb's bull, before they ended up calving along the river.

"You'll have to be staying here, Molly love, to watch over the place, hauling water for the stock. I'll be picking up one of the Garcìa boys in Peach Tree to help me herd, and it's a week or more I'll be away."

Molly wondered how she'd manage all by herself, in this bleak, isolated valley. She was used to being around so many people—her parents, her sister and brother, and them all living in the little cottage. Friends stopping by, the comings and goings, the village near. This business of being the wife of a rancher in this raw, new land, meant toil, and often loneliness. Not that she wasn't accustomed to work, but being alone for days on end was not to her liking.

Molly nodded. She'd not be afraid, she firmly made up her mind. It was her duty to keep the place while her husband was gone. And this was their land. No landlord to take all they had for rent. No lease running out each year. No threat of eviction over their heads. No rack renting. If they fixed up their cabin, or improved their land, they'd not be having their rent raised. This bit of America was their very own.

"Look, Jerry. I can plant my potatoes about there," she pointed out the spot. "And my cabbages over here. Would we be having a corn patch behind it?"

Jeremiah smiled his assent and Molly went on planning. "I'll have my chickens and a cow to milk. And, Jerry, if you would be planting some trees over there, one day they'll be shading the house."

128

Molly and Jeremiah spent their first day digging a second well for the livestock. As Jeremiah filled the bucket with earth, Molly pulled it up and emptied it. They worked through the heat of the day. By dark Jeremiah's head was no longer visible as he dug.

Next morning, Jeremiah was up at dawn, checking his red-wood stack for wood to shore up the well. Molly stepped through the cabin door and let out a shriek. "My chickens," she cried. "There's just feathers! Look, Jerry, look there!"

A short distance from the house Jeremiah saw the remains of two chickens, just a pile of feathers. "Coyotes did this, Molly, or bobcats," he said, angry at himself. "I'm a fool for not making them a safe place."

Molly was looking around for the rest of the chickens and found them hiding in the brush along the fence line. She shooed them back into the yard by the house.

"Jeremiah Cleary, I'll not be losing all my chickens to make a feast for those wild animals! You be building them a proper roosting place this very moment," she demanded.

"But Molly love, it's the new well I must finish first. We're in need of the extra water. I'll be getting to the roost tomorrow."

"Then I'll be bringing the chickens into the house tonight."

"You'll not!" Jeremiah protested. "There'll be no chickens in the house like some poor *spalpeen* laborer in Ireland. I'll make a proper roost tomorrow."

"You'll not." Molly firmly set her mouth and glared at her big husband. "It's now you'll be doing it. And I'll not haul another bucket of dirt until it's done."

Bedad, this woman is feisty, Jeremiah thought. And she no bigger than his thumb. If he had wanted a *colleen* with spirit, he certainly had one. *But I can't be letting her get the upper hand*.

"Well now, Missus Cleary. If you're not helping me with the digging, I'll be doing it myself."

Without even stopping for breakfast, Jeremiah went to work on the well. His anger got him through the first hours, digging the hole deeper, throwing the loose dirt in the bucket, climbing up his ladder, hauling up the bucket, emptying it and then repeating the process. Except when he had to go down with hammer, nails and redwood to shore up his progress. He was tired and famished when the sun was straight up. Sweat dripped from him. And he'd worked off his anger. But he'd be damned if he was going into the house to ask her to fix him any dinner.

Next time he climbed out, there was bread and cold meat, nicely wrapped in a cloth, sitting by the edge of the hole. *I ought to give it to the damn chickens.* But he was too hungry for silly pride. He ate the bread and meat, secretly thankful for her thoughtfulness.

He dropped back down into the well and began filling the bucket with dirt. But as he started to climb back out, he saw the bucket move. It rose to the surface and was returned empty. Jeremiah grunted with satisfaction. He filled the bucket again and watched it rise. So she'd given in, had she? That's the way of it, he thought. Just as with a good horse, you had to treat a woman with firmness. He'd not make mention of it, of course. But he'd fix that chicken roost first thing in the morning.

They worked in silence and stopped well before dark. He washed up without a word and settled himself at the table. Molly put a plate of stew before him. Jeremiah glanced up at her. He wanted to reach for her, to end this fight. But he was a bit ashamed and didn't know quite how to do it. She had spirit, and he was glad of it, and he loved her.

He reached out and tentatively took her hand. "Molly love, the work went much faster with you helping."

She allowed herself to be pulled into his lap. She didn't like a fight, either, and felt so relieved to have it over. She snuggled against his neck and let him stroke her hair. He put his arm around her and his hand brushed against her breast. He gently squeezed and Molly kissed him. Jeremiah lifted her and carried her to the feather bed. She sank into it.

He hurriedly removed his clothing, then gently undid the buttons of her dress and slid it from her shoulders. "Oh, Molly, *mavourneen,* my darling. I waited so long for you," he said.

The fight had left them both feeling bruised and anxious and they came together, at first rather tentatively, exploring each other, caressing, kissing, excited by the moment, but savoring it. "Jerry, I wasn't knowing being a wife is such a happy, wonderful thing," Molly said as she lay before him, unashamed, proud, letting the light from the lamp play it's soft, warm glow over her body. Their ardor mounted.

Now there was an urgency in their lovemaking. They joined fiercely and found a joyous release. As they lay side by side in the aftermath, Molly was thinking how deeply she loved Jeremiah and that she'd be with him for the rest of her life.

Exhausted by their lovemaking and the hard day's work, Jeremiah fell sound asleep. He didn't notice Molly slipping from the bed to stand beside it and look down at him. "I do love you, Jeremiah Cleary," she murmured softly. "But you are the most stubborn man."

He awoke at dawn to the rooster's crowing. He lay still a moment and heard it crow again. "That bird is very close," Jeremiah said to himself.

He got out of bed and looked into the main room. There, in the very center of the room, in their crate, were the chickens, awakening for another day. Jeremiah stared at them for a moment. Then he started to grin. But he couldn't be giving in, he decided, now could he?

He picked up the crate of chickens, carried it outside, and turned the birds loose for the day. Nothing was said about it and after breakfast, he and Molly worked side by side digging the well.

The next morning, he awoke to find the chickens back in the house. Again Jeremiah removed the crate and freed the chickens. Without a word about it, he and Molly went back to work on the well. It was completed that afternoon at thirty feet and the Clearys now had an ample supply of water for the stock. As soon as it was finished Jeremiah went to his redwood pile and selected boards for the chicken house. He had it knocked together before supper. Molly shut up her chickens in the new coop.

She and Jeremiah stood looking at it and Molly took Jeremiah's hand. She smiled at him and he grinned back. Then they both began to laugh and ended up hugging and arm and arm they went in for supper.

In the morning Molly smiled bravely as she helped her husband pack his saddlebags for his trip back to San Juan for the cows. She watched as he saddled Bouchal and gracefully swung up. Jeremiah leaned over and lifted Molly off her feet, holding her close as he gave her a lingering goodbye kiss.

Proudly, her eyes were on him as he rode off, up the Peach Tree trail, sitting tall and straight in the saddle. Just before he reached the top of the hill he turned and waved. She waved back. Then he was out of sight.

CHAPTER NINETEEN

MATTHEW CLEARY STRETCHED to ease his back and leaned on his shovel. His two partners looked up, saw Matthew resting, and stopped shoveling. It was miserable work, swinging the shovels full of dirt and gravel to feed the Long Tom, standing in freezing cold water from the chill of dawn in the high Sierras through the heat of midday on into late afternoon.

Matthew sloshed down to look in the riffle box. He shook his head at the little bit of gold dust that had accumulated there. "It's slow work, Matt," Swede Jensen declared.

"And just when was it you came to that brilliant decision?" Matthew asked.

"It's mounting up, Matt," his other partner, Mulie Higgins, insisted.

Stubborn Mulie, Matthew thought. He'd never give up. Neither would the big, burly Swede, slow-witted, perhaps, but strong, amiable, willing. They were good men to be partnered up with, but they weren't getting anywhere on these diggings. The amount of gold trickling into his little deerskin sack each night was pitiful. He was hardly making wages.

He arched his aching back again, picked up his shovel and resumed his work. But his mind was on his disappointment. It had been so promising when they'd set up here on Weaver Creek, twenty-five miles east of Placerville. There were a few other miners on the creek, but it hadn't been worked out like most of the streams in the decade or so since the big rush. At first he'd managed to send along some gold, almost five hundred dollars worth, to Lupe in San Juan Bautista in the custody of Wells Fargo. But he was thinking thousands, millions, not hundreds. Those big nuggets others had talked about were eluding him. Maybe it was time to move along.

Or go back to Lupe. Thoughts of her tormented him at night—Lupe's beauty, that olive complexion and long, black hair, the saucy smile on her red lips, her throaty chuckle at his jokes, the way she cocked her head to the side when she asked him a question, the way she moved within her dress when she walked. And her lush body in bed, meeting with his in abandoned passion. How the hell had he ever left her? Matthew asked himself.

"Was I ever telling you I'm married?" Again Matthew stopped shoveling. Work stopped.

"Ya, you been telling us most all the time," Swede Jensen answered.

"Why the hell don't you go home instead of pestering us about her?" Higgins wondered.

"Ya, we get more work done, just the two of us, without listening to you all the time," Jensen agreed.

"Suits me," Matthew said with a grin, throwing down his shovel. "Won't I be glad to be shut of this place? I'll be taking my share of the dust." The three gathered around while

Matthew divided the little sack of dust and a few tiny nuggets, shouldered his pack and, with a wave, took the trail back to Placerville.

He could take the stage to Sacramento, cross the bay and be home with Lupe in less than a week, he thought happily to himself as he strode along. He wasn't coming back with the fortune, but there's a bit in the poke. She'd be happy to see him.

He was in the assayer's office to measure his gold when an excited miner stepped up. He hefted a heavy, leather sack onto the counter. Matthew eyed it with envy. "Had some luck?" he ventured.

"Sure did," the miner replied. "Just panning and there it was, every wash."

"Where?" Matthew knew he shouldn't ask, but he couldn't help himself.

A veil came over the miner's eyes. He grunted, waved his hand vaguely toward the mountains to the north, and turned his back.

Matthew headed for the stage office to check the schedule and buy his ticket. But he stopped in the middle of the street to look intently toward the north, where the miner had pointed. Home could wait. He'd give it one more chance.

* * * * *

No longer did Lupe Cleary go to the post office every day. She'd given up hoping that Matthew would ever send a letter. She knew he couldn't write, but at least he could have somebody write for him, send her word. Some money had come, but not for many months, and now she was wondering if he'd ever come back. Or if he was dead. Or hurt somewhere. Maybe he didn't care about her. People had stopped asking her about him. She'd been ashamed to finally give up the little house they'd rented and move back with her parents.

Lupe was startled by the postmaster's voice as she walked past the post office. "Oh, Missus Cleary, Lupe, there's a letter here for you."

Surprised, Lupe Cleary took the envelope and, right there on the post office steps, eagerly tore it open. She found a postal money order for two hundred eighty dollars and a letter. *Dear wife, Hope this finds you in good health. I am fine. I have located a big strike north of Placerville and will be home as soon as I take out the gold. Your loving husband, Matt."*

She replaced the money order and the letter, and clutching the envelope, hurried home to the little *adobe*. There in the privacy of her room she re-read the letter, slowly. Coming home, he wrote. But first he must take out the gold. Always the gold. She knew people looked at her and wondered if Matthew Cleary was married to the bottle and to the gold, but not to Lupe Morales? Did he think she cared so much about the money? Did he think she didn't mind being alone? To be rich might be fine, but not without a husband. The more she thought, the angrier she became. She stamped her foot. Money wasn't going to keep her warm at night. Money wouldn't give her *muchachas*. She was ashamed to be walking in the town all alone, convinced everyone gossiped that he didn't want her, that he had deserted Lupe Morales! She got so mad she decided that if he came home that very night she'd slam the door in his face. If he tried to lay his hands on her, she'd scratch his eyes out—perhaps. She thought about Matthew's bright blue eyes, his handsome face with its happy smile, his Irish wit, his dancing feet, his strong arms around her, and his kisses. Lupe Cleary burst into tears.

* * * * *

Molly Cleary laid her head against the warm side of Aroon, her pet name for the cow, as she milked. Milking reminded her of home, and learning to milk when she was a girl, before their cow had been sold. She took part of the milk, then turned in the heifer calf to take the rest. She was the greedy one and stopped sucking occasionally to butt her mother.

"Stop it," Molly scolded. "You'll be weaned soon, you big *aulaun*. A lout, you are, and almost bigger than your mother." She carried the bucket of foaming milk into the house and placed it on the shelf to cool. The cream would be rising to the top and she would skim it off to churn butter.

Molly went back outside into the crisp December morning and picked up her spade. She was digging a vegetable garden while Jeremiah was off plowing the field for the wheat crop. Molly had plenty of chores to keep her busy. That wasn't it. It wasn't her hands that were idle. It was her mind. She had no one to talk with, no one to visit with. She stopped spading for a moment and let her eyes roam out over the valley. It was so empty. There were some cattle grazing not far away, and the horses in the pasture. But it would have been a blessing to see some smoke from another chimney. Just to know there were neighbors, a woman to visit with on occasion. She'd not seen another soul, except her husband, since they'd come into the valley, nearly four months ago.

She remembered how lonely she'd been when he was away those first days to bring home the cattle. But not afraid. She'd not admit to being afraid. Strange, it had been, so hot and dry. She still longed for the green of Ireland. She became used to the night sounds, and even welcomed the howls and yips of the coyotes. Perhaps they were lonesome, too, she mused, and just calling to their friends. But they'd better be staying away from her chickens. She knew Jerry was just up the canyon, but she'd not see him until noon when she took his dinner. And then she'd be alone again until supper time. Jerry wasn't much for conversation, puffing on that short pipe and watching her. He seemed to enjoy her talk, though. And his eyes on her were full of love. If only he'd speak more. If only there were neighbors, company dropping by.

It's your own company you're making inside you. She patted her slightly-rounded stomach. She'd felt a bit queasy in the mornings, not bad though, and she remembered the talk of that being a sign. Besides, there'd been no monthly bleeding these past three months. She squared her shoulders and took up her spade again. She'd not tell Jerry just now. Then she'd surprise him. He'll be pleased, she was sure of that. And it would be a son, a boy to help in the fields. There'd be another time for a girl for herself to fuss over.

After they ate supper, Molly told Jeremiah about the events of her day, what the cow did, how the calf made her laugh, and how she'd chased off the colt, him trying to play in the water trough.

Jeremiah suddenly interrupted her. "Molly, love. If you're willing, we'll be visiting Peach Tree for Christmas."

Molly was struck dumb. Going visiting? How wonderful. To see other people. And a Christmas celebration. Wonderful news. She rushed to her husband, jumped into his lap, and threw her arms around his neck. "Oh, Jerry, I'm willing, I'm willing!"

The Garcìa family had invited them. Felipe and Sophia Garcia and their family lived in Peach Tree Valley on the banks of San Lorenzo River, about six miles over the hill from the Cleary ranch. Molly thought they'd been very kind when she and Jeremiah had stopped at their rambling old adobe home on their way to Long Valley. Then Juan, their oldest boy, had helped Jeremiah drive the cows from San Juan and they'd planned the Christmas visit when they'd returned with the cattle. Jeremiah had ordered a horse-powered pump for the stock well from McMahan's store in San Juan Bautista, and it was to be sent, as soon as it came in, with whoever was hauling a delivery to the Garcìa place.

"Maybe by Christmas the pump will be there and we can bring it back," Jeremiah said.

"Yes, yes," Molly said gleefully, but she was barely listening. All that mattered was that they were going visiting and staying overnight. And celebrating Christmas. She was fairly bursting with anticipation.

The early rains had started the country turning green and the sparse sun shone through a break in the clouds as Jeremiah drove the two-horse team up the valley. Molly breathed deeply and feasted her eyes on the green-tinged hills. Today she just loved it in her Long Valley. It was a beautiful world and there was new life inside her. She couldn't remember being so happy.

Señora Garcìa welcomed Molly and Jeremiah, *"Mi casa es su casa,* my home is your home," she said in excited Spanish and with a great deal of fussing. She led Molly into the house, took her coat, showed her to the room she'd share with Jeremiah, insisted she have a glass of wine and presented the younger Garcia children—all of whom were asking a string of questions in rapid Spanish. Molly couldn't understand a word, but she responded to everything, in both Irish and English, and hoped for the best. Sophia Garcìa took both Molly's hands in hers and the two women started to laugh. In that laughter they'd found a common language.

The youngest Garcìa girl, the one called Carmencita, shyly took Molly by the hand, and led her out the back door. *"Venga aquì, por favor. Mira, mira. Perrocitas."* There in a large box was a litter of fat, squirming, cuddly puppies. Molly picked up one and nuzzled it. Carmencita did the same and they smiled at each other.

The men came in from outside carrying the antelope Jerry had killed, and hung out to age for three nights. He'd also trapped a bunch of quail for the Christmas table. And Molly had made a large pudding, the first she'd ever tried. She looked about the huge room, and was comforted to see the shrine of the Virgin Mary, and the crèche with the Christ child. There was an angel atop the gaily-decorated Christmas tree. A huge fire was blazing at the other end of the room, and they gathered there as Felipe Garcìa filled their glasses and cups and proposed a toast.

"Feliz Navidad." He explained in his halting English that this meant Merry Christmas.

Jeremiah raised his glass and responded, first in Irish, *"Nollaig shona dhuit,"* then said, "Happy Christmas."

The men went back outside to tend the horses, while Molly helped *Señora* Garcìa and her daughter arrange the big table and prepare the feast. Molly started to peel the potatoes, which the Clearys had brought, and suddenly felt like she was going to burst into tears. She thought of home, of Catherine and James, and her parents. How were they in the hills above Skibbereen? Were they about to sit down to a Christmas feast? Molly knew it wouldn't be anything remotely like this.

She'd written to Catherine about her wedding and the trip to her new home. But she hadn't said much about Long Valley. She'd said that Jerry was good, and kind, and loved her, and that she loved him back. He'd mailed the letter in September when he'd gone to San Juan. She might have a reply from Catherine waiting at the San Juan post office for Jeremiah to pick up one day soon.

Christmas dinner was a festive and abundant affair. Felipe said grace in Spanish, and *Señora* Garcia began passing the plates heavily laden with mashed potatoes, antelope steaks, *carne asada,* chicken *mole, frijoles, tamales.* After the hearty, delicious meal, while the women were clearing the dishes, Juan, the eldest Garcia boy, brought out his mandolin and picked the chords, singing, *"Noche de pas,* silent night — "

He had a sweet tenor voice that made the song especially poignant. Sophia Garcìa and her daughters joined in, and Molly hummed along to the familiar tune. Jeremiah and Felipe contentedly puffed their pipes by the fire.

That night, as they snuggled down together, Molly whispered into Jeremiah's ear. "Jerry love, you'd best see if *Señora* Garcìa can be visiting us come this May."

"Well now, and why is that?"

"And won't I be needing her help to be birthing your son?" Molly replied.

Jeremiah grinned in the dark and held Molly close. "And haven't I been suspecting that?"

In the morning Felipe and Juan loaded the new pump in the wagon and Jeremiah gave Molly a hand up to her seat. *Señora* Garcia and the children were gathered about, saying goodbye, but Jeremiah seemed reluctant to start his team. He looked toward the house expectantly and then smiled. Carmencita came running out, carrying a squirming puppy. She held it up to Molly, who reached down to take it and then looked inquiringly to Jeremiah. He smiled and nodded.

"He'll be company for you, Molly love, until the baby comes."

Molly thanked Carmencita and cuddled the puppy in one arm, waving goodbye with the other. There was a smile on her face for the Garcia family. But as they rode toward home there were tears of happiness in her eyes as she realized how sensitive to her feelings was her big, quiet husband.

CHAPTER TWENTY

THE BABY'S BIRTH was so easy, *Senora* Garcia was hardly needed and Molly was soon able to travel to San Juan. But after the five days of heat and dirt on the San Benito River road, Molly gratefully sank into the big tub of hot water and soaked as Emily cared for baby Will.

"Damn fine baby you got there, Cleary," was Weeb Jefferson's judgment as he watched Emily cuddling little Will.

That night the Jeffersons and Clearys enjoyed a hearty supper, sitting around the big table as usual with the *vaqueros*. "Have you been riding any more broncos, *Señor* Jerry?" one of them asked. But they were shyly polite with Molly.

Jeremiah left the next morning for the redwood mill and would be gone three or four days. He'd made an arrangement to haul shingles, posts and scrap redwood for their new neighbors, Delbert and Sally Thompson, who had come to homestead next to the Clearys. Molly was so grateful to have neighbors, especially somebody to watch their place so she could go with Jeremiah.

Calistro Salazar drove Molly and Emily into town in the surrey and Molly made arrangements with Padre Mora for Will's baptism at the mission. It was exciting to be in town, to see so many people and hear the talk. Emily took her to the San Juan post office and Molly held her breath until the postmaster produced two letters, one for Jeremiah and one from her sister Cauth.

You are fortunate, dear sister, and my prayers for you are being answered. We think of you every day and miss you, but it is good to know you are so happy and that Jeremiah is such a good man. Conditions are much the same here in Ireland, except that there are new laws that make it easier than ever for landlords to evict tenants, even those who paid their rents. This causes more talk of land reform so tenants will be able to own their farms, but it seems such a dream. James talks of something called the Phoenix Society in Skibbereen, but the leader, a man called O'Donovan Rossa, who ran the seed store, was arrested."

Molly was surprised her sister wrote of politics, but she wasn't surprised that her brother James was involved. He was the one with the fire burning inside him.

When Jeremiah returned she gave him his letter. He turned it over in his hands, held it to the light, squinted at it. "Postmarked Placerville," he said. And finally tore it open. He read a moment and then looked up at Molly. "Well now," he said. "This is from my brother, Matt. I'd about given up on him. A friend wrote it for him. He's still in the gold country."

Jeremiah read on. *I want you to know that I am in health and doing well. Hope you are the same. This claim shows promise. I'll return one day soon with a full poke. If you are not happy with your ranch, I'll buy you a new one. Your loving brother."* And below that Matthew had scrawled his signature.

Jeremiah sat with the letter in his hands, shaking his head. Matt and his big ideas. And not a word about his wife. As if she

141

knew his thoughts, Molly asked, "And what about Matthew's wife. Is she cared for with him off after gold? Should we be going to see about her, Jerry?"

"Aye, we'll be looking in on her later today," Jeremiah agreed.

Jeremiah and Molly met Padre Mora at the mission. He blessed baby Will with the holy water and baptized him "*in nomine Patris, et Filii, et Spiritus Sancti*," the age-old Latin the same in this Spanish mission church in California as in the Irish church on North Street in Skibbereen. Will didn't even cry, just looked at the priest with big, blue eyes like his mother's, and Jeremiah stood proudly by.

After the baptism, Jeremiah and Molly went in search of Lupe Cleary. They found her at her parents' home, but she didn't invite them in. "*Con mucho gusto*," she said in response to Jeremiah's introduction of Molly. And she shyly smiled. "Yes, I have a message from Matthew that he will return as soon as he picks up more gold." But she didn't know how soon that would be. "No, I have no needs," she replied to Jeremiah's question.

Jeremiah and Molly stood there a moment and then turned away. Lupe called after them, "Thank you for coming to see me." And the door closed.

"What a beautiful woman she is," an admiring Molly said. "But why did she act so strange, almost as if she was embarrassed because we went to see her?"

The Clearys left for Long Valley the next day with the wagon load of redwood and supplies and Calistro Salazar riding along horseback. Jeremiah had asked Weeb's permission to take Calistro to help the Thompsons build an *adobe* house just as he'd once done for Jeremiah.

"Damn right you can take him, Cleary, if he wants to go," Weeb said. "Damn good job for him. Damn fellow wants to get married to that Marìa Encinales girl, settle down, raise some more Indians."

While Calistro and Thompson were building the house, Sally and Molly spent time together and became friends. Molly appreciated the company because Jeremiah was off again, this time with the cattle drive to San Juan with nineteen steers of his own, part Spanish longhorn and part American breed, and stock gathered at the Rist ranch in Lone Oak and at Tully's in Bitter Water. The steers sold for nine dollars each and Jeremiah received forty dollars for a four-year-old gray gelding, which he'd put in the bridle just before the trip. He was proud of the ten double eagles jingling in his pocket as he went to the post office to check the mail.

Nothing for Molly, but there was a letter from her brother, John Hurley in Boston, addressed to both Jeremiah and Matthew Cleary. Well, Matt wasn't here so Jeremiah put it in his pocket. He'd read it later. First he went into McMahan's store to catch up on the news.

"War's broken out, Jerry. Didn't you know?" James McMahan asked. "Those southern boys fired on the flag at Fort Sumter."

"We can't be letting them rebels get away with that," somebody said. "We're gonna kick their ass."

"Oh yeah? Well, I'm from Alabama and I'm telling you one southerner can whip a dozen damn Yankees!"

A general argument broke out and Jeremiah thought the war was going to be fought right there in McMahan's store. Time to leave. But McMahan followed him onto the board sidewalk outside.

"A private word with you, Jerry." McMahan seemed to hesitate a moment. Jeremiah looked at him quizzically. Then McMahan said, "Your brother's here."

"What? Matthew—here in San Juan?" Jeremiah was astonished. "Why didn't you say so? Where is he?"

"Well now, Jerry. That takes some explaining."

"Explaining? What do you mean?"

"He's in jail."

"Jail? My God, man, what did he do?"

"Well, Jerry, he shot up Florney's Saloon, for one thing," McMahan said. "Drilled a whole row of bottles with one shot. Not bad for the amount of liquor in him." He paused for a moment. "And there were a few other charges."

"Like what?" Jeremiah asked, his blood rising.

"Like driving Rodriguez' hogs through the graveyard and yelling, 'wooo, wooo, hooo,' and ringing the mission bell at three in the morning."

Jeremiah was dumbfounded. Good Lord! His brother's antics had never included destroying other people's property before. What would make Matt act like that? Still on the liquor, was he?

"When did this happen? How long has he been back?"

"About three months or so," McMahan replied. "But the trouble was just last week. His wife doesn't have the money or she just won't pay it. The sheriff is holding him, waiting for you to show up. I'm sorry, Jerry, but they're going to ask you to pay for the damages."

"Me pay? How much?"

"I'm not knowing. Sheriff Stone wants to see you. I was to tell you," McMahan added. "They knew you were due soon with the cattle drive, and that you'd come here, or go to Weeb's."

Jeremiah was shaken, his concern evident, as he hurried to the jail. He found Sheriff Charlie Stone, in his little office, feet on the desk, rifling through his stack of wanted posters.

"Ah, Cleary, there you are." Stone's feet hit the floor with a thump and he pushed back his chair. "There's some relative of yours back there waiting to see you, if you want to claim him. Been a guest of ours." He pointed with his thumb, indicating the jail's lone cell.

Jeremiah's eyes narrowed. This was the man who'd held a gun on him one time. "It's my brother," he said in a voice that was quiet, but firm. "I've come to take him out. How much?"

"Easy there, Cleary. No harm intended," the sheriff answered. "He's all yours. If you can afford him."

144

"Once again. How much?"

"Well, Florney will settle for one hundred and twenty-five dollars. And then there's the room and board for the county. I'd say you can have him for one thirty."

My God, Jeremiah thought. That will take most of what I just made on the cattle. There go our savings. What would Molly say?

Jeremiah counted out the coin to the sheriff. Neither spoke. Then he took down his ring of keys and led the way back to the cell. As the key turned in the door, Matthew looked up from his seat on the cot. His smile of joy at seeing his brother quickly faded into a sheepish grin.

"Well, now, Brother. I'm glad to see you," Matthew said. "But these aren't quite the circumstances I'd planned."

"Matt, my brother." Jeremiah grabbed him in a bear hug. "I'm just happy to see you."

He took Matthew's arm, propelled him outside toward a shady spot across the plaza. "Tell me about it."

"Sure, Jerry. But there's so much to tell. Where will I start?"

"Try the beginning." Jeremiah's relief at seeing his brother, was tempered by the fact that he was now nearly broke, not to mention embarrassed by Matthew's latest prank.

"I wasn't having much success in Placerville," Matthew said, "so when I heard about a new strike, I lit out for it. I finally had some real luck, not a lot, but I found some color, and then a few nuggets. So I headed home. Lupe wasn't so damn glad to see me at first, wouldn't even let me in the house. But we made up and I got back on at the blacksmith shop. I can still shape iron."

"How the hell did you wind up in jail?" Jeremiah wondered.

"Well, some evenings I'd stop off at Florney's, just for one or two with the boys, and sometimes to play a little cards. Lupe didn't like that much and she'd rag on me." Matthew looked a little wistful, then brightened up.

"Say, Jerry, I got that ranch for you. I know that you have your own place now, but I had one for you. Honest, I did. Just like I promised. Two hundred and forty acres, right near here. My luck was holding good that night. I had the deed in my pocket. Then I was dealt a hand I could hardly believe. Draw poker and I held four jacks the first four cards. They all dropped out, except for one fellow. He raised. I pushed it all in, every dollar I had. We each drew one card. He bet first. I put the deed on the table and called."

Matthew stopped his narrative for a moment and sat shaking his head. "How can you lose with four jacks? Four jacks, Jerry! I was so sure." He stared into space.

"Well?" Jeremiah didn't know much about poker. He prodded his brother.

"He had four kings."

"So you lost?"

"Sure now, I lost. The winner bought a round of drinks. I guess I had several, and I sat there at the empty table. I couldn't believe it. And then it hit me. Of all the damned bad luck. That's all I ever seem to get is bad luck. I suppose it all came out in me at once, all my years of bad luck. And hating it. Anyhow, I took out the little pistol from my waistband and plugged a row of bottles behind the bar. It was a terrible splash and glass flew. I shot the backbar, too. I thought it was so damn funny and I laughed. Then I started potting the whiskey barrels on the floor, and seeing the liquor pour out the holes gave me great comfort.

"After that, I don't rightly know, they said I turned Rodriguez' pigs loose in the cemetery. Seems I remember something about trying to run off the spirits that were bringing me bad luck. I suppose I thought they were devils. I don't know why the hell I rang the mission bells. It seemed like a good idea at the time. I climbed into the belfry and that's where the sheriff found me."

Jeremiah was quiet for a moment, then said, "That's it?"

Matthew nodded silently.

Jeremiah stared at his brother and shook his head. "Well, well, well. And what does Lupe think of this?"

An expression of sadness came over Matthew's face. "She didn't even come to see me, Jerry. I guess I can't really blame her. I really love her, but it just doesn't work out." Matthew sighed, he just couldn't understand why. "But I'll pay you back, Jerry. Every cent you put out for me. With interest. Just as soon as I get on my feet again. I promise," he declared.

"Sure, sure," Jeremiah agreed, ready to change the subject. "Oh, there's a letter for both of us from John. What could he be wanting?" He pulled it from his pocket, ripped it open and began reading aloud to Matthew.

John was writing about the war. *Irishmen are joining up to fight for the Union. Dan Hennessy is helping to form a brigade under General Thomas Meagher in New York and I'm to be a captain. There's room for you and Matt to come along. Dan says after we lick the rebels we'll all go over to Ireland and kick out the British. Write and let me know if you're coming. Your brother-in-law, James Hurley.*

"War!" Matthew greeted the news with enthusiasm. "So John wants us to come soldiering with him. It won't be taking us long to finish off those southern boys and then we'll go across the water and chase the bloody Brits back to England."

Jeremiah looked at his brother in disgust. "My God, Jerry. You can't go running off clear across the continent to join the Army. And what about your wife?"

Matthew waved away his brother's concern. He could be going off to fight and beat the rebels and then the damn Brits. When he'd come home again he'd be a hero and Lupe would surely love him again.

But Jeremiah thought, War! How terrible. How could he go off to fight a war so far away and leave his family? Leave Molly and two children? And he had a ranch to work.

"How about it, Jerry?" Matthew asked. "Will you go with me?"

"I can't," he answered. "I have obligations, responsibilities. So do you. You should be thinking about your wife."

147

"Not going?" Matthew exclaimed. "And aren't you the one always telling me about democracy and this great country, so much better than we had it in Ireland. And aren't you the citizen now? And you're not the one to fight for it?"

Jeremiah swallowed hard. He didn't want to see this Union ripped apart by those who believed it was God's will for one man to own another human being, for one man to be better than another. He was sickened by the thought. But Jeremiah knew he was getting older, he was feeling it after a day of swinging that sickle. He'd better be leaving the soldiering to the younger ones without families. Besides, how would he keep his land if he left it?

"Well, I'll be going, even if you're not." Matthew stated. "One of us has to fight for his country."

Jeremiah was quiet for a moment, and then he asked, "How will you be getting back east? It costs money to travel."

Matthew hadn't thought about that. The question took him by surprise. He was flat broke. Whether he took a ship from San Francisco, or a stage coach to St. Louis and the train, it would cost money he didn't have. A look of defeat came over him. He thought a moment and then perked up.

"I think you should be paying my way, Jerry. Since I'll be representing us both, it's only fair."

CHAPTER TWENTY-ONE

"OH, NO, JERRY!" Molly cried. "How could you be giving your brother all of our money? We'll be having no savings."

Molly had joyfully greeted Jeremiah on his return from San Juan. She'd been preparing his supper as he recounted Matthew's latest escapade. But when he told her he'd borrowed money from McMahan to send his brother off to join the Army, Molly turned from the fire, put her hands on her hips, and vehemently protested. Jeremiah stood shame-faced before his angry, little wife.

"What else could I do, Molly? I can't be going off myself to fight for what I believe in," he tried to explain. "I can't be leaving you and the young ones, so I'm sending Matt."

"Matt, is it? Sure and this is just another excuse for him to be running off from his wife and responsibilities, and you're the one helping him do it!" Molly banged the pot on the fireplace and Will jumped, then toddled over to grab her by the legs. Little Jerry woke screaming. She picked up both boys, trying to soothe them. But the baby, sensing her agitation, cried louder.

"Now, Molly, don't be making yourself so mad," Jeremiah said. He'd never seen her show such a temper. "It's disturbing the baby."

"Disturbing the baby, is it? It's you disturbing me, Jerry Cleary," she said, her eyes sparking fire. She commenced to rock the child in her arms, as she continued. "Why is it you're paying to get him out of jail?" she shouted over the loudly crying baby. "You should be letting him rot, the way he's treating his wife, on the drink and gone all the time crazy after gold! Isn't our money hard come by and why is it you're wasting it?"

"He's my brother," Jeremiah said simply.

Molly started to speak again, but Jeremiah glared at her. "That's enough, woman."

Furious and frustrated, Molly glared back. But she sat down and put little Jerry to her breast. The sobbing baby began to suckle and the act comforted them both. Jeremiah ate his supper in silence. Finally, Molly spoke.

"I'm sorry to be carrying on so, Jerry. But it eases me so to know we've something set aside. I can't help but be thinking of those starving days without a shilling to our name."

"Aye, and I'm remembering them, too, Molly." He thought of it often, of somehow losing the land, of being penniless, of being helpless at the mercy of a landlord, of the hunger. Ireland was a reoccurring nightmare. But he didn't want to talk about it. Those terrible times were behind him. He couldn't forget them, but he'd not dwell on them.

"But it's here we live," Jeremiah said. "And we have the land. I'm grateful. A grand country, this America. If I was a younger man without responsibilities, I'd be off to soldier for it."

Molly nodded. She conceded that she'd much rather lose the money than lose Jerry to the war. She began to sing and the boy stopped nursing and fell sleep. Jeremiah never tired of hearing Molly's gentle voice, singing in Irish, *"Huzho-bye, baby, on the tree top... when the wind blows, the cradle will rock..."*

She put the baby down in the cradle, covered young Will and went to her husband. Jeremiah took her hand and pulled her into his lap. "Molly love, don't you be worrying now. Won't I be selling some horses and fat steers, and having a fine crop of wheat? We'll make up for the money."

* * * * *

Molly had been outside standing in the rain. She loved the rain. Sometimes she danced in it, laughing and singing as it drenched her, evoking good memories of Ireland. Now she stood dripping by the fireplace. A small hand clutched at her skirt. "Mama wet," little Will admonished her.

"It's all right, Will. Mama can dry off. Don't you be fretting now."

Mavorne, she thought, that boy worries about everything. Sometimes it's as if he's the mother and I'm the child. Those big eyes on me every move, and him trying to help, and so little he's in danger of being stepped upon. She glanced out the rain-streaked window, saw Jerry had turned Bouchal into the corral, and was forking out hay for him. In a moment he was stomping his muddy boots on the step, and taking off his dripping coat and hat. It had started raining in October and here it was nearly Christmas and it had hardly let up.

"*Bedad*, and it's wet out there, Molly. Never saw it so wet. There's a roaring creek flowing in Coyote Canyon, and the cattle are all brushed up. I couldn't see what cows have calved. I couldn't even find the half of them."

Jeremiah threw another pine log on the fire, the sparks jumped and sputtered as he spread his hands to the warmth. He noticed Molly changing her dress. "Been cavorting in the rain again, have you, Molly love? You'll be getting your fill of that this winter. I look to see us having a river of our own right through the yard if this keeps up. Tomorrow I'd best throw up some dirt for a dam to keep it out of our house." Jeremiah lit the lamps as the dark came early with the cloud cover and the rain. "It's a wild night we're in for, Molly love."

She was putting the supper on the table when the dog barked, and right after came a pounding at the door. "Cleary, it's me, Bert — ! Let me in." Delbert Thompson stood at the door, soaking wet, a frightened look in his eyes. "It's Sally. Her time has come early. I need help," he pleaded.

"Why sure now, Bert — " Jeremiah was thinking quickly. "Ride back on home and be with your Sally. As soon as I can hitch my team, I'll take Molly and the children down there. She'll be helping you and I'll go over the hill to bring Missus Garcìa. Be off with you now."

While Jerry was attending to the horses, Molly wrapped up some food, bundled up the boys, and got their things ready to travel in the rain. She was barely able to open the door against the wind, which whistled around her, and nearly tugged it out of her hands before she could push it shut. The moment Jeremiah reached the house with the wagon, she handed Will up to him, and then the baby, swaddled against the wet and cold. She hurriedly climbed aboard and they were on their way to the Thompson place at a mud-splattering trot.

Soon Jeremiah had his wagon back on the Peach Tree road, moving as fast as he could in the mud. Rain, driven fiercely by the wind, slashed at him, pelted him. He was hunched against it, squinting to see, but having to leave it to the horses to find their way along the tracks. The worst was sliding down the treacherous roadway from the top, winding down into Peach Tree Valley. Jeremiah trod on his brakes, locking them as best he could. The wagon slithered sideways against the bank, nearly tipped, then hung on the edge of the road.

He breathed a prayer of thanks when it righted, and the horses pulled it into the flat by the river. Now how would he cross the creek? It was dry most of the time, like a dead thing, but the rain brought it alive, twisting, roiling, flooding over its banks, ugly and dangerous.

Clouds closed off the weak moon and stars, but he found the ford in the blackness. He could hardly see it, but he could hear the roar of the water. The San Lorenzo was rushing bank to bank, flowing swiftly with the weight of water running out of every mountain canyon. It was impossible to cross with the wagon and it was still a mile down the creek to the Garcia place. He swung down off the wagon, unhitched Nellie, the near wheel horse, then tied up the rest of the team. He rigged the reins to her bridle, talking to the big, gentle, white mare as he did so. "Easy, Nellie, old girl. Let's be giving this a try. Now don't be letting me down."

Jeremiah swung up on the work horse, and took a tight hold of the collar and her reins. He kicked her sides and eased her down to the bank. She refused to take to the torrent, snorted and shied, but Jeremiah insisted. Nellie stepped into the river

152

and lunged, nearly throwing him into the rushing water. He righted himself as Nellie lunged again, almost going under. But suddenly they were out of it, up the slippery bank, and the old mare was moving at a lumbering gallop toward Garcia's. Jeremiah called out as he neared the ranch "Halloo — !" He saw the flicker of a lamp being lit as Nellie slipped and slithered into the yard. In seconds Felipe Garcìa was at the door. Jeremiah slid off Nellie and tied the mare to the hitching rail. In a moment he was in the house, where Juan was stoking up the fire, and Sophia Garcìa was heating coffee.

She agreed immediately to go help the poor *Señora* Thompson. "But *aye de mi*, how will I get across the river?" Felipe and Jeremiah figured the safest way was on Garcia's saddle horse. "But, Felipe, I haven't ridden a horse in ten years," his wife protested.

She and Felipe exchanged words in rapid Spanish, and it was agreed he'd take her to the river in the buggy and she would ride across on the saddle horse. Jeremiah went first on Nellie, and, when he was across, he tied off a *reata* to a tree. The other end had been secured to Sophia Garcia's ample form, now bundled against the rain, just in case her mount fell into the raging waters. But the horse carried her safely across, and she was boosted into the wagon. Jeremiah hitched up the team, put the horses to the climb up the Peach Tree road, and they skidded down into Long Valley.

It was almost dawn when they pulled into the Thompson place. Despite the screaming wind and the lashing rain, they could hear cries and shrieks from the little *adobe*. Sophia Garcìa hurried her bulk out of the wagon and through the door held open by a distraught Delbert Thompson.

Molly met her at the door exclaiming, "Oh, *Señora* Garcìa, God bless you for coming. There's trouble here and I'm not knowing what to do."

Molly pushed Jeremiah and Delbert out the door, back into the rain. And they went willingly, chased by Sally's screams. Delbert sat on the step, oblivious to the rain, his head in both hands. Jeremiah found an opening in the clouds and saw some stars. He offered up a prayer.

As Molly wiped the sweat from the young woman's forehead with a damp cloth, Sophia Garcìa began murmuring soothing words to Sally. She felt her swollen abdomen and examined her pelvis. What she saw frightened the midwife.

"*Madre de Dios*," she exclaimed. The baby was lodged in the birth canal, feet first. She moved Sally's arching body and reached for the tiny feet, trying to pull the baby. But it was stuck. Sally shrieked and contorted. Sophia made the sign of the cross, and tried again. The feet protruded and then the little legs, but the arms and the baby's head were jammed tight.

Sophia worked frantically, trying to free the baby. Sally struggled with her as the minutes went by. At last the baby's head showed and a final push by Sally brought forth a perfectly formed baby girl. "It's a *niña*," Sophia triumphantly announced to the exhausted mother, lifting the baby to clear the mucus from her mouth. She turned her over and gave her back a gentle pat.

But there was no responding cry.

She raised the baby by its feet and thumped her harder, but there was no answering life. She did it again and frantically, again.

The baby was dead.

Sally's scream of anguish rose above the howling wind. Her husband rushed through the door to her side. Molly stepped out into the rain, and into the arms of her husband. "Oh, Jerry, the baby was born dead," she cried. Jeremiah clung to her, held her close and stroked her wet hair. *And I'm knowing what he's thinking, that it could have been me in there suffering so with a dead baby.*

Molly and Jeremiah went back into the little *adobe* to join the sorrowing Thompsons. Sally sobbed uncontrollably in Delbert's arms, and Sophia Garcia knelt, rosary beads in hand, praying for the soul of the dead child.

"Sally, dear, I'm so sorry," Molly murmured, tears filling her eyes.

Bert Thompson rose from his wife's side. "Damn, this godforsaken country. I should never have brought Sally to this place. If we'd stayed in Nebraska this never would have happened."

Jeremiah didn't know what to say. They gathered the Thompson children and their own from the barn, bundled them up, and headed home. Sophia Garcia stayed to care for Sally. Jeremiah was silent, hunched against the rain, lost in his own thoughts. Molly knew this was no time to be telling him that there was another baby growing inside her.

CHAPTER TWENTY-TWO

"HOW DID THINGS GO there in Long Valley?" McMahan asked when Jeremiah was finally able to get his wagon along the river road and into San Juan. It had rained for eighty days straight and the winter of 1861-62 had been the wettest ever.

"We fared very well compared to what I'm hearing," Jeremiah answered. "Our cattle got by in the high country, and my wheat crop was the best yet. And I've a good harvest of hay set aside. But my neighbor, Thompson, didn't get planted early enough, and some in Bitter Water by that lake were flooded."

"That's the way of it around here," McMahan agreed. "Cattle drowned and so did the grain crops. But one man's poison is another man's honey." He watched as Jeremiah took out his bag of double eagles and stacked fifteen on the counter.

"James, this is what I borrowed last trip."

"Right," McMahan said, picking up the twenty dollar gold pieces. "You'll be making that up soon, Jerry. Cattle prices will be up with this war on in the east. And they're saying we'll be having soldiers stationed right here in San Juan soon and they'll be wanting beef."

"What's the battle to be fought here?" Jeremiah asked.

"There's some around who favor the South," McMahan explained. "They're having secret meetings, and there's rumbling they want to take California out of the Union."

"Well now, I'll not be holding with that." Jeremiah was strongly against slavery, and for him, the whole issue of North against South was the wrong of one man owning another. "There's not a man in my part of the county who feels so. We're Union men all the way. It's a grievous sin, that slavery."

"If you're such a blue belly, Mick, why aren't you in a soldier suit?" a man standing near the counter asked belligerently. His loud challenge caught Jeremiah by surprise.

"That goddamn Lincoln got us into this mess. Ain't that right, Mason?" another man said, moving toward Jeremiah and backing him up against the counter. "I sure as hell didn't vote for him. Suppose you did though, huh, Mick?"

Jeremiah's mouth grew tight and his eyes narrowed. He was proud of his vote, his first one as an American citizen, and he'd had to ride in a long way to cast it. But what business was it of this stranger? "Aye, that I did!" He was emphatic.

"See, I told you, Mason," the man said to his cohort. "I can spot a blue-bellied nigger-lover a mile away. Or smell him. We should run all these nigger-lovers out of San Juan, and I think we'll start with you, Mick."

Jeremiah felt the gorge rising, the red mist of rage in his eyes. He clenched his fist, and was about to swing it when McMahan stepped around the counter, and got instantly between them. "I'll be having none of this in my store, Henry. Out you go. And you, too, Mason." McMahan waved a large club, kept under the counter for just such a purpose, but rarely used. The two backed off, mumbling and cursing both Irishmen.

156

Mason glared defiantly at Jeremiah. "You'd better watch yourself, Cleary. We know you," he called over his shoulder as the pair went outside. Jeremiah gradually relaxed.

"I'm after thanking you, James. I'm not wanting a fight, but they were prodding me."

"Aye. They were. And that's the way of it nowadays," McMahan explained. "Feelings run deep over this war. There's quite a few people like that, but those two are especially bad, always starting fights. Some say they're really bandits, just renegades masquerading as southern sympathizers. And that's why the soldiers are coming, to keep the peace. You be on the lookout for that pair, Jeremiah. Now what is it I can help you with?"

Jeremiah pointed to a large, cast-iron stove, one with an ample oven and a spacious cooking surface. It was expensive—fifteen dollars—but Molly would love it. He wanted to surprise her. He didn't want to see her bending over that fireplace with her cooking pots anymore, and her with three *deeshy* ones now to care for since baby Timothy had come just two weeks back.

He and McMahan took the stove apart and loaded it in his wagon. He went about buying his own supplies, and loading the goods he'd been commissioned to haul for the other settlers. There was the sugar, twenty pounds at twenty-five cents per pound, and three dollars for a sixty-pound sack of beans, and another three dollars for thirty-eight pounds of coffee. He loaded four hundred pounds of flour, at a cost of three dollars per hundred weight, for Bitter Water families, and felt grateful that his own wheat hadn't drowned out. Molly had an ample supply to grind in her little hand mill. He consulted his list for special orders, and added syrup and tobacco, and then a box of horse shoes and some nails. Jeremiah started to climb to his wagon seat, thought of something, and stepped down to go back into the store.

"James, are you remembering that bolt of pretty blue cloth Molly was admiring last time?"

"Sure and I do," McMahan recalled. "That was sold." He saw Jeremiah's frown of disappointment. With a mischievous grin, McMahan added, "But could you believe it? There's another here just like it."

It was the morning of Jeremiah's second day along the river route toward home when a rider appeared around a curve just in front of the team. Another horseman moved out of the brush on the other side. They cut Jeremiah off, and he had to pull up. He dragged his rifle across his lap, but carefully, since he saw that both men were waving pistols.

"Hold up there, Mick! We think you're hauling contraband," said the first man, his horse fidgeting near the head of Jeremiah's team. "We're guerrilla soldiers of the Confederacy. And you're a goddamned blue belly! We're authorized to confiscate your wagon and these goods."

Jeremiah recognized Henry, the belligerent fool from McMahan's store yesterday. The other was Mason. Damn, he should have thought something like this might happen, he scolded himself. How would he get out of this? They had him covered with their weapons.

"We're taking this wagon! Step down," Henry ordered.

"I'll not," Jeremiah retorted. "This rifle is aimed at your gut, Henry. And this pistol here on the seat is for your friend. Now be away with you."

At that moment Henry's skittish horse pranced sideways and bumped against the wagon's near gray leader. He snorted, then reared up. The team plunged and the wagon lurched forward. The bump jerked Jeremiah's finger on the trigger and the shot struck Henry's horse, which went down with a squeal of pain, throwing his rider. The grays lunged against their collars and the white wheelers went with them. The team burst into a gallop and Jeremiah urged them on.

He shouted, "Run, run! Giddup Chip. Away Block. Go! Go!" And cracked his whip over their heads. The team was flying across the uneven ground. A shot rang out from behind Jeremiah. He heard it thump into a sack of flour.

He'd almost made the cover of a clump of trees when the second shot struck him. The shock of it drove him to the floorboards, but he kept a grip on the lines, and pulled himself back up onto the wagon seat.

Jeremiah reached the next river crossing before he checked the team. He struggled into the back of his wagon and settled himself behind the flour sacks. He ignored the pain in his shoulder to quickly reload and cover the back trail with his rifle. Blood poured from his wound, spreading and staining the flour. He stared at the back road, blinked and shook his head to lift the haze from his eyes. His lathered horses stood, breathing heavily. All else was quiet. He waited. A blue jay squawked and a hawk soared overhead.

His eyes followed it into the bright, blue sky. The blue sky turned red, and then black.

* * * * *

Molly straightened up from her milking stool, stretched to ease herself, and wiped the sweat from her forehead with the back of her arm. "There now, Will, go easy now," she cautioned her little son, who was trying to pick up the bucket filled with frothing milk. Sometimes he was more hindrance than help, but he always tried so hard.

Molly let Will's little fingers clutch around the handle next to her hand as they carried the milk bucket back to the house. But she stopped before entering to look again up the Peach Tree road. She set the bucket down and, with the palm of her hand, sheltered her eyes from the glaring sun. Will watched his mother intently study the road. But no amount of scrutiny could produce a speck of dust. There was nothing in sight.

She sighed and picked up the bucket. Another day without Jerry. He was four days late from San Juan. Molly knew he couldn't always make the trip in the exact amount of days every time. He was often a day or so late. Even, on several occasions, a glorious day early. But never four days overdue.

At first she hadn't worried. From the beginning she'd trained herself not to dwell on the things that could go wrong in this raw, unpredictable country. And Jeremiah was gone so often, on horseback, checking cattle, building fence, working in the fields, with the horses and wagon off freighting. She never allowed herself to wonder what she'd do if he didn't return. She didn't dare. But now that grim thought was creeping into her mind.

She covered the milk with a cloth and put it to cool. She checked baby Timmy, who was starting to fuss in his crib, letting her know he was hungry. Molly changed him and then sat down in her rocking chair and put her baby son to her breast. Will picked up the broom and entertained Jerry Jr., the little boy laughing as Will pretended to sweep him up. Before she fed the children and fixed something for herself, Molly again stepped outside to look up the Peach Tree Road. Nothing.

She lay awake long after she'd gone to bed. What could be keeping her husband? Perhaps some difficulty with the horses. Maybe something wrong with the wagon. An accident? No, of course, not, she told herself. Jeremiah is strong and capable, and as anxious to be home as she was to have him. He's a careful man. It must be some business that needed his attention. That's it, she decided. He had to stay back to do something special for Weeb and Emily. Or he stopped with the Bitter Water people to help them. He's in Peach Tree right this minute and will be driving in with the dawn. She took his pillow and held it in her arms for comfort.

But dawn came, and the red ball of the July sun climbed high and only the heat waves shimmered on the Peach Tree Road. Molly went about her morning tasks, but stopped every few minutes to go outside and look to the east. No matter how she tried to fight back the fear, that little grain of panic was growing. It knotted her stomach and soon filled her whole body. Jesus, Mary and Joseph, she prayed, help me know what to do.

She wondered if she should go to Thompsons for help. But how could she get there with the children? Ride a horse? Bouchal was there in the pasture. She knew he was gentle, but then again she'd never ridden. And she couldn't leave the boys. The panic in her breast mounted and soon clutched at her throat. She put her hand there to stop it. Mother of God, help me think. Think, Molly Cleary. Think!

The best thing I can do is stay right here and care for my children. If something has happened to Jerry somebody will find him, help him, bring him to me. She suddenly pictured Jeremiah being brought to her, hurt, needing care, or dear God, dead. She closed her eyes. Stop this silliness, she told herself. Jeremiah will be along later today, and he'll not want to be finding a dirty house, and no clean clothes, and crying babies. Molly returned to her chores with renewed energy.

It was late afternoon when the sound of Bodach's barking brought a leap of joy to Molly's breast. With a happy cry she ran to the door and flung it open. There was Delbert Thompson, on horseback before the door. "Good afternoon, Missus Cleary." He tipped his hat. He noticed the look of disappointment on her face, though she quickly tried to conceal it. "What's the matter, Missus Cleary?"

Molly explained that Jeremiah was nearly a week overdue from San Juan. Thompson nodded, smiled, and tried to reassure her that she had no reason to worry, that Jeremiah was all right, only detained by important business. He offered to ride over to Peach Tree to see if there was any word. But first he'd go home to fetch Sally and the children to spend the night with her.

A few hours later, even with Sally's comforting presence and all the little ones needing care, Molly's worry had turned to anxiety and moments of panic. She got onto her knees and prayed for Jeremiah's safety, then climbed into the big, lonely bed and fell into a fitful sleep. She had a terrifying dream in which she saw Jeremiah wounded, limping, bleeding, coming toward her on the road. She was running toward him, but never seemed able to reach him. The faster she ran, the further away he became. She screamed his name as she saw him fall in the road, but she still couldn't get to him.

Molly awoke, shaking, her heart pounding. She looked at the empty place beside her in the bed and tears welled up and cascaded down her cheeks. She shook with sobs. Sally ran to her and put her arms around her, holding Molly and patting her back.

When day broke Molly ran outside to search the Peach Tree Road. Molly's heart jumped as she sighted a speck of dust moving from the east. She watched it grow, but not grow large enough to be a wagon with four horses. It was a solitary rider. She recognized Delbert Thompson. He stepped off his horse and up to the house. Molly's eyes, red from lack of sleep, anxiously searched his face.

"I'm sorry, Missus Cleary. I rode as far as Lone Oak with Juan, the Garcìa boy, but there was no sign of him. Juan was going on, all the way up the river road to San Juan if needed. He'll find Jeremiah. Ride back with him. He'll be fine, you'll see. Probably wonder why all the fuss. We'll be laughing about this in a day or so."

But they weren't laughing about anything the next day. Nor the day after. While Delbert Thompson returned to his own place to do the chores, Sally and her children stayed with Molly, who dried her tears, but was in a daze as she finished her outside tasks, went about her housework and tended her children. Her face was grimly set as her mind prepared itself for some terrible news of Jeremiah.

It was mid-afternoon of the following day when Molly's everwatchful eyes spotted a wagon coming down the road. She stared hard and finally made out the gray leaders and the big, white, wheel mares. It was the Cleary wagon and team, for sure. Happiness and relief began to flood through her. But the driver, he didn't sit as Jeremiah did. Molly's eyes narrowed as she watched the rig draw closer, bigger, became recognizable.

It was Juan Garcìa handling the lines, his saddle horse tied behind the wagon. Molly, with Will by the hand and Little Jerry on her hip, waited, hardly able to breathe, fear and dread now clutching her heart. The horses turned into the Cleary lane and slowly, ever so slowly, pulled the wagon into the yard. Sally came from the house and stood by Molly's side. Neither of them spoke as they stared at the wagon.

Juan was alone. There was no Jeremiah in sight.

Molly's anguished eyes raised to Juan Garcìa on the wagon seat. She was about to ask the question, but the words caught in her throat. Then, she heard a voice.

"Molly love, and why is it now that you aren't greeting your husband?"

Jeremiah's voice. And coming from the bed of the wagon. Still holding the children, Molly rushed to the side of the big freighter. And there, tucked amid a load of supplies, on a mattress, lay Jeremiah Cleary. A wan smile appeared on his face when he saw Molly.

"Well, would you be looking at yourself there, Jerry Cleary, laying back and taking it so easy-like, riding in style, you are." Molly's voice broke and she gasped as the tears flowed. In her relief, she nearly dropped the baby. She handed him to Sally, let go of Will's hand and climbed into the wagon, to kneel by Jeremiah's side. Through her tears she saw his bloody clothing, his bandaged shoulder, his haggard face. But it was her Jerry!

Jeremiah was helped into the house and made comfortable in his bed. Molly fed him some broth after taking off his bloodied clothes, cleaning him and rebandaging his wound. Then Jeremiah told them what had happened.

"After those bandits waylaid me, I made a run for it, but they shot me. I forted up in the back of the wagon behind some flour sacks and waited for them to come up. But they didn't come. I passed out and came to when they were working on my shoulder. The hurt of it livened me up a bit."

His team had stood for several hours until discovered by the son of a settler, who'd been out looking for his goats along the river. Jeremiah was brought to the little house where the man dug the bullet out from his shoulder. His wife had cared for Jeremiah until Juan Garcia had come. Except for being weak from loss of blood, Jeremiah insisted he felt fine.

"But how did you get away from those two when they held guns on you, Jerry?" Molly wondered. "You with but one rifle and two of them?"

"Well now," Jeremiah explained with a grin. "With my rifle aimed at one, I told them my pistol was pointed at the other."

"And where would you be getting that pistol?" Molly asked.

"I had no pistol, Molly love. I meant to be borrowing one from Weeb. But would you believe it now? I forgot." They all laughed.

Thompson and Juan unloaded the wagon. Molly watched curiously as they carried in the heavy iron parts of the new wood stove. They started to assemble it and when she realized what it was, Molly gave a cry of pleasure.

"Oh, Jerry, a stove. It's a wonder, it is. Aren't I the blest one?" She ran to the bedroom to thank him with a kiss, careful not to touch the injured shoulder.

Sally called to her. "And just look at this, Molly — !" she said, carrying a bolt of cloth to her. "Your husband brought you the prettiest dress goods. The blue of it matches your eyes." She placed the bolt of cloth into Molly's arms and draped it over her shoulder. Molly whirled and wrapped herself in it, and ran back into the bedroom to gleefully show it off for Jeremiah.

"Oh, Jerry. The gifts are wonderful. But nothing compares to having you home."

He reached for her with his good arm.

CHAPTER TWENTY-THREE

SNOW WAS PILED on the streets of Boston by the time Matthew Cleary reached the city in the winter of 1861. He found himself too late to join John Hurley and Dan Hennessy and their company of Irish immigrants. The Irish Brigade had formed in New York and was already off fighting in the war. Cold, wet, nearly broke, Matthew spotted a huge poster calling for volunteers for a Massachusetts regiment.

"Bounty of $300," the big type read. Matthew made that out, but for the rest of it he depended on a man reading it aloud to several friends. "It says they'll pay us two hundred dollars in advance and the rest in cash before we leave Boston. They'll give us one hundred more when we are honorably discharged."

"Hey, that's a small fortune!" one man exclaimed.

"Sure is," another agreed. "And it says now is the time to avoid the draft by enlisting."

The young men went inside and Matthew followed. Soon he was Private Matthew Cleary, sent to join the 2nd Massachusetts Infantry with a group of replacements for men lost in battle. He made friends with other Irishmen in the regiment and one, Michael Flaherty, wrote a letter for him to Jeremiah.

Dear Brother, I didn't find John Hurley, but I joined a good Massachusetts outfit. We have some Irishmen and after this war we all will join up with the St. Patrick's Brigade for a crack at the Brits. It's not too bad here. We are resting up for the next battle. We play a new game where you hit a ball with a stick and run around bases until they catch you. It's called base ball and I am getting on well with it. When I get home I'll teach you. Food is good. Uniforms are warm. We drill a lot. Your brother, Matthew.

Matthew took the letter and scrawled his signature. He wanted to send a letter to Lupe, too, and Flaherty was ready, pen in hand, but Matthew couldn't find the right words.

"Just tell her you love her and miss her," Flaherty suggested.

"Sure now, Mike," he said — *that's true, but what else can I say? Has she forgiven me?* — "and I'll be telling her that a bit later. Let's just leave that letter for now."

"Suit yourself, Matt," Flaherty said. There wasn't another chance to send a letter to Lupe because the regiment was now on the move, marching into Maryland, part of Major General George McClellan's great Army of the Potomac, following Robert E. Lee's troops toward Sharpsburg. Matthew Cleary was lying on his belly behind a rail fence off the Haggerstown Pike, firing at dim forms in the morning fog. Bullets whizzed by him like hundreds of angry bees, some tugging at his tunic, and one knocked off his forage cap. From behind him rockets roared into the gray morning sky to crash in the Confederate lines. Answering fire exploded along the fence rail. Matthew wondered if he ever would have another chance to tell Lupe that he loved her.

Here and there a man was hit. Some cried out, others fell without a sound. Matthew heard a gasp, glanced at the man to his right and saw his face turn into a blotch of red. The soldier to his left shouted, spun around and fell forward onto the rails. Bodies began to pile up by the fence, but Matthew continued to load and fire, load and fire. The 2nd Massachusetts men were laying down a curtain of lead to meet the advancing gray-clad southerners.

"What's that damn fool doing?" somebody yelled.

There in front of him, Matthew saw a soldier in blue run toward a heap of dead and dying rebels to catch up the Confederate battle flag. He dashed back to the Union lines and held it up to their young colonel on horseback, who thrust it aloft and began galloping along the Haggerstown pike exhorting his troops.

"He'll get hit!" — "He's a target!" — "Get out of there, colonel — !" Men along the rail fence called out, but the foolhardy officer only turned his horse and raced back between the lines. Matthew saw him hit. The flag was flung from his hand. As he fell his foot caught in a stirrup. The gallant colonel was dragged past the cheering rebels.

"Damn fool!" a grizzled sergeant cried into the sudden silence. "Mind your fire now. They'll be coming on again. Be sure you aim. Make sure you're loaded. Hold the line, boys!"

Matthew carefully placed his bullet pouch by his side, the loads at easy reach. He heard the clinks and clicks up and down the blue line as rifles were loaded and hammers cocked. He peered through the rails, trying to make out the dim forms across the glade in the smoke and haze and fog. He could hear them. "Dress up that line, there. Be ready," a high-pitched voice floated up out of the Confederate lines. "Alabama, follow me," it cried. "Charge!"

The line of gray loomed out of the fog and the rebel yell screeched through the air mixing with the screams of the wounded, the roar of exploding shells, the cracking crescendo of rifles delivering volley after volley. "Steady, steady now, boys —" the sergeant called.

The earth in front of Matthew erupted, throwing up rubble and bodies. Arms and legs and blood spewed from the sky. High pitched shrieks and screams pierced the thundering symphony of shot and shell. The advancing men crumpled and fell, but still the line came on.

Matthew wanted desperately to cut and run from this part of hell. But he was confused. He didn't know which way to run. Bullets hit the fence, thudded into the dead bodies, struck the few still living. Matthew kept firing through the fence. Until his ammunition pouch was empty. Then he noticed a stillness all around him. He looked right and left along the fence, but he was alone, except for the dead and wounded. He started to rise up when a drawling voice stopped him.

"Where ya all goin', Yank?"

Matthew looked up at a Confederate soldier, his rifle pointed down at him, the bayonet nearly touching his chest. He couldn't run so he just sat there.

Matthew Cleary was a prisoner of war.

He was held for a short while in a warehouse in Richmond, Virginia. But then all the enlisted men were moved to an enclosure on Belle Island in the James River, a low, unhealthy place, filthy and damp, marked by a shortage of shelter, skimpy bedding, and poor food. It was no wonder that the prisoners cheered when in November 1863, they were ordered off Belle Island and into prison cars heading south. The cheering soon stopped. It was nearly five hundred miles, riding in box cars, sometimes walking for long, weary miles, and the survivors were near collapse when they entered a new stockade one night.

"Hey, Reb — !" Matthew Cleary called out. "What's the name of this place?"

"Andersonville."

* * * * *

In Long Valley the second year of a terrible drought wore on. The merciless sun had sucked all the moisture from the earth and left it baked and cracked. Molly was listlessly digging in her garden, wondering how much longer they could spare the water for her vegetables.

Vultures hovered and soared low over the valley, dropping down to sink their sharp beaks into the rotting flesh of dead cattle. Molly hated the sight of them, patrolling the hills, sensing that many more animals would soon drop to the ground and die.

Jeremiah was gnawed by the fear that he'd lose his entire herd. When the drought took hold, the Cleary cattle had grown to more than forty cows, three bulls and fifteen steers. Those still alive were terribly thin, just hides stretched over bones. There'd been few calves born the past fall. The cows had put all their energy into survival and had little left for breeding. Those that did calve had no milk in their shriveled bags and their tiny babies soon died. Some cows stood, legs spread, head down, until they fell to the bare, baked ground, and could no longer rise, another feast for the vultures.

"Those buzzards are part of God's plan, Molly. They have their duty to do. They cleanse the range, a filthy job, but necessary," Jeremiah had explained.

Molly shuddered and was grateful that Bodach barked and yelped when a vulture swooped low, casting a shadow over the yard, and landed in one of the little trees she was trying to grow by the house. Even the tree shuddered when the horrible bird landed.

Molly was letting the children play beside her in the garden before putting them down for their naps. Will and little Jerry had a game going in the dirt that only they understood and baby Timothy was toddling about on chubby, wobbly legs, falling down and laughing and getting up to try again. Molly watched him crawl toward the edge of the garden, and reach out with a plump little hand just as she heard the sudden, dry whir. The rattle rang in her ears. She'd heard it before and knew at once what it was. For a second she was frozen with fear. She stood mesmerized by that little hand reaching toward the coiled body, topped by the evil, triangular head. Then she sprang into action. She snatched up the baby an instant before the rattlesnake launched itself, the poisonous fangs striking harmlessly at the edge of her full skirt.

She pushed the baby behind her and grabbed up her spade as the snake coiled to strike again. In a primal rage of maternal protectiveness, she jabbed downward with all her strength.

She missed!

The snake struck again, hitting the blade of the shovel. But before it could recoil, Molly swung. This time she pinned the reptile to the ground, her blade cutting into its back. Unable to coil, the rattler fastened its beady eyes on Molly, its head weaving in and out, back and forth. Molly was afraid to move, afraid to raise her shovel, afraid she'd free the snake. For long moments they stared at each other. Then Molly, her rage and her courage surmounting her fear, lifted the shovel and chopped. Furiously she kept chopping the snake into pieces, into bits.

She stared at it, at the bits and pieces, the shovel ready to swing again. Nothing moved.

Molly's legs gave way and she sank to the ground. And there was Will at her side, a big stick in his little hand. She put her arm around his shoulder, and reached for baby Tim and Little Jerry, and sat there hugging all three, and sobbing. "Dear Lord, how am I to stand it? This heat and the terrible dryness, the dust all over everything. And now snakes." Molly felt a wave of homesickness wash over her. It filled her with a longing for the cool, green fields of Ireland with no snakes.

A small voice pulled her back to Long Valley. "Mama, Mama. It'll be all right. Will can help you."

"Thank you, Will. You're a brave boy." Molly pulled herself up and lifted little Tim, leading the other two back into the cool of the *adobe*. That evening Jeremiah saw the dog sniffing in the garden and came upon the bits of rattlesnake.

"What happened, Molly love?" he asked anxiously. "What happened?"

"Well now, it was nothing. I saw this snake coiled up there, and me with my shovel, and I chopped this way and the snake moved that way, and so I chopped the other way, and he darts about this way." Molly moved her head and her body about, her hands making chopping motions as she demonstrated for Jeremiah.

"He's looking at me, he is. And I'm looking at him. And then chop, chop, chop." Molly emphasized each word with a downward slash of her hands. "And that was the end of the old snake. There was nothing to it."

"Oh Molly love, it's a brave *colleen* I married," he said, giving her a hug.

After supper, Jeremiah looked in the mirror by lamplight and rubbed his hand across his beard. "I can't be standing this fur coat on my face in this heat, Molly. Are you minding if I rid myself of it?"

170

"Would I mind, you ask me? Sure and for these past six years haven't I wondered what he looks like, this man I married, all covered up with a great black beard?" Molly laughed to show she was teasing. "Shave away, Jerry. Then I'll know if the boys look like you without having to wait until they grow big, black beards themselves. And I can be letting you come near me without thinking myself caught in a bramble bush."

Jeremiah stropped his razor, felt its edge, soaped his beard, and screwed up his face to tighten the skin. He began the strokes that cleaned off the black bristles.

Molly smiled at the results. "Ah, and it's a handsome *dhioul* you are, Jerry Cleary, just like that young hedgemaster who had all the *colleens* in such a — "

" — Molly, love," Jeremiah interrupted her, a worried frown on his face. He abruptly said, "I'll be gone a few days. It's the cattle. I must ride out to find grass somewhere. If I'm not finding feed for them soon, they'll be too weak to travel to it."

Jeremiah left early that morning with his bedroll tied behind the saddle. He'd be gone two or three days riding through Pine Valley, over to the head of Peach Tree, and up into the hills, maybe as far as the high valley to the east.

After the hot, dry November, December had turned cold. A dry, bitter cold that ate at Molly's very bones. A fierce wind blew up, swirled the dust and sometimes the air was hard to breathe. There were mocking, teasing clouds that drifted over the valley, but never dropped rain. Molly wondered if she'd ever dance in the rain again.

Be counting your blessings, Molly Cleary. She looked lovingly at Will, who, at nearly five years old, was entertaining his two little brothers in a corner of the room. He seemed to have a knack for organizing simple games for them. Molly watched and smiled at their antics. *And we can feed them. Even with this terrible drought there's no hunger in this cottage.*

But it was for the poor animals they feared. If they died how would they be replaced? Although Jeremiah kept his worries from her, Molly knew. He had tossed and turned at night, frequently having nightmares about losing his animals and his land. Now he'd been gone four days searching for grass.

She built up the fire, spread her hands to warm herself, and turned up the lamp. It was a dim morning. She opened the chest by the bedside and took out the cherished letters that she kept tied with a little ribbon. She re-read the latest letter from Catherine. *Dearest Sister, We are well and our father sends his love. The big news here is of James, who is married now to Moira O'Malley, a fine girl from Ballydehob, and Da and I are living here with them.*

Molly looked up from the letter and frowned. That must be hard on Cauth, she thought, having a new mistress of her own house. She prayed, "Oh Lord, please let them be getting on together." When she'd read that letter to Jeremiah he had said, "Molly, my hope is that James will be as pleased with his Moira as I am with his sister."

It was John Hurley's letter from Boston that had troubled Jeremiah. John wrote about the Fenians, a secret group of Americans who had pledged to help free Ireland from the British. His brother James had joined a similar organization in Ireland. John claimed that there were organizers traveling throughout Ireland taking oaths to form a secret army, and that they expected thousands of the Irish now serving in the Union Army to return to Ireland after the war to lead the way when the rising came.

"It will never happen, Molly," Jeremiah scoffed. "The soldiers will be so sick of war, if this one ever ends, they'll not go in any numbers, and it will be another feeble attempt that will be crushed. You'll be hearing of more hangings and more men rotting in English jails."

"But, Jerry, what are they to do? Is it hopeless?"

"I know if I were still living there, trying to make my way against the landlords and the crown, I'd be trying something desperate." Jeremiah sadly shook his head. "I'm not blaming them, but it's a useless cause."

John's letter explained that he was one of those charged with raising money in America for the cause and would be thankful for a contribution. Jeremiah emphatically refused. "I'll not! I'm an American and I'll not be getting myself mixed up in useless politics. I'm not an Irishman, I'm an American. This is my country now."

Jeremiah lit up his pipe and sat there puffing, the smoke clouds billowing up around his head, sending angry signals that he'd said his piece. But then he relented a bit. "You know, Molly, if it were for food against their hunger, or for paying the rent, I'd be helping, if I could. But not for politics. Beside, Molly, we may be needing every bit of money we've saved just to keep us through this bad time."

"John isn't knowing about our drought, Jerry. Don't be blaming him," Molly said. But she did understand how her husband felt. *We are Americans. This is our country.*

Molly put Catherine's letter aside and went about her work, but she was starting to worry about Jeremiah gone so long in the high country. The old fear clutched at her—just like when he was days late from San Juan and finally came home wounded. She went to the door hourly and scanned the trail. Her eyes looked up, beseeching the sky for a cloud, one that would be heavy with rain. But there wasn't a cloud anywhere. Jeremiah didn't come. And the suffocating drought went on.

It wasn't until the afternoon of the fifth day that Jeremiah returned. Molly had never seen him so tired and discouraged. "There's not a blade of grass in Peach Tree," he said disconsolately. "García says they're cutting down trees in Lone Oak and Bitter Water so the cattle can eat the leaves. Carcasses lay about everywhere, and the stench of dead cattle in some places is so fierce I had to cover my nose with my bandanna. I rode all the way up into those high valleys this side of the San Joaquin before I found any grass at all. There's a little bit of green way high up in those canyons, but I'm not knowing how long it will last. Others will be driving their cattle up there. There's still a bit of water in some of the springs. It's the only chance we have to save a few head."

"Oh Jerry, when will you drive the poor creatures?"

"I'll be getting Bert Thompson and we'll move out in the morning," he replied. "The few cows he has left are mixed in with ours. I'll take that gray mare. Bouchal is used up for now, getting thin, too."

* * * * *

Late that fall two momentous events occurred simultaneously. Catherine "Kitty" Cleary was born in her parents' bed, while outside, as if to herald that arrival, a large thunderhead burst from the heavens and brought the blessed rain.

It poured down onto the roof, the fields, the hills, the whole valley. Molly laughed and cried at the same time. She snuggled deep into the feather bed and smiled at Jeremiah, who handed her the whimpering baby. Molly opened her nightgown and freed a swollen breast, offering it to the tiny child, who stopped crying and began to nurse. She'd finally had her daughter, named after Catherine, but immediately nicknamed Kitty.

"Listen, *allana*." Molly told her infant daughter. "You should stop your sucking for a minute and listen. That's rain you're hearing, dear child. Isn't that a grand sound? And Jerry, doesn't that rain have a lovely smell to it?"

Jeremiah looked up from his reading by lamplight, returned her smile and went back to his book about modern farming techniques. Weeb had given it to him on that last trip to San Juan.

"I'm not needing this damn thing, Cleary," Weeb had said. "I'm a cattle rancher, not a damn farmer. It's all about letting land lie fallow and alternating fields each year to get a higher yield. Hogwash, if you ask me. Why waste good land like that? Some damn college professor thought that one up. I hate damn farming. You take it, Cleary." Jeremiah had been reading it voraciously ever since.

When he blew out the lamp and lay quietly beside Molly that night he couldn't sleep. Although lulled by the sound of the rain on the roof, he was thinking about the new farming techniques and how anxious he was to try them.

CHAPTER TWENTY-FOUR

"WERE YOU ABLE TO SAVE any of your cattle, Jerry?" was the first question James McMahan asked when Jeremiah entered his store that spring.

"Aye, a few cows I drove into the high country," Jeremiah answered.

"You're lucky," McMahan said. "Most ranchers around here were wiped out. First the flood and then the drought. Some can't afford to re-stock. Too bad, but there'll be a big price on beef now."

"Wouldn't mind eating a steak myself. All the game died off. Had to kill my hogs and cure the meat. I'm sick of pork," Jeremiah said with a laugh. "What's the news?"

"Well, it's pretty quiet around here," McMahan said, "but those two fellows who shot you, Jerry—Mason and Henry—claimed to be Confederates?"

Jeremiah scowled at the memory. "And what about them?"

"They were captured down around Los Angeles for being road agents and hung," McMahan said.

"Well, well," Jeremiah said, "so they got what they deserved, did they?" He shook his head to clear the memory. "What's the news from back east now that the war's over?"

"The San Francisco papers say they're still having a ruckus in Washington. That Andrew Johnson fellow wants to pardon all the rebels and go easy on them, but some Congressmen don't hold with that. Now instead of just fighting the southerners they're fighting each other."

"Too bad old Abe got shot," Jeremiah said. "He'd have worked it out. Say, James, has there been any word around about my brother?"

"Not that I've heard. I'm sorry, Jerry," the storekeeper answered, taking Jeremiah's list of needed supplies and starting to fill his order.

Jeremiah was loading his wagon outside the store when a familiar voice hailed him, "*Señor* Jerry — ! *Un momento, pro favor.*" Rogelio Morales came across the street to him. "My sister wants to see you. She is very ill." Jeremiah's face showed instant concern. "You could go to her, perhaps?" Rogelio pleaded.

"Lupe?" Jeremiah was surprised. "Of course, I'll go." He hadn't seen Lupe since that day he and Molly had offered her help and been refused. He'd often wondered if she'd had any word from Matthew. He hadn't heard himself since that short note from his brother three years ago when he'd joined the Massachusetts Infantry.

Knocking on the door of the little *adobe* triggered a rush of memories, but Jeremiah put them aside when a withered, bent Mexican woman, a black *mantilla* over her white hair, opened the door. "*Señor* Cleary? You will come with me, *por favor?*" She indicated a doorway, which Jeremiah stooped to enter.

In the dimness of the tiny bedroom he could see a shadowy figure on the bed. As his eyes grew accustomed to the gloom he realized it was Lupe. But he was shocked. This wasn't the Lupe he remembered, this thin wraith who gave him a wan smile. The once sparkling black eyes were dull, the blooming complexion sallow except for the flush of fever on her cheeks. Those once full, red lips were drawn thin and white. The voice was Lupe's, but the words were feeble and said with great effort.

"Thank you, Jerry, for coming to see me."

Jeremiah was appalled at the sight of her. He went to his knees beside the bed and took her limp hand in his. "Lupe, Lupe, what's wrong with you?"

"It doesn't matter," her voice was a whisper now. She coughed. "What matters is that you are here and I have a great favor to ask."

"Anything, Lupe," Jeremiah replied. "What can I do to help?"

"First, let me tell you this. Once I thought I loved you. There was never anything truly between us, but I wanted it to be so." Her voice was low and he had to strain to hear her words. "When you left San Juan I was very sad. But your brother brought me out of my sadness. His funny ways and big dreams made me alive again. He looked so much like you, I thought I loved him — " Lupe had a coughing spasm and when it was over she seemed almost too exhausted to talk.

Jeremiah squeezed her hand, but he didn't know what to say.

"I found out that Matthew wasn't you," Lupe said. "But by then I had married him. When he finally came home from the gold mines, it was glorious and I thought we would be happy. But it wasn't to be. When he went away to be a soldier, I was with child."

"A child?" Jeremiah was incredulous. "Matthew is a father?"

"A beautiful, wonderful little girl," Lupe Cleary said, her voice stronger, her eyes brighter. "Her name is Conchita. She's four years old now. You will love her?"

"Me? Love her? Of course, I'll love her, she's my brother's child." Jeremiah was puzzled. "Where is she?"

"She is here," Lupe answered. "My mother cares for her now that I am too sick. But my mother is old and her time is short, maybe almost as short as mine."

"But, Lupe, you'll get well," Jeremiah protested. "You're young. Surely, this illness will pass."

"No, Jerry. I have the lung disease. There aren't many days left for me." She withdrew her hand and lay back on the bed to rest. There was silence for a moment. Then Lupe sat up and looked intently into Jeremiah's eyes. "I ask if you will love her, Jeremiah Cleary, because I want you to take her. Give her a home. Give her a chance in this world."

Jeremiah was astounded. Matthew had a daughter and the child's mother wanted him to take her, to raise her? He wondered how he could do this. What would Molly say? He tried to speak, but Lupe lifted her hand to stop him.

"I don't know if Matthew is alive or dead," she said. "If he survived the war and was coming home, he'd be here by now. But even if he did come back, he'd not be a real father to Conchita. This I know."

"Lupe, Lupe, I don't — "

"Jerry, you are the responsible one. It is you I trust." Again the black eyes lost their dimness and burned into his, pleadingly. "Please take my baby."

Jeremiah looked into her eyes and nodded. "Yes, Lupe. I will take her."

Lupe fell back, drained and weak. Jeremiah rose from his knees beside the bed. "When shall I — "

"Now," Lupe interrupted with an anxious whisper. "My mother has her ready. I couldn't bear to look upon her again."

Jeremiah took up one of Lupe's pale, limp hands and stood uncertainly for a moment. Then he leaned down and kissed her hot forehead. Lupe touched his cheek with her fingers. "*Que Dios te bendiga*," she murmured. "God bless you, Jerry."

* * * * *

Jeremiah was about to turn the team off the Peach Tree Road into his own lane. He felt that wonderful, excited feeling he always had coming home from a trip, filled with the anticipation of seeing his children and holding Molly in his arms. But this time it was tempered with anxiety. He had no idea what Molly would think when she saw this little person on the seat beside him.

She was a real little person to Jeremiah now. Obedient, quick to respond and anxious to help. Despite her thinness and eyes too large for her tiny face, she was an appealing little girl. She'd sat there beside him on the long, tedious drive without a complaint, and although he tried to talk to her, she rarely spoke. But one evening as he was bedding down for the night he heard a small voice coming from where she was curled by the campfire in her blankets. *"Padre Nuestra que esta en el cielo —"* Conchita saying her prayers. Lupe had taught her well, thought Jeremiah as he joined in " — hallowed be Thy name — " He went over and tucked her in, but saw her eyes roaming the camp, looking for her little rag doll. Jeremiah found it and brought it to her. *"Gracias, señor,"* she said with a shy smile, and hugged the doll to her.

Molly saw the wagon coming in the distance. She ran her hands through her curls, smoothed her dress and picked up baby Kitty. As she started through the door she was almost knocked over by Will and Jerry.

"Mama, mama — he's coming — ! Daddy's coming."

Will and Little Jerry ran into the house, shouting and running as fast as their young legs could carry them. They'd been on the lookout, watching the Peach Tree Road all afternoon, waiting to spot their father.

"It's Daddy! He's right there, up the road." They turned to dash back down the lane as Molly again started through the door. This time she nearly stumbled over Timothy, his chubby legs churning as he ran to the house. "Daddy coming! Daddy coming." Timmy contributed his share of the exciting news, and then he spun around to follow his brothers back down the lane.

Jeremiah stopped the team as the boys ran up. They stopped short, too. "Who's that?" Jerry Jr. asked, pointing to Conchita.

"This is your cousin," Jeremiah explained. "Climb up and say hello to her."

The three boys scrambled into the wagon, Will giving Timmy a boost. "Hi," he said. "What's your name?" Conchita stared at him.

"Her name is Conchita," Jeremiah told them, trotting the team toward the yard where Molly waited.

"That's a funny name." Timmy said.

Jeremiah pulled the team up in front of the house and jumped down to sweep his wife into an ardent embrace, but she pulled back, looking over his shoulder. "Who's the little girl?"

"That's Conchita Cleary."

"Who?" Molly asked.

"Matthew's daughter," Jeremiah answered. "I'll tell you all about it in a minute." He lifted the little girl to the ground and began to unhitch the team.

"She's our cousin, Mama," Will explained.

"Is she going to live with us?" Jerry Jr. asked.

"Can she play with me?" Timmy wanted to know.

Molly glanced over at the little girl standing quietly by the wagon, her eyes on the ground. "All of you go in and get washed up, ready for supper," Molly instructed her sons. "Take Conchita with you and fix a place at the table for her. I'll be along in a minute." Still carrying baby Kitty on her hip, Molly turned to follow Jeremiah, who was leading the team away. She looked back to see Will take the little girl by the hand and into the house. Molly caught up with her husband at the barn.

"Now, Jeremiah Cleary, you be telling me what this is all about."

"Molly love," Jeremiah explained, "I promised Matthew's wife, Lupe, that we'd take the child and raise her."

"You what?" Molly was astounded. "How could you ever be doing such a thing with me not knowing about it?"

"There was no time," Jeremiah said. "Lupe is dying and her mother is too old to care for the child. Who knows where my brother is, or if he's even alive. Lupe begged me to take her. What could I do?"

Molly was furious. "Your brother this and your brother that! Always Matthew." Eyes blazing, she glared at Jeremiah. "You gave him the last of our money so he could be running off from his responsibilities and now you're asking me to be taking over raising his child?"

"Now, Molly," Jeremiah said, shrugging helplessly. "What else could I be doing?" He pulled the harness from Maud, turned his back to Molly and carried it into the saddle room where he hung it on its peg. He busied himself there for long moments, hoping Molly would cool down, but when he came back for Nellie's rig, his wife was still standing there to face him, still fuming.

"A fine thing it is, Jeremiah Cleary, for you to be agreeing to take the child," Molly berated him. "It's not you that'll be doing the care of her! Off in the fields you are, or somewhere. And me already with four of my own."

"Woman, I'll be hearing no more of this!" Jeremiah suddenly shot back.

"Well done is done," Molly muttered. She turned away to stalk out of the barn, but over her shoulder she had the last word. "She can visit. But if that no good brother of yours ever shows up, I'll be handing her off so fast your head will ache." Molly stomped back to the house, slammed the door and rattled the pots and pans as she prepared supper.

But Molly awoke late in the night and heard a soft cry, like a kitten whimpering. She slid out of bed and checked on the children. There was Conchita, huddled in a ball, cuddling her doll, crying her little heart out, but at the same time attempting to muffle the sounds. Molly lifted her up, hugged her and carried her to the rocker. She held the child in her arms, rocking her back and forth, and softly singing until the sobbing stopped. Huge black eyes, wide open in the tear-streaked face, looked up into Molly's. "*Yo quiero mi madre*," Conchita said.

"Connie, Connie, I know you want your mama," Molly sighed. "But I'm your mama now." She continued to rock the little girl until she fell asleep.

The next morning Jeremiah smiled to himself when he saw Molly fussing over the shy Conchita, making sure she ate her breakfast, calling her Connie, and then telling the boys to play nicely with their cousin. It was Will who took her outside to organize a game for the four of them. But soon Connie was back in the house, hovering over the crib where Kitty lay, trying to find ways to help Molly.

After supper the next night Jeremiah was teaching the three boys as he usually did. He sat in his chair pulled up by the fire, looking into their little faces shining in the lamplight as he heard their lessons and then told them stories. Connie, however, sat apart, unobtrusive, in a corner, but trying to follow every word. Will, being six, was learning his letters, and Jerry, though only four, was trying. Timmy just listened. But the stories they were learning were from American history, not of Ireland, and always in English.

"One day they can hear of their heritage," Jeremiah explained, "but for now I want them to learn about democracy, about this country founded on the belief that all men are equal. They can't be too young to learn about that."

Jeremiah had obtained copies in San Juan of McGuffy's Reader, Town's Speller, Ray's Mental Arithmetic and Peter Parley's American History. These were the school books from which he taught his sons. But Molly had caught him, on the sly, reading the old Irish poems of Thomas Moore from a book he'd borrowed from James McMahan. "Well, you see, Molly love," Jeremiah had explained, " a man can be trying to grow a new skin without completely shedding his old, now can't he?"

Molly cleaned up the supper dishes and went about her chores singing some of the Irish songs but using English words. The children always loved them. Little Jerry was the one who seemed to have a talent for music in him. He left his father's side when he heard Molly and came to join her, his little voice singing, *"Cockles and mussels, alive, alive oh."*

Jeremiah laughed. "Well, now, it may be he's the image of me, as you say, Molly, but praises be, it's not my voice he has."

Molly cradled Kitty in her lap and the three boys knelt beside her. She noticed Connie by herself, across the room. "Here, Connie, come be with us now."

The little girl shyly, but obediently, crossed the room and Molly opened her arms to include her into the circle with the boys. Jeremiah, by the fire, led the evening prayers. "Our Father who art in heaven, hallowed be Thy name — " Molly and the children joined in, a chorus of "lead us not into temptation and deliver us from all evil." After the prayers came the remembrances of all the relatives, Uncle John and Aunt Rose in Boston, and Aunt Cauth, Uncle James and Grandpa Hurley, and Uncle Liam and Aunt Eileen in Ireland, and Uncle Matt wherever he was, and the rest of the litany of God bless this one and that one. The children strung it out as long as they could, even to Nellie and Maud, Block and Chip, Bouchal, Bodach and Aroon, the cow. Finally Molly lay down the baby, tucked in the boys and Connie.

Jeremiah lit up his pipe, and Molly, at last, relaxed by the fire. "I wish we did the prayers in Irish sometimes," she said.

Jeremiah frowned and shook his head. "These are American children," he said. "They'll be speaking the language of their country." She and Jeremiah hardly spoke Irish at all any more, only a few words now and then, when they had no others with which to make a point, or if they were keeping a secret from the children. Molly missed it, but she understood. They were an American family.

Molly brought out the cards for her favorite game. It was a new one that Jerry had learned from Weeb. It was called Pedro after Pedro Carlos of San Juan, who'd invented the game and taught it to his friends. Whenever Molly won, which was often, she grinned and teased Jeremiah and he'd pretend to be angry and slap down the cards. Then they'd break up laughing.

"Ah, it's a good life that you brought me to, Jerry Cleary. I'm appreciating it all the more this minute."

"Aye, that it is, Molly love. And you seem to be thriving on it, too."

Jeremiah stood up, stretched and leaned over to kiss his wife. They headed to the bedroom where Jeremiah, as he was taking off his pants suddenly realized there was something in his pocket. He took it out and saw it was a letter for Molly from Ireland. He'd picked it up in San Juan, but then forgot all about it with the excitement and turmoil of bringing Conchita home.

"Molly love," he said with an apologetic smile, handing her the letter. "I'm so sorry — I forgot to give you this."

Molly looked at the envelope and gave out a happy cry. "Oh, wonderful, it's from Cauth. Lovely," she said. "I've been waiting so long to hear from her." Molly sat down on the bed, tore open the envelope, pulled out the letter and began reading. Jeremiah continued undressing and was just about to get into bed when Molly's anguished, "No! No! Oh God, no," startled him.

"Molly love," Jeremiah turned quickly to her. "What's the matter?" He took her shoulders and held her.

"It's terrible — oh, my God, it's so terrible — "

"Tell me, Molly — what's happened? Jeremiah demanded.

"They've been evicted," Molly choked out the words. "The house is knocked!"

After generations on the little farm in Coolnagurrane, though the rent was regularly paid, even during the famine times, the Hurleys were put out. The year-to-year term had ended and there was no renewal. A new land agent was clearing the land and putting sheep to graze on it.

"After all those horrible times, how could they be doing this? We starved to pay the rent," Molly sobbed.

"Monsters, they are, that's how!" Jeremiah cursed in Irish. "God rot their heartless souls."

Molly's grief mounted as she thought of that little cottage in which she'd been raised. The room, with its fireplace and the tiny loft, which she'd shared with Cauth, now its roof crashed down, the thatch scattered, and the door splintered.

"What are they to do?" Jeremiah wondered. "Where will they go?" Molly handed him the letter.

Jeremiah read Catherine's tragic news. *James could do nothing. There was no appeal, and the constables stood by to see it was done without hindrance. Our father is filled with grief. He says little, but we can see that he feels his life is over.*

James is so bitter, I don't know what he'll do. I am so sorry to write you these words, dear sister, but you must know. We are all gone to a farm by Ballydehob, taken in by Moira's brother Kevin, and his wife Sheila. James will help work the land. It was good of them to take us in. But there hardly seems enough for us all. And the cottage is small. There's Da and me, James and Moira, her brother and his wife, and three children. We'll do our best. Bless you all, my love to you, and a special blessing on your little Kitty.

Molly lay in Jeremiah's arms that night and cried herself out. It's not fair, she thought. There's no justice, not in that part of the world. This news from Skibbereen again made her realize her own good fortune and she was grateful for it. But she felt a twinge of guilt knowing that whatever adversity she and Jeremiah faced it was nothing compared to the hardships and oppression being brought down on her relatives and thousands like them.

"Someday the landlords and the British will pay for this," Molly said angrily. "Someday they will be punished for what they're doing."

Jeremiah held his wife tighter. "Let's hope God doesn't wait until Judgment Day," he said cynically.

CHAPTER TWENTY-FIVE

Declan Hurley sat hunched on the hob by the fireplace in the little cottage near Ballydehob. It was mid-summer of 1866, but there was a chill in the air and he was warming his frail body by the fire, the one place he was sure to be found at all hours. But he made no effort to keep the fire going, to feed it a bit of turf, or stir up a blaze. He simply sat and stared. He took no part in the conversation that flowed about him now.

Although it was late at night the room was filled with people, mostly men from neighboring farms. Sheila O'Malley had put the children to bed in the loft hours ago, and now she sat with James' wife, Moira, Catherine's sister-in-law. Catherine herself was on a bench against the wall. The men sat cross legged on the floor or stood in a circle to hear what their visitor had to say. A single lamp cast a flickering glow over the room, its very dimness accenting the danger of the talk.

"Is there a man here who wouldn't strike a blow to free Ireland had he but the chance?" Michael Callahan asked. He was a short man, powerfully built, his face glowing red in the lamp light, his eyes gleaming with the fierceness of his message, his words strong, but quietly spoken. Callahan had been talking to groups throughout the west of Ireland in every *shabeen*, and in some public houses, and in any cottage where men gathered. Molly's brother, James Hurley, had been traveling with him, adding his own words when needed, and singling out men who would take the oath.

"They've shut down the *Irish People*, but not the voice of the Irish," Callahan continued. "They made a mockery of their own laws with the trials of O'Leary and Rossa and the rest. But the spark of liberty for Ireland still glows and the fire will ignite."

"How are we to be fighting the might of England?" It was Noelle O'Shea, ever the skeptic. "They shut you up in gaol just for reading the *Irish People*."

Callahan scowled. "What are you to do? How long are you to be meek and humble, sending off your food to pay the rents while your wives and children have no bread in the house?" He looked around the room, challenging them with his eyes, staring at each man. "You live like pigs, they say. And what if you put out stepping stones, or whitewash your cottage, if you build up your fences, or thatch your roof? Look how well he's doing, they say. And they raise your rents."

"You speak the right words, Callahan, to fire a man up. But O'Shea is right. What are we to do for weapons?" Dan Healy asked. "We can't be an army with just our bare hands."

James spoke up. "You all know me. What I am telling you is God's own truth. I have it from my brother John in Boston. The Irish in America are sending us boatloads of weapons. And them that learned the ways of fighting in their war just past are coming home to Ireland to lead us. And wasn't it Captain Dan Deasy himself in Skibbereen just last fall? And there are more like him, arriving to all parts of Ireland."

"I'm for it," Sean Barry exclaimed. "A man can't be a man the way things are."

"You're right. It's our own country, but we haven't a bit of it," Healy agreed. "Always bowing to the British. I'm sick to death of it. If we but had weapons we could fight."

"We have no rights," Seamus Walsh exclaimed. "The landlords take our farms on their whims, just like they did to James here. And the constabulary and the army stand by to enforce their whims."

"Sure," Callahan agreed. "And who is it pays for the army on Irish soil? The Irish, that's who. We Irish pay the keep for our own oppressors."

"The oath, the Fenian oath." Healy cried, his voice rising in anger.

"Let's take the oath." It was a chorus. Men raised their hands, stepped forward, eager now. Most knew of the existence of the secret Fenian Brotherhood, pledged to launch an insurrection against England.

"Hold up there," James said. He raised his hand and the room stilled. "That's not the way to be doing it. Someone will contact each of you. The oath is a private matter."

"Aye, and don't be telling the priest you've taken the oath," O'Shea exclaimed. "You'll be excommunicated."

"Its always the same, them telling us from the altar to obey the law, that it's right to pay unjust rents and suffer in this world for the rewards of the next. I don't want to hear that again," Barry said.

"Not from Father Hayes, you won't," Catherine spoke up. "He's changed. He's an old man now, but he's become as fiery as the young ones."

"It's the cardinals and bishops that are against the Fenians and the Brotherhood," James explained. "They take their orders from Rome. Many of the younger parish priests are with us."

"We'll take our religion from Rome, but our politics come from Ireland," Callahan's voice rang out.

A sudden knock on the door brought instant quiet to the room. The door opened a crack and a voice spoke quickly. "God bless all here and you'd best be leaving. Some constables are on the way."

Callahan had insisted a guard be posted. He'd learned in his travels that there were always informers about, and he'd been proven right again. The men hurriedly left, separating in silence, each heading across the familiar fields in different directions, finding their way in the dark. When the room had cleared of visitors, the Hurleys and the O'Malleys looked at each other for a moment, and then Moira threw herself into James' arms. She was trembling. "I'm so afraid for you, James."

"Don't be," he comforted her. "They don't know me. It's Callahan they're after and him long gone now."

"It's all of us I fear for," Sheila sobbed. She shook her finger at her brother-in-law. "You've brought danger to this house,

James Hurley, and I'm not liking it." She huddled against her husband's chest, crying to herself.

"Now, now, Sheila," Kevin tried to soothe his wife. "Quiet now, quiet. They'll be coming."

Catherine had brought out her tin whistle and began to play. She motioned to Moira, who finally caught on and started singing, and soon Sheila stopped her crying and added her voice. The men joined in, their deep voices in harmony.

"Gramachree macruiskeen Slainthe Gael mavorneen
Gramachree a coolin bawn, bawn, bawn — oh
Let the farmer praise his grounds. Let the hunter praise
  his hounds and the shepherd his sweet-scented lawn
But I, more blest than they, spend each happy night and
  day with my charm —"

A pounding on the door brought the song to a halt. "Open up there! Open up. In the name of the crown, open up!"

"It's unlatched — !" James called out. "Come in, if you're coming."

A constable threw the door open and thrust his face in. "This house is surrounded. Don't be trying to leave."

Catherine moved across the room to face him. "Surrounded, you say? And why is that? Leave? And why should we be leaving? It's our home you've invaded!"

The constable glanced around her to scan the room. "Where's Callahan? We know he's here. Don't be hiding him now. It'll go the worse for you."

"Callahan? There's no Callahan here." Catherine pointed her little flute at the officer and shook it in his face, furiously. "You should be ashamed of yourself, breaking in here like this, frightening peaceful people. It's but a quiet family gathering we're having, a bit of music for the evening. Now begone. You'll awake the children."

"Music, at this hour, is it?" He glared at them, then climbed up to see into the loft. The children were sitting up, looking down wide-eyed at the stranger. He stepped to the door and called out into the dark, "Any sign of anybody?"

"Not a soul, Captain," a voice replied.

"A dog barked over that way," reported another constable. "They may have escaped before we got here."

The captain looked back into the room, holding his stare on each of them in turn. "I know Callahan was here. You'd better watch yourselves, all of you, or you'll find out what it is to be arrested for treason." He banged the door shut and stomped off.

It was all over. They sat for a while, but nothing was said. James blew out the lamp and took Moira to their pallet in the corner. Kevin and Sheila did the same and spread their curtain. Declan Hurley still sat on the hob, staring into the dark. Catherine was shaking. She lay on her straw bed, but she couldn't stop shaking. *Get a grip on yourself now, Catherine Hurley. It's over.*

But it wasn't over. Catherine knew it would go on and on. The fire burned in her, too. Ireland must be free.

* * * * *

Two weeks to the day after they were visited by the constables, on an early fall morning, they found Declan Hurley dead right there on the hob by the fireplace. James, with Kevin's help, built a coffin for his father and they placed his frail body inside, and lifted it onto the table in the center of the cottage. The wake wasn't much, a simple affair. Some neighbors dropped by, said the appropriate words, and stood about as they moved the coffin to the cart, and started out on the road for Abbystrewery. It seemed right to do so, there were so many other family members at rest there. Father Hayes, bent by time and frail from his deprivations, intoned the prayers for the burial services, and added a few of his own.

"Oh God, it was the cruel system that brought the death of this good man before his time. Be kind to him, Lord, and be kind to us here on your earth. Give us the courage and the means to change those things that are wrong. This we pray in your Holy Name."

The sad little group followed the pony cart back to Ballydehob, Catherine walking along behind James and Moira, and the others, wondering how she would write all this to her sister in California. Molly will be expecting the news about Da's death. She knew he was failing. But Catherine didn't know how to write about herself and how unhappy she was.

The bit of money that Jeremiah and Molly had been sending her from time to time, most of it had gone to help with the O'Malley household — a way for Catherine to do her share. But she also gave some of it to James as a contribution to the Fenians. But she couldn't tell Molly anything about that. Fenianism was a secret. No telling what letters the postal authorities might be prying into, especially the British. No one knew for sure, but she wouldn't chance it. She'd like to tell Molly and Jeremiah that this time there was real hope for an uprising, that she and James were doing their bit for Ireland. Nor could she write that she felt like an outsider in the O'Malley home. It was Sheila's house and she resented the other women, even Moira, her sister-in-law. The three of them tried to put a good face on it for the sake of Kevin and James. But the cottage was too small to contain the constant tension between the women.

And privacy? Catherine gave the thought of that a bitter laugh. She was so tired of laying there on her pallet of straw and hearing the sounds of lovemaking in the night. *They think they're coupling quietly, but I'm knowing every move, hearing every endearing word, although I try not to. I'm jealous. I'm not knowing a man's touch and never will be doing so.* She couldn't bear the thought of not having babies of her own, a little cottage, a man to love. Tears flowed down her cheeks as she walked in the funeral procession. If anyone had noticed they'd think she was crying for Da. But Catherine knew she was crying for herself. At thirty-two years of age she was now considered an old maid, and few men around wanted an old maid. Certainly not any man that she'd be wanting for herself.

With that Catherine squared her shoulders. She had to stop feeling sorry for herself. This was her life and she'd have to get on with it. She'd get out her tin whistle when she got home and play a jig for the youngsters. She'd laugh and sing for them, and be their old jolly spinster Aunt Cauth. And she'd teach them the dance steps just as she'd once taught Molly.

CHAPTER TWENTY-SIX

SCRATCHED ON THE SMALL WOODEN CROSS was her name, Guadalupe Cleary, and the dates, 1835-1865. Matthew Cleary stood before the grave, wildflowers clutched in his hand, and wondered how it could be his Lupe under that mound. Lupe, so vital, so full of joy, so quick to laugh, but so sudden to anger and scold. Thoughts of her lush loveliness had sustained him through the terror of battle, the miserable long years of capture, particularly as a prisoner of war in that hell camp known as Andersonville, and then the endless trek home.

It was September of 1866 when Matthew Cleary finally reached San Juan. At war's end, with his release from prison, he was mustered out of the Union Army. Gone were any thoughts of joining Irish Brigade veterans to strike a blow for Ireland. Getting home was foremost in his mind. Sharing box cars with other returning veterans, riding in the wagons of sympathetic farmers, putting one foot ahead of the other for many weary miles, working at odd jobs when he could, he'd crossed the continent. All of his thoughts were of San Juan Bautista and the arms of his wife.

But the little *adobe* was empty. His inquiries took him to the priest and to this mound in the mission graveyard. Before leaving him at graveside, Padre Mora had seemed to hesitate, about to say more, but then changed his mind and left Matthew to his private grief.

Frail, exhausted, still emaciated, his tattered blue coat hanging limply from his stooped shoulders, his shaggy beard and once black hair now nearly white, Matthew Cleary stood at Lupe's grave. What went wrong? He'd planned to come home a hero to a loving wife. Nothing ever worked out for him the way it was meant.

"Lupe," he whispered. "I didn't mean it to end this way." He leaned down and placed the wilting poppies and lupine carefully by the cross. "I loved you, Lupe. In my own way, I truly did." He tried to pray, but nothing came. He wondered if he'd forgotten how. He simply felt empty.

Matthew Cleary stared numbly at his wife's grave for a few moments, then turned away, walked from the cemetery and down the hill, toward the San Benito River and on south. Long Valley was somewhere ahead. He had nowhere else to go.

* * * * *

"They're pulling out. Bert says he can't make it as a farmer and has a job lined up in Monterey," Jeremiah reported to Molly when he returned one afternoon from the Thompson place. "They'll be leaving in a day or so."

Molly was shocked at the suddenness of it, but not completely surprised. Sally had told her that Bert wasn't happy farming. "He just doesn't seem to be cut out for this life, Molly. This country has him beat, he says. Poor Bert, he hates it," Sally had said. "It's been worse since the baby was born dead. He blames this hard country. And we're just not doing so well, as you know." Molly did know. Jeremiah had been trying to help Bert, but he just wouldn't take to the new ideas. His crops were half of Jeremiah's, and he refused to invest in the better breed of cows.

"What will they do with their place?" Molly asked, saddened at the thought of losing her friend and neighbor of the past seven years.

"Sell it, Bert says. He's asking if we'll buy it. Land is valued at a dollar and a quarter per acre, but Bert will sell it all— house, cattle, throw in the equipment, for two hundred dollars. He wants the money to get set up in Monterey."

"What do you think, Jerry?"

"Sure, I'm for it. We have the two hundred. His one sixty acres is worth that and he must have six or seven cows. The *adobe* isn't much, but he proved up his homestead with it and he would be able to give us a deed. I could get some good crops on that place," Jeremiah said.

The next day Molly and Jerry took the children and went to the Thompson place to help them load up and say goodbye. Jeremiah paid the money, and Bert wrote out a deed, promising to register a copy with the county clerk in Monterey. Sally and Molly hugged each other, and Sally insisted she get Jerry to take her one day to Monterey for a visit.

"And won't that be a grand day?" Molly laughed. "And me not even going to San Juan these past five years."

Jerry helped Bert hitch up his mules and they gathered in the Thompson children who'd been scampering about with the Clearys. Good-byes were exchanged and the mules trotted off. Soon all that was left of the Thompsons in Long Valley was the dust billowing in the air behind their rolling wagon.

That had long blown away by the time Jeremiah was turning their own wagon into the lane for home. But there was another wisp of dust rising from the Peach Tree Road. Just a speck and Jeremiah's eyes narrowed as he followed it.

He halted his team and pointed. "Look, Molly, someone's walking down there. He looks to be having a hard time of it."

Molly, too, squinted to make out the figure of a tall, thin man, slowly stumbling along, putting one foot ahead of the other with great effort. Jeremiah hurried the team toward him and as they came closer, they saw he wore a tattered blue coat and pants that seemed sizes too large for his bony frame. He stopped as the wagon came alongside him. His shaggy gray hair showed under the edge of his floppy black hat above a pinched face with sunken cheeks. He seemed about to fall over and put one hand on the wagon to steady himself. When he looked up at the wagon load of Clearys with eyes burning feverishly bright, Jeremiah gasped.

"My God! It's my brother!"

Matthew's hold on the wagon slipped, his body slumped, and slowly he crumbled to the ground. Jeremiah leaped from the wagon and to his brother's side. "Matt, Matt, what's happened to you — ! What's wrong?"

"Ah, it's nothing much, Jerry." Matthew looked up with a feeble grin. "A weakness I get after a long walk on an empty stomach."

"Where've you been?" Jeremiah asked. "I hadn't heard of you for so long I thought you dead. Where —"

Molly interrupted. "Jerry, put the poor man into the wagon, he's sick and starved. Let's be getting him home and then he can be answering your questions."

Jeremiah picked up the six-foot Matthew in his arms and lifted him into the wagon bed, laying him among the astonished youngsters.

"Hello," Matthew said to the wide-eyed children. "It's me, your Uncle Matt." He tried to smile, but Matthew Cleary passed out.

They put him in Will's bed, his long legs hanging over the edge, and for three days Matthew slept, waking only to eat and to visit the privy with his brother's help. The color returned to his cheeks, his eyes came back to life and he watched with growing interest the baby, the three boys and the dark-skinned little girl. His feeble grin grew into a big, wide smile, particularly for Molly when she fed him her nourishing broth and later potatoes with vegetables and meat.

Soon Matthew was regaling the family with humorous war stories, but he spoke little of the battle at Antietam. His capture he made into a joke. "There I was, trying to catch a small nap, when this Johnny Reb comes up and says, 'Hello there, Yank,' and offers me the comfort of Confederate hospitality for the rest of the war." The long, nightmare years as a prisoner-of-war he compared to the Irish famine. "You're remembering how it was when the hunger was upon us, Jerry? That was the way of it, even worse, perhaps."

But he spoke in more detail about his arduous trek across the continent and the way it ended. Tears filled his eyes and he brushed them off his cheeks as he told of the priest leading him to Lupe's grave. He turned his head away to hide his emotions.

"I'm thinking it's time to tell him about Connie," Molly whispered to Jeremiah. They sent the children outside the house and went to Matthew's bedside. Both looked down intently, but neither spoke. "You be telling him," Molly urged her husband.

"Well now, Matt, there's something you must know," Jeremiah started, but faltered. "Sure and it's — ah, it's a father you are."

"A father!" Matthew bolted right up in the bed. "A father, you say?" He looked puzzled, but with a half grin, as if expecting a joke. "Go along with you. And how could that be?"

"It's God's truth," Jeremiah insisted. "After you left for the war, Lupe had a baby. A girl."

"She didn't!" Matthew searched his brother's face for some sign of a grin that would give it away that this was his idea of a jest. His gaze shifted to Molly. Both looked back at Matthew in dead earnest. Yes, they were serious all right, he decided. Slowly, it sank in. He had a child.

Matthew lay back against the pillow for a moment. *A little girl. How old would she be? What was she like? Maybe like Lupe?* A slight smile showed on his face. Then it grew into a wide, happy grin. He sat up and swung his feet to sit on the edge of the bed.

"Well now, I'm a father — and isn't that wonderful news!" Matthew exclaimed. "I'll be getting myself gathered up and head back to San Juan to find her."

"No need for that, Matt," Jeremiah explained. "She's here. You've seen her."

Expressions of amazement, understanding, then absolute delight registered on Matthew's face. "Connie," he whispered. "The child you call Connie. Sure, but I never guessed and her looking the image of my Lupe." He thought a minute and then a worried look replaced the delight. "Is she knowing about me?"

"She's not," Molly answered this time. "I'm sure Lupe told her she had a father somewhere, but we didn't know if you were dead or alive or if you'd ever show up. We took her to raise. But you're here now and you can be father to her." Molly glanced at Jeremiah who smiled and nodded.

Matthew was silent, thinking, digesting this momentous news. Emotion welled up in his throat and nearly choked him. He blinked and the wide smile returned to his face. "Could I be seeing my daughter now?"

Molly went for her and brought Connie into the little room by the hand. The child timidly approached the bed and stared at the man sitting there. Molly gently extracted her hand from Connie's clutch and stepped away, leaving father and daughter together. Matthew's eyes gleamed with wonder as he looked upon his daughter. There was Lupe, the same creamy, golden brown skin, the luminous black eyes in the heart-shaped face, the lustrous black hair. Her head was tilted to the side as she studied him.

"You're a little darlin'," Matthew whispered. "A beautiful little darlin'." He held out his hand, beckoning her to him. "Hello, Connie. I'm your da."

Connie's eyes had dropped to the floor, but she slowly raised them and again appraised him. "No, *señor*. My *padre* is away at a war. He may never come back."

"I'm back, darlin'. It's me, your own daddy. I'll never leave you again."

Connie shyly raised her big black eyes. *"Mi padre?"* she asked. Tentatively she reached out her hand and Matthew took it, drew her to him. The little arms went around his neck and clung for a moment, then she released them and ran to hide her head in Molly's apron.

"It will take time," Molly said.

But it didn't take much time at all. As Matthew's strength returned so, too, did his sense of fun and he sang silly songs and played little games with all the children. He told funny stories about his Army life — "You, there, Private Cleary. Straighten up. Wipe that silly smile off your ugly face" — and Matthew would square his shoulders and wipe his hand across his mouth to reveal a solemn, doleful look that had the boys rolling on the floor with laughter. That became their watchword for everything. Little Jerry would have Timmy at attention and tell him, "Wipe that silly smile off your face, Private Cleary." The two would collapse in giggles. Will would watch, serious, dubious, not really understanding why they found it so funny.

But he joined the others in listening to Uncle Matt's tales about his soldier friends and his exciting adventures in the Sierras finding gold. "Now don't you be filling my boys' heads full of that nonsense," Molly scolded. But the boys loved Matthew's stories and begged for more.

Connie kept her distance at first, watching her cousins' fascination with this man who claimed to be her father. But gradually she crept closer until she was part of the group, big eyes intent on him, thrilled that this was her daddy who delighted her cousins. Soon she was in his lap, laughing with the rest of them.

One afternoon Matthew was singing Irish songs and trying out a few dance steps for the boys and Connie. "Put your feet like this and your arms straight down at your sides like this," he instructed. Connie tried it, her little legs moving to the tune. Molly watched critically for a moment and then became caught up in the step herself, joining Matthew until they were breathless from dancing and singing their own music.

"Now don't you be keeping these lads from their chores," Molly ordered.

"Yes, sir, Sergeant," Matthew responded, forming up the children in a line. "Company, attention! Cow milking detail, fall out. That's you, Private Will. Pig slopping detail, report to duty station! That's you, Private Jerry. And you two, Privates Timmy and Connie, you're the egg collection detail! March — !" The children marched off to their duties, squealing happily. Molly smiled in spite of herself.

As Matthew grew stronger and healthier, he began walking around the ranch. He gathered a sturdy branch from a pine tree, picked up a block of redwood, a piece of cowhide, some straw and then begged some thread from Molly. "What are you making, Uncle Matt?" Will wondered. He was sitting beside his uncle on the stoop, watching Matthew carve the redwood into a round shape.

"Well now, this is a secret," Matthew told him, rolling his eyes mysteriously. He wound the redwood ball with straw and then tightly with string. Connie and the boys were watching intently as he cut the cowhide into an odd shape and began to stitch it around the ball. "What are you going to do with it, Uncle Matt?" Will asked.

"We're going to hit it with this." He reached under the step and brought out the strangely-shaped stick he'd carved from pine. "This is called a bat. Will, be getting me four of those jute sacks from the barn. The rest of you come along with me now."

They trooped after him into the corral and watched curiously while Will dropped the sacks in the positions Matthew specified. "Now there," he said, "this is a new game called base ball. We played it in the Army. I'll show you how. That's home plate and over there is first base. I'll be the pitcher here and you stand at home plate, Will, and see how far you can hit this ball with that bat. Connie can be the catcher and pick up the ball if Will misses and throw it back to me. Jerry and Timmy, you be the outfielders and catch the ball or stop it if Will hits it. And Will, if you hit it, you run to first base, that sack over there, and on to second and third and try to come home before somebody gets the ball and tags you with it. Ready now."

When Jeremiah rode in to put up his horse, the youngsters were running all over the corral, chasing the ball, laughing and shouting. He put his saddle away and watched for a while. But declined the invitation to join the game.

After supper when the prayers were said and the children in bed, he and Matthew sat on the stoop and puffed their short pipes. Finally Jeremiah spoke. "Matt, it's grand to see you spry again."

"Aye, Molly's good cooking and my knack for a sound sleep have made me whole again. I'm thanking you, Jerry."

"You'll be ready for some work then?"

"It was back to the Sierras, I thought I'd go," Matthew said. "But now I don't want to be so far from Connie. Maybe the forge in San Juan."

"I'm needing help here."

"I'm no farmer, Jerry."

"Well, you could learn," Jeremiah insisted. "I bought the Thompson place, you know, and it's more than I can manage by myself. I'd partner with you on it, share and share alike. You can have the house for your own. Connie could live there with you when she gets older. Meantime, she'd be right here and you could see her any time you want."

Matthew's pipe had gone out. He took his time to relight, thinking all the while. *I don't want to become a farmer. Following a horse all day around a field is not for me, plowing and broadcasting seed, cutting grain with a sickle. Hard work for little return. But what can I say? Jerry has been so good to me. He does need help and I can't be letting him down. And Molly, she watches me with an eagle eye. Sure and I'll be proving myself to her. And there's Connie. That settles it.* "Aye, Jerry, I'll give it a try. And I'm thanking you."

The brothers solemnly shook hands.

CHAPTER TWENTY-SEVEN

"WHOA, MAUD. WHOA THERE, NELLIE." Matthew Cleary stopped the two big work horses and reached for his bandanna. It was late December, but the afternoon was warm and sweat rolled off him. Following after the plodding horses, reins around his neck and hands on the plow handles to keep the share in the furrow, was damn hard work. Thirty acres didn't sound like much, but it seemed to Matthew that he'd been plowing forever.

He'd entered his new career with determination, if not enthusiasm, and was quick to learn from his brother. Although never comfortable with horses, Matthew managed the knack of harnessing and driving. Jeremiah had given him the experienced team and Matthew even enjoyed caring for the two gentle mares. Dawn until dark he worked up the ground. Some evenings he drove the cart up to Jeremiah's for a visit with Connie.

"Give me a ride, Daddy," Connie pleaded, and Matthew, tired as he was, would lift the little girl onto his shoulders and gallop around the yard to squeals of, "Faster, Daddy, faster." Molly would call them into the house for supper and then Matthew would return to the Thompson *adobe*, which was now his home. Other nights he'd stay longer to join the family for Jeremiah's lessons, listening to Connie recite her A-B-Cs, for the singing, storytelling and nightly prayers.

"Won't I be the first one to say how surprised I am at your brother," Molly admitted. "He's taking to farming and settling down better than I ever thought he would."

"Aye," Jeremiah agreed. "He's about finished broadcasting the wheat and asking me what a farmer does next. I'll be keeping him busy."

Matthew stuck with it through the winter fixing brush fences and pole corrals, mending harness, repairing wagon wheels. He enjoyed the sense of satisfaction as the green shoots of spring matured to ripe wheat for harvest. And he worked with a will through backbreaking days with the sickle and gathering the sheaves. But when the grain had been tramped out and sacked, Matthew was disappointed.

"Jerry," he asked, "is that the extent of our year's work?" He pointed at the stack of wheat-filled jute sacks they'd loaded into the wagon. "What do you reckon that lot will bring in San Juan?"

"Depends," Jeremiah said. "If the market holds from last year, could be three hundred dollars."

"Are you after telling me," Matthew asked, "that a year's work farming will only bring me one hundred and fifty dollars as my share? Is that all I'm breaking my bones over?"

Jeremiah bristled, "And haven't you been filling your belly regularly and having a sound roof over your head."

"Oh, aye, you can be throwing that up at me," Matthew retorted. He glared as he took the list of supplies from Jeremiah and climbed up onto the wagon seat. He waved goodbye with a smile to Molly and the boys and blew Connie an extra kiss. But he gave his brother a scowl as he shook out the lines and started the team.

When ten days had gone by and Matthew still hadn't returned Jeremiah began to worry, but he wouldn't admit it to his wife. "It could be anything holding him up, Molly. He'll be along."

"I'm not sure your brother should be the one you're trusting with our grain crop, Jerry," Molly responded. "No telling what mischief he's getting into."

When Matthew's team pulled into the yard three days later he was in an exuberant mood. He smiled and waved to everybody and hugged and kissed Connie. He began to unload the wagon and Jeremiah joined him, checking off the supplies. His eyes narrowed at one particular box, which stayed in the wagon for delivery to Matthew's place. But before he could say anything, Matthew flourished a wrapped package at Connie.

"Now you can't be opening it, darlin'. It's your birthday present."

"Birthday?" Molly asked. "How is it you're knowing when her birthday might be?"

"And wasn't I the one to go to the mission and ask Padre Mora to be looking in the baptism records?" Matthew answered. "July seventeen, it is, this very day. And tonight we're going to have a big party." He looked at Molly and winked as he said it, and she smiled and nodded her agreement.

Molly spent the afternoon over her big iron stove, preparing one of her precious chickens and baking a cake. Connie spent it in a fever of anticipation, looking at her package, squeezing it, shaking it, trying to guess. "Girls," the boys agreed, "are just plain silly." Jeremiah went with Matthew in the wagon to deliver his supplies to the Thompson place.

As soon as they were alone on the road, he handed Jeremiah a small buckskin sack containing golden double eagles and greenbacks. "Your half of the wheat money after the supplies were paid for," he explained. "Wheat brought a dollar sixty per hundred. Here's the receipt."

Jeremiah pocketed the sack, but was silent. He could tell there was more on Matthew's mind. He waited. Finally his brother said, "That's not much return for all the hard work. I'm thanking you, Jerry." He paused. "But I'm leaving."

"Leaving? How could you be leaving?" Jeremiah was astounded. "There's the land. The Thompson place is to be yours. And what about Connie?"

"I can be making a better life for her with this." Matthew pulled a packet from his pocket, soft buckskin wrapped around ancient paper. As the horses ambled along, he carefully opened it to show a crude map, frayed with age and much handling. "Look at this," he proclaimed triumphantly. "It's worth a fortune and I bought it for only one hundred dollars."

Jeremiah took the paper and studied it from all sides. The ink had faded and the legends were dim. "What the hell is it?"

"This is a map of how to find the Lost Padres gold in the Lucias. Many years ago when the Monterey coast was threatened by pirates, the padres at Mission Carmelo packed up all their gold and precious vessels and stored them in a cave in the mountains south of there," Matthew explained, his eyes bright with excitement. "They marked the entrance to the cave from a mountain called Ventana because there is a hole in it like a window. At certain times each year, at an hour past high noon, the shadow of that window covers the entrance to the cave. This map tells me how to find it."

"Bullshit," Jeremiah declared.

"No! It's the truth." Matthew was adamant.

"You paid somebody for this thing?" Jeremiah said with disgust. He handed the map back to Matthew. "Where'd you get it?"

"One night in Florney's I sat with these prospectors passing through and one showed it to me," Matthew answered. "I offered fifty dollars, but he didn't want to sell it." Matthew grinned with pride. "He finally took one hundred."

"You're a damn fool!"

"Well now, Jerry, you shouldn't be judging a man just because he's different than you," Matthew argued. "Brother, can't you see that I'm not cut out to be a farmer? I gave it a good year's try. But there's easier, quicker ways to make money. You can't be calling me a fool just because I'm seeing them and you're not."

Jeremiah shook his head. He knew it was hopeless. "So you're going to be off chasing your wild dreams again, are you?" He felt his anger rising. "Dammit, Matt, the worth is in the land. Part of this place would be yours, something real for Connie one day. What about her?"

Matthew smiled, his voice filled with confidence. "I'll be back for her as soon as I find the treasure. We'll be so rich I'll buy a mansion in San Francisco for her," Matthew enthused. "She'll have beautiful clothes, the best teachers, and she'll be a lady and one day marry some nabob. Connie will be just fine."

Jeremiah shrugged. He was resigned. "When is it you'll be leaving?"

"In a few days." Matthew turned the team into the Thompson lane. "Tonight we'll be celebrating Connie's birthday and I'll spend a few days with her and the lads and be finishing up some things here. Then I'm off."

They were unloading Matthew's things when Jeremiah lifted the box that had aroused his suspicions. He heard a gurgling sound and opened the box to find several bottles of whiskey. He whirled around and glared at his brother. "So, it's on the drink again, are you now? Stopped off at Florney's, did you?" Jeremiah spit the words out through clenched teeth. "You'll not be soaking up this stuff on my place!"

"Oh, it's your place now, is it? And what happened to share and share alike and this is to be your land, Matt, my brother, and all that lovely sentiment?" Matthew glowered defiantly at his brother. "What's it to you if I take a little drink in the evening after a long day? I told you before, you're not my keeper."

"Aye, that you did," Jeremiah said, half to himself.

Neither man spoke on the ride back to the Cleary ranch. They sat together on the wagon seat, in stiff, stony silence, neither looking at the other. Until the team turned into the yard. Then Matthew cleared his throat, glanced at Jeremiah and said, "Ah, there's one thing, Brother. I'll be needing a bit of a stake to get me to Monterey and buy an outfit. Just a loan, mind you. I'll be paying it back and all else I owe you ten times over and very soon. When I come back for Connie."

Jeremiah turned to face his brother in amazement. How could he be asking this? How could he be wanting more after all Jeremiah had given and all he'd offered? He'd always helped him at every turn and never refused. But not this time. He just didn't have it. And even if he did and could afford it, Molly would be vexed and angry and she'd be right. The bit Matthew had just given him from the sale of the wheat was their entire savings now. Loan, indeed. They'd never see a penny come back.

"I'll not," Jeremiah declared. "Every bit I had went to buy the Thompson place."

"What about the profits I just gave you?"

"That's all the hard money to my name just now," Jeremiah said in a low, firm voice, his lips barely moving in his determination. "But even if I had plenty I'd not be giving you more. This well is dry, Matt. You'll get no more from me for your crazy schemes."

"What?" Matthew was angry. "You'd be denying your own brother a chance at riches? Is it turning me out, you are?"

"Nay. I'm not after turning you out. Stay. Work the land. Make something of yourself besides a worthless drifter with a belly full of whiskey and a head full of wild ideas."

Like a knife thrust the words pierced through Matthew. "Worthless drifter, am I? Wild ideas, is it?" His face grew red. He jumped down from the wagon. "Well then, I'll be leaving here as I came, with just the shirt on my back." He turned and stomped off down the lane.

The angry voices brought Molly and the children from the house where they'd been preparing for Connie's birthday party. The little girl saw her father striding away and chased after him. "Daddy, daddy — !" she yelled as she ran.

Matthew stopped short. He turned and saw his daughter rushing to him. He choked back tears as he bent down and gathered the child into his arms. "There, there, Connie, sure and it's going to be all right," he said patting, and kissing her head.

"Where are you going?" She looked up with at her father with huge, trusting eyes.

His resolve nearly melted. *But how can I be backing down now? Not after making my big play.* "Connie, darlin', I must be leaving. You see how it is. I'll be back for you soon. I'm off to find a fortune and when I have it we'll go away together, just the two of us, maybe to San Francisco and we'll have a big house and lots of servants and all kinds of toys for you to play with."

"But, Daddy," she whimpered. "You said you'd never leave me, and what about my birthday party?"

Matthew kissed her teary face, hugged her, and then looked again into those big black eyes that were Lupe's and his own tears welled over. "There'll be other birthdays, Connie. And we'll be rich and you'll have all sorts of presents. We'll be together always. I promise." He put Connie down and rose from the dust. "Go back to the house now, darlin'." Connie nodded, but she still stood there so Matthew said, "Go on, Connie. Do as Daddy says."

Connie rubbed her eyes as she watched her father turn and walk away. But she didn't go back to the house, not until he'd walked all the way down the lane and turned off onto the Peach Tree Road and she could see him no more.

*****

A week later, after hiking and hitching rides on the river route, Matthew Cleary stood before Florney's Saloon in San Juan Bautista, flipping his last twenty dollar gold piece. After buying the map, the doll for Connie, and having a few drinks with the boys, it was all he had left from his year's work as a farmer. Should he risk it in the poker game or tuck it away and walk off for Monterey? It came up heads. He grinned and entered the saloon.

"Well look who's here? The farmer boy," the bartender greeted him. The men at the poker table looked up.

"Back so soon, Matt?" Charlie Folger asked, waving him over to the table.

Matthew pulled up a chair. "Deal me in," he said, flipping the double eagle onto the table and accepting a modest stack of chips. Simon Bronson, a rancher from Tres Pinos, grunted a hello and the other players nodded. The game went slowly. Five card draw, California poker, nothing wild, open on anything. Matthew's hands were average, three of a kind took one small pot, a pair of jacks another. Then he lost on three tens, but won again with a small straight going in. Most hands he had to fold before the real betting began. At the end of an hour his stack of chips was about the same as when he started and Matthew began to get impatient, drawing to inside straights, betting two pair against three of a kind. The pile of chips dwindled. Then Matthew got on a lucky streak and his winnings doubled. Maybe his luck had changed, he thought.

Bronson dealt the cards and then sipped a whiskey as he thumbed his own hand and waited. Folger, across the table nervously shuffled his and announced, "I'll open for ten." He looked around the table. Two other players to Folger's left threw down their hands in disgust. The dealer took a last look at his hand. "I'll call," he said, pushing his chips to the center. Matthew studied his three fives, looked hard at Folger and raised him five. Folger stayed and so did Bronson. "Cards?" he asked.

Folger held up one finger.

"I'll take two," Matthew said.

"Dealer takes three," Bronson said. "Your bet." He nodded to Folger.

"Ten more." Folger stacked the chips and shoved them forward.

"You're damn proud of that busted flush," Matthew said with a laugh. He left his cards face down on the table. "I'll back these three aces without looking." He picked two five dollar chips and tossed them out.

The dealer quietly added his chips to the pile. "I'll raise," he said, looking intently at the other two players. "Price of poker's going up. Twenty dollars."

Folger squeezed his cards through his hands, thumbing one at a time, stared impassively at the others for a moment and then called. It was Matthew's turn. He picked up his cards and quickly fanned them out, hiding his grin behind a sober facade.

He nodded to himself as if finally deciding. "Tell you what I'm going to do," he said. "I'm just going to raise you forty bucks."

The dealer thought for a moment and then said, "I'll see you and raise another twenty."

Folger wavered, but pushed in his chips to meet Matthew's forty and the other twenty. "Call," he said.

Matthew was feeling reckless. "Here's your twenty and another twenty."

Suddenly it was silent in the barroom. Conversations halted and all attention was on the poker table. The good-natured joshing among the card players had stopped. It was serious, deadly serious. The dealer thought a moment, counting his chips. Then he pushed the whole stack forward. "I'll see that and up it, ah — twenty–nine dollars."

Without a word, Folger met the raise and Matthew shoved in all his pile except for two white chips. He tried to laugh as he said, "Call," but it came out in a whisper.

"Read 'em and weep," Bronson said and laid down his three aces.

Folger gave a sigh of relief and showed his small straight. "I hit an inside straight, by God," he crowed and reached for the pot.

Matthew Cleary looked from one to the other. He put his hand on Folger's. "Hold up, there, Charlie," he said. "First look at these." He spread out three fives and two eights. His tight smile turned into a big grin. "Drinks are on me, boys. Full house takes the pot."

The barroom came alive again. Amid congratulations from the patrons and the grumbling of the poker players, Matthew cleared his winnings off the table. He paid for the round, downed his own shot in one gulp, set the glass on the bar and walked out, headed for Monterey and the south coast. His cave filled with treasure was waiting.

CHAPTER TWENTY-EIGHT

"AH, JERRY, ISN'T THIS JUST GRAND, to be having all this room?" Molly whirled around, dancing with her broom. "And look at my floors, would you now. Aren't they lovely?" She'd been sweeping her new pine floor, cut by Jeremiah and Calistro Salazar over in Pine Valley and split out with great care last winter after the Salazar family had taken over the Thompson place. Calistro had also helped Jeremiah add two new rooms to the Cleary house, one for Will, Jerry Jr. and Timmy, and another for Connie, Kitty and Annie, now nearly three. Baby Danny still slept in the cradle in the main room, although he'd been weaned from Molly's breast and was trying to walk.

Jeremiah was amused as he watched his wife dancing her pleasure about the room. He realized that it had been some time since she had moved so lightly. Too often he'd noticed her fatigue. All the hard work and a baby nearly ever year or so was beginning to tell on her. That half-laughing statement she'd made to Sally Thompson, "I haven't even been to San Juan for five years," continued to ring in his ears. And now two more years had passed.

"Molly, love, I'll be hauling grain to San Juan next week."

"Oh, Jerry, I'm knowing you must go, but I'm dreading it so," she said. "I miss you when you're away."

"Miss me, will you? And why is that? Aren't you the one to be going with me?"

"Me? Going with you? But Jerry, if your taking me and the children, where will be you carrying the grain sacks?"

Jeremiah had a surprise for her. He'd made arrangements for Maria Salazar to care for the children. "This is a grand time for you to be having a holiday without a baby clinging to you or one coming on."

Molly enjoyed the wagon trip down the San Benito River route because it reminded her at every turn of their honeymoon. She was also thrilled at the prospect of seeing Emily and Weeb, visiting in San Juan and going to Mass.

As soon as they arrived in town, Molly asked Jeremiah to go first to the post office. She was hoping for a letter from her sister. But there was no letter awaiting her.

"Could something be wrong, Jerry? It's not like Cauth to fail to write. Is something going on in Ireland I'm not knowing?"

"I'm sure nothing's wrong, Molly love. If there's any problem it's with the mails. You can't be depending on them. Now stop your worrying."

Sunday morning they attended Mass at the Mission and learned that Padre Mora was being transferred to San Miguel Mission. He promised that he would break his journey at the Cleary ranch and baptize the children. On their way back to the Jeffersons', Jeremiah suggested she change into her good dress, the blue one, that evening. "Remember, Molly love, that first time we walked together around San Juan? The night before we were married?" Molly nodded absently. "And we were looking into the window of the Plaza, and you said it was much too grand for us?"

She suddenly brightened. "Oh, Jerry, I do. It looked so elegant."

"Aye, Molly love, and it was me who promised you that one day we'd eat there. I don't think you believed a word of it, but tonight I'm making good on my promise."

That evening he again borrowed the Jeffersons' surrey and they headed for San Juan, Molly in her blue dress with the lace collar, and Jeremiah in his frock coat, high white collar and black string tie. As they rode toward the Plaza, Molly was almost as nervous as she'd been on that day ten years ago when her boat arrived in San Francisco. Nervous, excited and happy. But afraid, too. *They'll all be knowing I'm but a simple Irish girl. I'll be making a fool of myself for sure.*

Jeremiah tied up in front of the Plaza Hotel. He was nervous, too. He handed Molly down from the surrey and she placed her hand on his arm as she'd seen it done, and he

211

escorted her across the lobby, and into the restaurant. It was aglow with light from the chandeliers and the candles on each table, which flickered across the white tablecloths, and glinted off the crystal glassware.

The smiling head waiter came up to them. "Good evening, sir. How nice to have you with us this evening. I have a nice table for you."

It was a table for two by the window, looking out into the dimly-lit plaza square. Jeremiah seated Molly as he'd seen the gentry do, and took his own place, glancing around the room as he did so. There were other diners and some nodded to him. He didn't know them. Just being polite, he thought, so he nodded back. He tried to watch them without seeming to.

But Molly kept her head down, her hands folded in front of her. She looked at her hands. *Oh dear God, and me with my hands so red and rough. They'll see I'm no lady.* She quickly clasped them in her lap, beneath the table cloth. And all these knives and forks. And the spoons of different sizes. And the glasses and plates. What was she to do? She took a quick glance around and swiftly returned her eyes to her place. She hardly heard Jerry as he ordered for both of them with the help and suggestions of the attentive waiter.

First a glass of Burgundy wine. But why was he pouring such a little bit in Jeremiah's glass? Molly wondered. Was he thinking the entire bottle was for her? Jeremiah wondered, too. The waiter looked inquiringly at Jeremiah, who was holding up his crystal goblet, expectantly.

"You may taste it, sir," the waiter said politely.

Jeremiah drained the glass. It tasted fine to him. He nodded. The waiter smiled and moved to Molly's side and poured wine into her glass. He then refilled Jeremiah's glass and placed the bottle on the table.

Molly, too, wondered what this ritual was all about, but decided not to ask until they were alone later. *Jeremiah has the manners of a lord. Where did he learn such things? From his books? I mustn't shame him. He'll not be knowing how strange I feel. But this is no place for the likes of me.*

"To us, Molly love. To you, and me, and to our children. And to this nation. A toast to our happiness." He showed her how to clink their glasses together. "Health," he said. "*Slainte!*"

Jeremiah smiled at her and she anxiously returned his smile as a waiter brought a long loaf of freshly-baked French bread and a bowl of butter. A second waiter placed a tray before them filled with olives, pickles, green onions, salami, cheese and smoked beef tongue. Molly studied the array of silverware next to her plate and wondered which one to use. Jeremiah's concern was for the bread. Should he cut it? He covertly glanced around the room and saw another diner tearing the bread with his hands so Jeremiah picked up the warm loaf and carefully pulled apart a piece for Molly and himself.

"Jerry, I'm not baking bread so good as this," she said tasting the flaky, crisp crust.

"Yours is every bit as good, Molly love, only different."

She located the soup spoon and carefully lifted a mouthful of consommé. It had an onion taste, strange to her palate, and she felt so nervous she was afraid she might spill another spoonful so she folded her hands in her lap.

Jeremiah took another sip of wine and looked across the table at the wife he cherished. She was so beautiful, her curls shining, the color of her cheeks blooming in the candlelight, the blue of her good dress matching the blue of her eyes. So trim, so womanly, and after having six children, and all that hard work. He thought his heart would burst with the sheer joy of loving her. Molly felt her husband's eyes on her and the love that shone from them encouraged her to enjoy their unique dining experience.

Molly took another swallow of wine and as soon as she put down her glass it was refilled by a watchful waiter. By the time a carving board holding a roasted leg of lamb was wheeled alongside their table, Molly was relaxed and curious. She noticed a small side dish. "That looks to be green jelly, do we put it on the bread?" she whispered.

Jeremiah shrugged and glanced around. "On the meat, I think," he whispered back.

Molly studied the generous slices of lamb on her plate surrounded by golden brown potatoes and green beans. "This is lamb, Jerry? I don't believe I've ever tasted it before." She sliced off a bite and as she chewed her expression showed her pleasure. "Once we had sheep at home, but just for the wool and to sell. I'm partial to this, Jerry. Why don't we keep sheep?"

"The coyotes would love that," Jeremiah answered with a laugh. "Sheep wouldn't last a week in Long Valley."

By the time dessert came Molly was full, but Jeremiah had ordered strawberries topped with thick, rich cream and she couldn't resist. "And aren't you the one now, Mister Cleary, knowing how to show a girl a grand time?" Molly said, her eyes twinkling, a mischievous grin on her face.

Jeremiah brought out his short pipe and went through the ritual of lighting up. He sipped his coffee and puffed with satisfaction as the waiter arrived with the bill on a tiny silver tray, which he left in front of Jeremiah. He studied the piece of paper and then brought a half eagle out of his pocket. The five dollar gold piece would cover the meal and the wine and leave enough for a handsome tip, as Weeb had suggested. Jeremiah winced at the amount, but seeing Molly's enjoyment made it worth whatever the cost.

The next morning they drove their wagon to McMahan's store and loaded the supplies Jeremiah had ordered. Molly had climbed back up onto the wagon as Jeremiah was checking the harness one last time when the postmaster came running toward them.

"Oh, Missus Cleary. Wait, Mister Cleary! Wait!" He was panting and talking at the same time. "I'm glad I caught you. This letter came for you two months back, and I set it aside, hoping somebody would be going your way to deliver it. I clear

214

forgot it when you were in yesterday, Missus Cleary. I'm so sorry." He handed up the letter to Molly and she thanked him.

As they rode off, Molly looked anxiously at the return address on the envelope. "It's from my brother John in Boston. Oh, Jerry, what could be the matter?" She tore it open and quickly scanned the letter, her heart pounding. "It's James. Terrible trouble. James is in jail. He was with the Fenians in some battle near Cork. It was a rising, but nothing went well in the snow and rain, and the British put it down. James was captured in the mountains and sentenced to seven years in prison." Molly's tears started down her cheeks. "Oh, Jerry, seven years!"

Jeremiah put an arm around his wife as they drove. But there was no comforting her. "Molly love, if I were still in Ireland, I'd probably be a rebel myself — "

"What's the use?" Molly shot back, anger mixed with anguish. "What's the use of fighting. They get you one way or another. Knock your house, kill you, throw you in jail!"

Jeremiah sighed. The memory of the lovely supper the night before was being completely washed away by Molly's tears. Despite the extravagance of the previous evening, Jeremiah suggested they turn around and go back to town. "We can send a postal money order to Cauth. She'll be needing it," he said.

* * * * *

It had been a gray, drizzly December day in Ireland and now the rain had turned to sleet. It drummed against the thatch, threatening to hammer its way into the tiny cottage. The occupants huddled by the fire where it was warm, drinking hot soup. That morning Catherine had purchased a joint of beef with the money sent from California. With that postal order and another from John and Rose in Boston, Catherine was more than able to keep up her share of expenses in Ballydehob. With the bit of meat, and with vegetables from their own garden, she'd made a good thick soup. It was a treat.

215

Catherine knew Kevin depended on her contributions and thanked her for them, but her sister-in-law Sheila didn't like having her in the house and made little pretense of her feelings. And ever since James' trial, over a year now, all Moira could do was mope and wring her hands. It irritated Catherine no end, all Moira's wailing and moaning. She knew there was no use crying about it all day. Life isn't fair, so get on with it, she wanted to shout at Sheila.

"This is a grand soup, Cauth. Just the thing to warm a man on a cold night, and fill him at the same time," Kevin said, although his wife was glaring at him over the compliment.

"James is not having such a soup where he is," Moira whined. "He'd not be there if he cared more for his poor wife, and less for that hopeless cause."

"He's a man, and he stood up and struck a blow for Ireland. You should be proud of him," Catherine scolded Moira. But she knew it was no use.

She thought of the letter she'd just received from Molly. She'd written about Baby Daniel, a chubby toddler, Molly said. And now there were six children plus the little cousin, Connie. They were so far away. Tears welled up in her eyes. She hated getting herself in these moods. *Oh God, help me be what it is you want of me. Give me the strength.*

There was a knock on the door, so quiet it was hardly heard above the storm.

"Who could that be at this hour on such a night?" Sheila wondered. She held up the lamp to light the doorway. Kevin pulled the latch and the door swung open. There stood a dripping figure, huddled against the rain. He looked vaguely familiar.

"Come in, come in. You'll drown out there," Kevin said.

The man stepped inside, ragged, soaked, water puddling at his feet. "God bless all here," he greeted. They'd heard that deep, gruff voice before. Its fierceness had filled this very room when he exhorted them to fight for Ireland's liberty. It was Michael Callahan! Still on the run.

"You're not welcome here, Mike Callahan. Leave us in peace," Sheila ordered.

"You're the reason my James is suffering in British hands!" Moira charged.

Catherine looked angrily at the two women. "Let the poor man come in by the fire." She crossed to the door, still held open by a shocked Kevin, and drew him in, then swung it shut. "Give the man some soup and let him warm himself." She led Callahan to the hob, and fed more peat to the fire. Callahan shrugged himself out of his wet coat and hung it to dry. He spread his hands before the blaze, and then gratefully took the cup of soup that Catherine handed him.

"There's no danger to you. I wasn't followed here, and I'll stay but a little while. I'm expected in Skibbereen, a safe haven for a bit. I'm thanking you for this fire and warming soup."

"It's the little we can do for a man who still fights for Ireland," Catherine said.

"And you, Miss Hurley. We've heard of you and your courage. What other woman stands in the door of a cottage being knocked and defies the authorities?"

"A futile gesture, it was," Catherine responded. "They but dragged me out of the way and pounded in the door. I'm just a weak woman, and it angers me. Were I a man I'd have been there with you and James."

Just a few months past, Catherine had been so incensed at the sight of families being put off the land, she'd led them to protest, standing beside the pitiable creatures to face the soldiers who'd come to evict them. They'd shrunk away, skulked off, but she'd stood her ground in the cottage door, and been forcibly flung aside.

"Damn rebels," the British officer had remarked as he took a pinch of snuff. "Some of their women are as bad as the men. Let the slut go."

"Would that the whole of Ireland had the spunk of you, Miss Hurley. Had they that, the rising would have won the land."

Callahan's voice had the same ring, the quiet force, the same convincing appeal that Catherine remembered. "Don't think the Fenians are finished. There are thousands of us throughout this land and we won't give up. There'll yet come the day when Ireland will be free of the damnable British."

"What can I do?" Catherine asked.

"What you're doing. Keep up the spirits of the people. Help those who are being put off their lands. Encourage them to resist. One day there'll be new laws to restrict the landlords, to change the system. The people must have hope." Callahan put down his soup cup and pulled on his wet coat.

"One more thing." He turned to Moira. "And you'd be the wife of James Hurley? We have word from his prison. He's well and sends his love."

"Thanks be to God," Moira said.

"And thanks to you, Callahan, for bringing us word," Kevin added.

"Beannmmacht Dè leat, oiche mnaith dhuit," Callahan spoke in Irish as he went out the door. "God bless you and goodnight."

"Fod saol agot," Catherine called after him. "May you have a long life." But she doubted it.

CHAPTER TWENTY-NINE

"WE'LL BE HAVING THE BEST calves in Monterey County," Jeremiah bragged to Molly when he and the two older boys rode in and shut the new bull into the corral. It had taken them nearly three weeks to drive the bull and four cows home from the new railhead at Gilroy.

"I'll be turning him out tomorrow afternoon, when the other cows come in to water, so he will bunch up right off," Jeremiah explained. "He was the stubborn one to drive, especially in the middle of the day. We had to keep the cows moving off or he'd brush up. But just be looking at him, Molly, and isn't he the grand one now? Isn't he worth it?"

The new Hereford bull was a beauty. Red, with a white head and great, curving horns, he had white markings down his back, and under his belly, and on the tip of his tail. The bull was walking along the corral fence, shaking his head and proudly arching his neck.

"Aye, Jerry. He's a beauty and doesn't he know it? Just look at him snorting around the corral," she answered.

"He's on the prod all right," Jeremiah said. "I told the boys to stay well clear of him."

The next morning the sun was shining brightly and the air had the crisp bite of autumn.

On this October day in 1869, Molly Cleary was up with the dawn to cook breakfast for her husband and children and send them on their way for the day's chores. Jeremiah was off that morning to cut brush and patch a gap in the fence on the north side of the ranch. He saddled one of the gray geldings he was training and rode off up the canyon. Will, Jerry Jr. and Timmy were busy in the barn, minding their father's warning about the bull.

Molly fairly sang as she washed the dishes while Connie dried, with the not quite helping hands of Kitty, who actually wiped a few, although Annie tried to pull the towel away from her. Two-year-old Danny was underfoot, but Molly was used to that. It seemed that one baby had always been underfoot. Molly was so full of energy this morning. Her family was together again and it was such a glorious day. Even the diffi-cult chore of scrubbing the *adobe's* pine floors didn't intimidate her today.

"I'll scrub those floors, Aunt Molly," Connie offered.

Molly smiled at this dark child who didn't quite fit into the family. She was always trying to help, always so obedient, but she had a strange sadness in her big black eyes. And whenev-er the other children teased her, Connie would declare,

"Someday I'm going to San Francisco and be rich and live in a great big house. As soon as my father comes back."

"Ah, your father's never coming back," Little Jerry taunted.

"He is so," Connie insisted, big tears rolling down her cheeks. She'd run off and stay by herself for hours. Molly would finally find her and hug her. "You know we love you, Connie. This is your home and we're your family," Molly would tell her, thinking *the devil take you, Matthew Cleary, for leaving your child*.

Now she smiled at the eager eight-year-old. "We'll do the floors together, Connie. The job will go faster that way."

"I help Connie," Annie declared. She was never far from Connie's side.

"Go along with you now," Molly said. "You be helping Kitty keep an eye on Danny." She shooed the little girls and the baby brother outside. "Play out here while the floors are wet," she ordered.

Molly took the bucket to the well while Connie got out the soap and the scrub brush. She watched as the three children began making mud pies with the water spilled near the well. They'd be a mess to clean up, but at least they were out of the way for a little while. She added soap to the bucket of water and poured some on the floor. Molly knelt down and started scrubbing with Connie beside her. She heard Bodach bark. He must not have gone off with Jerry, she thought. He probably was playing with the children.

She went back to her work. But the dog barked again. And again. "What is that fool Bodach barking at?" she asked of Connie as she straightened up, arching her back to ease it, and went to the door to look. She gave a startled gasp.

"Oh, my God, dear God!"

There was little Danny in the corral with the Hereford bull, holding out to him some wisps of hay. The bull was across the corral. Pawing the ground. Head down, shaking his horns and snorting. Between them was Bodach, barking angrily, protecting Danny, but making the bull madder by the second.

Molly rushed to the gate, then slowed. She didn't want to startle him more. Keeping her eyes on the bull, she slipped through the gate and edged along the fence toward her son. "Come to Mama, Danny. Come to Mama."

The bull charged, the dog nipping at its heels. Molly saw the bull coming as she reached for Danny. She pushed him under the fence just as the bull struck her in the back and threw her into the air.

She hit the ground with such force all the breath left her body. She gasped for air and struggled to her knees, trying to crawl under the fence. The bull charged again. This time he hit her with his horns, tossed her, and she landed on her back. The bull drove at her with his head down. A horn entered Molly's chest and she was pinned to the ground. The bull ground his head against her. She tried to scream, but no sound came. The bull flung his head and again tossed her body into the air. Molly landed with a sickening thud, unconscious, bleeding.

The girls' screaming brought the boys from the barn. Will reached his mother, while Jerry distracted the bull and allowed Will to pull Molly through the fence. "Jerry, jump on Bouchal and ride fast for Dad," Will instructed his brother. "Connie, help Tim take care of Danny and the girls."

Will knelt by his mother. She was still, unconscious, but breathing. Blood was pouring from her side. He didn't know what to do. "Ma, Ma. It's Will. I'm here. I'll take care of you. You'll be all right."

Will took off his shirt and wadded it, placing it over the huge, gaping wound. He drew his mother's skirts down over her legs, and took her head in his lap. "Dad will be here in a minute. He'll know what to do. He'll fix you, Ma."

Ten minutes later Jeremiah galloped into the yard, slid his horse to a stop and jumped off. He ran to his wife. "Oh, Molly love, Molly love." Jeremiah knelt beside her crumpled body. He saw Will's bloody shirt wadded up against the hole in her chest and a wave of fear flooded through him. He gently lifted his wife and carried her carefully into the house.

Before they reached the bed, Jeremiah was covered with blood. He put Molly down and searched for some clean cloth, stuffing it into her terrible wound, just under the right breast. In seconds the cloth was a sodden red mess. Molly opened her eyes. She focused them on her husband.

"Jerry, I hurt — I hurt."

"It will be all right, Molly love. I'll fix it."

But he knew he couldn't.

In fact, Jeremiah knew there wasn't anything he could do. There wasn't anything anybody could do. A helpless dread chilled him. But he had to do *something*. "Will, go for Missus Garcìa. Jerry, ride for Calistro and Marìa. Bring them!" Jeremiah prayed they would know how to stop the bleeding and close the wound.

The children stood by the bed, too stricken to move. Tears poured down Will's cheeks as he held Danny in his arms. Jerry and Tim were ashen, looking wide-eyed, unbelieving at their brutally injured mother, her blood soaking the bed. The girls were sobbing, but not fully understanding, Connie with an arm around Annie, clutched Kitty's hand.

"Go now, boys. Hurry!" Jeremiah yelled, and they jumped into action. Will handed the baby to Tim and ran from the house, Jerry just behind him.

Jeremiah sat on the bed, changing cloths, stuffing them into the wound, trying to stop the fountain of blood. Wiping Molly's forehead with a wet rag. Holding her hand. Whispering to her, "Hang on, Molly. Help is coming. It will be all right." And praying, "Dear God, save her, save my Molly."

She tried to speak. Jeremiah couldn't understand what she was saying. Her voice was so weak. He placed his ear to her lips. "Cauth, Jerry — Cauth — Send for Cauth. Care for children."

"No, Molly. No!" Jeremiah pleaded. "Don't be leaving me! Oh, God, don't be taking her, please, God. I love her so."

"Jerry — Want priest — Love you — Love you forever."

Jeremiah looked into her blue eyes and saw the light go out of them. They glazed over and were blue no longer.

He sat by the bed. He was numb. He called her name, over and over. He shook her.

"Molly — !" he shouted. "Molly — Molly — !" His voice seemed to come from the very depths of his soul. Jeremiah shuddered, but no tears came.

He sat there holding his wife's hand, feeling it grow cold. That was where they found him when Calistro and Marìa Salazar arrived. And he was still there, sitting quietly, hours later, holding Molly's stiff, bluish hand in his, when Felipe and Sophia Garcìa reached the Cleary ranch.

Sophia gently reached out, took Jeremiah's hand and lifted him up. He shook her off, but rose from the bed. He strode to the fireplace, and reached above the mantle for the Spencer rifle. The box of shells was nearby, and he inserted several of them into the stock.

Jeremiah went outside to the corral, and levered in a shell. Taking careful aim, he fired. The Hereford bull dropped, shot through the head. His legs jerked a few times and then stopped. Jeremiah stood, numbly staring at the huge dead animal, but not seeing it, not seeing anything.

CHAPTER THIRTY

JEREMIAH SAT, FACE FROZEN, eyes glazed. He hadn't moved all afternoon. Marìa Salazàr and Sophia Garcìa prepared Molly's body for the casket of redwood, which Calistro and Felipe were making. The two women tenderly washed away the dried blood and placed her in the blue dress. They combed out her black curls, choking back sobs as they worked. It was finished. Molly was laid out on the big table, candles placed beside her. By now it was dark and the candles, and light from the lamp, cast shadows on the walls, and flickered across the dead woman's body.

Marìa had seen to the younger children. They were washed and clean clothing laid out for them for the morning. The boys took care of themselves and had that scrubbed look, despite their tears. They all stood by the table, Will holding Danny's hand, and stared at the person lying there.

Was that really Mama? That couldn't be Mama. Mama would be fixing supper. Mama would be singing to them. Mama would be making jokes for them, making it fun to do their chores. Mama would be scolding them, protecting them, loving them. Mama would be talking and laughing with Dad. Why was she lying there so still and cold looking? They knew. They knew their mother was dead. But they didn't really know.

Jeremiah knew. It pounded in his brain. It coursed through his veins. He looked down at his dead wife, so still there in her pretty blue dress, her eyes closed, long lashes hiding those dead, blue eyes. He couldn't bear it. He looked away. His gaze was straight ahead, fixed on the wall. He knew Sophia Garcìa was leading the prayers, the others responding in Spanish. He heard them, but he didn't hear them.

Calistro led him away. He had a question that had to be answered. Felipe stood with a shovel. Where was the grave to be? They would dig it now, for the morning.

"No!" Jeremiah spoke for the first time in hours. "A priest she was wanting. Consecrated ground. I'll take her to the priest."

"But, *señor*, San Juan is too far," Felipe protested.

"San Miguel," Jeremiah said. "Padre Mora is at San Miguel."

With that Jeremiah again lapsed into silence. He sat on the stoop while the others tried to eat the supper that Marìa and Sophia had prepared.

"Here, Dad."

It was Will, handing him his pipe, filled with tobacco and tamped. Will lit it for him and sat there with him. Neither said a word. Jeremiah finished his pipe and put his head in his hands. He didn't notice that Will fell asleep right there on the stoop and that Marìa helped the boy to his bed. Jeremiah didn't feel the cold. He simply sat there all night.

At dawn he rose, and caught his horses. He harnessed the team and had the wagon waiting when the others came awake. The women dressed the girls, braided their hair, and readied little Danny, saw that the boys brushed their hair, and fed them all a warm breakfast. Jeremiah sat waiting on the wagon's high seat, lines in his hands, quiet, grim.

Felipe and Calistro lifted the casket into the wagon bed, and the children climbed up, Jerry and Tim helping Kitty and Annie, who clung to Connie, Will holding Danny. Sophia Garcìa handed up a bundle, food for the trip, a cask of water and blankets. Jeremiah shook out his lines and the horses pulled.

"*Via con Dios*." "Go with God. Good-bye." The Garcias and the Salazàrs said almost in unison. Then they stood in silence, watching the wagon roll down the valley. It wasn't until the last wisp of dust had disappeared that they turned. The Garcias got their wagon ready--it was time for them to head back to Peach Tree. Calistro and Marìa had to take care of their own children and oversee the ranch.

All day the Cleary team plodded along, first on the track down Long Valley, and then following the bank up the Salinas

River. The dust rising behind the wagon marked their progress, but it was slow, keeping to the edge of the foothills and through the fields of mustard, away from the dunes where the October wind blew up gusts of sand. It was afternoon when they passed the buildings of Rancho San Bernardo, and late in the evening when they finally saw a cluster of lights from a ranch some ten miles further south. They drove into the yard, pulled up in front of one of the houses, and Will called out, "Hello — "

A man, holding up a lantern, and a woman stepped from the house. When Will explained the circumstances, and they saw the casket and the children, the woman said, "Come in, come in. I'll have something hot for the children in no time at all."

She fed the children and settled them all in makeshift beds near her own youngsters. When they were asleep, Jeremiah finally broke his silence to thank the couple for their hospitality. But he declined their invitation to sleep inside the house.

"It's my last night with her. I'll be spending it here, beside her, in the wagon."

Jeremiah rolled himself up in a blanket, there on the bed of the wagon beside the body of his Molly, and looked up at the stars. So like those other nights he'd spent with her in this very wagon, his wedding night and all those other times along the San Benito River. But so very different. This night a box of redwood was between them. His throat ached with unshed tears. He nearly choked on them, yet they didn't flow. The anguish in him was so deep, so intense, he felt he would burst, but there was no release. He lay there for hours staring at the stars. Finally, he fell into an exhausted sleep until the sun touched him.

The funeral Mass in San Miguel mission church was said the next afternoon by Padre Francisco Mora, who had returned that very day from Mission San Luis Obispo. He was in the mission compound watching as the Cleary wagon approached. His eyes lit up when he recognized Jeremiah and he called out a greeting. *"Buenos tarde, mi amigos.* Good afternoon. I'm happy to see you, my friends." But the delight went out of his voice as his eyes searched the wagon for Molly and came to rest instead upon the wooden box.

He shifted his gaze to Jeremiah, staring down at him, stoic, silent. "*Señor* Cleary, what — ?" The gentle priest looked from Jeremiah to the sad-faced children, quietly sitting beside the casket. For long moments no one said a word. Then finally it was Will who spoke.

"Mama is dead."

Padre Mora made the sign of the cross. "*Aie, que lastima!*" he exclaimed. "What a pity." He looked from Will back to Jeremiah and asked, "How?"

Again it was Will who answered. "Mama was gored by our new bull. Danny was in the corral and Mama went in to save him. The bull killed her." A sob caught in Will's throat and he, too, fell silent.

The Franciscan priest said a short prayer for Molly's soul as he studied the seven children in the wagon. "*Pobrecitos,*" he said. "You poor little ones." They stared back at him from tear-streaked faces, Will holding Danny, Little Jerry and Timmy with Kitty, and Connie, her arms around Annie. Jeremiah still sat with the lines in his hands, staring straight ahead now.

Padre Mora called for help, to put up the Cleary team and to carry the casket into the church. Jeremiah finally stepped down from the wagon and followed the priest, the children walking behind him. Padre Mora went to prepare for the Requiem Mass while the Cleary family huddled on their knees before the altar, the little group of mourners making the huge *adobe* church seem even larger.

The old Franciscan had seen much sorrow in his ministry, but he was especially saddened by this tragedy. The Clearys were like family to him, ever since that day twelve years ago in San Juan when he'd married the tall, shy Jeremiah to Molly, the pretty Irish girl. And now she was gone to her rest far too soon. Never would she see her sons and daughters grow into

227

young men and women. His voice broke as he recited the Latin liturgy.

At Molly's grave in the mission cemetery Jeremiah remained stoic. His children had exhausted their tears. They stood in silence at the edge of the open grave, and watched their mother's coffin being lowered into it.

Jeremiah's lips moved. "God bless you, Mary Margaret Hurley Cleary. You'll always be with me," he told her in Irish and turned away.

Will and Jerry had the team hitched early the next morning and they all climbed into the wagon. It was a two-day trip back to the empty house in Long Valley. It was late in the afternoon of the first day when Danny began to cry. "I want my mama. I want my mama," he demanded, tears rolling down his fat cheeks.

Will tried to quiet his little brother. But Jeremiah paid no attention. His eyes were fixed vacantly ahead of him. He was somewhere else, far away, unreachable.

The team trudged along, the only sound was the rattle of the harness, the creak of the wheels and the little boy sobbing, "I want my mama."

CHAPTER THIRTY-ONE

WILL TOOK SOME VENISON CHOPS from the big crock, scraped off the lard as he'd seen his mother do, and placed them in the frying plan. If Jeremiah noticed the smell of frying meat, he gave no indication. Nor did he eat when Will, with Connie's help, fed his brothers and sisters, and set a plate before his father.

"You need to eat, Dad," the boy insisted. Jeremiah slowly shook his head but said nothing,

In the days that followed, Marìa Salazàr often prepared food and sent Calistro over with it, good stews and *chile verde, enchiladas,* and big pots of *frijoles.* She came herself when she could, cleaned the house, left a supply of *tortillas*, and showed Will how to warm them. Jeremiah didn't seem to even notice her. He picked at the food, went through the motions as he did with everything else since Molly's death. He automatically went about doing the necessary chores, hardly aware of anything or anyone around him, not even his children.

Will sent Jerry and Tim out on horseback to check the cattle while he and Connie watched over the younger children. When they returned, Little Jerry went straight to his father. "Dad, the cows drifted through that fence up the canyon, the one you were fixing. I put them back through, but they'll just drift out again unless you fix it."

Jeremiah glanced at his son but didn't answer him.

Will went to Calistro when he realized his father would surely not mend the fence. "My father just doesn't seem to care anymore," Will told him. "I don't know what to do. You do, Calistro. I think you'd better be doing whatever needs to be done."

"He'll be himself again one day soon, Will. The sadness will always be there, but he'll be all right," Calistro tried to reassure the boy. "I'll cut brush and fill that gap. You take care of your brothers and sisters."

The rains had come, and mid-January Calistro went into the fields by himself to plow. Jeremiah spent his days sitting on the *adobe's* stoop, or leaning on the corral fence, gazing for hours at the spot where Molly had been gored.

If I hadn't been wanting to improve the herd I'd never have brought home that damn Hereford bull and Molly would still be alive. Curse the day I learned about such bulls. Curse the time I took to bring the beast here.

He was there by the corral when Little Jerry came to stand beside him. Father and son stared silently at the place where Molly had fallen. Then Little Jerry asked, "Dad, why? Why did Mama have to die?"

Without speaking, Jeremiah turned away quickly and walked off.

At night it was Will who led the prayers and tucked the girls into bed. It was Will who held Danny when he cried for his mother. It was Will who fixed the meals and tried to do the washing. It was Will who built the fires and set the others to their tasks. Connie helped as much as she was able, particularly with little Annie, but it was Will whom she depended upon.

Jeremiah sat in his chair, unaware of his grieving children. He seldom spoke and then only when absolutely necessary. The children gave up trying to get his attention. Their father was locked up somewhere far away. And wherever he was, they could not reach him.

Finally, one evening he sat staring into the fire, as had become his habit. He noticed Will close to the firelight, fumbling with some fabric, and trying to thread a needle. "What is it you're doing, Son?"

Will jumped, startled by his father's voice. It had been so long since Jeremiah had taken notice, spoken, or asked a question. "It's Kitty's dress, Dad. She tore it. I'm trying to mend it for her," Will answered.

"Mend it?" Jeremiah was puzzled, but disinterested. His voice sounded hollow, as if it came from some distant place.

Jeremiah looked around the room. For the first time in months he noticed how dirty and ragged his children looked, their hair unwashed and unkempt. Jeremiah rose from his chair and walked through the house. He saw the half-made beds, the dirty dishes, the floors that needed cleaning. Even with the occasional help of Marìa Salazàr, and with Connie's willing hands, Will hadn't been able to keep up. Jeremiah suddenly realized how valiantly his eleven-year-old son was struggling to hold the family together.

"Oh, my God, our poor children!" Jeremiah exclaimed.

He stumbled to the door and went outside into the darkness. He laid his head against the wall, and finally the tears came. With deep, wrenching sobs, he cried out his anguish, and his shame. He had been so blind, so selfish in his grief.

"Ah, Molly, I'm so ashamed," he called up to the stars. "And you'd be so ashamed of me for neglecting these little ones. Please forgive me. God forgive me," he cried out through the torrent of tears.

When the shuddering sobs ceased and he got his breath, Jeremiah looked up and there, illuminated by the lamplight inside the house, stood the seven children in the doorway, their eyes fixed on him. Jeremiah went back into the house and sat in his chair. He called them to him.

"I've not been taking proper care of you," Jeremiah said in a shaky voice. "I'm so sorry." He took a deep breath. "That is changed, right now."

Tears were still running down his face as he apologized to them. "Will, you've been the man of the house, and I'm proud of you, and thanking you for it. Now I'll be helping you, and we'll bring some life and order back into this house as your mother would want. She loved you all so much that, as she was dying, she asked me to send for her sister, Catherine, your Aunt Cauth, to come and take care of you. I'll be getting to that very soon."

As he opened his arms the younger children eagerly and joyfully ran into them. They embraced Jeremiah and climbed into his lap. Their father had come back to them. He would love them, help them, protect them again. Will placed a hand on Jeremiah's shoulder and patted him, as if to show how manly he'd become. Connie stayed back until he beckoned to her and took her into his arms, too. But Little Jerry stood apart, unable to trust the father he felt had abandoned them all in their grief.

Jeremiah noticed Little Jerry's reluctance to come to him. "What's the matter, son?" he asked and reached out to pull him into the family group. But Little Jerry pulled away and refused to answer. Jeremiah watched his young son turn and run out of the room. He'll come around, he thought. It'll take a while, that's all. He's the sensitive one and his feelings run deep. He needs time. Jeremiah's big arms wrapped around the other children and he studied each closely, looking into their faces, tenderly patting a head or touching a cheek. "You dad's here," he said. "I'll be right here."

CHAPTER THIRTY-TWO

CATHERINE HURLEY STOOD in the doorway of the cottage at Ballydehob. She clutched a letter to her breast. She looked across the green fields, over the hedges and rock walls, past the tiny farming plots and the houses, all the way to the waters of the bay shimmering in the distance. But she didn't see them. She couldn't see anything past the tears.

Molly was dead!

Catherine couldn't believe it. Her mind refused to grasp the words Jeremiah had written, even though she'd read the letter a dozen times in the last hour. The words in harsh black ink on the white paper, damp with her tears and beginning to run.

Her beloved little sister, always so full of life—how could she possibly be dead? The mischievous girl who had shared her life growing up in the cottage in Coolnagurrane? Who kept up her spirits through the famine times. The girl who had left to become a woman, a wife and mother, and had continued to share her life with her sister through the eagerly-awaited letters they'd been writing to each other for more than twelve years. The tears kept streaming down Catherine's cheeks as she thought of a place more than five thousand miles away, one she'd never seen, but felt she knew. And there, seven children needed her. To be needed. Now that should be cause for joy. But there was no joy in this.

Of course she'd go. "Molly asked me to send for you. It was her dying wish," Jeremiah had written. And there was the postal money order, more than enough for a steamship from Cobh, and the train journey from Boston to a place called Gilroy. It was her duty to go, to be a mother to Molly's children, to care for them, and raise them as Molly would have done. But still Catherine was filled with conflicting emotions. There was deep sorrow at the death of her sister, and a sense of obligation to take her place raising the Cleary children, of course. But there was more than that, and Catherine tried to shut it out of her mind, to turn it away.

Deliverance, it was!

God save her, she thought. She felt a sense of deliverance because of Molly's death. She'd not be spending her life here, after all, unwanted in another woman's home, useless except for the comfort she could give her suffering neighbors, and the occasional happiness of being Aunt Cauth to Sheila's children. But they didn't need her and Sheila would be much happier with her gone. Moira, too, for that matter. Every time Catherine did the least thing for the cause, or spoke out against the injustices she saw around her, Moira looked at her with accusing eyes — blaming her because James was "rotting in prison."

What a wife she was for the fiery James, a whining woman with no gumption. Catherine was sure James would become involved in something, some rebel action, some protesting group, when he got out of jail. They'd be watching him, for sure, but James wasn't the one to humbly submit like the rest of these *gommach*, poor frightened fools that they were. She'd not be here to help him now, not that there was much a woman could do. She'd have a new purpose to her life, one she could perform. She could be a mother. And what else was it Jeremiah had written?

Catherine walked across the field and sat on the fence. She unfolded the crumpled letter. *To protect you, I offer you my name and my home shall be your home. I will provide for you as my wife.*

Now what was that? she wondered. Sure now, it meant marriage. He was suggesting it wouldn't be proper for her to live in his house on a far-off ranch and not be married. Catherine remembered Molly's words in her letters about what a fine and decent man Jeremiah was. And she certainly knew how generous he'd been to her family. They would soon be missing that. Maybe they'd be appreciating her a bit more when she wasn't there to give it to them. Catherine chided herself for this petty, uncharacteristic resentment.

She'd have to write to Jeremiah and let him know she'd accept his offer. This was March and she must wait until the worst of the Atlantic storms were over. She'd book an American ship from Cobh to Boston, if one was to be had, and stay a while with her brother John before attempting the long trip by the new railroad to California. Surely Jeremiah had written to the Hurleys about Molly. And she must let James know. But would a letter reach him in Kilmainham? She knew many of the letters to Fenian prisoners were never delivered.

Catherine was quiet during supper, but if the others noticed the strained whiteness around her mouth and the sadness in her eyes, they didn't comment. As Sheila rose to clear the table, Catherine said, "Wait. I have something to tell you all."

Sheila sat back down, but impatiently asked, "What is it now? More trouble for us?"

Catherine was silent, but a choked sob escaped her. She controlled herself, but still didn't speak. Kevin encouraged her, "What is it, Cauth? What troubles you?"

Catherine raised a grim face and replied, "My sister Molly is dead."

"What? What is this you're telling us?" They were all shocked and Moira put a sympathetic hand on Catherine's arm. "How? Where?" she asked.

"I have a letter from Jeremiah," a more composed Catherine explained. "He said Molly was killed by a wild bull. She was gored. He asked me to go to him and raise the children. It was Molly's dying wish."

Stunned, the two women and Kevin O'Malley stared at her. Finally, Sheila asked, "Will you go? To America? To California?"

"I will," Catherine replied. "He's sent the passage money. I'll be leaving as soon as the weather clears. I'll get to Cobh and find a ship."

It was quiet around the little table as they considered this momentous news. Finally Kevin asked, "But Catherine, you'll just be a housekeeper and nanny for seven children. Are you sure that's what you want?"

"I'll be needed," Catherine replied simply.

"Well now," Sheila injected, "there are certain proprieties, you know. It wouldn't be proper for an unmarried woman to share his home."

"Don't you be worrying about that," Catherine retorted angrily. "My virtue is my own. Besides, he's asked me to marry him."

"Oh," Sheila said. "And so soon after his wife's death?"

"For God's sake, woman, hold your tongue!" Kevin ordered. Catherine glared at Sheila and then shook her head—the woman wasn't worth answering. "Catherine will be going to do a wonderful thing, to care for Molly's family," Kevin stated emphatically. "We'll miss you, Cauth, and so will the cause around Ballydehob."

"Oh, the cause, the cause," Moira cried. "If it weren't for that cause, I'd have my husband with me."

But later she drew Catherine aside to admit, "I never had your strength, Cauth. You've held us all together. Thank you. I wish you all the best."

"I must get word about Molly's death and my leaving to James," Catherine said. "Callahan could get a letter in to him. But I don't know how to reach Callahan."

"I do," Kevin quietly admitted. Moira gasped, "Oh, dear God!" Sheila stared in amazement at her husband.

"I'll write the letter," Catherine said. Kevin nodded.

She went to bed that night knowing that the rebel spirit would still be alive in Ballydehob. Catherine lay awake on her straw pallet in her corner of the cottage and prayed for Molly. She silently said every prayer she could remember, anything to keep her mind off her own deliverance. But it was so quiet that a whisper from the O'Malley corner reached into her consciousness.

"Well, I don't care," Sheila muttered. "I'll be glad when she's gone."

"But you'll be missing the money," Kevin hissed at his wife.

Thank you, Kevin, Catherine thought. *And I'll be missing you.*

CHAPTER THIRTY-THREE

MATTHEW CLEARY WAS INTENT ON CATCHING A FISH. He crouched low behind a boulder and cast his line into the fast water below him, letting it carry the grasshopper impaled on his hook toward the shallow end of the pool where the trout lay feeding. The sunlight, filtering through the tall redwoods, glittered and danced on the water, illuminating the grasshopper as it skipped from shadow to light. Peering over the edge of the rock, Matthew could just make out the big rainbow. He held his breath as the fish made a run at the lure and felt the sharp tug when it hit. But he left the line slack and let the trout take it toward a clump of ferns at the end of the pool. Then Matthew struck back. He set the hook and the rainbow began to battle, racing back and forth across the pool, jumping into the air, fighting the hook, landing with a splash, but finally tiring in the shallows. Matthew threw down his laurel branch pole and took the line hand over hand, hauling in the fat trout, just over a foot long.

After cleaning the fish, he untied his line and tossed the pole aside, wound up the line and hook, carefully placing them in his pocket. Since he'd learned to fish for trout in the Sierras, Matthew was never without his line and a few hooks. That fish would make a fine supper. He walked downstream to his camp where his mule was staked to graze in a small, but lush meadow.

Matthew was camped on the headwaters of the Carmel River, at the foot of Ventana Double Cone, the mountain with the window in it. This was the same base camp he'd used the year before when he'd climbed Ventana to sight in on the shadow of the window. Although he couldn't read them, the words on his map were ingrained in his mind. *At one hour past high noon at the time of the Summer Solstice, the sun shines through the hole in the mountain and a shadow covers the entrance to the Lost Padres Cave.*

Last year he'd marked three spots deep in the canyon, but none of them had proven to be the entrance to any cave. Disgusted and discouraged, Matthew had gone back to Monterey to wait through another fall and winter, helping at a blacksmith shop in exchange for room and board. He wanted to return to Long Valley, make his peace with Jeremiah, be with Connie, but he couldn't. *How can I be going back without finding the treasure? I can't pay back my brother. I can't take Connie away and be a real father to her, buy her presents and a grand house in San Francisco. I can't fulfill any of my dreams until I find that treasure.*

So with the last of his money, Matthew bought an old mule to carry his pick and shovel, pot and frying pan, blankets and a few supplies. Besides, he'd need the mule to carry out the treasure. He'd named the stubborn animal Johnny Reb because it was always eyeing him, threatening to bite and kick, and balked most times when he led it. They'd taken the trail out of Carmel Mission and followed the river deep into the forest.

Reb greeted Matthew with a raucous braying when he arrived back in camp. "Shut up, you old bastard," was Matthew's response. He always had the feeling that Reb was laughing at him. "You're just like my brother, never a good word to say. I'll be showing you both. I'll find that cave and I'll fill your pack bags so full of gold you'll be groaning instead of laughing at me."

Matthew had been camped here all alone for a month now, marking off the days until the sun would be right. The solitary life was not for him—he missed people. Talking to the mule, singing songs to himself by the campfire after a few shots from his bottle, just left him morose and more lonesome than ever.

He wondered if Connie missed her daddy. And how Jeremiah and Molly and the children were. Connie was better off with them, he thought. "There're the only family I have," he told Johnny Reb one night, "and I want to be with them, too." Why did he always wind up in a wrangle with his brother? But that

238

one word Jeremiah had said about the treasure map—"bull-shit"—stuck in his head. What if Jeremiah was right? What if he'd really been a fool to buy a map to a cave that didn't exist for a treasure that never was?

No, he wouldn't allow himself to believe that. If he did, it would kill the dream, every dream he had. And dreams were *all* Matthew had. Tomorrow was the day. By his reckoning the summer solstice was tomorrow. Conditions would be exactly right for the shadow to mark the cave. Tomorrow he'd prove himself right and Jeremiah wrong. Then he could go home. Home to Long Valley and Connie.

Following deer trails and the ancient path of Indians to the ridge, Matthew climbed to the top where the natural bridge of earth connected the two peaks, forming the window from which Ventana got its name. Long before the sun was straight overhead, he was in position. As the sun climbed higher and higher, Matthew's excitement mounted. One hour after the sun reached its zenith, that was the time.

Stretching into every niche and cranny of the deep canyon below him, the shadows played tricks on Matthew. First one seemed to cast the image of the window and then another. He mentally marked the possibilities. There, by the dry gulch filled with manzanitas. No, there where it's dark and wet and the ferns climb the rock. By that old, gnarled oak, at the base of that cliff. Which was it? He checked again. And again. And the moving shadows teased him. The time passed.

It was late afternoon when he returned to Reb's greeting. "Don't you be laughing, you miserable old *aulaun*." Matthew told the mule. "I'll be finding it, if I'm having to check them all."

The next morning, leading a disgruntled Johnny Reb, Matthew climbed up out of the redwoods onto the hot hillsides where the shadows had led him. Tying the mule to a limb of a shady oak, he searched through the manzanita grove. When that failed to turn up a cave opening, he located the distinctive oak tree he'd marked in his mind. But two hours hunting around it left him tired and discouraged. There was one other possibility, the one with the ferns. Now where was that?

Dejected, ready to give up, Matthew finally spotted the rock surface with the ferns clinging to it. At first he could see no break in the face, no place for an entrance to a hidden cave. And then, suddenly, there it was, a crack covered by ferns, shaded by bay trees. But the crack was filled by rocks, some as big as boulders. Matthew hurried back to untie Reb and lead the unwilling beast forward, carrying the pick and shovel.

Through the heat of the afternoon, Matthew labored taking out the rocks, clearing the rubble from the entrance. It took all of his strength to roll the last boulder aside and disclose an opening large enough to enter. His heart thumping, his breath coming in gasps, Matthew crouched low and walked through on a sloping rock floor into a cavern. His eyes grew accustomed to the dim light and he quickly searched the interior. Nothing. Empty.

He was about to cry out in disappointment and frustration. But then he saw up ahead of him, at the far end of the cave, another opening. He hurried to it. Bent nearly double, he managed to enter. But it was pitch dark inside.

There was nothing he could do but go for his lantern. Since it was now late afternoon he'd have to come back the next day. Reb snorted in derision when Matthew came to lead him back to camp. He spent a sleepless night in anticipation of what he'd find in the morning. Would the second cave contain treasure chests spilling over with gold and silver coins, with precious jewels and golden chalices? Or would the horde be scattered over the cavern floor? How many trips would he have to make to Monterey with Reb's loaded pack to bring out the treasure? What if somebody stumbled on the cave before he could get it all cleared out?

He took time at dawn only for a cold biscuit and jerky, not wanting to waste time building a fire, and then carefully wrapped the lantern against breakage. He hurriedly threw the pack saddle on Reb and drew the cinches tight, despite the mule's vehement protests, and hung the bags over the saw-bucks. Matthew didn't bother with the canvas and lash and left camp at a trot, pulling the reluctant animal.

The cave was just as he left it. Matthew took the lantern from the pack and entered the first cave before lighting it. The light flickered and grew as the wick caught and he turned it up to cast a yellow glow before him as he stooped to enter the second cave. Inside, he lifted the light to shine all around. Matthew, his breath short, heart pounding, hands shaking, moved slowly into the center of the cave. The light danced on each small area, but didn't penetrate the blackness beyond. Gradually, slowly, he moved the lantern beam to illuminate every portion of the wall and the ceiling. Bare. It was all bare.

The air left Matthew's lungs in a deflated gasp. He slumped onto the rock floor, the lantern beside him. Matthew's dreams, the hopes he'd cherished, the possibilities he'd nurtured, all evaporated in the stale air of the cavern. He lay on the floor barely breathing. The rays from the lantern spread along the bottom of the cave and, at the far end, gleamed on something bright.

Matthew's eyes followed the weak rays. Suddenly, he saw it. His heart started pumping again, furiously. The hair stood stiff on the back of his head, a chill followed the course of his spine. He jumped up with a startled oath.

A skull grinned at him above the breastplate of a Spanish soldier.

"Jesus, Mary and Joseph," he whispered, and made the sign of the cross.

Matthew steadied himself, and a great joy filled him. Had this ancient soldier been left here to guard the gold and silver? Matthew raised the light and shone it into the face of the long-dead man. There was the breastplate, showing the rust of years, and shreds of leather that had once been boots and wisps of decayed cloth clinging to the bones. Lifting the lantern to survey the scene, Matthew saw other bones scattered about. And skulls. More than one person had died in this cave. But why? And where was the treasure chest?

It had to be here somewhere, he thought, and a new-found hope leaped into his breast. He hurried out to return with his pick and shovel. All the rest of that day he picked at the hard rock floor of the cave, tapped the walls for secret openings and banged on the ceiling. Gradually he came to accept the cruel fact that the cave, except for the skeletons of the long dead, was empty. A last whack on a protruding rock brought an echoing clang. He pulled the rock aside and a shovel fell to the cavern floor.

Matthew examined it. He couldn't believe what he saw.

It glinted brightly in the lantern light. It didn't have a speck of rust. The manufacturer's name was stamped on the hardwood handle. *J.P. Huggins, Chicago, Ill. 1867.* He couldn't read the words but he understood the date. Matthew dropped the shovel to the floor. "Gulled, by God," he muttered.

It didn't matter to Matthew what tragedy had occurred here in those ancient times. It had to be over gold and silver, but someone else had found it first. And then duped him into the bargain. He crawled from the cavern and left the dead to the ages.

A disconsolate Matthew Cleary packed up and led Reb on south toward the Los Burros country, panning the coastal streams as he went, checking the rock ledges with his pick. Gold. It was here somewhere. He couldn't go back until he found it.

CHAPTER THIRTY-FOUR

A LTHOUGH IT HAD BEEN THE RAILHEAD for more than a year now, the arrival of a train in 1870 was still an event in Gilroy. People began to gather, stepping from the depot out onto the platform, others strolling from the town toward the railroad tracks. Wagons and buggies gathered. Youngsters raced up and down, excited by the prospect of the big steam engine that would soon pull the line of cars into the station.

But Will, Little Jerry and Tim stood by their father, solemn and quiet. And stiff in their brand new clothing bought the day before in San Juan on a shopping trip with Emily Jefferson and their father. He'd overruled the idea of suits as impractical, and instead had Emily pick out overalls and shirts. There they stood, in clean work clothes, hair brushed under their broad-brimmed hats, pint-sized replicas of Jeremiah, anxiously looking up the tracks. The boys silently wondered about the woman they were waiting to meet. Would she be stern with them? Would she change things at the ranch? Would she be like Mama? Would she look like Mama? Would she gush all over them and want to hug and kiss them like Emily always did?

The expected whistle sounded in the distance and the excited youngsters up the track came running back to announce, "It's coming! The train's coming — !" Small in the distance at first, it grew larger and larger, and then was upon them, its whistle shriek blasting the sky. The huge beast, huffing and puffing, screeched to a halt, its sliding wheels sparking the tracks. Cinders flew about. Smoke billowed out of its stack. It stopped and sat there in front of them, hissing and breathing steam. And then the car doors opened.

The conductor and brakemen stepped out, porters placed step-stairs by each door. Passengers began to alight. The waiting crowd moved forward, and into the arms of arriving relatives and friends. But the Clearys stood back, apart from everyone. Jeremiah tried to watch the doorways of all four passenger cars. Would he recognize Catherine?

His heart leaped! Molly was stepping down from the train onto the depot platform! Molly was walking toward them! It was Molly, her head cocked with an inquisitive look. Jeremiah shook his head to clear out the vision. Of course, it wasn't Molly. But it was Molly's walk and she carried her head as Molly had.

But this was Catherine. She was taller than Molly, and thinner. She was dressed in black, with a black bonnet covering her hair. Of course, Jeremiah realized, she'd be wearing mourning clothes. He fingered the black ribbon encircling his arm. He stepped forward to greet her.

"Catherine."

"Jeremiah."

He took both her hands in his and they stood there, looking at each other, both fighting back the tears. Jeremiah thought she looked stern, her mouth set, until it relaxed in a bit of a smile. It was Molly's smile. Jeremiah dropped her hands and turned away. "Be greeting your Aunt Cauth, boys." His voice was gruff.

"How do you do, Aunt Cauth. Thank you for coming," Will said, stepping forward offering his hand with awkward formality.

Jerry looked at the platform floor, but managed, "How do you do, Aunt Cauth."

Tim raised his eyes and looked into those of his aunt. He could see she was a lot like his mother, with blue eyes that were warm and kind. He wanted to cry and to hug her. But he knew nine-year-old boys mustn't cry, and he didn't dare do any hugging and kissing in front of his brothers. He mumbled his greeting.

Catherine realized the boys had been well-rehearsed. She smiled as she watched them run off to retrieve her one bag from the platform and argue over who would carry it.

244

Jeremiah took her arm and led her to the surrey he'd borrowed early that morning from Weeb Jefferson. As the boys lifted up the bag and climbed into the back seat, Jeremiah helped Catherine into the front. They took the San Juan road. No one spoke. Jeremiah gave all his attention to the team, a matched pair of grays he'd once broken to harness and sold to Weeb. Catherine sat beside him. She didn't know what to say or how to ease the tension between them.

She finally ventured a question. "And how far is it to your ranch?" The soft brogue was so like Molly's, though it didn't have the same lilt to it. Her voice hit Jeremiah so hard he couldn't answer.

Sensing his father's discomfort, Will answered. "It's a long way, Aunt Cauth. We're going to the Jefferson place in San Juan for tonight and we'll leave tomorrow for our ranch in Long Valley."

"The Jefferson place, is it? Your mother wrote me about it," Catherine responded. "They're your good friends. But after that? Is your ranch far?"

"We'll have to camp on the way," Will explained.

"Camp, is it? And I've never been doing any camping. What is that now?" Catherine asked, smiling tentatively. She had struck a line of conversation that might work. Will told her they'd be four nights on the road and Dad would fix their meals over an open fire, and they'd all sleep on the ground, except Dad would make a bed for her in the wagon.

Catherine nodded. "That sounds just grand." She kept her doubts to herself. She glanced at Jeremiah, whose attention was doggedly on the road ahead. He was remembering a similar conversation with Molly nearly thirteen years before. He thanked God that he'd brought his sons along. *With them it's not the same. They make it different. I couldn't stand it, if it was the same.*

Will spoke up again, this time surprising Catherine with his words. "Dad says you and him will get married at San Juan mission in the morning before we leave. Will that make you our mother?"

"Well now, I suppose the exact way of it is I'll be your step-mother," Catherine replied. She wanted to explain that she'd be more like a nanny, not a real wife to their father. But it wasn't something she could make the children understand. "But I'm also your Aunt Cauth."

The three boys exchanged relieved looks. They'd not have to be calling her Mama. That would have been tough to do, no matter that she did look a bit like their mother. Little Jerry ventured a question. "Mama said you can play the tin whistle. Did you bring it?"

Catherine smiled at her nephew. "Sure, I did that. It's there in my bag, and I'll get it out to play a tune for you one night, perhaps while we're doing this camping. Your mother wrote me that you like music and have a fine singing voice, Jerry."

"Yes, ma'am."

"And you, Will, do you like to sing?"

"Ah, Aunt Cauth, I can't carry a tune. Mother said I take after Dad."

"I like to sing, Aunt Cauth." Tim spoke out, wanting to please his aunt and get in on the conversation. "But I don't really know many songs."

"Then I can teach you some."

They rode along in silence for a few minutes. Catherine could see out of the corner of her eye that Jeremiah was still not ready to join in the conversation. She turned again to Tim in the back seat. "Your mother wrote me that you are becoming a fine cowboy, Timothy. Be telling me about cowboys. We have cows in Ireland, and we have boys. But cowboys I'm not knowing."

"We ride horses and watch over the cattle," Tim explained, proud to be singled out for this important question. "We have to gather them and keep them from straying off our land. Sometimes we have to rope them with our *reatas*."

"Aw, you can't rope, Tim," Little Jerry scoffed. "He's just learning," he said to his aunt.

Tim glared at his brother. "Oh yeah, well I can rope as good as you — !"

Catherine interrupted in order to keep a fight from starting. "And you, Will, your mother said you can drive a team of horses, that you'll be as good a farmer as your da someday."

"Yes, ma'am." Will smiled at the compliment.

Catherine had been looking at the countryside as the horses trotted along. It was a beautiful spring day, the grass at its greenest, and there were wildflowers by the roadside. She thought the passing scene quite beautiful, not at all like the dry, treeless, wild and desolate place of Molly's early descriptions. She wondered if Long Valley would be like this?

"Please tell me about the ranch house, Will. And the ranch. What's the difference between a ranch and a farm? We have farms in Ireland. But no ranches."

"Well now," Jeremiah suddenly said, before his son could answer, "it's the size has something to do with it. Farms in Ireland are small. Ranches here are many acres. A rancher may do some farming. Most grow grain. But a rancher also runs a herd of cattle, and most of the ranch is open land for grazing. A farmer now, he just farms his grain."

"Ah then, you'd be a rancher, Jeremiah," Catherine said.

"Aye, that I would."

"And we also raise horses," Little Jerry chimed in. "We run a herd of mares and foals, both for work horses and cow horses."

"Cow horses!" Catherine exclaimed. "You're having fun with me, you are. How can an animal be both a cow and a horse?"

The boys let out whoops. Now that was a good one. They laughed. Then, not wanting to hurt Aunt Cauth's feelings, all three started at once explaining the term cow horse. Even Jeremiah smiled. He let Little Jerry explain. "A cow horse, Aunt Cauth, is a horse that has been specially trained to work cattle, to follow a cow."

247

Catherine looked a bit puzzled. What strange terms, she thought, work cattle and follow a cow? Why on earth would you be wanting to follow a cow? Follow her where?

"We call them cow horses because they're good at heading off cows." Will said. "They follow them, and when a cow turns to get away, our horses turn with them, and cut them off. We rope the cattle from our cow horses, and when we take our dallies around the saddle horn, our horse holds the cow right there. A good cow horse has to be well-reined and have a soft mouth, carry a spade bit, and react with just the touch of the reins on his neck," Will said, then added proudly, "Dad trains them."

Catherine pondered the strange expressions. Horns on saddles. Dallies. Reined. There was a lot she'd have to learn. But she'd not worry about it. She didn't come here to be a cowboy. "What about the girls and the baby?" she asked.

"They're with Marìa Salazàr," Will said. "Dad thought it was too far to bring them. Kitty wanted to come. She kicked up a great fuss because she wanted to see you."

"And me to see her. And Annie and Danny. And your cousin— Connie. I was wanting to see all of you," she added. "And it's grand I have such fine young men as my nephews."

They lapsed into silence. But now it was a comfortable silence. They were all more at ease, lulled a bit by the clip-clop of the horses' hooves on the well-traveled, hard-packed road. Tim broke the silence by asking, "Do you like dogs, Aunt Cauth?"

"Well, I've never had one. But I suppose I do."

"We have a dog," Tim said. "But he's getting old. His name is Bodach, that means clown in Irish." The boy grinned and glanced at Catherine. "He's a cow dog."

"Now don't you be starting that again, you young scamp!" Catherine laughed. "And I'm knowing Bodach must be named for a clown."

She smiled at Jeremiah, who gave her a perfunctory nod. They hadn't spoken any Irish yet and she was wondering

248

about that. "And I know you have an old horse named Bouchal, and that means boy, now doesn't it?"

"Aw, sure it does, Aunt Cauth," Will agreed. "Course you know Irish. But we don't know much. Dad doesn't want us to learn it. He says we're Americans." Catherine thought that strange and, again, looked over at Jeremiah, but his eyes were fixed on the horses' rumps. They put the miles behind them, and it wasn't quite dark when they pulled into the Jefferson yard. When Emily saw Catherine she burst into tears.

The next morning they were married at early Mass in the San Juan mission church. James McMahan again stood up with Jeremiah and his wife with Catherine, and Weeb and Emily Jefferson were in attendance, but there the similarities to his first marriage ended. Thank God for that, thought Jeremiah, as he stood before the altar beside his dead wife's sister.

Kneeling in the front row behind him were his three sons and in front of him at the altar was a different priest, a Franciscan he didn't know. There was no subdued gaiety as there had been with Molly. He had no knot of excitement in the pit of his stomach, nor the glow of pride he'd felt when he looked at his bride. The wedding vows in this mission church were so achingly familiar, yet so different today. This was a somber affair.

Catherine was dressed in her mourning black and Jeremiah had the black ribbon around his arm. Molly had been radiant in her wedding dress, her eyes sparkling, her mouth breaking into that mischievous grin. Molly had been bubbling with enthusiasm for life, but Catherine was quiet, solemn. Jeremiah wondered what she was thinking.

Catherine looked at him and was struck again by how straight and tall he stood, how strong he looked, and handsome, his features defined by grief, his mouth hardened in a grim line, his hair gray at the temples, his eyes troubled, but kind. She felt safe with Jeremiah. But this wedding was like nothing she'd ever imagined. *In those far off days when I let myself dream of marriage, it was a happy occasion, full of color, music and mirth, and to a man I loved who loved me. Here I am in a strange land before a strange priest who doesn't even speak my language, being married to my dead sister's husband, a man I can respect and serve, but who will never be a real husband to me. And I'll have care of a large brood of children not my own. God, help me love them and cherish them as Molly would. And let me be a good helpmate to Jeremiah.*

Catherine carried this thought through the wedding, suffered Emily Jefferson's weepy hug and the murmured good wishes of Weeb and the McMahans. She was grateful when Jeremiah helped her to the seat of the loaded wagon and the presence of the boys. Their chatter about San Juan, the river route, and their description of ranch life in Long Valley lifted Catherine's spirits. She answered the boys' questions about Ireland and her life there. But Jeremiah didn't say a word.

Cauth's voice, so very like Molly's, and her manner of speech so similar, brought too many memories—they only served to refresh his grief. Especially the memory of that first time with Molly, on this very trip, when he couldn't talk because her presence had him tongue-tied. This time he couldn't talk because the lump of sorrow stuck in his throat. He concentrated on the team and let the boys speak for him.

That evening he set up camp and built the fire while the boys cared for the team. Catherine tried to be useful, but not knowing what to do, finally sat down on a fallen log and admired Jeremiah's efficiency as he prepared supper. He allowed her to help wash dishes and they shared their first brief smile.

He showed Catherine to her bed in the wagon and lay awake long after the boys were sleeping soundly in their blankets by the dying campfire. The stars were glittering and the light of a half moon shone on the wagon standing in the clearing. The sound of a hoot owl in a dead oak nearby was all that broke the silence. Jeremiah's thoughts were of his wedding night with Molly and, when he finally dozed off, her presence was real, right there in camp with him.

He heard Molly calling him!

Jeremiah awoke with a start. He sat up, his heart racing. All was quiet. The campfire had died out. The moonlight had left the wagon in shadow. The owl atop the dead oak was now silhouetted against the sky.

Again it hooted.

CHAPTER THIRTY-FIVE

"No!" WILL CLEARY HAD A STUBBORN set to his jaw as he stood in front of his sister Annie. "Mama didn't spank us."

Catherine had reached for the racing Annie, who'd come skidding in from outside, across the wet pine floor, tracking dirt and scattering soap suds, just seconds after she'd warned all the children to stay out until the floors were dry. She was about to give Annie's bottom a sharp slap. But Will had suddenly positioned himself like a soldier on guard, the frightened Annie peeking around her brother's legs. Catherine's heart melted at the sight of the twelve-year-old boy protecting his baby sister.

"All right, Will," she conceded. "Annie will remember. Won't you, Annie?" Catherine bent down and coaxed the child into her arms. She hugged and kissed the girl who now cuddled against her breast. As she watched Will go back to his chores outside, she frowned.

"Mama didn't do it that way," was Will's standard judgment no matter what Catherine did around the house, from skimming the cream off the milk to putting up meat in the larder, from sweeping the floor to stacking the dishes. Everything she did, Will was watching her to make sure she did it right, or getting there a second before her, jumping in to do it himself. And always telling her how to care for the children.

"It's bedtime for Kitty and Annie," he'd announce before she'd think to send them off.

Or he'd notice Timmy's overalls needed mending, or tell Little Jerry to brush his teeth, or take Danny into the house for his nap, or lead his sisters by the hand to the outhouse. Dear God, what a sense of responsibility this poor little boy had developed. She could understand it. He seemed to have mothered them all when Molly was killed. It was a heavy burden for a young boy, but Will had manfully borne it. Still, she couldn't have him overruling her on everything, having the children look to him for guidance.

When the crisis with Annie had passed, Catherine called to Will and invited him to sit down. "Will," she said, " I need your help."

His serious, big brown eyes looked straight at her. "Sure, Aunt Cauth. What can I do?"

"Well, Will, I know that you've been the one in charge of things around here whenever your father isn't here and that you've been doing wonderfully well caring for your brothers and sisters. That's a big job for a boy. And now I'm here to help you."

Will nodded, intent on her face, wondering what she was getting at.

"Where I come from, Will, we don't have all the things that you have here. We don't have the different kinds of food or things to cook with, or wooden floors to sweep and wash and beds to make. So I must learn about all these things and you can teach me."

Will nodded again. "Sure, Aunt Cauth."

"The sooner I learn everything I have to do, and how to care for your brothers and sisters and cousin, the sooner you'll be free to go back to helping your father. I know he needs your help with the cattle and horses and the farming. So until you think I'm ready to handle the house and the children, you and I can be partners, doing things together. And when I've learned enough so you don't have to worry, you can turn it all over to me."

"Sure, Aunt Cauth," Will agreed. "I'll help you learn all this stuff. Dad does need me outside soon as I can be spared here."

"Well, that's grand, Will. I knew I could be counting on you," Catherine said with a smile. But the sigh of relief she kept to herself—she finally was on her way to taking charge of her new home.

That evening after the children were all asleep, Catherine said to Jeremiah. "He's a wonderful young man, Jerry, and so determined to carry the world on his shoulders. We're going to get on just fine now."

"And the other children?" Jeremiah wondered. "How do you fare with them?"

"Grand," said Catherine. "They've the same mischief as youngsters everywhere. Just like Sheila's were in Ballydehob. But, Jerry, it's Connie that worries me a bit."

"She's not obedient?"

"No, Jerry, just the opposite," Catherine explained. "She's obedient and willing for any task I set. Too willing. It's as if she's always after earning her keep, that she's doesn't feel she's one of the family."

Jeremiah was disturbed. "But Molly loved her, never showed a difference between her and the others. Nor have I."

"I'm thinking it's her father caused it," Catherine said. "We were doing the dishes last night and she confided in me. 'When my father comes for me,' she said, 'we'll have servants to do the dishes and we'll be living in a big house in San Francisco.' I've heard the other children scoff at her for expecting Matthew to come back and take her off to some grand life — "

"Aye, it's the others who have the right of it, I'm thinking," Jeremiah interrupted. These days the mention of his brother always set him off. And it upset him even more to realize that Matthew had filled the child's head with his grandiose nonsense. Jeremiah wanted to change the subject. "Cauth," he said, "as far as Will is concerned, I'll have more for him to do helping me. That'll keep him out of the house."

It wasn't long before Will began attending to the work horses, helping his father in the fields and riding with him to check cattle. He grew far less concerned about how his aunt was maintaining the house and managing the children. Occasionally, Catherine would catch the boy's eye on her as she mended clothing, or cut up vegetables, or helped the girls get dressed. But now he'd give her an approving grin.

Her fastest way to win over the children, though, was to bring out her tin whistle and play tunes for them. They were learning some of the old songs from Catherine, and remembered some Molly had sung with them. Though Jeremiah listened, he couldn't tell one song from the other, but he could clap his hands to the jigs and reels that Catherine played. How she got music out of that little pipe was a mystery to him. And she played it so fast. Especially the one they all liked, the *Kerry Polka*. He had to smile remembering the night little Kitty had slipped down out of his lap to kick up her chubby legs and do the dance steps Molly had taught her to that very tune.

Jeremiah watched as Catherine played. The music brought out the fun in her, the sternness around her mouth had melted into a smile, her brow was unfurrowed, her eyes sparkled like Molly's. Well, not just like Molly's, he thought, but there was now happiness in them sometimes. He gazed for a moment at her body, full and graceful, as she did the steps or swayed to the music. He caught himself thinking that his wife was an appealing woman.

Wife? Well, sure now, and she is my wife. But I mustn't think of her that way. She was his dead wife's sister. It would be unfaithful to Molly's memory. Wouldn't it?

He'd wondered if Catherine would accept him. A touch as they passed, an intimate smile, that special concern she showed for his welfare made him think she might. And that time he'd felt her eyes on him as he worked with the colt.

Catherine was interested in everything that happened on the ranch. It was all so new and exciting to her. She'd taken a respite from her chores one day and was watching at the corral fence when Jeremiah caught the new colt. He was demonstrating for the boys how to handle a newborn. He picked up the spindly-legged little thing as its worried mother nickered from her stall. Jeremiah ran his hands around the colt's belly and lifted it into his arms. He carried it to the fence in front of Catherine and put it down, straddling it, holding it between his legs, softly talking to it, stroking it.

She watched his hands, so strong and capable, callused, work-worn hands, but kind, gentle hands, she thought. They played over the colt's body, around its neck, petting the head, over its back, down its legs.

"I do this to teach the colt not to fear me, that my hands won't hurt," he explained to her. Catherine was fascinated by those hands as she followed their every stroking movement. She was as soothed by them as the relaxed colt.

"Here, Cauth. You be doing it," Jeremiah invited. Will opened the gate for her and she entered the corral. She knelt by the colt, tentatively put out a hand and touched the soft muzzle. She stopped, as if afraid to do more. Jeremiah took her hand in his and rubbed it across the colt's back, its withers, around the legs. His hand was firm, but gentle and warm. She imagined that hand on her own body. Catherine looked up into his eyes. Just for a moment, she thought he imagined that, too.

CHAPTER THIRTY-SIX

IT WAS ONLY MID-AFTERNOON, but Catherine was exhausted. She had gone into the bedroom and flopped down on the bed. She wondered how her little sister had managed to do all the things that needed doing on the ranch. She had always been the stronger of the two, but here she was for ten months now, tired, sore and aching all over, all the time.

In Ireland there hadn't been that much to do around the cottage and there were three women to do it. She'd helped in the fields, but had never worked this hard, every day, all day. Then in the evening after supper the children wanted her to play tunes for them on her whistle, or sing the old songs, and she hardly had the energy for it.

She let herself lay down on the bed, just for a minute, she cautioned herself. But, oh, it felt so good.

It was a lovely feather bed. But Catherine always felt a pang of guilt when she sank into it. This had been Molly's bed. It was in this bed that she'd slept with Jeremiah. Here is where her younger sister had learned the secrets of marriage, felt those hands on her body, shared the love of her man, conceived their children. Catherine felt the heat rising in her own body at the images that were rioting in her mind.

But then she realized that Molly had given birth to her children, and ultimately died in this same bed. Catherine's vision of two people entwined in lusty embrace instantly faded away. She felt ashamed and humiliated for having such thoughts, for being unfaithful to her dear, dead sister.

Stop it, Catherine Hurley, she scolded herself. She looked about the room. Her room now. "I'll be putting your things in this room," Jeremiah had told her as he carried her one bag from the wagon when they first arrived at the ranch. There wasn't a trace of Jeremiah left in the room. But Molly's touches were everywhere. The picture of Jesus, Mary and Joseph above the bed, the big chest that still held some of her clothes, the rag rug on the floor, a small mirror on the wall, the vase that held wildflowers. Catherine had to smile at that.

The flowers were Kitty's offering. She'd picked them on the hill behind the house, poppies and lupine, blue and gold, and placed them in her hand. "Mama liked me to bring her flowers," explained the little girl. "Would you like them, too, Aunt Cauth?"

Hot tears had sprung to Catherine's eyes. "Thank you, Kitty. The flowers are lovely." She'd quickly turned so Kitty wouldn't see her tears and filled the vase with water from the bucket, arranged the flowers, and placed them on the chest by the bed. The flowers were long wilted now, Catherine noticed.

She took a deep breath, stretched and rubbed her arms. She had to be back to work or the children might think she'd taken ill. Catherine walked into the main room with the big cast-iron, wood-burning stove, the fireplace with its mantlepiece, and the place for Jeremiah's rifle, gone now with him off hunting a deer. There was the bewildering assortment of pots and pans hanging from the wall, and she was still learning what to do with all of them. The big table stood in the center of the room, and around it enough chairs for all. Catherine again shook her head at the luxury of such things. There was a door into the little room where Connie, Kitty and Annie slept, and through that the boys' room with its outside door, in which Jeremiah had constructed a loft for Will and Little Jerry. He'd made a trundle bed for Danny under Tim's, and placed a bunk for himself in that small room. Awkward and uncomfortable, he'd slept there ever since he'd brought Catherine to Long Valley.

Catherine adjusted the blankets, the comforters and quilts, lingering a moment to fluff up Jeremiah's pillow, then she swept the hard-packed dirt floor. She was grateful these rooms didn't have a pine wood floor to scrub. And the garden. That Molly had been a wonder. Catherine admired all the evidence of her sister's industry. Since her death, it hadn't been kept up, but now the boys were helping to put in the corn and potatoes.

Kitty and Annie watched over the chickens and gathered the eggs. Tim took care of the pigs, and Will and Jerry milked the cows. Two of them were in milk just now, and that meant hours at the churn for Catherine if they were to have butter. And Jeremiah did like his buttermilk.

Catherine stood in the center of the room and looked around. She could be doing some ironing. But that would mean building up a fire to heat the irons. It was too hot for that. She also must decide what to cook for supper. This was always a problem for her. With such a variety of food available, she was always intimidated by its preparation. Then she became angry with herself for being ungrateful. *You had nothing in Ireland and you complained. You have everything here and you're still complaining.* She ran the choices through her mind. Venison steak? There was still some in the larder. But they'd had it last night. And before that was ham. A stew? Too late to start one now. What were those things Marìa Salazàr had sent over? Something with meat and cheese. *Enchiladas*, she'd called them. They had to be eaten.

That settled, Catherine's eyes again roamed the room. They focused on the huge tub standing against the far wall. All was quiet in the house, except for the buzzing of a fly against the window. Jeremiah was off in the hills and the boys were cleaning the barn. Connie, Kitty and Annie were playing outside, and Danny was still sound asleep. She checked the fire and the big kettle of water. Hot enough, she decided, and it was a warm spring afternoon. *Catherine Cleary, you'll be indulging yourself.*

She carried the huge tub to her bedroom, placed it on the floor, and poured hot water into it. She felt a brief twinge of guilt—all that work that needed to be done. She added enough cold water to make it just the right temperature and quickly took off her clothes. Gingerly she lowered herself into the tub. With her knees to her chin she could just fit. Catherine relished the feel of the warm water on her body. With her hands she scooped it up and poured it on her firm, full breasts, her knees, let it flow across her smooth stomach.

She stood up in the tub and found her bar of soap, lathered it in her hands, and ran them down her long legs, over her belly, between her legs. She soaped her breasts, cupped them, and felt the nipples harden at her touch. She imagined, for a fleeting moment, Jeremiah's head against her bosom. She sat back down in the tub and soaked for a moment. She rinsed off and stood up, dripping into the tub.

Catherine reached to the back of her head and took out the pins, letting her long, black hair fall below her shoulders. *Jeremiah now, if he should see me like this, would he think of me as a woman? I'm thirty seven-years old, but no hag.* She ran her hands down her sides and across the curve of her hips. *I could be carrying babies there.*

She was startled to hear a door slam. Her heart thumped. She hurriedly covered herself with the towel. Was it one of the children? Could it have been Jeremiah? The bedroom door was open a crack. Could he have seen her?

She began to dry off with the towel. And she began to cry. She was mourning Molly, but she was coveting her dead sister's husband. Her husband now. But in name only. And yet this was the man she was beginning to love. To be in love with.

She was so confused. She'd better think of the children—they were her purpose in life, to care for Molly's children, not to be yearning for what she couldn't have. She pinned her hair back and took out the black dress. She'd wear her mourning dress. She'd be reminding herself of Molly. Catherine dropped to her knees and prayed for the strength to do her duty.

That night a pine log crackled and sent sparks up the chimney, its red glow gleaming across the room where Catherine was darning the boys' socks. Jeremiah watched her, trying to erase from his memory that glimpse he'd had of her nakedness.

Supper had been good, he thought. Catherine was starting to get the knack of cooking. Jeremiah looked over at his sons and his niece, who were reading their books by the lamplight. Kitty and Annie were playing with the dolls Catherine had made for them. Jeremiah was very aware that the house was orderly, the children happy, loved and well cared for. She'd been grand these past ten months, he realized. And it hadn't been easy for her, what with everything so different here, so strange for her. Jeremiah couldn't help but be grateful for the way she took to the children, and they to her. She'd even managed to win over Will, who was now her staunchest ally.

His reverie was broken by Little Jerry's voice. The boy looked up from McGuffy's Reader with a question. But it wasn't about today's lesson. "Why did the British starve the Irish, Aunt Cauth?"

"Well now, Jerry, it wasn't that they started out to starve us. It just worked out that way," Catherine explained. "They didn't think we were human. They didn't treat us like people. They owned all the land and charged us rent for it. All our animals and our crops were sold to pay the rent and we had only potatoes to eat. When the blight destroyed all the potatoes we had nothing to eat."

"Oh," Jerry said. It was obvious he'd been thinking of this and not the story in his reader. "Why did they own all the land?"

"Because they conquered Ireland and took the land for themselves," Catherine answered. "Ireland was once one of the best, happiest places in the world before a man named Cromwell killed thousands of Irish and made serfs of the rest. Ours was a country of scholars, poets and — "

Jeremiah interrupted. "Be getting back to your lessons, Jerry. And the rest of you, too."

He wished Catherine wouldn't tell such stories about Ireland. About the damnable British, and famine times, and the rebel cause. They don't need to know all that. They're American children. *I put that behind me, and it's something much better I'm building here for my children.* Catherine shouldn't put those ideas in their heads. He'd try once more to explain that to her, tonight after the children were asleep.

Watching her now, her face lighted by the fire and the lamp, Jeremiah was struck again by her resemblance to Molly. It must be something in the way she acts, he decided. It wasn't her face, so much. Although her eyes were that same blue, they didn't have the same mischief in them. Her nose was different and there weren't the freckles. Her mouth now, that was firmer, sterner. Until she smiled. Then it was Molly's smile and that tore at his heart. Catherine was taller, too, and slender. And her hair wasn't curly. Tied up in a bun that way, it made her look severe. But when she took out the pins, and shook it loose, letting it cascade down her back as he'd seen her do several times, yes, then she became quite a handsome woman.

The image of Catherine standing up in the tub, her back to him, her long hair hanging down, returned to him, but he shook it off. There were so many images of Molly in his mind there was hardly any room for Catherine. A year and a half had passed since Molly's death, and she was still with him. Walking beside him as he plowed, bringing him dinner to the field as he reaped, with him as he rode horseback after cattle, and always in the wagon wherever he went. But no matter how hard he tried he couldn't bring an image of Molly to his bed. He was achingly lonely there.

He called Connie and the boys to him to check their lessons. They were studying the Constitution and the Bill of Rights, and Jeremiah was hammering hard on the liberties Americans enjoy. "This is a democracy, boys, and one man is as good as the next. And when you reach voting age, be proud of your vote and don't give it thoughtlessly." They'd heard this particular theme many times and could repeat it word for word, especially Will, who loved learning about politics and history. "Now who can tell me the first amendment in the Bill of Rights?" Jeremiah asked his children.

Will held his tongue to let Timmy answer, "Freedom of religion, speech and of the press."

"Right, Timmy. But what else?"

"Ah — ah — ," then it came to him in a rush. "The right of assembly and petition."

They went through the amendments, each youngster contributing in turn—bear arms, private property, no search and seizure, trial by jury—"These rights mean you'll never be tugging at your forelock and bowing to any man," Jeremiah declared proudly.

Little Jerry was quick with his lessons, Jeremiah thought, eager to learn, but there was something about the boy which worried his father. *He reminds me a bit of my brother, Matthew. A dreamer, God help him, with big ideas and romantic notions.* Perhaps it had to do with the music in Jerry and the fact that he was far too interested in Catherine's stories of Ireland, clinging to every word about the rebel cause and Irish bravery.

It was time for prayers and Jeremiah led them, first the rosary, and then all the God blesses, especially for Mama in heaven. He looked up to see Catherine lift Danny, who'd fallen sound asleep by the fire. "You'll be coming now, too, girls," she called. "Time for bed." Kitty and Annie slid out of their father's lap, where they'd curled up after prayers, and Connie got up from the floor where she'd been at Jeremiah's feet since the lessons.

"You boys, as well," Jeremiah said. "Big work day tomorrow." They put aside the McGuffy Reader and the history books. "I'll need you to help with the team in the morning. We'll be needing six-up, so hitch old Nellie and Maud with Block and Chip, and put those black colts in the middle," Jeremiah instructed.

The children were bedded down for the night and Jeremiah was just tamping out the bowl of his last pipeful when he looked up and saw Catherine. She was walking toward him in her nightdress, her long hair loose, floating down her back. She came right up to him and stopped. Their eyes locked together. They were both very still, each afraid to move. Jeremiah thought she looked beautiful in the glow of the firelight.

"Jerry," Catherine finally said, her voice almost a whisper, "I know that you're still mourning Molly. And I'm mourning her, too. But — " Catherine took a deep breath, " — I'm a woman, and your wife, and I'm wanting babies of my own — and — " Her voice was shaking so she lapsed into silence as she searched his face for a hint of the same feelings she had.

Jeremiah stared at her for a moment. Then he got up, walked past her and out of the room. Catherine was mortified. She was too ashamed to cry. She hurried to her room and shut the door. She lay, curled on the bed wondering that she could have done such a thing. How she could have asked him and been refused. She didn't know how she'd ever face him again.

Her tears had just begun to fall when the bedroom door opened slowly. Jeremiah stood there on the threshold in his nightshirt. He went to the bed, reached out with both hands and lifted Catherine off the bed. He noticed how tall she was when he gently pulled her against him. Taller than Molly. But the fleeting thought left him as quickly as it had come. He ran his hands through Catherine's long hair, pushing it back from her face so he could look into her eyes. With his fingertips he traced her forehead, her eyelids, down her cheeks and across her mouth.

"Ah, Cauth, Cauth. You're a lovely woman. And you are my wife." He held her tighter, his voice an urgent whisper. "And I want you."

She raised her lips to be kissed. And gave herself up to whatever happened next.

CHAPTER THIRTY-SEVEN

"Aunt Cauth — ! Aunt Cauth — ! Some men are here." Seven-year-old Kitty ran into the house, spilling the bucket of water she had just drawn from the well.

Catherine Cleary looked up from her scrub board. "Who could that be?" she asked. She stretched and grabbed at the small of her back with both hands. Her swollen body made her back ache mercilessly, no matter what she did to try and relieve it. Catherine, at thirty-eight years of age, was carrying her first child, and trying terribly hard to bear it well, despite the constant tiredness and discomfort that attended her night and day.

Well, if the men were here to see Jeremiah, they'd just have to wait, Catherine thought, wiping her hands dry on a dish cloth. This day he had taken Will and Timmy with him, with a load of redwood stakes, up into the canyon to build fences. But not Little Jerry, who disliked fence building. He was staying at the Garcia place, helping Felipe and Juan search for wild cattle in the high country.

Kitty was tugging at her skirt, "Hurry, Aunt Cauth." And Connie, who'd been playing outside with Annie and Danny, pushed the youngsters into the house, a frightened look on her face. "Men out there!" the wide-eyed Danny exclaimed.

Catherine wasn't prepared for the sight that greeted her. The large Mexican *sombrero*s and the *bandoleros* filled with bullets were the first things she noticed. Then she saw the fierce-looking mustaches, the dusty *vaquero* clothing, and the tired horses. There were five men. Some carried rifles in their hands, others had the weapons tucked into scabbards on their saddles. All of them wore holstered pistols.

"*Buenas tardes, señora.*" A small man, dapper even with the grime of hard riding all over him, swept off his big hat, and bowed from his saddle. "Good afternoon."

264

The others dismounted and, without asking permission, led their horses to the water trough. One of the men hauled a bucket of water from the well, and they all took turns drinking, spilling water, pouring it on each other, splashing, and laughing. The leader was still astride his horse. He rode a large, handsome black with white stockings to the water trough and let him drink, all the while looking into the corral where Jeremiah's colts were caught up. He studied the horses.

"*Señora,*" he announced. "My men are hungry. You would feed us, perhaps?"

It was phrased in broken English, but Catherine understood it. This wasn't a question. It was a demand! Catherine nodded, realizing these men were dangerous and she'd have to keep her wits about her. She sent the girls into the back room, Connie taking Danny by the hand and silencing his questions.

Without waiting for an invitation, or even a reply, the men tied their horses to the hitching rail and along the yard fence, and strode into the house, their spurs jangling noisily on the wood floor. They slapped the dust from their clothes and sat down at the table, their rifles by their sides. The small man, the leader, pulled a chair over and joined them, staring at Catherine. He took in her pregnant figure, nodded approvingly and smiled. A wave of his hand indicated the stove, and he sat back. "*Carne, por favor,*" he politely insisted. Cauth had been around the Salazàrs enough to know this meant meat. At least he's saying please, she thought. Perhaps if she just fed them, they'd go away.

She went to the crock, took out venison chops, removed the lard, and placed them in the frying pan. She bent over to pick up a stick of wood to add to the fire and found the small Mexican by her side, picking up the wood, and feeding the fire. He bowed to her and went back to his seat. The others watched Catherine intently, one of them getting up occasionally to look out the door, up and down the valley. Catherine had some beans on the stove and stirred them. She cut slices of bread and placed them on the table with the freshly-churned butter.

The only sound in the room was that of the chops sizzling in the skillet. Catherine noticed the children peeking in the door, watching wide-eyed, and sent them back to their room with a frown and a wave. She placed the pot of beans on the table, put the chops on plates, and handed one to each of the men. One man grabbed her hand and pulled her toward him. Catherine's heart began to pound. A sharp reprimand from the leader stopped him and he let her go.

"*Vino*," demanded another.

"We have no wine," Catherine said, "but we have buttermilk."

"A baby's drink," scoffed the one who had grabbed her. He cursed and again was admonished by the leader.

Frightened, Catherine stepped back and stood by the stove. She watched the men eat. They were crude, sloppy, scarfing down the food. Except for the leader, who chewed slowly, enjoying the meal, his eyes roaming around the room. He noticed the Spencer hanging above the fireplace, rose and walked to it. Taking it down, he looked it over carefully, levered the action, sighted it on Catherine, and laughed at her startled gasp. He replaced the rifle and sat back down to finish his meal. Catherine was now terrified but tried desperately not to show it. Then her anger quelled her fear. Anger at this intrusion, at the demands of these uncivilized men. If only they'd finish their meal and leave before Jeremiah returned with Will and Tim. She feared for the safety of her family. What would Jeremiah do if he found these ruffians in his home? Maybe they were bandits.

"Your husband, *señora*. Where is he?" the leader asked.

Catherine, her heart still beating too fast, wasn't sure how to answer. She settled on the truth. "Up the canyon, building fence. He'll be back soon."

Perhaps they'll finish eating and leave if they think Jerry might be coming, she thought. It seemed to work. They scraped back their chairs and rose from the table, their boots clumping on the floor as they strode through the doorway and into the yard. "Dear God, let them leave," Catherine's lips silently formed the words as she watched them.

They went to their horses. Catherine quietly let out a small sigh of relief. But what were they doing? Unsaddling? Why would they do that? They took their *reatas* off the saddles and entered the corral. To Catherine's wide-eyed astonishment, each Mexican swiftly roped one of Jeremiah's colts, the ones he'd been breaking to rein, the ones nearly ready to sell, the three grays, the bay and the sorrel. They left Bouchal.

"*Demasiado viejo*," one said with a laugh. "Too old."

The horses were caught with little effort, each being well-trained to the rope, and by the time Catherine realized what was happening, the Mexicans' own tired mounts had been turned into the corral. Jeremiah's horses were being saddled.

"No — !" Catherine yelled furiously. She ran from the doorway straight toward the little man—the leader who was lifting his saddle onto one of the grays. She beat on his back with her fists. "No! No — ! You can't take my husband's horses!" she shouted and pounded on him.

He turned and grabbed her by the arm. With his other hand he slapped her. Slapped her hard, across the face. Then he shoved her away. Catherine stumbled and fell heavily.

"*Gracias por la comida, señora*," he said. "But you must not get in my way — not ever!"

Catherine sprawled in the dust. She barely missed being trampled by the horses as the riders swung into the saddles and yelled, leaving the yard in a clatter of hooves, at a gallop up the Peach Tree Road. Catherine lay there a moment, then started to get to her feet. She was on her hands and knees, watching the riders disappear with Jerry's horses, when the pain struck her. It hit her so hard she lost her breath, so hard she couldn't rise. She was gasping when Connie ran out to her.

"Aunt Cauth, what's the matter? Did he hurt you?" Now Kitty was by her side, too, trying to help her stand up. Annie and Danny came running, frightened, crying at what had just happened.

"It's all right, it's going to be all right." Catherine tried to soothe them but could barely get the words out, her breath coming in quick, short gasps. She struggled to her feet and put her fist into her mouth to keep from screaming in pain. Connie and Kitty helped her into the house and to the bed. She mustn't frighten the children. That was her last thought before passing out.

She was there on the bed, moaning as Kitty applied wet cloths to her forehead, when Jeremiah came home. "My God, Cauth, what happened?" He bent over her, then knelt by the bed, taking her hand.

"The baby, Jerry. It's coming a bit early," Catherine murmured between labor pains. "I had a fall. You'd best get *Señora* Garcìa."

"Daddy, some bad men were here," Annie explained. "They made Aunt Cauth cook for them and they took our horses."

Jeremiah dropped Catherine's hand and hurried to the door. He looked over at the corral and studied the horses, all strangers except for Bouchal. He came back to the bedroom and again knelt by the bed. "Who were these men?" he asked, his mouth pulled taut.

"I don't know, Jerry. Mexicans. They had rifles and pistols. They called the leader Tiburcio, a small man." Catherine gasped out the words. "He's the one who pushed me."

"When were they here? How long ago did they leave?"

"About noon. They made me fix them dinner. They were here about two hours," Catherine said as another spasm gripped her.

"Aunt Cauth tried to stop them from taking the horses," Kitty told her father. "That's when he hit her."

Jeremiah felt his anger rise, enraged at the thought of someone stealing his horses. Jeremiah straightened up from the bed. He quickly went into the main room and took down his Spencer, loaded it, filled his pocket with shells, and went out the door. He started for the corral to get Bouchal. But there was the wagon, standing in the yard, Chip and Block still in harness. Will and Tim were standing by, awaiting instructions. When Jeremiah saw them, he stopped, turned uncertainly, and looked back at the house.

"My God," he said aloud. "What am I doing?" He was about to ride off on Bouchal, in a red haze of fury, tracking the Mexicans who had stolen his horses, and there was his wife in the pain of childbirth. What sort of a man had he become? He looked at the rifle in his hands and then at the boys.

"Will, you be helping Connie care for your Aunt Cauth and the little ones. Tim, take Bouchal and ride down for Calistro and Marìa." Jeremiah placed the Spencer on the wagon seat and ran back into the house.

He leaned over Catherine and stroked her hot brow. "Cauth, I'm leaving now. I'll bring back Sophia Garcìa. She'll know how to ease you." Catherine nodded and closed her eyes. He patted her hand and kissed her on the forehead. Then he whispered in her ear, "I'm so sorry this happened, but everything is going to be all right now, I promise, Cauth."

CHAPTER THIRTY-EIGHT

IT WAS DUSK WHEN JEREMIAH crossed the dry river bed of the San Lorenzo and pulled up at the Garcias' house. Felipe and his son, Juan, and Little Jerry were outside to greet him as he climbed down from his wagon.

"Hello, Dad," Little Jerry said running up to his father. "What's happened? What're you doing here?"

"It's your Aunt Cauth. It's her time for the baby — "

"Is she all right? Is Aunt Cauth all right?" Jerry demanded.

"Sure, she'll be fine. " He turned to Felipe, his voice shaky with rage. "Some *banditos* stole five of my horses this afternoon. They came this way. Any sign of them?"

"No *Señor* Jerry, we've been in the mountains," Felipe replied. "These *banditos*, what did they look like?"

"I didn't see them. They forced Catherine to cook dinner for them, and left their worn-out horses in my corral, and took my colts, the ones I've nearly finished." Jeremiah's face was flushed with anger.

"These horses left in your corral, *Señor* Jerry, there was perhaps a large, black gelding with white stockings?" Juan asked.

"Aye, there is such a horse."

"Ah, Vasquez!"

"Vasquez?"

"*Si, señor*, I believe that would be Tiburcio Vasquez and some of his men. It is known that he rides a black horse with white stockings," Juan said excitedly.

"By God, that's him. Catherine said they called their leader Tiburcio. He struck her! Knocked her down when she tried to stop them from stealing my horses!"

"The *cabrón*!" Juan said contemptuously.

"I know of him!" Felipe exclaimed. "Everyone knows of him. He and his band rob stage coaches and rich travelers. They are said to hide in a cave up in the Jolon country. Sometimes we see them crossing over through here to visit with their friends by the New Idria mine. They've been seen around San Juan and Gilroy, too."

"These are *muy malo hombres*, *Señor* Jerry," Juan added.

"Bad men, are they?" Jeremiah said. "I'll be looking them up and getting my horses as soon as I take your wife back to help Catherine."

"I'll go with you, Dad," Little Jerry said. "I can shoot!" But Jeremiah walked off toward the house, calling over his shoulder, "You stay here and help the Garcias." Sophia Garcìa waited for him on the porch. He took off his hat and greeted her, explaining with his limited Spanish, that Catherine was having the baby.

There were lights at the Cleary ranch as Jeremiah turned the horses into the lane. He'd half expected to come home to a dark house with everyone sleeping and a new baby by Cauth's side. He'd thought of Sophia Garcìa simply as a precaution. Molly had hardly needed her help, the babies came that quickly. Marìa Salazàr opened the door, holding the lamp as they climbed down from the wagon. She spoke rapidly in Spanish to Sophia and the two women hurried in to the bedroom.

Jeremiah busied himself with the team, unhitching in the dark. He led Chip and Block to the barn and found the lantern. He unharnessed the big work horses, and hung the collars on their pegs, arranging the harness for its next use, and forked hay into the mangers. Maybe by the time he finished in the barn, the baby would be here. Would it be a boy or a girl? Jeremiah smiled to himself. Another girl would be grand. But so would a boy. Boys were a great deal of help on a ranch.

Jeremiah headed toward the house, carrying the lantern, expecting to hear the cry of a newborn any moment. Then he heard them, the familiar birthing sounds coming from the bedroom, the heavy breathing, the subdued cries, Sophia Garcia's encouraging words. What was happening? Was there trouble? Jeremiah went to the door, opened it a crack and looked in. He was shocked to see Catherine writhing in pain, her body drenched in sweat, her face contorted. Sophia Garcìa was wip-

271

ing her forehead with water from a bucket. She looked up at Jeremiah's anxious face.

"*Està bien, Señor* Cleary," she assured him. "A little longer. Sometimes it takes a little longer. You go now. Sleep. *Sera la puerta, por favor.* Shut the door so as not to wake the children."

Bien, she tells me. But it doesn't look very good to me, Jeremiah thought as he obediently shut the door. Poor Cauth. She was suffering so. He didn't remember Molly ever having it this hard. What's happening? He stretched out on his old bunk in the boy's room and finally dropped off into a troubled sleep. He came awake with a start when the rooster crowed in the chicken house at the first crack of dawn. For a second he thought it was that time long ago when Molly had brought the chickens into the house. Then he suddenly sat straight up in bed, aware of the present and of what was happening, and listened for a baby's cry. There was no sound. Jeremiah hurried to the bedroom door just as it opened and Sophia Garcìa came out holding her finger to her lips.

"Shh," she cautioned. "The *señora* is sleeping for a moment. She is so tired. Nothing is happening, *señor.* Sometimes it is that way with a woman who is having her first at such an age. *Quantos años tiene la señora?*"

"She's thirty-eight-years old," Jeremiah replied. "My God, is that too old for her to be having a baby?"

"No, *señor.* But sometimes it is harder for the woman. It takes longer." Sophia Garcìa slumped down in a chair, letting Jeremiah put on the coffee pot and start fixing breakfast. He wished Marìa Salazàr was still here to do this, but she had to return to her own children the night before.

Catherine appeared to be sleeping when Jeremiah looked in on her, but suddenly she stiffened with pain. Her hands clenched. She stifled a cry. He hated to see such suffering. She immediately fell back into an exhausted sleep. She looks so tired, he thought. He shut the door softly and went back to help prepare breakfast.

The day moved so slowly. With Will and Tim, Jeremiah busied himself with the horses. He sent Tim to throw hay to the
Mexicans' horses in the corral and to feed Bouchal in the barn
to keep them from fighting. He trimmed hooves and helped
Will shoe Maud and Nellie. The old, white work horses, about
thirty years-old now, were so gentle, lifting their big feet for
young Will's rasp and hammer.

Connie, holding Annie's hand, and Kitty with Danny had
come to watch the horse shoeing. "Is Aunt Cauth all right,
Daddy?" Kitty asked anxiously. She'd wanted to help, but
Sophia Garcia had been adamant. "This is no place for
muchachas. Connie, take the children outside. *Andale*. Go on."

"She'll be fine, *alanna*," Jeremiah replied, showing his own
concern by lapsing into Irish. All day he kept his ear open to
the sounds from the house. An occasional cry would send him
to the door with an inquiry. The afternoon lengthened into
dusk and Marìa Salazàr came back, this time with Calistro
and their children, bringing a large pot of *chili verde* and *tortillas* for supper. Sophia spoke in rapid Spanish to Marìa.
Jeremiah couldn't make it out, except something about water
breaking.

The Salazàr children were hard to keep quiet so Jeremiah
took all the children into the back bedroom for reading lessons
and evening prayers. Night came and still no birth. Sophia
Garcìa never left Catherine's bedside now. When Jeremiah
looked in, she glanced up with a worried expression and shook
her head. His questions were met with incomprehensible
Spanish and a helpless lifting of her hands. "No *se, señor*." If
Señora Garcìa didn't know, who did?

Jeremiah sent his children home with Marìa and Calistro,
all crowded together in the little errand wagon. He threw
another pine log on the fire and sat by it anxiously. He heard
a low moan from the bedroom, which tore at his heart.
Suddenly he could stand it no longer. Over Sophia's protests,
he came into the room and sat by the bed, watching Catherine.
She opened her eyes, but seemed not to see him. The pains

came in waves, one after another without a break, hardly giving her time to catch her breath before the next one hit.

Jeremiah remembered sitting by this very bed, helplessly watching Molly. And losing her. He could not bear to lose Cauth, too. He began to pray.

Taking her hand, he watched her struggle, and her quiet courage overwhelmed him with tenderness. He felt her pain and, with sudden clarity, realized how much she had come to mean to him. "Oh, God, please help her," he cried.

Sophia began pushing on Catherine's swollen stomach. Catherine arched her back and cried out. Finally, with one more strong convulsion, the baby was forced out. Sophia quickly cleaned out its mouth, held it upside down, and a lusty cry came forth. Jeremiah was too shaken to even look at the baby. All his attention was riveted on Catherine.

She finally opened her eyes and gave him an exhausted smile. He put his face against hers and said, "Ah, Cauth, Cauth darlin', I love you so."

CHAPTER THIRTY-NINE

CATHERINE CRADLED HER INFANT son as he hungrily suckled her breast. She gave Jeremiah a contented, drowsy smile. Every muscle and bone in her body ached. She was numb with fatigue. But she had her baby, her own baby.

And Jeremiah had said he loved her. It was the first time.

He looked at Catherine with joy and relief, and a new-found admiration for this woman whom he'd seen simply as a nanny for his children and a housekeeper. Now she had become the center of his world. He meant it when he said he loved her.

"A name we'll be needing to call the boy," Jeremiah prompted as he watched Catherine nurse their infant son.

"It's after my brother in Ireland I'd like to call him," Catherine said, smiling weakly down at the baby.

Jeremiah nodded approvingly. "I like that name. James, it is then."

Catherine shook her head. "It's the Irish way of it, I'm thinking," she said. "I was hoping to call him Seamus."

"Oh!" Jeremiah was bothered by this. He'd have preferred a simple, common name, not an unusual one that would proclaim the boy's Irishness. A name that might set him apart.

"Jerry, if he has the courage of his Uncle James, and a name that speaks of his Irish heritage, he'll have the spunk to make his way in the world, now won't he?"

Jeremiah didn't like it, but he couldn't tell her the reason. And as for spirit—or spunk, as Catherine called it-—no one had more of that than she did. The baby would be getting his share from her. Besides, he could deny this woman nothing. Not now.

"Well then, Seamus it is," he agreed and tried to hide his disappointment.

He went outside and leaned against the corral fence, watching the five strange horses clean up the hay Will had thrown them. He studied the mixture of brands on their hips, front shoulders, necks. He wondered what he could do with these animals, these stolen horses in his corral. Of course, no one was going to brand him a horse thief. But he didn't relish the prospect of riding a hundred miles to the county seat in Monterey to report them to the sheriff, as well as the theft of his own bunch. But first he had some business with Tiburcio Vasquez, if he could find him.

Jeremiah waited three days, making sure Catherine had gotten stronger and was able to be up and around. Then he made arrangements with Marìa Salazàr to care for the younger children and to help Catherine. He filled his saddle bags with dried meat, some hard biscuits, coffee and a pot, and got out his old bedroll. He cleaned and oiled the Spencer, worked the lever and checked the sights. He loaded the seven cartridges in the stock and filled his pockets.

Catherine watched his preparations with growing alarm. "Jerry, those are hard men. They're so heavily-armed. I'm afraid for you." She was almost in tears. "Must you be doing this?"

"I must," he answered.

He kissed her, holding her close for a long moment. He patted his new son's head, and then picked up his outfit, and went to the barn. "Bouchal, old boy, it's you and me again," he told the horse, once a solid gray, but now nearly white at eighteen years of age.

Will and Tim silently stood by, watching their father get ready. He'd already refused their offer to go along. Jeremiah was cinching up when Little Jerry rode into the yard, returning from the Garcias. He realized immediately where his father was headed. "I'll change horses and go with you, Dad — !" he called out.

"You'll not," Jeremiah said with finality.

"But you'll be needing help against those *banditos*," Jerry insisted. "I could take the army rifle. I know how to shoot it."

"No!" Jeremiah shouted. "This is no task for a boy. You stay here and be helping Will and Tim. And that's an end to it."

Jerry stood with his brothers and watched his father ride off, up the Peach Tree Road. Then he turned to put up his horse. "I'm not just a boy," he muttered angrily. "I did a man's work cowboying for the Garcias. I could do a man's work getting our horses back, too."

A whole week went by. Catherine worried constantly about Jeremiah's safety. The only thing that gave her comfort was caring for her baby son. Maria's presence helped too, but at night she slept fitfully, waking up frequently to find herself alone in the bed. Finally, on the eighth day Jeremiah returned, slumped in his saddle, dusty, obviously as tired as his old horse. He'd found no trace of his stolen animals, and no one he'd asked around the New Idria country knew anything about them.

"No comprende, señor." "Yo no se." "No habla Ingles," were the responses to his questions.

Not one would admit to knowing Tiburcio Vasquez or any of his men. The *banditos* were protected by a wall of professed ignorance or silence. Jeremiah was disgusted. Now he was facing that long trip to the sheriff in Monterey. As he rode into the yard, his whole family rushed up to greet him.

And it was then that Jeremiah looked over toward the corral and saw an amazing sight. He had to rub his eyes to make sure he wasn't dreaming. For there, in the corral, were Jeremiah's own five horses. The black and the other mounts were gone. He looked at them, dumbfounded. Catherine smiled at the expression on her husband's face.

"Jerry," she said, "you can't imagine how afraid I was when I saw them ride in. It was just as before, the boys were off working, Maria had gone home, and it was just me here alone with the children. And the *banditos* looked so fierce, just like last time. Well now, there I was, standing at the door, and not knowing what to do!"

Jeremiah couldn't speak—his amazement grew as Catherine continued. "I simply watched them as they roped the horses in the corral and changed their saddles. They turned our horses

277

in and mounted their own. It was so swift. Their leader, that Tiburcio, bowed to me from his saddle, and said something in Spanish that I didn't understand. He waved his big hat and then they all galloped off. The dust was so thick I couldn't see for a bit, and when it cleared they were gone!"

That evening Calistro came over with Marìa. He and Jeremiah looked over the horses to assess the damage. They were tired and thin, to be sure, and a bit foot sore, needing to be shod, but unharmed. The two men leaned against the corral fence. "I did not want to get your hopes up, *Señor* Jerry," Calistro said, "so I never told you before. But I have heard of this. This *bandito*, this Vasquez, *señor*, sometimes he does this thing."

"He's a strange one, all right," Jeremiah said. "But he's got loyal friends in New Idria."

"Si, señor," Calistro agreed. "He's always safe there."

* * * * *

Seamus Cleary was a happy, laughing baby, and Catherine couldn't get enough of him. Her strength came back slowly and Jeremiah arranged for Marìa Salazàr to come for a few hours every day to help with the work. One day Catherine was holding the fat, gurgling boy and cooing to him while little Danny, standing nearby, stared at her with his thumb in his mouth, a new habit.

"Ah now, and you're Mama's little *macushla*, you are," Catherine said to her son.

A small voice beside her chirped up, "Could I be your little *macushla*, too, Aunt Cauth?"

She looked down at Danny and pulled him to her side. "Sure, and you are my little darling, Danny."

"Could you be my mama, too?"

Catherine put the baby in his crib, sat down and pulled Danny onto her lap. "Danny, darlin', I'm the same as your mama. I want you to call me Mama, if you're wanting to."

278

Danny snuggled against her. He gave a happy sigh and mur-mured, "Mama" against her breast as she hugged him. But she felt terrible. Had she been so taken up with her very own that she was neglecting these other children?

Although Catherine was getting stronger by the day, Jeremiah continued to treat her as if she were a porcelain fig-urine, afraid to touch her for fear she'd break. And though they shared a bed, he was careful not to embrace her. Catherine ached for the comfort of her husband's arms. It had been three months since the baby came, she fretted, and he was still afraid to even kiss her.

That night when Jeremiah blew out the lamp and slid into his side of the bed, Catherine moved over, closing the distance between them. He couldn't move away, there was not enough room in the bed. She curled against him. Neither said a word. Jeremiah breathed deeply and lifted aside her long hair. He put his lips to her skin and kissed the back of her neck. Catherine moved herself even closer to him, and felt his arm go around her, and his hand cup her breast. She felt him grow hard against her.

"Oh, husband. Oh, how I've been missing you," she whis-pered as she turned to him.

CHAPTER FORTY

JEREMIAH AND HIS THREE OLDER SONS sat on their horses and watched the activity swirl around them. It was spring of 1873 and the town of Soledad, named for the nearby, long-abandoned mission, our Lady of Solitude, was rising in the center of the Salinas Plain.

"Look at that, Dad!" Jerry Jr. exclaimed, pointing to the edge of the fledgling town where a Southern Pacific engine sat on brightly gleaming iron rails, whistling its impatience and belching steam and smoke, waiting to be uncoupled from the string of boxcars and rolled onto the turntable for its return trip to San Francisco. "Now that's a sight," Jeremiah agreed. The boys wanted to ride closer, but their horses were too spooked.

Farm wagons and buggies had gathered from the nearby ranches for their occupants to gawk at the carpenters hammering, sawing, lifting beams and nailing great slabs of redwood siding into place. Broad-hatted, overall-garbed men and sun-bonneted women were appraising merchandise as fast as the new shopkeepers could stock the shelves of their half-finished stores. Here and there tents were still standing, the first business establishments of Soledad.

A stagecoach from southern California pulled up to the brand-new Railroad Exchange Hotel, the street already thick with dust despite the spring showers. Passengers stepped down from the coach onto the fresh-cut plank sidewalks. Teamsters were backing their horses and moving their freight wagons to unload lumber, building supplies and merchandise for the new stores.

Jeremiah marveled along with his sons. So much had changed in this part of the country since he'd first ridden into it. He'd heard about the railroad coming and the new town on the banks of the Salinas River when he'd last gone to Peach Tree, which was itself a little village now. He and the boys had ridden down to see for themselves, to check the facilities before the June cattle drive.

"Look there, Dad!" Little Jerry exclaimed, his eyes wide with excitement. "They're building cattle corrals, all right."

"Aye, this will be a shorter drive for us, by half, than going all the way to San Juan," Jeremiah said with a satisfied smile.

Will had guided his horse over to an open lot behind a store where a variety of farm equipment was on display. A number of farmers walked among the implements, discussing their good and bad points. Will motioned for his father and then pointed to a strange contraption. "What's that?" he asked.

"A reaper, and the big farms are using them. It cuts the grain and bundles the sheaves. Saves hand labor," Jeremiah explained as he inspected the modern machine.

"How many horses does it take?"

"Four, I'm supposing. But it might work better with six." Jeremiah looked at the price tag, a hundred and fifty dollars, and began trying to figure a way to afford the reaper. He could be hiring out with it to cut grain for the neighbors since there were now other ranchers in Long Valley. That was another one of the many changes. New settlers had come into Pine Valley and over into Wild Horse, too. And they were taking up every bit of the remaining vacant land in Lone Oak and Bitter Water. Most of the old San Lorenzo land grant had been purchased by a man named Henry Miller, who was already being called Cattle King of the West, and cattle carrying his Double H brand were all over Peach Tree Valley. Now Miller was buying up all the nearby little places, too, even the Garcia's. Felipe, Sophia and their family had all moved to Monterey, leaving their big, comfortable *adobe* house deserted.

Many of the new homesteaders were accepting Miller's offers and selling out, as well. Jeremiah wasn't surprised. He had seen it coming. The settlers had arrived from the east with big hopes, deluded by the dream of free land, but with no idea of the hardships they would face. Several of these new Long Valley settlers had become discouraged by the lack of water and the endless hard work, and decided, as Delbert and Sally Thompson had, to give up the struggle. Jeremiah had bought out the others, too, and now owned more than a thousand acres, half of it good farm land, the rest good grazing, in addition to the unclaimed range land he controlled. All of it was more than he and Calistro could manage, even with help from the boys. It was time, he knew, to start using more modern farming methods.

That night as they camped under Chalone Peak, Jeremiah, lying awake under the stars, mulled it over in his mind. There was no way he could afford the reapers and seeders, the threshers and new gang plows, or the new mill to pump water, run by the wind. Not without going to the bankers. As they rode through Bitter Water toward home, he was adding up the amounts in his head.

Jeremiah hated the idea of being beholden to a bank and paying interest. But that little sack of double eagles, and those new greenbacks in the trunk at home, weren't enough to buy what he knew he needed. Maybe he should ask Weeb Jefferson. Weeb knew about banking. At least he knew a damn sight more than Jeremiah did.

After the cattle were shipped out of Soledad that summer, Jeremiah sent the boys home and rode on alone to San Juan to confer with his former employer and good friend. "Damn good idea, Cleary," Weeb Jefferson agreed. "You'll never get ahead without capital. Sometimes a man has to take a risk. Shoot the damn works. I did and it paid off."

Two weeks later Weeb met Jeremiah in Salinas and introduced Jeremiah to William Vanderhurst, one of the organizers of the new Salinas City Bank. They went into the Abbott House next door to discuss crops and cattle prices over dinner. After the meal Vanderhurst took Weeb and Jeremiah back to the bank, where he introduced the manager, Charles Wetzel, a tall, sparse, bald-headed man with cold eyes that penetrated through steel-rimmed spectacles perched on his thin nose.

"Damn good man, this Irishman, Charlie," Weeb said, looking at Jeremiah as if he were a son who'd made his father proud. "You won't be taking a chance on him. This equipment he wants is a damn good investment." Weeb left the banker's office so the two men could continue their discussion in private.

Wetzel listened attentively to Jeremiah's plans for upgrading his equipment. The only question he asked was about horses. "What about the stock to manage all this? You're going to need eight-horse teams, maybe several."

"I have them, Mister Wetzel," Jeremiah said confidently. "I've been breaking work horses these past sixteen years, and selling them for good profit. I'll just be keeping the lot for my own use now. But I do plan to buy a Percheron stud."

"How much do you figure for him?" Wetzel dipped his pen into the ink bottle on his desk and made some notations on a piece of paper.

"A purebred Percheron, such as I want, is bringing a thousand dollars."

Wetzel arched an eyebrow and pursed his lips. "Hmmm," he murmured. "That's a sizable investment for a horse."

"He'll pay his way," Jeremiah insisted. "His services for the neighbors' mares will bring in good money, and my own grade of work horses will improve."

Wetzel thought a moment and then finally nodded. "All right then, we'll figure that in." He did some quick arithmetic, and then pushed the paper across the desk so Jeremiah could see the figures. "Will four thousand dollars be a satisfactory amount?" Wetzel asked.

Jeremiah studied the figures for a moment and then answered, "That will do it."

"All right," Wetzel said, adjusting his glasses. "Now the terms are these. Interest will be at eight percent and there must be an annual reduction of principal."

"I understand," Jeremiah agreed.

"Good then. We'll prepare loan papers for your signature. Funds will be available in the morning."

Jeremiah started to rise and offer thanks to the banker, but was stopped by Wetzel's question. "You do have a copy of your deed so we may prepare the mortgage?"

"Mortgage?" Jeremiah was stunned. He stood before the banker, unable to mask his surprise, and then slowly sank back into the chair.

"Well now," Jeremiah said, "I had supposed there would be a lien on the equipment, sure. And the stud horse, too. But I had not considered a mortgage on my land." Disappointment clouded his face.

"Oh yes, Mister Cleary. I'm sorry if that wasn't clear to you. I thought Mister Vanderhurst had explained."

"He did not." Jeremiah was irritated and struggled against the anger that was turning his face red. He tried to consider his position. "But — ah — Mister Wetzel, the value of the equipment, that should be enough to secure the loan? And the stud horse?"

Wetzel removed his glasses and took out a white handkerchief. He wiped the lenses as he carefully spoke. "Oh, I'm sorry, Mister Cleary, but machinery wears out and should you be unable to pay, the bank has no use for worn-out equipment." He replaced the spectacles on his nose, adjusted them, and then continued. "As for horses, they can be injured or they simply get old and infirm. Yes, sir, land is the security we require."

Jeremiah rose from his chair and stared hard at the banker. "I'll not be putting a mortgage on my land," he stated emphatically and walked out of the banker's office, letting the door slam hard behind him.

That evening a dejected Jeremiah joined Weeb Jefferson at supper in the Abbott House. He told him about his unsuccessful meeting with the Wetzel.

"So what's the damn risk?" Weeb asked.

"That it's a dry year and I'm not making a crop. No feed for my cattle."

"We have them," Weeb agreed. "It's a chance you take in this damn country. But somehow we make it."

"Aye, but we go through hell some years not knowing. After all this time working to own land, I hate the thought of putting it at risk to some beady-eyed banker."

"Well, Jerry, you have to make the decision," Weeb said. "I look at money as just another tool I need for ranching. If you go along without any damn capital, a little bit at a time, you'll be old and used up and never acquire anything." Weeb shoved a forkful of meat into his mouth and chewed thoughtfully for a moment. Then he looked at Jeremiah and said, "Sometimes a man has to shoot the damn works."

Jeremiah chewed his own steak for a minute, swallowed, and said, "I've not been the one to gamble much."

"Me neither, Jerry," Weeb said. "Just once. When I put all I had into that San Juan ranch. It paid off for me. Could for you. But it's a tough decision."

"Maybe."

That night Jeremiah went to his bed in the Abbott House still not sure what he should do. He could take the early train back to Soledad, ride on home, and give up his grand ideas of large-scale farming. Then again, he could take the risk and mortgage his land to buy the implements and the stud horse. He hardly slept, fretting and changing his mind back and forth throughout the night.

But in the morning he had decided what to do. He walked into the bank and stood before Wetzel's desk. The bank manager motioned for him to sit. "Pleased to see you back, Mister Cleary. Have you changed your mind?"

"That a mortgage on my land is fair, Mister Wetzel? I have not." Jeremiah declared. "But if it's the only way I can get the money, I've decided to take the risk."

Once he left Wetzel's office, Jeremiah was anxious to be home. There was another new baby in the house, a girl born the previous month, two years after Seamus came into the world. But this time the birth was easy, and fast. Catherine

285

was soon up and about, strong and happier than ever. The only thing that had momentarily upset Jeremiah was Catherine's choice for the name of their new daughter.

"It's Mary Margaret," she said proudly.

The name hit Jeremiah as though he'd been struck by a blow to the pit of his stomach. Was it hurt or a pang of pleasure? He couldn't speak.

"It's for our Molly, Jerry. I want her remembered," Catherine said as if trying to explain.

Remembered? Of course, she's remembered, Jeremiah thought. Molly was locked in his heart. He never spoke of her, although Catherine did, many times, and often told the children about their mother. But when the youngsters asked Jeremiah questions about Molly, he couldn't bear to answer. He simply turned away in silence. He knew they didn't understand.

"Molly." Jeremiah had to take a deep breath. He could hardly get the name past his lips.

"We could name her Mary Margaret, but we could call her Peggy," Catherine said, sensing Jeremiah's discomfort.

"Peggy?" Jeremiah was relieved. "Aye. Peggy." He worked it around his tongue. "Now there's a grand old-fashioned name. I like it. Sure, Cauth darlin', we can be calling her Peggy."

It was after dark when Jeremiah rode into the ranch. Catherine had supper waiting, but before he ate, he put up the gray he'd ridden. Bouchal was there in the barn so Jeremiah threw the old white horse a forkful of hay, too. "Well now, Bouchal, old boy, when you and I rode out that time to look for land, I never thought I'd be having dealings with a banker and putting our ranch up at risk."

Bouchal flicked an ear at his master's voice, but otherwise paid no attention. He munched his hay while Jeremiah leaned on the stall door and talked to him. "That beady-eyed fellow at the bank doesn't think much of old horses. But you and I have come a long way, old boy, and I don't mind telling you that this mortgage business has me fearful. I can't be telling Cauth or the children. I'm not wanting to worry them. This is something between you and me. If you've got a horse god, Bouchal, you better be helping me pray for a few good, wet years."

Jeremiah went in to supper and to a restless night, seeing Wetzel's eyes piercing him from behind those steel-rimmed spectacles every time he closed his own.

CHAPTER FORTY-ONE

"TELL US AGAIN, AUNT CAUTH, why did they throw Uncle James in jail?"

All the children loved to hear about Ireland, but it was fourteen-year-old Jerry Jr. whose eyes grew wide with excitement when she told about the risings and the rebel bravery. The family was gathered around the table for the noon meal, except for Jeremiah who'd ridden over to Peach Tree to check for mail.

"Well then," Catherine said, as she sat down to her place at the table. "Your Uncle James was a member of the Fenians, a secret group of patriotic men pledged to free Ireland from the heartless rule of the British. When the call came to rise up against them in the spring of eighteen sixty-seven, my brother answered and joined the Cork brigade. Their job was to tear up the railroad tracks near Cork City and disrupt communications and British reinforcements. But some dirty informers told the British of the plans and the soldiers were waiting for them." She grimaced at the memory. "Shots were exchanged and some of the Fenians were killed or wounded. My brother escaped with a few others into the hills, but it was snowing and freezing cold and they had no shelter. They tried to hide from the redcoats, but they were captured and tried as traitors to the crown. Those patriotic Irishmen were sentenced to prison for seven years. Your Uncle James is out now. But, you can be sure," Catherine said proudly, "with his courage, he's still a rebel."

"Is Uncle James a hero?" Will asked.

"Aye," Catherine said. "He's a hero to the Irish people."

"Will there ever be another rising, Aunt Cauth?" Little Jerry wondered.

"I'm sure there will," Catherine replied. "Men like my brother and Callahan and many others, even Kevin O'Malley, have the spirit of freedom burning in them. You're not knowing here—where freedom is taken for granted—how important that is. Your father has been teaching you that."

They all nodded. "But why did they evict you all from Grandpa Hurley's farm?" Kitty asked.

Catherine sighed. They'd heard it all before. But she told them again, "It wasn't because we hadn't paid the rent, you know. That was paid right on time no matter what the sacrifice. We had just a year-to-year-lease and the landlord simply would not renew it. He wanted to put sheep to graze on our farm. So he sent the constable and some soldiers and put us all out on the road. We barely had time to gather our belongings before they knocked in the roof."

"Damn the British!" Little Jerry exclaimed.

"Shh, Jerry," Catherine admonished. "You're not to be using such words."

They'd finished the noon meal, the girls were clearing the table and the boys were ready to go back to work outside, all except Little Jerry. "First, one song, Aunt Cauth. I'll get my mandolin."

The boy had a real gift for the pot-bellied instrument, which Juan Garcia had given him and taught him to chord. But Little Jerry had the ear to hear a melody just once and be able to play it. He struck the notes and Catherine sang as she washed the dishes.

Yes, we are free, to plough the sea
and dig the earth for treasure;
And when we do, the ruling few

Can take our gains at leisure.
We are free to weep while tyrants sleep,
And starve while they are feasting;
And when we do, the ruling few
Feed us with scorn and jesting."

It went on for several stanzas, Cauth's sweet voice filling the room. Little Jerry was picking the chords and his strong, young tenor helped carry the melody. Tim added his voice, and Connie, Kitty, and Annie joined in. Will, though, just listened and tapped his foot.

Now Cauth swung into another, more fiery song she remembered from her youth, hearing it roared out in the cottage of Coolnagurrane. It was popular after a pint or so with those who recalled the rising of 1798. Little Jerry sang along with her as he picked the mandolin accompaniment.

"The minstrel boy to the war has gone,
In the ranks of death you will find him;
His father's sword he has girded on,
And the wild harp slung behind him."

They didn't hear Jeremiah ride up and tie his horse. He stood framed in the doorway. Startled, they all turned to look at him, the song dying on the children's lips. Jeremiah, too, remembered the song. He'd liked it in the old days. But now he angrily shook his head and glared at them.

Only Little Jerry and Catherine finished singing the lyrics, harmonizing, *"Thy songs were made for the pure and free, they shall never sound in slavery."*

"So this is the way you're spending the day when my back is turned?" Jeremiah roared. "Is there no work to be done that you can spend the afternoon screeching at each other? Be off with you!"

The youngsters scattered, except for Little Jerry, who slowly returned his mandolin to its place, looking defiantly at his father as he went through the door. Catherine busied herself at the sink, ignoring Jeremiah, who silently helped himself to the dinner leftovers.

Finally he spoke. "Cauth, you know my feelings about those rebel songs. I don't want the children to be learning them. There's no need. They're Americans, dammit. I'm not wanting their heads filled with romantic notions about Ireland."

"But, Jerry, these song are their heritage. They spring from the hardships and heartaches of life in old Erin. They should hear her songs."

"I'll not be having them singing songs about a useless cause," Jeremiah declared, his face getting red, his jaw tensing.

"Useless cause, is it?" Catherine's voice raised an octave. "Useless, you say. And it's my very own brother who's suffered for it. There's no more holier cause than the freedom of the Irish people."

"Well now, it might be holy, for all of that. But it will never succeed." Jeremiah's voice rose, too. He was nearly shouting and the children who were still in the house were cowering. "The crown is too strong! And it doesn't matter a wisp in hell to our life here in America!"

"Well, it matters to me, Mister Cleary." Catherine was so angry, a vein in her temple throbbed and her eyes brimmed with outraged tears. She banged down the frying pan. "And if the children want to be hearing my stories and songs, sure then, I'm the one to be doing it. And you can be putting that in your pipe and smoking it!"

"You'll not." With that Jeremiah gave his wife one last stern look, strode from the house and slammed the door with a resounding bang.

He was busy around the ranch all afternoon, working off his temper, and didn't come in until after dark. Silent, withdrawn, he took his place at the supper table, but hardly ate. Without a glance at Catherine he went to his chair by the fire and filled his pipe. As he puffed on it and waited for the youngsters to come for their lessons, he mulled over the argument they'd had. Couldn't Cauth see what she was doing? He'd seen the shine in Little Jerry's eyes. God knows what that could lead to.

The children had recited their lessons, said their prayers and were all off to bed when Jeremiah brought forth the letter he'd picked up at Peach Tree. He gave it to her as a peace offering.

"It's from Boston," he said.

Catherine took the letter and sat down near Jeremiah, sharing the lamp. She read a bit and looked up at him. "It's from John. He's suggesting one of the children might be of an age to be going off to school somewhere, and asks if we'd want to send them to Boston."

"Boston!" Jeremiah was shocked at the idea. Boston had no good memories for him, not the way they treated the Irish there. "And by all that's holy, why would we ever want to send a child of ours to Boston?"

"John claims there are grand schools for Irish students and that they'd not have to board. They could stay with him and Rose." She handed the letter to Jeremiah.

"They'll not. I'm not sending a son of mine to that city where he'll have to toady up to those snobs. A school for the Irish, is it? And why is it just for the Irish? Why not a school for everyone? Is it the Irish aren't good enough for the other schools?"

"Now, Jerry, that's up to you." Catherine was not argumentative, in fact, she was in a very conciliatory mood that evening. "But it's a wonderful offer John and Rose are making, and perhaps it just might be time to be thinking of more schooling for the older children."

"It's me that's teaching them what they'll be needing," Jeremiah said adamantly.

"That's always a wonder to me how you can be doing that and them learning so much. And then don't I remember, it's yourself who taught me?" Catherine smiled at him and spoke softly. "And aren't we the lucky ones to have you to teach our children? But what about the other youngsters in the valley now? There's more than aplenty to have a school right here."

"And is it the teaching of all the valley children that you're asking of me, woman? I can't do it. There's a ranch to run, you know."

"No, Jerry, of course I'm not thinking that you have the time to teach them all. But, perhaps, you could talk to the other fathers and suggest a way to establish a school. We'd not want our little ones to ride all the way to Peach Tree, would we now?"

"Aye, they have a school in Peach Tree. And there's been one in Bitter Water these past four years," Jeremiah remarked, as he re-lit his short pipe. Catherine left him alone to be thinking on it. She'd leave the discussion of schooling for the older children until another time.

That night in bed, things were still strained between them. They lay without touching each other and neither one could sleep. Finally Jeremiah turned to her and said, "Cauth darlin', you know I'm partial to the music. It's a wonderful thing for the family of an evening to have the songs. But it's the rebel tunes I'm not liking."

Jeremiah put his arm on her shoulder and tried to turn her to him. But Catherine only gave him her back.

CHAPTER FORTY-TWO

THERE WAS A SPRIGHTLY LIFT TO MATTHEW CLEARY'S FEET, and joy in his heart, as he fairly skipped along the well-beaten trail. He was leaving Los Burros mining district behind him, heading for civilization and a visit with his brother. Surely, the past eight years was enough time for Jeremiah to be forgiving, to forget what he'd once so scornfully said. Especially since, for the first time, Matthew was returning with money in his pocket, a few nuggets in his money belt, and a poke full of gold dust in his pack. Won't Jerry be surprised and impressed, he thought with a chuckle.

Along Anthony Creek he stepped off the narrow trail to allow a packstring to pass. It was Byron Plaskett, a prospector he knew, leading seven mules loaded with supplies for the miners.

"Hello, Cleary. Where' ya headed?" Plaskett asked, stopping his laboring animals for a blow.

"Jolon," Matthew replied.

"Not pulling out? Leaving your mine?"

"Sold it," Matthew said, a bit of bragging in his voice. "Willie Cruikshank bought me out. I have a share in his Tarantula mine. I'm heading for civilization for a while. But I'll be back. There's more gold waiting for me back there."

"Well, I'll be damned," Plaskett said. "Willie, huh? He must think you found the Mother Lode if he bought you out."

"Well, there was a vein with good color and I panned some nuggets. Before I go back, I want to look up my brother. He's a rancher over there in Long Valley." Matthew gestured to the east.

"Good luck — " Plaskett called out as he started the mules, and wound his pack string up the switchbacks.

Matthew strode on down the trail, his legs moving with a rhythm that showed he'd covered many a mile on trails such as this, first in the gold fields around Placerville, and the past eight years roaming these Santa Lucia Mountains. He'd finally had some luck, enough to interest Cruikshank, who traded him an interest in the his hard-rock Tarantula Mine, right next to Matthew's claim on Alder Creek. He guessed there might be as much as five hundred dollars in his pocket by the time he had his dust and nuggets converted to good old USA certificates. Plenty to pay back his brother, with interest, as he'd promised, for getting him out of that scrape in San Juan, for the generosity he'd shown through the years and, God knows, something toward Connie's keep.

Matthew hit San Miguel Creek and followed the trail to Jolon, arriving at Dutton's Hotel in time for supper, a good rest, and an early stage to Salinas, where his first business was converting his gold to cash. He'd never had so much money, not since he and Jeremiah had hoarded every penny in Boston so long ago. His next stop was the barber shop where his beard was amply lathered, and deftly sliced away, and his hair neatly trimmed. A luxurious soaking in a bathtub in the back room eroded the grime, gathered since his last ablutions in the icy cold water of Alder Creek. Matthew headed for Hale's Department Store, where the solicitous salesman outfitted him in the latest fashions.

He stepped back onto Main Street in a red and brown checked suit, a red waistcoat, high-collared white shirt, and black bow tie. *Jeremiah will never know me now.* His feet felt strange in high button shoes as he gave an experimental skip. A brown bowler hat, set at a jaunty angle, topped him off. He tipped it with aplomb at every woman he passed. He was just in time to catch the afternoon train to Soledad.

He whistled a rollicking tune and did another little dance step right there in the aisle of the train before taking his seat. The rhythmically rolling train lulled Matthew into a joyful daydream. He imagined the reunion scene with Jeremiah and Molly. *He'll see, by God, that I'm a success, too. Well, Big Brother, I'll say, here's that money I owe you, and we'll just double it for the interest, and call it square.*

He wondered about his daughter. What would Connie look like? Would she be happy to see him, or had he been away too long? Maybe she'd forgotten him. He calculated she was abouty fourteen by now. Would she look like Lupe?

The wonderful vision of a youthful Lupe stayed with him even after he arrived in Soledad. That night he ate supper at the Railroad Exchange Hotel. He sat alone at a corner table, but his mood was so expansive, he ordered a bottle of wine with his steak. After supper Matthew fired up a cigar and settled back with a glass of brandy. He had another, but it tasted flat without conversation to spark it up. So he looked around the hotel dining room for some other lone man, but there was no one.

Too early to go to bed, he decided. He'd just have a *deoch an dorais*, one for the road, before calling it a night. Matthew still often thought in Irish, having spent so much time alone along the creeks with only his pan and that damn mule for company. He found an empty spot at the bar in the Gray Eagle and called for a whiskey. The bartender placed a bottle of Ned's Best in front of him and Matthew spun out a twenty-dollar gold piece.

"A shot or the bottle?" the barkeep asked.

Matthew shrugged. "I'll keep it. Settle up later," he said, taking the whiskey bottle by the neck, and carrying it to an empty table.

Two hours later found Matthew explaining to a cowboy sharing his table, "Not me — you won't get me on the back of a horse unless you're carrying me out of the mountains, trussed up for the undertaker. I'm a miner, not a rancher."

"A miner? Ever find any gold?" the cowboy asked with genuine interest.

"You bet I did," Matthew boasted. "Plenty. And I'm headed for Long Valley to see my brother, pay him off a little debt. Helluva guy, my brother. He's a rancher. Has a big spread, lots of cattle and horses."

Matthew was holding forth as the young puncher's friends joined the table. He called for another bottle and flipped another gold piece. Plenty more where that came from. These were good boys. When they suggested "going down the line," Matthew bought another bottle and followed.

Elsie's Doll House wasn't a fancy place. Not that Matthew was any great judge. He'd been in such an establishment in Sacramento, once on San Francisco's Barbary Coast, and several times when he'd trailed in to Monterey. He didn't care much for them. Besides, he was usually flat broke. But tonight he had money. So tonight he'd try it all. The girls lined up and the prettiest one, a slim redhead with an amazing bosom, smiled invitingly at Matthew, as if she was choosing him over the young cowboys. He grinned back. Of course, she wanted him to pick her out, he thought. They'd take an old Irishman every time over one of those young buckos.

He looked around for his bottle, but couldn't locate it. So he ordered another and took it up to the room on the second floor of Elsie's Doll House.

"You're a real sweetheart," she murmured in his ear, running her hands through Matthew's newly-trimmed hair. "I'm Lily, what's your name, honey?" she asked as she shrugged out of her loose fitting wrap and lay back on the bed.

Matthew introduced himself, almost fell as he tripped over his pants, and reached for the lovely redhead. By the time Lily had expertly accomplished her goal, Matthew was in love.

"How much for all night?" he asked when he finally had recovered his breath.

She let out a high-pitched giggle. "Are you sure you can afford little Lily, you big Irishman?" Her eyes got wide when he showed her his wad of bills.

"Don't you worry about money, darlin'. Old Matt is loaded and just the one to be showing you a good time."

Matthew napped and drank and talked, frolicked with Lily, and dozed again. It was dawn when the idea came to him. A grand idea, just grand.

"Lily, my darlin', I'm off to see my brother and you're coming with me. He'll be amazed to see his little brother with such a beautiful woman."

"Not me, Matt Cleary. You're an old sweetheart, all right. And I love you dearly. But I'm a working girl and I need the money. My job is right here. You go along now while I get my beauty sleep."

"Money? Don't be fretting yourself about money, my girl. Old Matt will take care of you. I'll return you here in a few days and stuff that sweet spot between your titties full of green-backs."

It didn't bother Matthew that they'd missed the morning stage. He wanted to arrive in Long Valley with a bit more class, anyhow. But it wasn't easy to talk the livery stable owner out of a rig. He didn't want to rent a horse and buggy to a drunken Irishman with that blowsy redhead from Elsie's place. But Matthew finally settled on a two hundred dollar deposit and away they went on the road past Chalome peak toward Bitter Water. Matthew, in his wrinkled new suit, stained from the spilled whiskey, and Lily in her crimson taffeta evening dress, her tousled, dyed-red hair attesting to the previous night's debauchery. Although they'd left Soledad without eating breakfast, they had plenty of liquid refreshment to sustain them on the long drive. And Matthew needed the bottled courage to manage the horse.

Lily was beginning to think this was a harebrained idea when they arrived in Peach Tree late that afternoon. They stopped at the store and got directions to the Cleary place from the postmaster. "Jeremiah Cleary's brother, huh?" he mused to some bystanders. "I'd like to see the look on old Jerry's face when that pair shows up."

"What will you tell them about me, dearie?" Lily wondered, wishing she was back in her room in Soledad.

"You're my wife. My bride, you darlin' girl," Matthew slurred. "Just be your sweet, ladylike self and they'll think me a lucky man." Lily, who'd sobered up some on the long trip, now took a pull on the bottle to get back her courage.

It was nearly dark when they pulled into the Cleary yard and Matthew saw three young boys coming from the barn, one with a milk bucket. "H'ar ya," he greeted them.

"How d'ya do, sir." It was a chorus as the curious boys gathered around the rig. They didn't recognize Matthew, who was having trouble sorting out his nephews through bleary eyes.

"Uncle Matt?" Will wasn't quite sure. He took in the gaudy clothing, not like anything he'd ever seen. And he couldn't figure out who the lady was. But it *was* Uncle Matt, all right. So Will offered to care for the horse, while Jerry and Tim ran to the house to announce the visitors. "It's Uncle Matt — " they yelled. "Uncle Matt's here!"

Matthew stepped down from the buggy and nearly fell. But he righted himself and, with a courtly flourish, helped the embarrassed Lily to alight. Jeremiah came hurrying from the house, reached his brother and gave him a bear hug.

"Matt, Matt, how good to see you. How are you, Brother?" He tried to hold Matthew at arm's length and found the full weight of his brother in his hands. Jeremiah's eyes narrowed as he appraised Matthew's condition. Saying nothing, he looked toward the woman. Who was this frowzy, heina-haired female? He had a pretty good idea!

Matthew introduced her with a gesture of his arm that nearly knocked her over. "This is my wife, Lily." He bowed and nearly fell. "Lily, meet the best brother a man ever had, Mister Jeremiah Cleary." But Matthew's speech was halting and he lurched to catch himself on entering the house. He stopped and swayed on his feet for a moment.

There was Catherine at the door, her ready smile to greet her brother-in-law changing to consternation as she recognized his condition. Matthew stared at Catherine, uncertainty and confusion crossing his face. "Molly?" He tried to focus on her. Was this Jeremiah's Molly? He swayed and bumped against the door frame. He tried again, "Molly?"

"No, I'm Catherine, Molly's sister. Molly is dead. I'm Missus Cleary now. And you're Jeremiah's brother, Matthew?"

By that time Matthew had wobbled into a chair. He sat, staring vacant-eyed, blinking, confused. Lily stood on the steps, pulling her shawl up to cover her bare shoulders and low-cut bodice, nervously watching the scene before her. No one spoke.

The children had all entered the room now, Connie among them. She stood behind the boys, a puzzled look on her face. "Daddy?" she asked. "Daddy?"

Matthew turned toward her and again tried to focus. "Connie," he said, squinting. "My darlin' little girl. Connie, come here to your daddy."

But Connie stood still, frozen in horror, at the drunken man slumped in the chair. He rose and stumbled toward her, his arms open to embrace his daughter. The other children parted to allow him through. But he staggered and fell at her feet. Connie put her hand over her mouth to stifle a cry and turned her head away. Then she couldn't stop her choking sobs and ran from the room.

Jeremiah stood, white-faced, his jaw tightening as he watched his drunken brother try to struggle to his feet. They all stared at him in silence.

"Missus Cleary — " It was Lily who spoke up. She looked directly at Catherine, standing tall and stiff. "I apologize. I shouldn't be here. Matthew wanted me to say I'm his wife, but, of course, I'm not. I'm sorry to be intruding."

Jeremiah turned to Lily. He felt genuinely sorry for her. "It's not you, miss, who should be apologizing." He stared at his brother, sitting on the floor in a near-stupor, and was torn between contempt and pity, outrage and compassion. *How could he have done this, even so deep into the drink, how could he have brought this woman into my home, presented himself in such a state before my wife and children and his own daughter?*

He angrily shook his head and then his innate kindness returned. He'd see this through somehow without letting his anger get the best of him. "We'll have supper and a place for you to stay," he said to Lily in a gentle voice. "Matthew will be leaving in the morning."

"Leaving?" Matthew looked up with bleary eyes. "Leaving?" He barely comprehended all that had taken place. "Not good enough for you, huh? Me and my wife aren't good enough for the mighty Jeremiah Cleary? We'll be leaving right now then — !" He struggled to his feet, but then slipped and fell. Face first. Out cold.

Jeremiah laid him down in the boys' room and the family sat down to a strained and silent supper. Connie didn't appear at the table. Lily, embarrassed, hardly looked up from her plate, except to whisper, "Thank you." They found a bed for her in the girls' room.

In the morning a sobering Matthew realized the enormity of his drunken behavior. His usual bravado had deserted him and, after a hurried breakfast during which no one spoke, he stood, shamefaced, before Jeremiah. "I made a real mess of the whole thing, Brother. I'm sorry, and I'll be getting myself and this woman away from you and your family as fast as I can."

Matthew looked around at the children, obviously searching for Connie. He turned to Catherine. "Can I be seeing my daughter just one last time?"

Catherine disappeared to find Connie, but quickly returned. "She doesn't want to see you," Catherine said.

Matthew sighed and sadly nodded.

He and Jeremiah went outside and stood together as Will brought out the livery horse and hitched up. Matthew reached into his pocket and realized he had a few bills left. At least he could pay off that debt. And then another thought struck him. He owed that money to Lily. He'd promised it to her. Matthew withdrew his hand from his pocket as another idea came to him.

"Oh, Jerry," he said. "I just remembered. There is one good thing. That money I owe you. When I sold my claim, I put your share with my own and invested in a sure thing. It's hard-rock mining in the Los Burros Country. We have shares in the Tarantula Mining Company. They're cutting into a great vein of gold quartz. You'll soon get your money back ten times over."

Jeremiah waved his hand in disgust. "Matt, you're nothing but an *amadan*," he said, using an Irish word for a fool in the depth of his emotion. "A drunken fool, at that. Stay away from me and my family. I don't ever want you around here. And I mean it. Not unless you swear off that stuff."

Matthew looked at the ground, then slowly raised his eyes to Jeremiah. "I can't, Jerry. I just can't."

CHAPTER FORTY-THREE

CATHERINE STOOD IN THE DOORWAY watching Kitty impatiently brushing the snarls out of her hair, trying to tie back the rebellious golden curls. It reminded her of Molly, the many times she'd tried to arrange her sister's unruly hair when they were girls in Coolnagurrane. Just catching up to Molly had been a chore. And Kitty was so much like her, always on the go. Always wanting to be outside, doing something with that fool horse, riding astride as if she were a boy, wanting to chase the cattle around the hills just like her brothers did. She didn't care a fig for trying to be a lady no matter how hard Catherine tried.

Although Kitty's hair was reddish gold and her mother's hair had been black, Catherine thought the look of her was so much of her mother it fair hurt. At thirteen, Kitty was starting to show the woman she would become. Her blue eyes, her fresh pretty look, even the freckles across her nose, and her wide, mischievous grin, were vivid reminders of Molly. Occasionally Catherine noticed Jeremiah look at Kitty and then quickly turn away, as though his daughter's resemblance to her mother was almost more than he could bear. Catherine sighed. *He loves me. I know that, but the memory of Molly will always be strong within him.*

Catherine went into the bedroom to help Kitty with her hair. She wished the girl was more like her cousin. Quiet, demure, gentle Connie was already a beauty at sixteen, dark skinned, with lustrous black hair so long she could sit on it, and big, black eyes, fringed by long lashes. She was serious, even brooding at times, and her smile slow to come. Well, it was no wonder, Catherine thought, losing her mother so young and that terrible time of Matthew's last visit. The girl had to do some painful growing up.

But Connie tried in every way to be ladylike and she just didn't understand Kitty's impetuous nature and desire to act like a cowboy. Catherine felt Connie had more in common with gentle, sweet, brown-haired Annie.

She gave Kitty's hair a final stroke and set down the brush. "Now Kitty, put on your bonnet before you go back in the sun or you'll be all over freckles," Catherine warned the rebellious girl who reluctantly crammed the bonnet down over her curls, turned away and hurried out the door, nearly getting knocked down by her brother Jerry, storming into the house, his mandolin clutched in his hand.

"That father of mine — !" he said. "Who put the burr under his saddle blanket?" Little Jerry was fuming. Before Catherine could respond, he went on, "All I was doing was taking a bit of a rest from cleaning the harness and he's all over me."

"Well now, Jerry, was it playing your mandolin in the barn again that upset him?"

"Upset him? That's not the half of it! I'm sixteen years old and he treats me like a little kid."

"Jerry, you must understand that your father is under so much stress these days. There's been no rain yet this fall and last year's crop but cut for hay. And there's himself with the payments due to the bank." Catherine shook her head. "He's badly worried, Jerry. We all are."

"Aw, I know, Aunt Cauth, we're all watching the sky for rain clouds. I just wish he'd talk to me about it. Or about anything."

"It's a strange country, this," Catherine observed. "One year the crops are a wonder and the cattle get fat, and the next your father can hardly grow a crop."

"But he won't talk about it," Jerry persisted. "He just lays out more work for us to do. I can talk about things with you, but not with Dad."

"Jerry, your father is a good, hard-working man and he loves you. It's showing it that's hard for him. He's always telling me about building up this place so there'll be a fine future for you and your brothers."

"I guess so. But I'm wondering about that. Will and Tim may be happy following the south end of horses going north, but I don't think that's what I want to do."

"And just what is it you're wanting, Jerry? You seem to like the riding and roping, and working the cattle."

"Aw, that's just fun, Aunt Cauth. I don't know about making a lifetime of it."

"Well now, what is it then?" Catherine gently prodded. "What is it you're dreaming about?"

"Now you're sounding just like Dad. He's always calling me a dreamer."

"Dreams aren't bad, Jerry. They can be like goals in life. Even the impossible ones sometimes come true," Catherine said reassuringly. "I certainly know that. What are yours, Jerry?"

"Well, promise you won't laugh?"

"Sure, and I promise."

Jerry's eyes lit up. His words poured out quickly. "I want to go to school somewhere, maybe go on to a university. I could be a lawyer or something like that. Maybe go into politics like Uncle John." Catherine was struck by how ambitious he seemed. "And then, you know what, Aunt Cauth?" She shook her head and watched Little Jerry pace around the room with growing excitement. "I'm going to go to Ireland and do something, something big, something special to help Uncle James free Ireland of the British!"

Oh, dear God, Catherine thought. *What kind of ideas have I been planting in the boy's mind? I've only been telling him the stories of Ireland, telling all the children. But he's been taking them to heart, the most rapt of them all.*

She had stopped telling the stories and singing Irish rebel songs. At least when Jeremiah was around. But when he was off for a few days on a trip to San Juan or Soledad, Catherine might take out the tin whistle and play for the children. And when she sang, Jerry would accompany her on his mandolin.

"See who comes o'er the red-blossomed heather, green banners kissing the pure mountain air. Head erect. Eyes afront. Stepping proudly together. Out and make way for the bold Fenian men."

That is their history, she'd tell herself. Jeremiah didn't understand that they had a right to know about their roots. It would even make them appreciate America more if they knew about Ireland. The children seemed to understand that. But Little Jerry—had she been molding a rebel?

Catherine looked into the boy's face, so serious and proud, his eyes blazing with determination. "Well now, Jerry, that's a great dream. But I wouldn't be telling your father about it just yet. Not with his worries about the drought and the crops."

Jeremiah scanned the skies for the hundredth time that day. Not a cloud. Without a little rain he couldn't even begin to plow. Then, even if it did rain, he'd be late planting. Another scant year would cause trouble at that damn bank, as Weeb would say.

The first season that the Clearys farmed with their new equipment, there was an abundant rainfall which resulted in a bumper crop. Jeremiah, his sons and Calistro couldn't thresh all the grain and the hay filled the barn. Jeremiah had been a happy man, and just a bit proud, when he had appeared two summers ago at the bank in Salinas to make a substantial payment on his principal.

"Good afternoon, Mister Cleary," a smiling Charlie Wetzel had greeted him. "Good to see you. Wonderful crop, you had. Come in, come in. Sit down. Cigar?" He raised the lid on the humidor that sat on his desk.

First class treatment he gave me that year, Jeremiah recalled. *You'd think I was Henry Miller, himself. And wasn't I the posh one, sitting there in my new suit? Puffing on that big cigar?* Jeremiah ruefully shook his head. But the following year was a different story.

"Well, well, Mister Cleary," Wetzel had said, unsmiling. "So hay was all you got? Too bad, too bad. Now about this payment? You can pay only the interest, is that it? Yes, I suppose we can let the principal stand for this year. Perhaps this next season will be a wet one. We certainly hope so."

Then he looked Jeremiah squarely in the face, his eyes growing cold and hard. Jeremiah wasn't able to forget that look. "I must make you aware that you will be required to reduce the principal next year," Wetzel said in a voice as hard as his eyes. "You do understand that?"

No cigar, that time, Jeremiah wryly remembered. He'd had to pay out all the money saved from the sale of his steers just to meet the interest. What would he do this time if it didn't rain soon? And, what would the bank do if he couldn't pay them? Take his land, sell it at auction? He couldn't be worrying Cauth about it. But fretting about this was a bother. He wasn't sleeping and he was getting short tempered. He'd not have to be so hard on the boy just now.

Jeremiah got mad at himself. This whole loan business had been too risky. But he was the one who took the risk. He was the one who got all puffed up, feeling so grand, and got too big for his britches. He was the one who had to have all the new inventions, who had to buy up the neighbors land. He was the one who insisted Weeb introduce him to Wetzel, and he had been the one to agree to the mortgage on the land. Nobody held a gun to his head. He had only himself to blame.

Jeremiah looked again at the blue, cloudless sky that held no hint of rain. *Now all you've worked for these past twenty-eight years could soon be gone. Lost! Where will you go? And you with a wife and nine children? Start over again, will you, Jerry Cleary? At your age? Fifty one, it is? Where will you be going, Jerry Cleary, when they take away your land? It's a fine mess, it is, you've made of your big dream!*

Jeremiah spent the rest of the day with Will working with a new team. At least, he still had horses to sell. But that made him think of his Percheron stud, another big expense, another cause for worry.

"Watch what you're about there, Will," Jeremiah snapped at his son. "You've been taught better than that. That's no way to be handling a horse."

"I'm doing the best I can, Dad," Will said defensively, but he realized that his father wasn't really upset with him. He was upset with the weather and only rain could relieve his anxiety and calm his worst fears.

* * * * *

Jeremiah stepped into the little store which held the Peach Tree post office. He was greeted by the postmaster and a few farmers who were gathered there. It was three weeks since he'd prayed for rain to save his land. "Hello, Cleary, did it rain enough for you to get your crop in?" the postmaster asked.

"Well, sure now and it did. But it was hard work. That little bit of rain didn't soften the ground much. How about you fellows?" he asked, looking at the farmers.

"Not me," said one of the men. "Hell, I can piss more water than we got so far. What good's it do to get a crop in the ground if it ain't gonna grow?"

"Couple of letters came in for you, Jerry," the postmaster said. "Looks like this one's from Ireland."

Jeremiah found a nail keg in the corner and sat down to look over the letters. The one from Ireland made him curious. He held it up to the light, looking for a clue. Not from James. He knew that handwriting. And Liam wasn't the one to ever write. He carefully opened it. *Dear Jerry, This is being written to you by my son, Patrick, but the words are mine. All are well here and hope you and yours have good health and prosper. But we are in dire straits or I would not ask this of you. The potato crop has failed again. I have no money and the rent is due. I sold all that I could to meet the rent last gale day. I have been given until March 1 to pay the 30 pounds or lose the holding. I'll not get another extension. If you have this sum to spare, I will be further beholden to you. Respectfully yours, your brother, Liam Cleary.*

Jeremiah held the letter in his hand and stared at it for a while. It was a bad time to be putting out money, but, of course, he'd help Liam save the family holding. It must be fifteen years since he'd sent a postal money order to Skibbereen. Things must be very bad or Liam would not bring himself to ask for help.

Jeremiah read the second letter quickly. Bad news comes in bunches, he thought. But this wasn't unexpected. It was from Emily Jefferson. Weeb was dying and wanted to see him.

Jeremiah hurried out of the post office, mounted up and rode back to Long Valley thinking about the last time he'd seen Weeb. He'd been frail, but cheerful when they'd gone to meet the bankers. He'd feared for him that day in Salinas, Jeremiah recalled. At eighty-three, Weeb had suddenly become an old man.

As soon as Jeremiah told Catherine about Weeb, she began hastily to pack for the trip to San Juan. "Maybe I can be helping Emily," she said.

Although it was late December, there wasn't a cloud in the sky when Jeremiah and Catherine went down the river route in the wagon. First they stopped in San Juan at the post office so Jeremiah could send a money order to Liam Cleary in Skibbereen. Then, dreading that they might be too late, they hurried on to the Jefferson ranch.

Emily came into the yard to greet them as they stepped down from the wagon. "Lands sakes, I'm glad to see you. Weeb has been wanting to talk to you, Jerry. It's the biggest thing on his mind." She led Jeremiah to the huge bedroom in the back of the house where her husband lay, looking small and white in the center of a big bed.

"Hello there, Weeb, how you doing?" Jeremiah could see how his friend was doing, but he didn't know what else to say. He stood beside the bed and offered his hand. Weeb's fingers had been plucking at the bedsheets, but now he raised a trembling hand to Jeremiah and attempted a smile.

"Any damn rain yet, Jerry?" he asked in a weak, labored whisper. Jeremiah had to lean close to the old man to understand him.

"Any day now, Weeb," Jeremiah answered.

"Been worried," Weeb murmured. "Gave you all that damn advice. Take a chance. Buy land — equipment — big debt. Apologize, Jerry. Shoulda kept my damn mouth shut."

"No, Weeb. It was good advice," Jeremiah insisted. "But I made my own decision. Sure now, it's going to rain and we'll have grand crops. You'll see."

"Not me," Weeb said. "Damn Doc McDougal can't do a damn thing. Parts worn out. Too damn old." He was still holding onto Jeremiah's hand, but finally dropped it and his fingers returned to plucking at the blankets. "If it doesn't rain — got you into trouble, Jerry — sorry."

Weeb turned his head away for a moment and then looked back at Jeremiah, tears welling in his eyes. "Best damn man I know, Jerry — got plan to help if it doesn't rain — " Weeb was still, exhausted by the effort to speak, his eyes closed. But as Jeremiah stepped back from the bed Weeb whispered again. "Emily," he said, "She'll tell you."

Jeremiah and Catherine stayed on with Emily Jefferson, Catherine helping her in any way she could. Jeremiah kept busy with a few chores around the ranch assisting the *vaqueros*, although they were a new bunch he hardly knew.

"That Emily is a wonder," Catherine said one night when they were alone in the guest room. "Didn't I think she'd be carrying on and wailing about, she's such an emotional one. But she's just as calm and steady as could be. It's as if she's comforting me."

It was on the fourth day that Weeb Jefferson simply closed his eyes and didn't re-open them.

"Well, Weeb's gone," Emily said matter-of-factly. "He wanted me to be sure to tell you his plan, Jerry."

Jeremiah nodded sadly. "Aye, he mentioned to me he had a plan."

They were sitting in the main room of the house, across from each other on the large, tan leather chairs. "He's been very troubled that he gave you a bum steer, Jerry," Emily said, "advising you to buy all that equipment and more land and put a big mortgage on your place. He started fretting when last year was dry and really got worried when it didn't rain much this year." Emily paused and sighed. "You're like the son we never had, Jerry," her voice breaking a little, "and Weeb felt he gave you bad advice. He wanted you to have an alternative, if you lose your ranch to the bank."

Jeremiah started to frown and Emily put up her hand. "Wait now, Jerry. Hear me out. I'm planning to go back to Illinois to my people there. Weeb called them a couple of damn no good nephews," Emily said with a slight laugh at the recollection, "but I like them. And so we thought you could move in here and manage this place. Buy it from me gradually so I'll have an income. It would be yours if you want it, Jerry. Otherwise, I'll sell it."

Jeremiah was surprised, and so touched he couldn't speak for a few moments. Finally he managed to thank her. "That's a grand offer, Emily. Let me be thinking on it."

That night in bed he said to Catherine, "I just don't know, Cauth. Haven't those two been fine friends to me? And now look at this, will you? It was my lucky day when I took Weeb's freighter job and me just off the boat. But if I take the offer, I'll be giving up my own land. It would not be the same."

"Sure, Jerry, but what if it doesn't rain and you don't make a crop?" Catherine asked. "How will you be satisfying that Wetzel fellow at the bank?"

"Aye, it vexes me to be thinking of it. But if I do lose my land to the bank and come here, I'll still be broke and every dollar I make would have to go to Emily to pay her off. She'd be needing her money." Jeremiah thought a moment. "No, Cauth, if Emily sells the place, she'll have her money straight away. There are plenty of buyers with cash who'd want a grand cattle ranch like this."

Next morning at breakfast, Jeremiah explained to Emily that he'd take a chance on his own ranch and have faith it would rain. He thanked her again and tried to express how much she and Weeb had meant to him, all the years, right from the very beginning. But he turned away and left the room, unable to get the words out. Catherine said it for him. "Jerry feels that knowing you two was all the luck any Irishman would ever be needing."

The Clearys stood next to Emily, the ranch hands and most of the population of San Juan as the services were read over Weeb Jefferson that afternoon. He was buried under an oak tree on a little knoll. Mourners looked past the preacher, down toward the river where Jefferson cattle were rustling among the willows for the few blades of grass. And their eyes searched the skies for clouds. As they left the graveside their thoughts may have been on Weeb, but their conversations were about the weather. "No sign of rain yet," they all agreed.

All the way back up the river, guiding his horses through the crossings and pulling the grades, Jeremiah fretted about his decision. He tried not to let Catherine know how worried he was. But she saw him keeping one eye on his team and the other searching for rain clouds. At night as they camped, he woke frequently, but saw only stars in the clear sky. When he tried to go back to sleep, Wetzel's hard eyes watched him.

They were passing through Lone Oak when they heard the first sounds. Jeremiah cocked his head to listen. "Cauth, that's thunder, by God!" he exclaimed. And they turned to see the storm clouds blowing in behind them. Wind increased, the sky darkened and then lightening flashed on the nearby ridges. Jeremiah grinned and took out the slickers he'd brought along. "Would you be looking at these now," he told Catherine. "Wasn't I the one to be knowing it would rain?"

"And was there ever a doubt in my mind?" she agreed, laughing with him.

By the time they made Peach Tree the storm had turned into a deluge and despite their slickers, the Clearys were soaked when they pulled up in front of the store.

"Hello there, Cleary, Missus Cleary," the smiling clerk said. "And what brings you folks out on such a beautiful day?"

The store was filled with ranchers and people of the little village, all gathered around the potbellied stove and all grinning from ear to ear. From the saloon across the way they could hear the raucous whoops of Henry Miller's cowboys celebrating the rain and a day off. Jeremiah and Catherine shrugged out of their slickers and stepped to the fire to warm up and dry off.

"So what do you think of this rain, huh, Cleary?" one rancher asked.

"It's grand, just grand, that's what it is," Jeremiah said with a big grin. "But now we need a bit of sun to make the grain sprout."

"You damn farmers," the clerk said with a loud laugh, "you bellyache about no rain and now you want sun. God himself doesn't know how to please you."

Everyone in the store laughed.

Jeremiah and Catherine took advantage of a lull in the storm for the last lap of their homeward journey, but the storm came back in full force as they started down into Long Valley. The wagon slithered and slid on the slick road and Jeremiah used all of his skills to keep it upright. But the smile stayed on his face. "A few more storms like this, Cauth, and we'll be having another bumper crop," he said, the water dripping off his hat. "Maybe I won't have to be selling off those good heifers, after all."

"And maybe we can be thinking of buying a buggy to ride in instead of this wagon," Catherine suggested, clutching the wagon seat as the big freighter swung in the mud behind the team.

Jeremiah took his attention from the horses for a moment to turn and grin at her. "And how about that new house you've talked about, Missus Cleary? Two or three wet years and we'll be out from under that bank and we can be thinking about house plans."

"But first, Mister Cleary, it's wringing myself out a bit," Catherine said, "and then it's a hot bath that are the things foremost on my mind."

CHAPTER FORTY-FOUR

LITTLE JERRY MOPPED THE DUST from his eyes and his forehead with his red bandanna. He retied it securely around his face and up over his nose. He hated riding drag and had even suggested to his father that it was time for Danny or Seamus to start doing it. But no, his father had said, it had to be a good cowboy to keep the herd moving and see that no stragglers dropped back. So here he was, back in the dust. At least his father was giving him some responsibility.

The day was oven hot. Jerry felt the sweat dripping down his back, and the river sand blowing against him in the fierce afternoon wind, stinging right through his shirt. It was hard to keep the cattle moving against the strong wind. They continually wanted to stop and put their tails against it.

But finally they were almost there. It was a three-day drive to Soledad, moving the cattle slowly along the foothills, and by the river, so they could graze as they went. And so much shorter than the old cattle drives to San Juan that used to take a week or more. Jerry Cleary liked being a cowboy, but the dirty jobs around the ranch were what he hated—mucking out the barn, cleaning harness and shoeing horses, doctoring sick animals, digging post holes, nailing up fences. He certainly didn't want to do those things for the rest of his life. His dreams—his goals Aunt Cauth called them—they were for more education. He'd long ago learned everything he could in the new Long Valley school. He wanted to take the entrance exams to some college. That much he knew. What he didn't know was how he'd ever find the courage to talk to his father about it.

He looked though the dust to see his brothers, Will and Tim, turn the herd into the stockyard gate where Jeremiah was counting in the steers. The San Francisco cattle buyer walked over from the Railroad Exchange Hotel and hailed Jeremiah, who had ridden his horse to the water trough.

"Well, Cleary, I hope you didn't run all the fat off of them getting 'em here," he said good-naturedly.

"You wouldn't be paying me for it, anyhow," Jeremiah retorted.

"What's your count?"

"Ninety-six," Jeremiah replied, as the cattle buyer studied the milling steers.

"I see you're still growing your own cowboys," the cattle buyer said as he jerked his thumb at nine-year-old Seamus, who was along this year for his first cattle drive.

"Sure, but it doesn't save on wages. You should see these boys eat," Jeremiah said with a proud laugh.

"I know." The cattle buyer grinned. "Fed out a few of them myself. Let's go over to the Gray Eagle, wet our whistles, and settle up."

Jeremiah stepped down from his horse, loosened the cinch, and removed the bridle. He handed the tired animal's lead rope to Will and looked at his sons, "You boys take the horses to the livery stable and have them grained. I'll meet you there. Go ahead and look around town," he called out. "I'll be ready to head back shortly."

Little Jerry frowned. "Oh, dammit, Will. He's wanting to turn right around and ride out. I was hoping he'd let us put up in Soledad at the hotel for the night, maybe eat in a real restaurant."

"Not Dad." Will laughed. "Too expensive. But you'd better stick your head in that water trough and melt off a few layers of dirt or somebody will try to plow you."

Soledad might not have been much of a town by some standards, but it looked huge to the Cleary boys. They clumped along the board sidewalk, looked into the store windows, walked past the harness shop, and watched the blacksmith busy at his forge, shaping a rim for a wagon wheel.

"Hey, Jerry, did you ever see anything like this?" Will was pointing to a roll of wire with sharp little points stuck in it at intervals. "This stuff would keep the cattle from straying for

314

sure." He read the label pasted to the wire. "Kelly's Diamond Point Wire. Price two dollars forty cents per quarter mile." Will turned to his brothers. "Dad should see this. We could buy enough for three wires around to fence off a section for less than a hundred fifty."

Oh, great, Jerry thought. Four miles of pickets, and digging, and pounding, nailing up the wire. That's no job for a cowboy. But Will would love it. So would Tim. The brothers headed back for the livery stable to check on the feeding horses and meet their father. Jerry walked along with Will. "Did you ever think of going to school?" he asked his older brother.

"I did go to school, Jerry, but that teacher said there wasn't any more he could teach me. You, too. You know that."

"Naw, that's not what I mean. I mean a real school. Like a high school and college."

"Why would I want to do that?" Will looked puzzled. "We don't need any more schooling to work the ranch."

"Well, I guess that's okay for you. But it's not what I want to do," Jerry said. "I'd like to get more schooling, maybe be a businessman, or one of those lawyers. Maybe even a doctor."

Will stopped suddenly and faced his brother. "Wow! I didn't know you felt that way. I could always tell you didn't like the farming much, but you're a good hand with cowhorses. You could train them and handle the cattle end. Tim and I can do the farming."

"Aw, it's more than that, Will." Jerry sighed audibly. "I want to get out of Long Valley. I'd like to see the cities, maybe even go to Ireland." There, he'd said it. Jerry watched Will's reaction. The boys stood there on the boardwalk, letting their other brothers walk on ahead. Will looked hard at Jerry and saw how serious he was. He knew that his brother loved Aunt Cauth's stories and songs. They all did. But Jerry most of all. Maybe it was the music.

"Have you told Dad how you feel?" Will asked.

"Naw, I don't have the guts. He'd have my hide."

315

"I don't think so, Jerry. Not about school. But he'd think you crazy about wanting to go to Ireland. You know how he feels about that. I'd have to agree with him there."

Jerry took a deep breath and plunged in. "Will, would you talk to him for me? Dad listens to you."

Will thought about it for a few minutes. "We'll see," he finally said. "If the chance comes up."

Father and sons camped that night in the big grove of oaks by the river near the place where Jeremiah had crossed twenty years before, when he'd first set off looking for his own piece of land. Each of them had a bedroll tied behind the saddle and some food in the saddlebags. They didn't even bother with a fire, and they set off early in the morning on the twenty-five mile ride back to the ranch.

Jeremiah was in a thoughtful mood as they rode. He glanced from time to time at the son named after him and wondered what was in the boy's head. Will had taken his father aside at the camp the night before and told him of his conversation with Jerry.

"He's different than we are, Dad," Will had tried to explain. "He wants something else out of life. He wants more education." He paused. "And to get off the ranch."

"Get off the ranch!" Jeremiah was shocked, dismayed. "Why? It's a good life he has and a future. There's plenty of land for all of you and you can be homesteading more."

"Well, I just promised him I'd bring it up to you," Will said. "Give you some notice, Dad, so you can be thinking about it when Jerry asks you himself."

Jeremiah had thought about little else all morning. The boy was full of romantic ideas—as for more schooling—he'd already passed all the tests that the school teacher could devise. A lawyer or a doctor? Didn't he know it's the land that matters? *I worked all my life for it and it's here. It's to be theirs. Why would he be wanting to throw it away? He doesn't know how precious it is.*

But schooling was a different matter. How could he be against further education when he himself wanted to learn everything he could from the time he could talk? *And then being a teacher, myself. Is it from me he gets this yearning? Oh, how I'd miss the boy.*

Jeremiah thought about it for several days before finally bringing it up to Catherine. "That school in Boston your brother wrote about, Cauth. Are you thinking that would be suitable for Jerry?"

Catherine was surprised. "Is it schooling he's been talking to you about?"

"Well, no," Jeremiah admitted. "He had Will speak for him. I'm not knowing why the boy's fearful to talk to me. Will says he wants off the land, doesn't want to be a rancher. Wants to be a lawyer or some such thing."

"Well, my brother's offer still stands. John and Rose would take him in and enter him at St. Brendan's. He could take the college tests after a year or so."

"Cauth, I'm just not knowing," Jeremiah said. "I hate the thought of him going so far away. We'll be missing him around here. Who knows what wild ideas he'll get in his head hanging around those Irish lads in Boston. But how can I be standing in the way of his education?"

Catherine remained silent and let Jeremiah work it through in his mind. Then he said, "Perhaps he'll be getting his fill of schooling and city life and be wanting to come home, back to the land. It may make him appreciate what he has here."

"Aye, Jerry. That's possible," Catherine said. "But you have to face it that all your sons aren't the same. Jerry is a bit different. You should let him try his wings." She paused. "Shall I be writing to John and Rose?"

Jeremiah nodded his reluctant agreement. He had no idea how relieved Catherine was, not about the boy going off to Boston, but that Jerry's dream of one day going to Ireland never came up.

CHAPTER FORTY-FIVE

THE ENTIRE CLEARY FAMILY had taken the wagon to Soledad to see seventeen-year-old Jeremiah Cleary Jr. off to school in Boston. Since they'd camped along the way, Catherine had insisted they stop by the river just outside of town so they could clean up, scrub off the dust and change into the clothes that she had ironed, carefully folded and placed in the huge chest carried in the wagon. Catherine helped Jerry pick out a new suit in Soledad, and then they'd all gone into the hotel dining room for dinner before the train came. There had been a strained silence during the entire meal, broken only by the waiter taking their orders.

Jeremiah proudly surveyed his family gathered around a large table, the boys with a scrubbed look in clean work clothes, Jerry distinctly apart from them in his new suit. He'd grown so tall and lean, Jeremiah suddenly realized he looked like a man. *And he'll soon be leaving us. And I'll not have said how proud I am of him and that I love him. He's my son. I used to hold him on my lap. I could kiss him and hug him. He'd come running and jump into my arms. I want to put my arms around him now so badly it fair hurts. And now I don't even know how to talk to him.*

Jerry sat stiffly, afraid to move with the unaccustomed high collar and the tie, his hair slicked back, his boots polished. The girls were so pretty and fresh in newly-ironed calico dresses, Kitty and Annie with their long hair in braids tied up with ribbons and Peggy with a red bow holding her loose, black curls. And Connie, he noted, looked every bit the young lady with her hair piled high on her head to display her graceful neck, a piece of white lace at her throat, as befit an eighteen-year-old.

Jeremiah wanted to tell them all how nice they looked, particularly his well dressed, handsome son. But the words stuck in his throat and came out, "Jerry, do you have your money?"

Of course he had his money. Aunt Cauth had sewed it into the waistband of his new trousers. "Yes, sir," Jerry said.

"You be sure to write, Jerry," Catherine reminded him for the tenth time.

"Yes, ma'am," he answered.

They ate in silence. Each very polite. Dining in a restaurant was a new experience. And Jerry's leaving had affected all of them.

Kitty had been critical of Jerry's desire to leave the ranch, but Connie understood and envied Jerry's opportunity. Annie was painfully conscious of this first crack in the family structure. Peggy, at six years of age, knew she'd miss her fun-loving brother, but had no concept of how long he'd be gone. The four boys were all puzzled by this brother who wanted something beside the precious land. They'd discussed it with him, but they were tolerant and wished him well. However, now sitting in this restaurant in Soledad, none of them could talk about it. Jerry was so different from them. It was almost as if he were already gone.

"Hello there, Mister Cleary. How nice to see you." Jeremiah looked up with an irritated frown at the young man who had approached the table.

"I'm Christopher Baxter. We met at Peach Tree. I'm here to catch the stage to Monterey and I just wanted to say hello."

"Ah yes, Mister Baxter." Jeremiah rose from his chair and introduced him to Catherine and the children. "We're here to see my son off on the train. He's going to Boston for school."

Baxter smiled and nodded through the introductions, but his urbane smile faded when Connie lifted her long lashes and met his eyes. With great effort he stopped staring at Connie long enough to ask Jerry, "What will you be studying?"

"I'm thinking about law," Jerry answered.

"Admirable, admirable. That's my profession. Best of luck to you," Baxter said. "Well, nice to have met you all." His eyes again were captured by Connie. "Goodbye, Miss Cleary."

"And who in the world was that?" Catherine asked as soon as Christopher Baxter was out of earshot.

"That's the son of the lawyer who represents Henry Miller," Jeremiah explained. "I met him at the store last month. He's going into practice with his father. Old San Francisco law firm. Big money. Miller and Lux is their largest client. So they're giving him a taste of ranch life."

"How old is he?" Catherine asked.

"Late twenties, I'd say. Why?"

"Oh," Catherine said. "I have the feeling we'll be seeing him again." She glanced over at Connie who responded with a blush.

As all the Clearys walked across the street to the train depot, father and son side by side, Jeremiah again tried to tell his son how proud he was, but again, all he could ask was if Jerry had his train ticket.

The northbound train had rolled off the turntable and steps had been set out for boarding passengers. Jerry put down his carpet bag and his mandolin case, kissed the cheek of each sister, Annie's wet with tears, and his cousin Connie. He gave each brother a firm handshake. He embraced Catherine and kissed her. "Thanks, Aunt Cauth. Thanks for everything," he said.

Then he turned to his waiting father. "Bye, Dad," he said awkwardly as he stuck out his hand.

* * * * *

"Give us another song, Jerry."

"Another round of *God Save Ireland*, Jerry."

Jeremiah Cleary, Jr. was in his element, playing rebel songs on his mandolin and roaring out the lyrics with his friends. *"Climbed they up the rugged stair, rung their voices out in prayer...then with England's fatal cord around them cast....Close beneath the gallows tree, kissed like brothers lovingly...True to home and faith and freedom to the last."*

Jerry's classmates from St. Brendan's were gathered in Jerry's room at his Uncle John Hurley's home in Boston. Most of their fathers worked for the city or were in Boston politics. Dan Kelly, Pat Casey and Sean O'Reilly, Gavin Flaherty, Mike Flynn and Padriac Hennessy, son of Uncle John's good friend, Dan Hennessy, alderman of Ward Three. They were all going out later that evening to hear the champion of the Irish people, Charles Stewart Parnell, speak at a rally in Boston at Faneuil Hall. Parnell and John Dillon, and their colleagues from Ireland, had come to America to raise money for the Land League. It was a new organization, which, they were all sure, would be instrumental in finally gaining rights for Irish tenants.

"You should have been here to see Michael Davitt last year," Pat Casey said to Jerry. "We all went to the meeting." Casey's eyes were lit with excitement. "There were thousands there. You should have heard that man speak."

"What did he say?" Jerry was eager to hear.

"He mostly told his own story," Pat Casey said.

"Yeah," Paddy Hennessy joined in, "his family was evicted before he was even five years old. Put out on the road, their cabin knocked, and they were left to starve, all because they couldn't meet an impossible rent."

"He's been working for the people ever since," Dan Kelly explained. "Been in jail. Convicted in eighteen-seventy and sentenced to fifteen years, but they let him out last year, and he's still protesting against the landlords' excessive rents. He's the one who started the Land League."

Many of the old Fenians, Jerry's Uncle John among them, served on the sponsoring committee, and saw to it that the students had seats up front for the rally. Jerry looked around at the audience of more than a thousand Boston Irish who packed Faneuil Hall to hear Parnell. Many were just off the boat, others had been long established in America and had political clout, owned property and had money. It was these more affluent ones whom Charles Parnell hoped to reach. But he also knew that those just over from Ireland—barely out of the clutches of poverty, with fresh stories of British oppression—would be the ones to whip up their American-Irish relatives and open their pocketbooks for the cause.

"The object of the Land League," Parnell told the approving crowd, "is to reduce rack rents, to facilitate the ownership of the soil by the occupants. The landlord system will never be fair to the Irish yeomanry." His voice rose dramatically. "With land reform we'll be having home rule." A huge cheer welled up from the audience. Parnell waited for the auditorium to quiet down. "This is another time of sore distress for the rural people of Ireland," his deep voice intoned. "Crops, particularly the potatoes, have been very poor. You all know what this means. You've lived through it. But many did not. It means more famine in the land, more evictions. And even while the people suffer, the landlords impose higher and higher rents, many times above Griffith's Evaluations."

"What's that?" Jerry whispered to Kelly, who was sitting next to him.

"A system the British had in eighteen-fifty of putting a value on holdings, what a house or farm would be worth," Kelly whispered back. "That would be considered a fair rent. It's supposed to be the same today. But they're charging two and three times as much—it's called rack renting."

Jerry nodded and turned his attention back to the mesmerizing speaker on the platform. Parnell's voice rang out. "The Land League encourages tenants to consider first the needs of their families before satisfying the claims of the landlords. They must not allow their wives and children to go hungry. They must keep a firm grip on their homesteads."

"Down with the dirty rack renters — !" a voice yelled from the back of the auditorium.

"Send out Captain Midnight! He'll show them," another cried out.

"The bastards! Cut a few British throats — !" a man bellowed from one of the front seats.

Parnell raised his hands for silence. "The Land League does not advocate violence," he said firmly, his eyes searching his listeners. "We denounce acts of violence, but we urge peaceful resistance to evictions. Control your rage. You can help by contributing. Money is needed to further this political aim. Meanwhile, people are starving. These are your parents, your aunts and uncles, your brothers and sisters," Parnell exhorted the huge crowd. "They need your help."

Jerry Cleary jumped up, leading the tumultuous applause, clapping till his hands hurt.

When Parnell and his men left for Baltimore, Jerry Cleary and his friends from St. Brendan's followed along.

When Jerry had asked his uncle's permission to travel with the group, John Hurley gave it willingly. "Good for the lad," he told his wife Rose. "Give him some exposure to the world and he can meet important people. He'll work for a good cause. Beside the new school term hasn't started yet."

From Baltimore the young, idealistic Irishmen traveled by train to New York City for another rally. They worked the crowd and helped with the collections. Jerry Cleary soon was a hit with Parnell's people. Whenever they gathered in their rooms, Jerry would bring out his mandolin and lead the singing of the rebel songs. More than once he privately thanked his beloved Aunt Cauth for having taught them to him.

"A few of your songs, Jerry, are worth more than all our speeches," Parnell remarked one evening after a rally in Manhattan.

When Jerry reached New York a letter from Catherine caught up with him. She wrote that crops were good—there'd been enough rain, thank God—and cattle prices were up, too. Everybody was well. Jerry looked surprised as he read the next few lines. *It's beginning to appear that we'll be losing Connie from the ranch, too. Remember that young lawyer who spoke to us in Soledad? His name is Christopher Baxter. Your father gave him permission to call on Connie and he is a frequent visitor to Long Valley.*

That fellow? Jerry thought about it a moment. He was too old for Connie and she was too young to be courting seriously. Then he remembered that Connie and he were nearly the same age. He smiled and went back to the letter.

We've moved into the new house, Catherine wrote. *It was finished in the spring and it's just grand. It is large and roomy with a big kitchen, and a large parlor with a fireplace. It has a porch all around. There are six bedrooms. Your father and I have one, of course, but there is one for Will and Tim, and another for Danny and Seamus. Connie and Annie, Kitty and little Peggy share two rooms in back. Aren't we the grand ones?*

But there is one room that is vacant. It will always be warm in winter because it is just off the kitchen. Your father moved all your things in there, and he says that is your room, ready for you when you come home. You know how he is about speaking his feelings, but I know he loves you and misses you very much. We all miss you. We trust you are doing well in school. Please write soon and tell us all the news of John and Rose and Boston. With love, Your Aunt Cauth.

Included with the letter was the postal money order to cover Jerry's tuition and his expenses for another term at St. Brendan's.

When Parnell's tour of America was finished, he had more than seventy thousand dollars for the Irish cause. And shipped along with him, out of New York, were tons of food and clothing.

Among the passengers was Jeremiah Cleary, Jr.

CHAPTER FORTY-SIX

"CONNIE, I HEARD FROM MY FATHER," Christopher Baxter said. "It's time for me to join the firm in San Francisco," He paused nervously. "So I'll soon be leaving Peach Tree."

It was after supper and the couple had been given the privacy of the parlor in the new Cleary ranch house, luxurious by local standards. Christopher Baxter anxiously looked at Connie for some encouragement, but she sat demurely, hands folded in her lap, downcast eyes shaded by those long, black lashes. He cleared his throat. "I've spoken to your father."

Connie raised her eyes and looked squarely at him. "You have?"

"Yes, I asked for your hand in marriage. He said it was up to you. So, will you marry me, Constance Cleary?"

There was a long silence and then Connie took a deep breath and again looked up in his face. "My name isn't Constance." Christopher Baxter looked puzzled. "It's Conchita Cleary." Christopher nodded tentatively.

"And Jeremiah is not my father."

"What?" Christopher stared at Connie in shock. "What are you saying?"

"Jeremiah Cleary is a fine, kind man who has been like a wonderful father to me," Connie spoke softly. "I'm his niece, his brother's daughter." She waited for a reaction, but Christopher was too stunned to say anything. Connie decided she may as well tell him all of it now, even though he'd probably walk away. She took a deep breath and plunged in.

"My mother was a beautiful, courageous Mexican woman who loved me deeply and took very good care of me after my drunken father left her to go off prospecting for gold, and then during the war he joined the Union Army. I was four years old when my mother died. My father was gone so Jeremiah Cleary took me in. He's the only real father I've ever known. And Aunt Cauth has been like a mother." Connie looked defiantly at

Christopher Baxter, expecting him to be put off by her revelation. He surely wouldn't want a wife who was half Mexican.

He rose from his chair and began to pace the room. Long moments passed and Connie, sitting straight and fiercely proud, watched him, puzzled, confused. When he didn't speak, she was about to ask him to leave. But suddenly he turned, went to her and knelt by her chair. He took one of the hands knotted into a fist in her lap. He gently pried it open. He brought the fingers to his lips. "I love you, Conchita Cleary. I want you to be my wife."

All the defiance went out of her and tears filled her eyes. He kissed them away. "Where is your father, Connie? Do I need his permission, too?"

She began to laugh, a bitter, brittle laugh, but tears still spilled onto her cheeks. "I have no idea where he is, Chris. He left me with broken promises many years ago. He said he'd come back for me, that we'd be rich and live in a big house in San Francisco."

Christopher smiled. "I'll give you the big house in San Francisco," he said.

"Oh, Chris, that was just a childish dream I cherished," Connie said. "I don't need the riches or the mansion. I just need a place where I belong, that belongs to me."

"I'll make that place for you, Connie," Christopher said. "But you haven't answered me." He took her face in his two hands and looked deeply into the black eyes. "Conchita Cleary, will you marry me?"

She smiled. "Yes, Christopher Baxter, I'll marry you."

* * * * *

Matthew Cleary had come into Monterey several months previously, disgusted with the small amount of gold his mine was producing. His money soon played out and he went to work again at the blacksmith shop to earn enough for supplies so he could return to Los Burros mining district. He was living in the room behind the smithy, but hadn't saved much for a new stake because nearly everything he earned went to quench his thirst. He'd staggered red-eyed from his rumpled bed one Sunday morning thanking God it wasn't a work day. He was standing on the corner of Alvarado and Franklin Street wishing he hadn't finished the last of his Old Ned the night before.

Matthew started to walk across the street as an open Landau, pulled by a smart team of two burnished bays, rolled around the corner. He jumped back to keep from behind hit, but caught a glimpse of the passengers as they passed. There was a driver and a middle-aged couple. But between them sat a young girl wearing a stylish suit of powder blue, a bonnet to match atop her dark hair, her beauty touched by the early morning sun.

It was Lupe, by God!

Matthew was shaken. He stood uncertainly for a moment and then started to run after the carriage. But it quickly disappeared around the corner and he stopped, looking after it and breathing heavily. He felt as if he'd seen a ghost.

"What's got you in such a dither, Cleary?" It was one of his drinking companions from the night before, stumbling along the street toward him.

"The girl in that carriage. Who was she?" he asked.

"Whadda you care who that was? Those swells got no use for the likes of you, Cleary. That was some of that Baxter outfit, probably on their way to church at the mission."

"But the girl? Who was the girl?"

"Maybe she's the one I heard about, a gal from some ranch down in south county that's gonna marry into the outfit. How the hell do I know?"

Matthew stayed near that street corner all morning until the carriage returned and he followed it to a home on Alvarado. He watched from behind some bushes across the street as the young girl was helped down from the Landeau and gracefully ascended the steps to disappear into the house. The hair stood up on the back of Matthew's neck. His hands shook. It was Lupe! But it couldn't be Lupe. She was under that mound of earth in the San Juan graveyard.

Connie! It had to be his daughter, now a beautiful young lady, the reincarnation of her mother.

Matthew had to see her, hold her, talk to her, tell her he loved her, how much she'd been on his mind all these years. He started toward the house. But halfway across the street he stopped.

He looked down at his broken brogans, at the tattered Levis he wore. He ran his hand across his face, feeling the ragged beard and realized the picture he made, an old, dirty, unkempt drunk. Matthew hurried back to his hiding place. He couldn't appear to Connie in such a condition. Matthew looked at the house, at the door through which she'd disappeared. He wanted so badly to see his daughter. But he couldn't. Not like this. He couldn't let her see him like this. Tears welled up in his bleary eyes.

Matthew Cleary made a vow. He stood before the house with Connie inside and swore he'd stop drinking. He'd save his money and get that stake. He'd return to his mine on Alder Creek and work it until he prospered. Then, in a new suit with a gold watch chain across the vest, his pockets heavy with money, he'd present himself to Connie, a successful man, the father who loved her.

* * * * *

The wedding was held in the big mission church of San Carlos de Borromeo near Monterey, where Connie had been the house guest of Christopher's aunt and cousins for a month before the ceremony, which was considered the social event of the year.

All the Clearys attended the wedding. Jeremiah, in a new three-piece suit purchased just for the happy occasion, gave the bride away. She was radiant, her dark coloring and lustrous black hair set off by a lacy, white veil and white dress, its long train held up by two attendants, one of Christopher's little cousins, and the other six-year-old Peggy Cleary. Annie Cleary, only fourteen, was proud, but embarrassed, to be chosen her cousin's maid of honor, and Will Cleary was invited by Christopher to be his best man. Except for Jerry Jr., the rest of the Cleary family sat smiling with pride in the front pew.

The reception was a lavish affair, held in the garden of Christopher's aunt's home on Alvarado Street. Music and dancing took place on the specially-constructed pavilion. Champagne flowed and toasts were offered to the bride and groom. Will had worked for weeks to perfect his toast and, sweating nervously in his tight collar and heavy coat, raised his glass. "To the new member of our family and my new friend, Christopher, and to my cousin Connie, who is really more like a sister to me, I wish them a long life, much happiness and a family as wonderful as ours."

The new Mr. and Mrs. Christopher Baxter stepped up into the waiting Landau behind the liveried coachman and two beautiful bays for the ride to Salinas and the train to San Francisco. Wedding guests gathered around, throwing rice and calling out their good luck wishes.

Connie noticed the tall, thin man in rough miner's clothing who peered at her from the fringes of the crowd. But she didn't recognize her father.

CHAPTER FORTY-SEVEN

THERE WAS A THUMPING IN JERRY'S CHEST and his breathing was rapid. But neither was caused by the steep path he was climbing. He was excited. But he was taking his time, savoring every bit of the scene as he trudged up Knockauneen hill from Skibbereen to Coolnagurrane. He'd been looking forward to this moment ever since he knew he was really on his way to Ireland. *This is me, Jeremiah Cleary, Jr., walking the same path as my father and mother once did, the same path as their father and mother, and theirs before them.*

He came to a turn in the path and stopped, looking around carefully. It was just as Aunt Cauth had remembered and described to him. The old Hurley cottage stood there right off the path, but all that remained were the crumbling rock walls and the gable ends. The roof was gone, knocked off fourteen years ago. Jerry studied the ruins. This has been his mother's home. And his Aunt Cauth's home. The place where his uncles grew up. His grandparents had lived here, and their parents, and it was so tiny and looked so pathetic.

He climbed a bit further, and there, just around a bend, he saw it—the Cleary holding. Jerry stopped again to look and catch his breath. The cottage, whitewashed, its thatch in place, stood in front, just off the path, and behind it the cow shed, and a pig sty, the fields beyond with sheep grazing, and a cow in the pasture. Some men were turning the lazy beds in the distance, and there on the stoop, before the open door, catching the weak rays of the afternoon March sun, sat an old man.

Jerry cautiously approached. The old man removed his short clay pipe, waved it in Jerry's direction and nodded. "H'ar ya?"

Jerry politely responded, "God bless all here," and studied the man. The resemblance was there, all right. This looked like an older version of his father, not as tall, perhaps, and thinner, but surely it was a Cleary. But Liam Cleary would only be a few years older than his father, thought Jerry. This man seemed much older.

"Uncle Liam?" he ventured.

"Uncle Liam, is it? And who is this that's calling me Uncle Liam?"

It was his father's voice, but gruffer, rougher and the brogue was much thicker. Jerry had been raised hearing Jeremiah's brogue, grown softer and musical with his years in America, and Aunt Cauth's accent was gentle. But this was harsh, and hard for him to understand.

"I'm Jeremiah Cleary, Junior from California," he replied.

The man appraised him, silently looked him over, up and down, and then pronounced, "Well now, and I do believe you are. *Cèad mìle fàilte!* Welcome, lad, a hundred thousand welcomes."

He stood and called through the open door, "Eileen, Eileen, it's a visitor we have and from America! My own nephew, Jerry." By this time Liam had Jerry in a bear hug and the young man hardly was able to greet his Aunt Eileen, who smiled warmly and invited him in.

She spoke in Irish and then, realizing he didn't understand, switched to English. "Take a stool, lad, sit down, sit down. There's enough stools for all. There now. And a glass of cool buttermilk?"

Jerry hated buttermilk. He never could understand his father's craving for it, nor could he develop a taste for it himself. But now he accepted the glass, only to be polite. He sipped and looked around the inside of the dreary little house. How small it was. And sparsely furnished. Only this table, and a few stools, and some straw in the corner. He supposed there was another room behind the fireplace, and he could see a loft above. A small stack of sod was piled by the hob. A pot of something hung cooking from the hook over the fire.

Since arriving in Ireland two months earlier, Jerry had grown accustomed to seeing terrible poverty and realized that this holding of his ancestors was better than most. But coming from America, and his comfortable ranch home, then going to school in Boston, Jerry was appalled that people were forced to live as most did in Ireland.

He didn't know what to say. He was saddened by his surroundings and kept his attention on his hand holding the old, cracked glass filled with buttermilk. The situation was saved by two lanky young men about his own age, who suddenly filled the doorway, stooped, and entered the cottage. They stood shyly before him, twisting their wool caps in their hands.

"Patrick and Terrence," Liam boomed. "It's your own cousin, Jerry, from America, I want you to meet."

The boys nodded and smiled at Jerry, who rose to greet his cousins. After firm handshakes and claps on the shoulder, they all three stood speechless, self-consciously grinning. Jerry was suddenly very aware of his new pants and coat to match. And of his heavy, woolen knit sweater. His cousins' garb was rough and patched, and they were barefoot despite the March chill. He noticed their eyes on him, missing nothing.

"Well now," Liam said. "Well now. And your father, how is himself?"

"He's just fine, Uncle Liam. Fine." Jerry didn't want to admit that his father might not yet know that he was in Ireland. "He'd prefer I stayed in school in Boston. Or, better yet, that I'd go home and work on the ranch."

"I can understand that. A father misses a son. But what are you doing here in Ireland?"

"I'm working with the Land League," Jerry explained.

"The Land League, is it? And what good is it doing to be maiming cattle, and crippling horses, and such?"

"No, no, Uncle Liam. Those things aren't our doing. That's not what we stand for. Parnell asks for passive resistance to evictions. The death threats of Captain Midnight don't come from us. We advocate the boycott."

"The boycott? And what's that? I've not heard of this boycott."

"It's in Mayo that it started. Some agent named Captain Boycott took unfair action against the tenants and everyone took a stand against the man," Jerry explained. "No one would shoe his horses, or work for him, no matter the wage he offered. No one would grind his wheat, or sell him goods. They shut Boycott out completely. He had to leave Mayo. That's what Parnell proposes be done to landlords and agents who charge unfair rents, or try to evict. Or to those grabbers who take over leases after evictions. They call it boycotting."

"I see, I see. Would that work here in Cork?" Liam wondered. "It's evicted we'd be right now and out on the road, the lot of us, if it hadn't been for your father, Jerry. He's a grand man, sending home the money in famine days, and again this last time. God grant him long life."

Eileen crossed herself. "God bless him," she said in Irish, and started to ladle potatoes out of the pot, placing them on a plate to cool. "We'll be having a bite of supper," she said.

"Aye, your father and your Uncle Matt saved us with their money from Boston in those hard days." Liam began to peel a potato. "You be thanking him for us again next you write him."

"You write him your thanks Uncle Liam," Jerry responded. "I know he'd like to hear from you."

Liam looked up from his potato peeling. "Well now, the truth of it is, lad, I'm not much of a one for writing. I never learned the proper way of it. But my boys now," he nodded toward Pat and Terry, "they learned from Michael Harrington at the Skibbereen school. Your da now, he was the one for learning. Matt and I had no need for the books, saw no use in it. What do you hear of your Uncle Matt?"

"He's a gold miner. But we haven't heard from him for several years."

"A gold miner? Aye, I'd heard he went searching for gold. And did he find it?"

"I don't really know — " Jerry let his voice trail off.

"Well, you have the look of him, you know."

"That's what Aunt Cauth says."

"Ah, your Aunt Cauth. That Catherine Hurley, she was the spunky one."

Jerry was amazed at the way his relatives ate potatoes. They only dipped them in salt water for flavor. He glanced at his cousins and his Aunt Eileen, silent, except for their chewing. One potato was enough for him, but he wanted to be polite so he reached into the pot for another. But he passed on the buttermilk and said, "Aunt Cauth has told me so much about things here, I feel as if I've been here before."

"Catherine has been the one telling you the stories, has she? And what about your da? Does he talk much of the old days?" Liam wondered.

"No, Uncle Liam. He never says much about Ireland at all—Aunt Cauth says he's trying to forget the bad times."

"Aye," Liam agreed. "I can understand him putting those times behind him. But the Irish now, you've not learned to speak it?"

"No, we never learned it. Dad and Aunt Cauth rarely use it. Dad wanted us to learn only English. He claims Irish is useless in the world nowadays." Jerry's face reddened when he realized what he'd said, but he continued. "He wants us to be American in every way."

Supper ended, Liam pushed himself up and announced, "I'll be checking the animals in for the night. Come along, Jerry, and tell me about things on your farm, or ranch, as you call it in California." Liam turned to his sons. "And you, Patrick, will you invite some of the neighbors to come by and meet your cousin? You, too, Terry. Be sure to tell young McGurk. He just might bring around a drop or so, if he's the man his father was. A bit of a *hooley* we'll be having to celebrate," Liam decreed.

He'd been eyeing Jerry's mandolin case and asked, "And is that your suitcase, lad?"

"No, it's my mandolin."

"A mandolin, is it? Well, that's just grand. And can you play it?"

"Some," Jerry said modestly.

334

"Lovely, lovely. Terry, you be telling Dennis O'Shea about the mandolin and maybe he'll bring his father's old fiddle. Who'll have a whistle? Oh, this will be a grand time."

And it was. The little cottage was soon crowded with people, young and old, all with questions for Jerry about America, and fond remembrances of his father and mother—-"that dear Molly, a frolicsome lass,"—and his Aunt Cauth, "there was a rebel spirit in that one."

"Ah, sure, and your father was a fine lad," Patrick Flynn assured Jerry. "That he was. When he left here I told them all he was certain to be a great success in America." Others at the party claimed to have been at "the waking of the two of them, off to Amerikay, Jeremiah and Matthew, grand lads they were."

But it was an old man, gnarled by time, who hobbled in and peered up at Jerry, who affected him most. Liam introduced him. "This is Dennis O'Farrell, back from a life in Dublin, who knew your da."

"Aye, his teacher I was," the old man explained. "A fine, bright pupil, I remember him to be, and a good humored one, my best student. When I heard it was his own son visiting I had to look you over, lad. My best to your father and long life to you."

O'Farrell, bent over and with a game leg, limped to the fire, and Jerry, touched that his father was so well remembered by this man from his distant past, watched him nod off, sitting right there on the hob with the party noisily swirling about him.

Then Dennis O'Shea plucked his fiddle strings for a quick tune-up and launched into a reel that had everyone tapping their feet. Jerry was shy about bringing out his mandolin, although he recognized the tune as one his aunt used to play on her whistle. The *poteen* was passed around. "*Slàinte*," they toasted and Jerry tried a swallow. He nearly choked. He hid his sputtering as best he could, but not from a red-headed girl in the corner, who grinned broadly at his discomfort.

335

To cover his embarrassment, Jerry took out his mandolin and quietly tuned it to the fiddle. O'Shea moved into *Brennan on the Moor* and gave Jerry a nod. This was one he knew well, a favorite of Aunt Cauth, and Jerry sang along as he chorded the accompaniment. "*His name was Willie Brennan and in Ireland he did dwell...A brace of loaded pistols he carried night and day...He never robbed a poor man upon the king's highway...But what he'd taken from the rich, like Turpin and Black Bess...He always did divide it with the widow in distress...Brennan on the Moor, Brennan on the Moor, a brave, undaunted robber was bold Brennan on the Moor.*"

They all joined in when Jerry struck up "The Rising of the Moon" and smiled their approval, especially the buxom redhead, who had moved over in front to watch him play, and now sang lustily, "*For the pikes must be together at the rising of the moon.*"

Jerry had learned the words to *Dear Old Skibbereen* and judged this a good one for the crowd. They all responded by joining in. Then he roused them with "*God save Ireland, said the heroes...God save Ireland, said they all...whether on the scaffold high or the battlefield we die...Oh, what matter when for Erin dear we fall.*"

"Good for you, lad," they praised. "Good one, that." They clapped and stamped their feet, and applauded Jerry for his playing, and for knowing the old rebel songs. Eileen Cleary looked toward the redheaded girl. "And now you, Nora. Give us a song."

"Aye, Nora, give us *Nell Flaherty's Drake*," Liam requested.

Nora tossed her thick, red mane and stepped to the center of the room with a swish of her petticoat. Dennis O'Shea gave her a note on his fiddle and she swung into her song about the "*wicked savage, to grease his white cabbage, who cruelly murdered Nell Flaherty's drake.*"

She smiled boldly at Jerry as she sang the curse, "*May his pig never grunt, may his cat never hunt, may the ghost ever haunt him at dead of the night...May his hen never lay, may his*

ass never bray, may his goat fly away like an old paper kite..."
When she started the song everyone in the room was grinning
in anticipation, and, by the time she finished, they were all
roaring with laughter.

When the party finally broke up, each guest went out the
door wishing Jerry a long life, "*Fad saol agat.*"

Nora's father rushed her along before Jerry could say a word
to her, but his smile brought an answering one. That night he
lay on his straw pallet by the fireplace, and although he was
tired to the bone, sleep would not come. Images swirled
through his mind—the people he'd just met, his relatives and
their friends, and the redheaded Nora; all mixed together with
anticipation of the next day when he'd be out with the Land
League protesting an eviction. The knot of excitement that had
built in the pit of his stomach kept him awake for the rest of
the night.

CHAPTER FORTY-EIGHT

A N EARLY MORNING MIST shielded the rising sun as Jerry
Cleary left Coolnagurrane shortly after dawn. He was to
meet his Aunt Cauth's brother, James, north of Skibbereen on
the River Ilen. They would be joined by several others walking
to Drimoleague. He was excited at the prospect of finally doing
something—they would be on the scene at an eviction. The
Land League had decreed there'd be no more evictions without
witnesses. The more people who saw the tyrannical acts the
better, Parnell had said. But he'd insisted that there be no violence. Passive intimidation was the method of protest. It
might not stop the evictions, but it would have political effect.

As he strode along, Jerry thought about Nora and the saucy
way she'd tossed her head when she sang that funny song, and
her pretty smile, her lovely figure—the kind that the boys

would talk about back at St. Brendan's. Nora had taken his eye more than any girl he'd ever met. And he hadn't even properly met her. Her father had rushed her out of the cottage so fast he didn't have a chance to talk to her—didn't even know her last name. But he knew where to find her. And he'd be back.

But right now he had other things to think about. He'd have to write his father and aunt and explain how he came to be in Ireland. Explain about the money. By now they surely knew where he was. Uncle John must have written them when he didn't return to Boston. He'd asked Paddy Hennessy to explain to Uncle John for him. It just happened. They invited him to join Parnell's group, and the money for passage, and some extra, was there in his hand. It seemed right. He'd explain why this experience would turn out to be a better education than any history lesson he'd learn in school. And, of course, he'd return to school eventually. But this was his big chance to help Ireland. Aunt Cauth would understand. But would his father? He doubted it.

He felt some pangs of guilt about the money his father had sent to pay tuition for the next term at St. Brendan's. How would he make it up when he got home? How would he face his father? The last thing he wanted was to further alienate Jeremiah.

The meeting place on the river came into view and Jerry could see his Uncle James with a group of men waiting for him. He waved and hurried toward them, all thoughts of Nora, and school, and his family in California faded away. He became focused on the next day's mission and his heart pounded with excitement and purpose.

They arrived at Gavin Ginnity's cottage that afternoon. The peppery little man met them at the door, waving an ancient flintlock pistol.

"Put that thing down, man. We're here to help you!" James Hurley exclaimed.

Ginnity squinted at them, studied them and then slowly lowered his firearm. "All right, then. You can come up," he said, beckoning.

"Where in God's name did you get that relic?" Hurley asked. "Let me see it."

He put out his hand and Ginnity reluctantly gave him the gun. It was rusty, parts were missing, and there was no flash pan, no powder, nor shot.

"This looks like it was left over from the Flight of the Earls," Hurley said with a laugh, referring to the exodus of defeated Irish leaders two hundred years before. He handed it back to Ginnity. "Put it away, man. Or better yet, bury it before it gets you in trouble."

"Trouble, is it?" Ginnity said, his voice rising with anger. "Sure, and there's trouble enough with the high and mighty Sir Richard Wimberly wanting me off my land. This will warn the bastards, the filthy *Sessenach*. " Ginnity again waved the century-old pistol. "They'll not move me!"

James Hurley didn't know Gavin Ginnity, only that he was a widower whose two sons had emigrated to America. He looked ancient, nearly as old as his pistol. Ginnity was small, shriveled, bent, but wiry and tough. He'd been out with the rebels in every rising since '48, survived the famine, and tenaciously maintained his little holding.

But now, his farm and several others along the nearby road, all the property of Sir Richard Wimberly, were to be cleared by the authorities to provide grazing land for sheep. As cause for eviction, rents had been raised well beyond the ability of the small tenant farmers to pay. Sir Richard was a rack renter of the worst sort.

Ginnity's face was now red with rage. "Oh, sure, I could be paying his damnable rent money as soon as my sons send it. Good lads, they remember their old father," Ginnity said. "But be damned if I will! Three times the evaluation he's asking, and only because I've whitewashed this old cottage and moved the dung pile. I'll die first." Again he waved the broken pistol.

"Calm down, Ginnity," Hurley said. "Calm down a bit. No one is going to die."

"Oh, now and who is it to be telling me what I can and can't be doing?"

"My name is James Hurley from Ballydehob."

"A Fenian, were you not?" Ginnity's old eyes peered at Hurley for the first time.

"Aye, you could call me that," Hurley replied.

Ginnity's face softened. He smiled and nodded. "Well, well then. You've done your bit, you have. I'm honored you're with me. Come in, come in."

James and Jerry, and the other men entered the tiny cottage. All except James found seats by the fireplace and on the floor. James took Ginnity aside to explain the reason for their presence.

"The word got out about Wimberly's plans for the morrow. They're to march out from the Drimoleague barracks at dawn to serve you here, as well as Bryan, Maloney and Walsh down the road. We'll make our showing here as this is the first place they'll come to. The boys will be here from Drinagh and Aghaville, and some from the Skibbereen area. I'm told that they're even walking over from Bantry." Hurley paused, intently watching Ginnity for a moment, seeing that the old man was taking in every word.

"So there should be as many as a hundred men or more here, and some women, by dawn. We'll line them up across the road and in front of your cabin, Ginnity," Hurley explained. "They'll have to march through the lot to serve the notice. It may stop them. And it may not. But no one is to strike a blow. We want no violence. We all lose that way."

"And yourself? Will you stand by me at the door, Hurley? I'd be proud to have you by my side," Ginnity said.

"Nay, I can't," James replied. "I'd be proud to stand with a fighter like yourself. But if I'm seen I'll be arrested and I've had my fill of jail. My role is in the organizing. I'll be across the road and out of sight. My nephew here, he'll stand with you."

James pointed to Jerry, who rose and stood by his uncle. James put his arm around the young man's shoulder and led him to Ginnity, who shook his hand. Jerry felt a surge of pride.

"Done then," Ginnity said. "Now I'll place a pot of *praties* on the hook, and while they're boiling we'll share a drop of the finest. Made it myself."

A few hours later Jerry fell into a fitful sleep, fully clothed, on the bed of straw in the corner of Ginnity's cottage. Visions of the redheaded Nora, mixed with his father's frowning face and soldiers marching up the road, caused him to toss and turn until he realized that he'd not sleep for the second night in a row. It was still dark, a late moon giving what light there was, when he stepped outside the cottage. It was then Jerry saw the shadowy figures massing by the roadside. More kept arriving from all directions, and by dawn a large crowd was in place. James Hurley had positioned them along the road and in front of Ginnity's cottage. Jerry defiantly took his stand in the doorway alongside the beleaguered little man and anxiously watched the road.

It wasn't long. First they could see the morning sun glinting on the rifles. Then the sound of tramping feet and the cadence calls reached their ears. *Here they come.*

Jerry's pulse quickened. All his senses were on alert. He felt the adrenaline flowing. He glanced down at the proud, tough little man, who barely came up to his shoulder, determinedly standing by his side.

James Hurley saw the constable on horseback riding beside Charles Warren, the landlord's agent. Sir Richard himself wouldn't take the time for such mundane affairs, Hurley thought bitterly. He's probably at ease in some London parlor. He watched the soldiers pass from his secret vantage point.

Twenty men, their red coats agleam in the early sun, marched in step behind the sergeant as they moved between the rows of Irish peasantry lining the road. The crowd, silent until now, began to call out, angry voices heckling the soldiers.

"D'anam don diabhal," they yelled. "Damn you, leave the people be — !" "Have you no pity? Bad *cess* to all of you — !" "March back to your holes, you dirty pack of vermin — !"

"Easy now. Keep in step," the sergeant ordered. "Pay no attention. Hep, two, three, four. Eyes front."

The people began to move with the soldiers along the road, brushing against them as they passed, trying to impede their progress, hissing, booing, cursing them. Looking down the road, Jerry could see young boys darting in and out, crossing the road, dashing between the files, disrupting the ranks. And women were walking, too, keeping pace with the soldiers, their loud, shrill voices shouting insults.

When the riders arrived at Ginnity's home, they were met by a wall of people guarding the cottage. The men on horseback couldn't move ahead without trampling the protesters. The horses became skittish, stepping sideways, fighting their bits and neighing, their riders angrily trying to control them. The air was filled with the sounds of confusion.

"Disburse there — ! Fall back. Out of the way — ! This is the law," the red-faced constable shouted as he waved a piece of paper. Jerry realized it must be the eviction notice.

The contingent of soldiers had drawn up just beyond the line of people, halted by the clenched fists, the determined stand, the weight of numbers. They were uncertain, almost afraid, perhaps not really wanting to hurt anyone.

"Move your men along, Sergeant," Agent Warren ordered. "Do your duty, Constable, move this rabble. You there, step aside for the law!" The people hooted and hollered and shouted him down. But then an order rang out, heard above the roar of the crowd.

"Fix bayonets — !"

There was the clank and clash, the sounds of steel being locked in place. Then an awful silence fell. After the raucous noise, the silence shattered the morning. It was so still it resounded. Frighteningly.

"Forward — !" the sergeant shouted. "March!"

With bayonets fixed in place, the soldiers moved ahead. The crowd, fearful now, parted before the naked blades.

Suddenly, Jerry Cleary realized that he and Ginnity were all that was left between the might of England and the cottage door.

The crowd was quiet as Warren stepped down from his horse and the constable began to read the eviction notice.

"To hell with you and your damnable paper!" Ginnity yelled. Jerry felt him move at his side.

"He's got a gun!" Warren cried.

A shot! The report echoed through the crisp morning air.

The taller of the two men guarding the cabin door staggered forward, stumbled and sprawled full length on the frosty road. A man broke away from the crowd, dashed through the ranks of the soldiers and reached the fallen man. He rolled him onto his back. He looked back at the soldiers. "You bastards! You shot him!"

Blood slowly welled up on the young man's chest, soaking his shirt and spilling onto the ground, staining the hard-packed earth. It bubbled and frothed from his mouth. His wide-open eyes glazed over.

Jeremiah Cleary Jr. was dead.

"My God, you've killed him!" the man cried out.

The crowd was still. Shocked. Then somebody yelled, "That was James Hurley's nephew! He's just a lad."

Across the road, James Hurley started to run to his fallen nephew. But he stopped himself and quickly returned to his concealed observation place. He sank to the ground, moaning in grief, his head in his hands.

The red-coated ranks stood in silence, smoke curling from one rifle. "It was self-defense," a soldier said. "He had a gun."

"You didn't have to kill him," a woman screamed in anguish.

The sergeant held up his hand, facing his men. "Quiet there. Silence in the ranks."

"Constable, do your duty." It was Warren, up on his horse, back in command. "Get that pistol."

The constable took it from Ginnity's hand and raised it up to show Warren. "A worthless relic," he said. "This hasn't been fired for two hundred years."

"Too bad," Warren said. He looked at the constable. "Now get on with it. Serve your notice and knock the house. We've three more to do this morning."

CHAPTER FORTY-NINE

TIM LOPED THE YOUNG HORSE across the Cleary corral, slid him to a stop, and backed him up. Then he reined him left and right, the gelding swinging on his hind feet. Tim gathered him up and trotted to where Jeremiah and a horse buyer named Charlie Manning were leaning on the fence.

"Looks good to me." Manning nodded approvingly. "I'll take him."

"That's just fine," Jeremiah said, shaking Manning's hand. "And if there's any trouble with him, you bring him back." It was the same guarantee he gave with all the horses he sold, whether they were for saddle or harness. Cleary horses had a reputation now throughout Monterey County, and buyers came frequently to the ranch when they needed well-broke stock to do their cow work. Jeremiah didn't sell as many buggy and work horses as he had in the past, although, with his Percheron stud, they were larger and stronger than the average. Now that he was farming on such a large scale, he needed them himself. But he'd passed on to his sons the training techniques he'd learned from Celestino at Jefferson's so long ago and the Cleary saddle horses brought top prices.

Will Cleary rode into the yard just as Manning was leaving with his new horse tied behind the buggy. He waved to Manning and swung off his horse. "I had to ride over to the

Peach Tree store for some things, Dad, so I picked up the mail. Two letters here for you and Aunt Cauth."

"Thank you, Will. Kindly give them to your Aunt Cauth. She's in the kitchen. I'll be in shortly."

"All right. I'll leave them off and be on my way back to my place," Will said. He'd almost finished the cabin on his own homestead up the valley. Jeremiah smiled. "Good, Son, Good."

A few minutes later Jeremiah came into the house, but was brought up short by the terrible sounds of sobbing from the kitchen. Catherine was alone—Will had already left. She was sitting at the table, clutching one of the letters in her hand and crying uncontrollably.

Jeremiah rushed to her. "Cauth darlin', what's the matter?" But Catherine couldn't answer him.

Jeremiah pried the letter from her fingers and sat down next to her to read it.

It was from James Hurley in Ireland. *Dear Catherine and Jeremiah. It grieves me terribly to give you this news, which I know will break your hearts. Your son Jerry, is dead. He was accidentally killed here in Ireland by a bullet meant for another man. He was out with me and a group of Land League volunteers protesting an eviction. He was standing beside a tenant, who foolishly brandished a worthless weapon. A soldier fired the shot, which missed the tenant but killed Jerry instantly. I can assure you the boy suffered no pain.*

I have seen to his burial with Catholic services in Abbystrewery cemetery. I am unable to convey my sorrow and my sense of responsibility. This was a peaceful, non-violent mission, and I foresaw no danger in allowing young Jerry to accompany me. But I can never forgive myself. You may consider that he died for Ireland and that must be of some comfort. With deep sorrow, I remain, your brother, James Hurley.

Jeremiah read the entire letter through with a puzzled frown on his face. Jerry wasn't in Ireland. He was in Boston, in school. He wasn't with James. He was with John. This didn't make sense to Jerremiah. There must be some mistake.

Jeremiah was about to read it again when he noticed a second letter on the table by the sobbing Catherine. It was unopened. Jeremiah picked it up and held it to the afternoon light. It was from John Hurley in Boston, postmarked several weeks before the letter from James.

My dear sister and Jeremiah. It pains me to tell you that your son Jerry has taken ship to Ireland. He had gone to New York to attend a rally for Parnell with some of his school friends, all young men of good character and sons of my own friends. He had my permission to join them because St. Brendan's was not yet back in session and I felt the experience would be valuable for him. He was then invited to join the contingent with Parnell returning to Ireland and, without my knowledge, he did so. I am led to believe that he used his school allowance and tuition money from you to secure passage. I learned from Dan Hennessy's son that Jerry intends to write to you to fully explain what he has done and that he plans to return to school, where, as you know, he was getting excellent grades —

Jeremiah slumped in his chair and let the letter fall from his fingers.

"My son Jerry is dead." He whispered it to himself. Then he just sat there, stone faced, numb.

Catherine stopped sobbing. She wiped her eyes and looked at Jeremiah with ineffable sadness and compassion. She rose from the chair and stood beside her husband. She placed her hand on his head and started to stroke his hair. She wanted him to bury his face in her breast and cry out his pain. But instead, with a violent shrug, Jeremiah threw off her hand. He looked at his wife with an anger and fierceness she had never seen before.

"My son is dead. It's your fault!"

"My fault?" The grief-stricken Catherine was stunned, unable to comprehend his words. "My fault?" she asked through her tears.

"*You* filled his head with romantic notions of Ireland — ! *You* filled him with your rebel songs and your stories!" Jeremiah

346

spat out the words from between clenched teeth. Anguish mixed with rage as he spoke. "It was you who insisted he be sent to your brother in Boston for school! He'd be here with us today, he'd have stayed on the ranch, if it weren't for you!"

Jeremiah stood up, ramrod straight and glared at Catherine. The contempt and rage she saw in his eyes made her gasp. Her tears flowed out with a heartache she could hardly bear. "Oh Jerry, no — ! Please don't say that! Oh God, I'm sorry — I'm so sorry."

Jeremiah's icy silence cut through her like a knife. He turned and went out the kitchen door onto the porch. Catherine followed him, but he refused to even look at her. Lost in his anger and grief, he stumbled down from the porch and to the corral. There at the fence, he slumped against the boards, staring at the ground, at the place where Molly had been gored. But he wasn't seeing the image of his bleeding, dying young wife. He was seeing his son, lying on the ground in front of a miserable little Irish cottage. Dead for a worthless cause.

Catherine stood on the porch and watched him for a long time, tears blinding her vision. Then she slowly turned away. *I've lost him. I've lost both my Jerrys.*

CHAPTER FIFTY

"I MISSED HIM MORE YESTERDAY THAN EVER. Every time somebody threw a loop, I thought of Jerry."

Will was sitting in the kitchen with Catherine and talking about the Cleary branding that had taken place the day before. They'd worked through two hundred and twelve calves and it had been a long, hard day. Usually it would have been fun, too, but this time memories of Little Jerry were too vivid in everyone's mind. Neighbors had come from miles around—cowboys from the Peach Tree and from the Trescony across the river, ranchers from Pine Valley, Wild Horse Canyon, Lone Oak and some from even as far away as Lewis Creek—in wagons and buggies, with their wives and children, their saddle horses on a lead. The women brought salads, cakes and pies to go with the beef and beans served by the Clearys when the work was finished.

The calves had been parted from the mother cows early in the morning and fifteen calves at a time were let into the big branding corral. The ropers worked in pairs with three teams in the corral at once, one roper catching the head, and the other picking up the hind feet.

Will worked the ground, leaving the roping to Tim and Danny. That's when he realized how much he missed Jerry. His brother had loved to rope and he could swing a sixty-foot rawhide *reata* with the best *vaquero*. Will shook his head sadly and put more wood on the fire. The branding irons had to be kept red hot. He grabbed an iron with the Cleary brand—a quarter circle triangle—and ran to where they had a calf down, stretched between the ropers. Two men held it for dehorning and castrating and Seamus carried the ball bucket. Will applied the iron to the calf's left hip, smoke curling up from the burning hair.

On his way back to the fire, he saw his sister Kitty at the fence, excitedly watching the action amidst the clouds of dust, the smoke from the fire, the confusion of horses and milling calves, the sounds of bawling cows and the lusty language of the men. Will scowled his disapproval at his sister, but she just smiled and waved to him. He shook his head at her and looked over toward Jeremiah, who was busy with his knife on another calf and hadn't noticed his daughter.

Most of the women stayed inside the house, visiting with each other, and helping Catherine and Annie. Even eight-year-old Peggy had chores. But Kitty had stolen away. Will knew that household duties and women's talk were not for her when cattle were being worked. But a woman's place was in the kitchen. Will frowned as he saw a number of ranchers cast disapproving glances at his sister.

But he saw more looks of approval, particularly from some of the young cowboys. For at age seventeen, Kitty was a beauty. The long, gingham dress couldn't hide the curves of her ripening figure and the sun bonnet couldn't control the escaping, red gold curls. Her large, blue eyes followed everything with curiosity, and her quick smile was usually radiant. But not just now, Will noticed.

"Damn being a girl," he heard her mutter.

Will saw one cowboy, bolder than the rest, ride over to the fence and doff his hat. "Good morning, ma'am," he said. "Nice day for a branding."

"Yes, it is," Kitty agreed. The young puncher touched spurs to his horse and moved off, swinging his loop to pick up both hind feet for his partner. "Two hocked him. Good job, Buck," the other cowboy called.

So Buck O'Keefe had an eye on his sister. Well, Will thought, Buck was all right. Will glanced back at Kitty and saw that her father had finally spotted her and had fixed her with his paternal frown. Kitty sighed. She left the fence and returned to the house.

Will grinned at his sister's discomfort, turned back to his fire and the heating irons. And again felt the deep pangs of emptiness and sorrow over his dead brother. If only Jerry was here—God, how he missed his brother.

Will slept in his own cabin now, but he stopped off at the ranch the next morning to see his aunt. He could sense the burden of grief and guilt she carried and he knew she needed some company, someone to talk to. His father certainly wasn't doing that. The distance from Catherine that Jeremiah had imposed created a palpable tension. Will often wondered how Aunt Cauth lived with it. He wished he could do something to bring them back together, but his father was unapproachable, grim and silent. Will went over to the big wood stove and picked up the coffee pot simmering there. He poured another cup for Catherine, filled his own, and sat back at the table, facing her.

She smiled lovingly at him. He was so solid, so dependable, kind, and caring. Just the way he looks, Catherine thought. Shorter than his father, but wide-shouldered and sturdy. Not handsome, but rugged. He was like a young oak. She thanked God for Will.

He had just mentioned Kitty's escape from the house during yesterday's branding. "But she's happier today," he said. "She's helping Tim and Danny move the cows and calves back into the hills." Catherine smiled as Will spoke, but said little. Then he brought up the painful subject.

"It's still hard for me to believe Jerry's dead, Aunt Cauth. I sometimes find myself looking down the road expecting him to come riding up."

Her eyes filled with instant sadness at the mention of Jerry. "I know. I do the same thing. I miss him every day and I know your father does, too. But I don't think he'll ever forgive me for the part I had in his going. I can't forgive myself."

"Oh, Aunt Cauth, you mustn't feel that way!" He loved this woman and he couldn't stand to see her so tormented. "It wasn't your fault! We all learned the same stories and songs. All of us loved hearing about Ireland." Will reached across the table and took his aunt's hand in his. "It was just that Jerry had this restless streak. He wasn't satisfied here on the ranch. If it hadn't been Ireland, it would have been somewhere else."

"He might not have gotten killed somewhere else!" Catherine exclaimed. "Why didn't he just stay in Boston? In school?" Catherine's voice had a sad, but bitter edge to it.

"Jerry told me a long time ago that he wanted to go to Ireland," Will said.

"I know, Will. He told me, too. But I'm the one who planted the seed in his head," Catherine said. "And I must live with that."

It had been more than a year since Jerry's death and Jeremiah showed no signs of softening toward Catherine. He treated her with cold politeness. He never called her Cauth, always Catherine, or Mrs. Cleary. He never talked to her unless it was absolutely necessary, never held her, never even touched her. Catherine's guilt was deep and intense, but she yearned for understanding, and she ached to hear Jeremiah call her "Cauth darlin'" once again.

That first afternoon, she'd been outside, walking the grounds, trying to control herself so she could move on with her chores. She'd returned to their bedroom and knew something was different. Catherine stood in the center of the room and looked around. What was it? What was missing? And then she realized.

She threw open the closet door and saw that Jeremiah's clothes were gone. Everything of his was gone. Not a trace of her husband remained in their bedroom. Catherine frantically searched the house. And there, in the empty room off the kitchen, were Jeremiah's things, his clothes hanging in the closet, and stacked in the bureau drawers, the extra boots on the floor, an old hat on the bed. The chaps flung across a chair. The pipe and tobacco on the bed stand. Jeremiah had moved into the room they'd saved for Jerry.

Catherine fell to her knees by the bed. The pain in her breast, already awful, was like a knife giving its final twist. She was too stunned, too hurt to cry anymore.

The family prayed for Jerry that night when they gathered for the rosary. But Jeremiah didn't lead as he usually did. He sat silent and aloof while the others knelt, and left it to Will to direct the evening prayers. Catherine watched him and wondered. *He blames me. But does he blame God, too?*

She tried to atone, to win him back. She did everything to please him, cooking his favorite meals, dressing and wearing her hair in the way she knew he favored. She poured over her monthly magazine, *Demorest Family Weekly*, reading about the gracious touches of an American home, how to be a hostess to visitors, business and social, the ladylike skills he required of her on his visits to the county seat. The rebel songs and stories of life in Ireland were a thing of the past. She tried to be an American in all things, studying the history and politics, even the music of her adopted country.

On one occasion, she tried to create again a musical evening with the children. They started to sing some of the American songs they had learned in school and had taught to Catherine. But when she began to play her tin whistle, Jeremiah abruptly got up and left the room. The song died on the children's lips and Catherine, herself, had to turn away to hide her flowing tears. That was the last time they played music in the house. Jeremiah's silent disapproval was too loud, and, as Tim once noted, it wasn't the same without Jerry's voice and his mandolin.

Whenever Catherine felt overwhelmed by this terrible exile and alienation, she would walk up to the line of scrub oak trees on the hill above the ranch. There she'd sit, and think and pray. Looking down on the busy place gave her some perspective on her problems. This day was as gray as her spirit. She felt suffocated by her guilt, unable to reach out to others, unworthy of their love and trust.

"Dear God," she implored, "I can't go on like this. Please help me. I feel so empty, so useless and unloving."

As she sat staring down the valley, the stillness of the afternoon seemed to soothe her. She felt a peace touch her being. A quiet sense of God's presence enveloped her. She began to pray for each of the children and for Jeremiah. As she thought about their needs, the guilt began to loosen its grip on her heart. She came to realize that, in order to really love her family as they needed to be loved, she had to let go of the guilt, it was impossible to feel guilt and love at the same time.

She spent a long time on the hill that day. When she finally came down, she knew she had been given the strength and direction to move on with her life.

CHAPTER FIFTY-ONE

"AUNT CAUTH, DO YOU THINK I'm ever going to have a beau?" Annie asked plaintively.

Catherine was standing at the kitchen table, rolling out dough for a pie. She looked at sixteen-year-old Annie, who was slicing the fresh peaches for the pie that had become one of Catherine's specialties and Jeremiah's favorite.

"Of course you'll have a beau, Annie dear. Lots of them. Why on earth wouldn't you?"

Annie had grown tall and slender, but her figure had not yet blossomed into womanhood. She had intelligent brown eyes and long brown hair, now tied up in a pretty red ribbon. But hers was a plain face, not the heart-shaped one of Kitty. Still, Catherine thought her nose was pert, and her complexion creamy white. She was no raving beauty, but she wasn't unattractive.

"Gee, Aunt Cauth, didn't you see the way I just stood around at the Peach Tree dance?"

Catherine had noticed it and her heart had gone out to Annie. The dance was a family affair and all the Clearys were there, but Catherine had sat on a bench against the wall the

353

entire evening. Jeremiah stayed with her, of course. She had to give him that. But he didn't dance with her, nor with anyone. He just sat and watched. It was a long evening for Catherine.

"All the fellows flocked to Kitty like she was the queen bee," Annie continued, "and that Buck O'Keefe couldn't stay away from her. Even Will had a girlfriend to dance with. I never even knew Will could dance."

"That was Buck O'Keefe's sister, Honora from San Juan," Catherine said. "I met her and she seemed very nice."

"Well, maybe so," Annie pouted. "But the only one who asked me to dance without being forced to was that fat Freddy Bruxton, and he sweat so I could hardly stand him. Kitty didn't miss a dance."

"Kitty can't help it, Annie. She certainly doesn't seem to encourage them."

"Oh, I know." Annie agreed. "She kept bringing boys over to dance with me all evening, and I know she made Toby Wilkins sit with me for supper. But it's not the same. I wish I was pretty like Kitty and Connie."

Catherine took down the large baking pan and carefully placed the peach slices onto her pie dough. "Well, your day will come, Annie. You're attractive and you're very nice. Besides you're intelligent."

"Oh, just great," Annie said with a mocking laugh. "That's what they all want, an intelligent girl."

"Well, the truth is, I think you are a very special person," Catherine insisted. "You don't have to be like Kitty or Connie, or anybody else. The right man will come along someday and appreciate you for yourself."

"Do you really think so? Well, if it does happen, it won't be one of those cowboys, and certainly no clod-hopping farmer. I don't think I'm cut out to be a ranch wife."

Catherine was startled by Annie's remark, and curious. "What do you think you are cut out for, Annie dear? What would you like to do?"

"Go to school, I think. Maybe learn to be a teacher."

Catherine had noticed her often helping Seamus and Peggy with their schoolwork. The girl really enjoyed it. Catherine thought she seemed to have a natural gift for teaching.

"Would you talk with Dad about it, Aunt Cauth?"

"Well now, I think it would be better if you bring it up to your father yourself," Catherine replied.

Jeremiah was sitting by the fire that night, puffing on his pipe, when Annie, shoulders squared and chin jutting out with determination, came over and stood before him. She wasn't exactly afraid of this stern man—he'd always been a kind and loving father, especially when she used to sit in his lap as a youngster—but he'd been so quiet and aloof lately. Annie took a deep breath. "I need to talk to you, Dad."

"Why sure, Annie darlin'."

Annie sat on the floor and leaned her arms on Jeremiah's chair, looking up into his eyes. Another deep breath. She was trying to figure out how to put it, the phrases she'd practiced just wouldn't come. But when she saw her father's tender, encouraging smile she blurted out, "I want to go away to school. I'd like to become a teacher."

Jeremiah puffed on his pipe for a moment, staring off into the room. School was it now? Another one wanting schooling. But, of course, he couldn't be faulting his own children for desiring an education. It was what he'd wanted, too. But a girl now, was it right for a girl?

"Well now, Annie, and why would you be wanting to teach?"

Annie's face lit up. "Oh, Dad. I know I could be a good teacher, and I don't want to spend my life on a ranch. Not like Kitty. I want to see other things, go other places."

"But we'd miss you, Annie. Your Aunt Catherine and I, and your brothers and sisters, we'd not like to lose you."

"Oh, Dad. I'd come home and visit. It would only be for two years and then I'd be a teacher. Maybe I'd even get a school near here somewhere."

"Let's see now, Annie. You're about sixteen. If you still have a mind for this teaching when you're seventeen, perhaps we can look into that school at San Jose for you."

Annie threw her arms around her father. "Thank you, Dad." She kissed him heartily and skipped out of the room.

He'd never seen her so happy, but he wondered why his children seemed afraid to talk to him these days. It didn't used to be that way. They would come running and jump into his arms. There were always hugs and kisses, until the boys decided such things weren't manly. And now Danny, too, seemed afraid. That very same day he had also told Jeremiah how much he wanted to go on to school. Jeremiah was surprised at how nervous his son was when he asked to go to the high school in Santa Clara where several of his friends were going. He'd said yes to Danny and the boy was obviously relieved and happy. But Jeremiah couldn't shake his awareness that his children had become afraid to talk to him.

Was it his grieving over Jerry that created this chasm? He missed his son so much and was still so angry at what he felt was the futility of Jerry's death. *Is it this difference between Catherine and me they feel?*

Jeremiah got up from his chair and walked past the large parlor where Catherine was reading her magazine by lamplight. Her gray-streaked hair was still long and luxurious, tied in a graceful knot at her neck. She wore a gingham dress, clasped at the throat by a cameo brooch, a clean apron at her waist. She still had a lithe, firm figure. She was a handsome woman, a lady, and Jeremiah had to admit she'd been the most attractive matron at the Peach Tree dance. And she was a fine, loving mother to all the children. There was no doubt he respected her.

But forgive her? He tamped his pipe. He could not!

CHAPTER FIFTY-TWO

ANNIE WAS SETTING THE TABLE for supper as Catherine bent over her wood stove, turning the meat in the big skillet and ladling the pan drippings over it to keep it moist.

"Where's Peggy?" Annie asked. "She's supposed to help me set the table."

"Finishing her homework, I suppose," Catherine said. Annie didn't really care. She'd be off on her great adventure next week, taking the train from Soledad to San Jose, to enter the teachers school just as she'd always wanted.

She set just five places at the huge table. Kitty had ridden over to spend the night with Betsy Wexler, Tim was staying with Will to help at his homestead and Danny was in school in Santa Clara. The family was suddenly shrinking. She missed Connie, although they wrote each other frequently. She hoped they'd be able to visit, San Jose being fairly close to San Francisco. But the rest of the Cleary children were hardly ever all together any more. And in a week she'd be gone, too.

"Supper — !" Catherine called. Jeremiah came into the kitchen and took his place at the head of the table. "Peggy! Seamus! Supper!" Catherine called again. She wondered what was taking her children so long. That hungry pair were usually first at the table.

They finally arrived and sat down but both looked uncomfortable. "I'm not hungry, Mama," Peggy complained. "My head hurts." She returned to her room right after Jeremiah said the blessing.

Seamus picked at his food for a few minutes, then excused himself to finish his homework. Catherine raised a quizzical eyebrow at Jeremiah, but he didn't seem to notice anything strange. He completed his supper and sat back with his pipe. Something was wrong with those two, Catherine knew it. But measles, chicken pox, mumps and assorted colds had already swept Long Valley school. She'd nursed the children through them all. So what could this be?

Seamus and Peggy were both asleep in their beds when Catherine checked on them. She blew out their lamps and, with a sense of relief, left their rooms. But in the morning both children were listless at breakfast and not ready for school.

By noon Peggy was throwing up. Stomach flu, Catherine diagnosed. But Seamus was coughing and said his throat hurt. She felt their hot foreheads. Both had fevers. Peggy admitted her throat also ached, and soon Seamus began retching and needed a basin by his bedside.

Annie took turns with Catherine soothing their hot brows with cool compresses. When Jeremiah came in for supper, Catherine said to him. "I don't know what it is, some type of flu, perhaps, and they'll be well by morning." But her worried frown belied her words.

In the morning, as Annie was helping to bathe Peggy, she noticed a red rash spreading over the girl's body. Catherine checked Seamus and found his skin taking on a scarlet color, too. They both were hotter to the touch. Catherine rushed to her bookshelf and brought down her copy of *The People's Common Sense Medical Advisor* by R.V. Pierce, M.D.

She compared the children's symptoms with those in the book. No appetite, headache, a thirst, diarrhea, and vomiting, sore throat, fever, and now a rash. She couldn't be sure. Dear God, don't let it be, she prayed. But Seamus and Peggy, according to the medical book, had all the symptoms of scarlet fever.

"Highly contagious, it runs its course in a week to two weeks," she read aloud to Annie. "There is no other disease so simple, and yet so often liable to prove fatal, than scarlet fever. For this reason we shall advise the attendance of the family physician." Family physician, Catherine thought ironically. The nearest doctor was in Soledad, thirty-five miles away! Dear Lord, what was she to do?

She couldn't let any of the others be exposed. Jeremiah had to stay away, too. She'd have him get word for Tim to remain at Will's, and tell Kitty not to come home from Wexler's. She and Annie would just have to nurse the children as best they could.

She followed the directions in the book and, from her supply of medicinal herbs, found pleurisy root and boiled it into a strong tea. Taken with a teaspoonful of Dr. Pierce's Extract of Smartweed, this was meant to drive the rash to the surface. It was difficult getting the brew down her children's swollen throats, and they lost most of it, heaving and choking. Annie continued bathing the two with cool water, holding them as they retched, and tirelessly emptying the foul basins, washing them and the bedclothes, soothing them with assurances that soon they'd be better.

Catherine sent Jeremiah to the barn for the night, and the next morning at dawn he rode off to warn Kitty and Tim, and to advise neighbors to stay away from the Cleary place. "Quarantined, we are," was his message. But he found other families with the same plight, their children sick with the fever—an epidemic had hit Long Valley school. Jeremiah returned home that evening, silently praying that Seamus and Peggy had improved.

But they hadn't. The house was dark except for the lamps burning in the two bedrooms, and Catherine met him at the door. "You'd best be staying in the barn again, Jerry. I'll wash myself up good and put some food out for you."

"You'll not." Jeremiah was adamant. "These are my children. I'll come inside and do what I can." He began bringing in the buckets of water, cleaning the basins, setting out a cold supper from left-overs he found in the pantry.

Catherine and Annie were sponging the fevered children with cool water, into which a small amount of soda had been added to relieve their itching skin, now angry scarlet over their entire bodies when Jeremiah came into the room and saw them. He was appalled and frightened.

Seamus lay unseeing, his eyes glazed, his skin fiery to the touch. He hardly had enough strength for his racking cough, and could no longer raise himself to retch. He could barely manage to turn his head to the side of the bed. But with nothing in his stomach, there was nothing to expel. The violent dry heaves had left the boy extremely weak.

Memories of his tiny brother and sisters, dying of hunger and fever in Ireland so long ago, flooded back to Jeremiah. He saw it all again, the three wretched little bodies laid into one tiny casket, the hurried prayers at the grave. The fever! The dreaded fever had taken them. "Oh, dear Lord, not these two. Please spare my children," he pleaded. "It was me swearing the fever would never take my own children. I'd protect them, I would. Dear God, please be showing me what to do."

All that night he stayed with the children, first relieving Catherine at the bedside of Seamus, and then Annie with Peggy. But both Catherine and Annie were too exhausted to sleep, too frantic with worry. Just before dawn Catherine found herself near Jeremiah, looking down at Seamus, finally quiet, almost in a stupor. Catherine took Jeremiah's hand. He didn't seem to even notice. She moved her hand to his shoulder and patted him. He shuddered, shook her off and left the room.

Even at a time like this, he'll not let me comfort him. He's so hard, but suffering so inside. What a stubborn man, but I love him still.

Jeremiah went to hitch up his surrey, but as daylight broke Will came on horseback into the yard. "Dad — I'm riding to Soledad for a doctor," Will announced. "There are four or five other families with sick children. He'll surely come for that many."

"You'll not," Jeremiah declared. "It's my job. I'm leaving now. You ride to the neighbors. Tell them I'll be back tomorrow night with a doctor."

All that day, and throughout the night, Annie helped Catherine nurse her brother and sister. It was nearly midnight when Peggy's fever finally broke. For the first time, the girl's body relaxed and she fell into a heavy sleep. But the fever in Seamus continued to burn. If anything, he was getting hotter.

Annie sponged him off again and felt his body jerk. Was it from the touch of the cold water? Seamus convulsed. His arms flailed the air. His legs twisted up, and his body writhed and contorted. Annie threw herself on him to keep the boy from falling off the bed. "Aunt Cauth — ! Come quickly!" she screamed as Seamus shook and jerked.

Catherine hurried in from the kitchen and took her son's thrashing body in her arms, soothing him, rocking him, singing Irish lullabies. Gradually he quieted, only to suddenly convulse again. It went on like that for the rest of the night and throughout the next day. Annie and Catherine took turns holding Seamus to keep him from hurting himself, praying the whole time to God and all the saints to ease the boy's fever.

The nights and days became a jumble in Annie's mind. Wasn't this to be the day she was to leave for San Jose Normal School? It didn't seem important anymore. The only thing that mattered now was bringing down this terrible fever, getting Seamus to swallow a little broth, and some cold drinks to ease his thirst. Thank God Peggy's fever had broken. The girl had taken some broth and was sleeping restfully. But Annie didn't understand why Seamus was still so sick.

It was at dusk the following evening when Jeremiah pulled the surrey into the yard and jumped out, hurrying the doctor into the house.

"This is Doc William Stover, kind enough to come for us," he told Catherine. "How are the children?"

"Peggy's doing fine, her fever's gone — " she said as she led the way into the room where Annie held Seamus — "but our boy — Oh, Jerry, he's bad. Seamus is so sick!" Jeremiah stood back, silent and stoic, while the doctor examined his son.

Dr. Stover brought out a thermometer, shook it, checked it, placed it into the boy's mouth, and held him quiet for a few moments. When he removed the thermometer, he turned it to the lamplight and saw it read just above 106 degrees. Alarm and sadness registered on Dr. Stover's face. He turned to

Catherine. "Missus Cleary, how long has he had this high fever?"

"It's been several days now," Catherine answered, struggling to contain her fears. Dr. Stover shook his head. He went to examine Peggy.

"Your diagnosis is correct, Missus Cleary. Scarlet fever. The girl is fine now, but I'm afraid the boy's disease has progressed to something else." He asked Catherine for a glass of sugared water and, as she hurried into the kitchen, the doctor rummaged in his medical bag. He took out three ounces of citrate of potash, and when Catherine handed him the water, he dropped it in. Then with much difficulty, Seamus was made to swallow the drink. "This should reduce the fever," the doctor said.

They all stood by the bedside, anxiously watching as nearly an hour passed. Jeremiah still seemed impassive, but he was torn apart inside. Catherine gripped her handkerchief and prayed with Annie. The doctor's eyes never left the boy. He took his pulse and his temperature. There was no change in Seamus. He burned as fiercely as ever, moaning and jerking.

"We must break the fever," Dr. Stover said, and asked Catherine to make some hot tea. He managed to force most of it past Seamus' congested throat. Then, he instructed Catherine to bring him several more blankets. He began piling blankets on top of Seamus and wrapping them tightly around him. Another ten minutes passed and then the boy started to sweat. Soon perspiration soaked his bed. By midnight the fever broke. He stopped convulsing. He cooled and was finally resting, his breathing returned to normal again. As they all watched, Seamus fell sound asleep.

"Ah," Jeremiah emitted a heavy sigh of relief. "The crisis is past. He'll be fine now, won't he, doctor?"

"Perhaps," Dr. Stover answered.

Jeremiah was startled by the doctor's answer. "What do you mean by that?" he asked.

"Well, sometimes with high fevers you just can't tell," Dr. Stover replied. "We'll just have to wait and see."

Catherine and Jeremiah exchanged worried glances as the doctor suddenly was very busy with his medical bag, replacing items, preparing to leave. He looked up to say, "Expect their skin to scale off now. That's part of the healing process."

"And what about my wife and daughter?" Jeremiah asked. He had to know the worst. "Do we expect them to catch this terrible thing now?"

"I don't think so," Dr. Stover said. "Usually it develops within three or four days after exposure and the first days are the most contagious. You're well past that time," the doctor gave them a small smile. "I believe you're all spared."

Jeremiah took Dr. Stover to the other ranches, where the families with infected children were desperately waiting, so relieved when they saw Jeremiah's surrey coming into their yard. Eventually Will took the doctor back to Soledad.

In the days that followed, the Clearys attended two funerals in Long Valley. Small coffins were lowered into the ground in family graveyards as neighbors stood beside grieving parents. Jeremiah thanked God that his children weren't victims of Long Valley's scarlet fever epidemic of 1883. But there was one thing Jeremiah couldn't stop wondering about and he knew that Catherine, standing beside him at this latest graveside, was worrying about the same thing. When he'd asked if Seamus would be all right, Doc Stover had said, "We'll have to wait and see."

CHAPTER FIFTY-THREE

JEREMIAH WAS IN THE BARN tending sick horses, spreading salve on collar galls and wire cuts, rubbing liniment into hocks ailing from kicks, bumps and bruises. To keep full teams in harness it seemed he needed twice as many horses, some were always in the sick pen. He grumbled because his boys weren't around to help him, each off somewhere on their own business. He snubbed up a big work mare, ran a tube down her throat and poured in oil, trying to cure her colic. She fought and kicked at him.

"Dad — Dad — " Jeremiah heard the loud cry and ran to the barn door. He looked up the hill and there was Tim, busting his horse down the Coyote trail, a cloud of dust billowing behind him. "There're three men moving in on the Coyote spring — !" Tim yelled breathlessly as he slid his horse to a stop in the yard. "They're camped there with a wagon, Dad. I spotted them from the ridge!"

"Well now," Jeremiah said calmly, "they might just be passing through and set up camp for the night."

"No chance, Dad," Tim said, still excited. "They're stringing wire."

"Stringing wire?" Jeremiah's eyes widened. His voice turned from incredulous to angry. "On my land? Cutting off my spring? Are you sure?"

"I stayed up there long enough to see that," Tim insisted. "And they have a tent. I'm not sure, but it looks like they butchered a beef."

Taking over my spring, is it? Stringing wire to cut my cattle off from water? Killing one of my steers? Jeremiah felt the rage taking hold.

"I'll get my horse." He caught up the blazed-faced sorrel, quickly saddled, and hurried to the house. Tim followed his father inside and watched anxiously as Jeremiah took down the Spencer and loaded it with seven big, fifty-four caliber shells, then rammed the rifle into the scabbard.

"Dad, can't we just tell them it's our spring and ask them to leave?"

Jeremiah thought for a moment. Technically that spring wasn't actually his. He owned the land all around it, but the Coyote spring itself was still government land. Jeremiah had hoped that Will would homestead it when he became twenty-one. Or Jerry. Instead Will had wanted farming ground up the valley, and Jerry had been dead for five years now. Tim was twenty-three, more than old enough to homestead, but he hadn't gotten around to it.

"Son, Cleary cattle have been watering at that spring for nearly thirty years, and to reach that canyon means crossing Cleary land. By God, they're trespassing. I'm going to run the bastards off my land."

He and Tim took the trail up out of Long Valley and topped the ridge. They looked down into the canyon and saw their boxed spring feeding their redwood water trough. Jeremiah stepped from his saddle and drew his Spencer. He sat on a rock for a better look at the scene below.

About two hundred yards down, just above the spring, two men were stringing barbed wire on a row of posts set up across the canyon. A third was at the spring filling a bucket. Jeremiah watched as the man carried the bucket of water to the barrel lashed to the side of the wagon. He poured the water into the barrel and started back to the spring.

Tim stayed on his horse and kept his eyes on his father. He saw Jeremiah lever in a shell and lift the heavy rifle to his shoulder. "Dad — no!" he screamed, "Good God, don't shoot him! Wait — "

Tim jumped from his horse as Jeremiah took aim. Tim reached for his father's arm. But he was too late. The Spencer roared.

"Oh, my God!" Tim cried.

But then he saw the water pouring from a huge, gaping hole in the barrel. The three startled men stood stock still, two by the wire and the other by the spring, stunned by the rifle shot. They looked up at Jeremiah, who levered in another shell. Jeremiah walked down the hill toward them, leading his horse, the rifle pointed at them. Tim followed anxiously.

"Don't be moving now," Jeremiah ordered the threesome. He carried the Spencer in front of him, swinging it from side to side to cover the men, who still remained motionless. When he reached the camp, Jeremiah ordered them to gather in front of him. He saw they were unarmed. "Stay put," he commanded, and let his eyes roam around the camp. He noted the tent set up by the wagon, the cooking utensils by the fire pit. And something else.

"Tim. Check that hide over there."

Tim tied his horse to the wagon and walked to the back. There was a hide spread across the tail gate, bloody side to the sun, but red and white hair showing. Tim ripped it off and turned it over. "Quarter circle triangle, Dad," he called back.

Jeremiah narrowed his eyes at the men. "So! It's fencing off my spring and slaughtering my beef, is it?" he shouted at them, feeling his blood rising again. "This is my land! You've no right to be here!"

Jeremiah breathed deeply, trying to get a grip on his temper. The big gun trembled in his hand. He glared at the squatters and steadied the rifle.

"Easy, Dad, easy," Tim warned.

His son was right. He couldn't kill these men over water. But Jeremiah knew he'd been close to it. He'd order them off and see that they left. And that would be an end to it. Jeremiah slowly lowered the rifle. "You're on my land. Pack up and get out."

"It's not your land, old man. This spring is on free government land." The one still holding the bucket found the courage to speak.

"We looked it up in Salinas," the other said. "We're going to file on it."

"You'll not!" Jeremiah's temper flared again. He raised the Spencer to his hip and covered the three again. "Cleary cattle have been watering here since I came to this country nearly thirty years ago. That's my land your wagon made tracks across. Now be hitching up and getting the hell out — !"

Jeremiah's finger tightened on the trigger and again the Spencer roared. The bullet struck the ground at their feet, blasting the dirt and throwing dust over the men. They jumped and started for their team, which was standing near-by in harness for hauling posts and wire. They moved even faster when they heard Jeremiah lever in another shell.

"You can leave the fence posts and wire right where they are," Jeremiah instructed. "I'll be taking them for my trouble. And I'll be keeping any weapons you might have as payment for my beef. Tim, kindly look into the wagon."

Tim discovered a loaded Henry and an old Sharps. He pumped out the shells from the Henry and unloaded the Sharps, tying them to his saddle. Tim released his horse from the wagon and swung up.

Jeremiah and his son watched as the three men took down their camp, loaded the wagon, and quickly hitched up. They climbed into the wagon and one took the lines, calling over his shoulder as he started the team, "We'll see whose land it is, old man! We'll be back."

The Clearys watched for nearly an hour as the wagon fol-lowed the tracks down Coyote Canyon and turned onto the Pine Valley road. They tracked it by the dust to make sure it was leaving the country before they turned their horses toward home.

"Change horses and be on your way to the court house your-self, Tim. Right now. File on that quarter section before that lot gets there," Jeremiah said.

It was already dusk when Tim left the yard at a gallop, thinking it was a good thing the court house had been moved closer, from Monterey to Salinas. He soon settled his horse into a lope down the Long Valley road toward the Salinas River. He held this pace for several miles, keeping to the east side of the river, along the foothills, then walked his horse some to let him rest, and loped again. He alternated that way most of the night, stopping only for a quick nap. He unsaddled, hobbled his mount and rolled up in the saddle blankets while the horse cropped grass nearby. At dawn Tim hurriedly saddled and put his horse to a full gallop for Soledad nine miles away. He had a quick breakfast at the Railroad Exchange while his horse was grained at the livery stable. He had less than twenty-five miles to go and could be in Salinas by early afternoon. He passed Gonzales in good time, walking and loping his horse, watching the road behind him.

It was somewhere near where Chualar Creek met the Salinas River that Tim noticed a change in his horse's gait. The bay was limping. He stepped off and raised the mount's left front foot. No shoe. He'd obviously thrown it somewhere since leaving Soledad and now the animal's foot was sore. Now what the hell could he do? Tim wondered. He knew he couldn't ride the horse like this, but it was still nearly ten miles to Salinas. He'd not be much for walking in these boots. But he had no choice except to walk and lead the bay. The afternoon wore on and Tim was still plodding along, now nearly as sore-footed as his horse. He knew his father would come down on him hard if he didn't make it. The land meant everything to him, especially that spring.

He anxiously watched the back trail now, worried that the three squatters might catch up to him—pass him right there on the road, and beat him to the courthouse in Salinas. Tim hoped someone with a rig would come along and offer him a lift. But all that passed were horsemen, who commiserated or kidded him, as they rode by.

Tim looked at the sun, now setting behind Toro Peak. His only consolation was that the three squatters couldn't do anything at the courthouse until the next morning. His feet hurt, but he limped along. "We're some pair," he told his horse. "A couple of cripples. But we'll make it. We'd better, or the old man will have both our hides."

It was well after dark when they limped into Salinas. Tim's blistered feet were on fire and his horse could barely stumble along. He found a livery stable and pounded on the door until the sleepy night man responded. Tim bedded down in the hay alongside his horse, afraid to pull off his boots for fear he'd never get them back on his aching, swollen feet.

At dawn Tim got up, brushed the hay off his clothes and hobbled to the county courthouse. He was the first one through the door when it opened up. He went straight to the clerk and gave him the piece of paper that Jeremiah had written so long ago, describing the one hundred and sixty acres, including Coyote Spring. The clerk accepted the claim without question and wrote out an official document. A relieved Tim thanked the clerk profusely as he left.

It was mid-afternoon, when Tim, relaxed and leisurely riding his newly-shod horse, spotted the wagonload of squatters coming toward him on the old stage road. He pulled off onto a nearby knoll and watched them pass, tapping his saddlebag containing the precious papers, and smiling to himself.

But Timothy didn't enjoy the happy feeling very long. He had too much time for thinking. And thinking always led to Amy Barnes. He'd been riding over to Pine Valley to see her for two years now and he just couldn't figure that girl out. What was it she wanted out of life? She had said she loved him, let him kiss her, even touch her breasts a few times. Tim thought of those times, holding Amy tightly, the way she moved against him, her teasing tongue in his mouth. And then she'd pull away, laughing in that sassy way she had, and toss her long, blonde hair.

"Oh, Timmy," she'd say. "I can't be stuck here all my life. I want to go to the city, be where the excitement is. I can't marry you. You'll always just be a farmer." Damn her, the way she teased him. Tim wondered if he'd love her so much if she wasn't so pretty? Most of all he wondered if he'd ever change her mind.

And what would she say when he told her that he was now the owner of his own piece of land? He could hear the trill of her laughter. "In Coyote Canyon, Tim?" she'd say, and laugh again. "And you rode all night and walked all day just for that piece of land? And now you're going to build a cabin there and prove up? You must be joshing, dear."

But to Tim it was far from a joke. Owning land was serious in the Cleary family. This was an important event in his life and to his father. When he finally arrived home he proudly showed the claim to Jeremiah. He'd practically memorized it, but they read it together.

Be it known that on the sixth day of September, A.D. 1885, before me, J.P. Willerford, county clerk of the County of Monterey, and notary public in and for the said county, and the State of California, appeared Timothy Patrick Cleary.....and under the Homestead Act of the United States of America of 1862, he has taken possession of, and now occupies, for the purpose of cultivation and grazing, the following tract of land, to wit: Situate in said state and county in the township of Peach Tree — This land embraced does not exceed one hundred sixty (160) acres and.....

Now all Tim had to do was build a cabin, further develop the spring, and graze cattle there for five years, and he would prove up, the property would legally be his, part of the Cleary family ranch. Jeremiah was pleased. But Tim knew Amy Barnes would just laugh.

CHAPTER FIFTY-FOUR

THE CLEARYS SAT ON THE VERANDA of the new Pleasant View Hotel in San Lucas, the new town that had sprung up in 1886 on the banks of the Salinas River at the mouth of Long Valley. Jeremiah wore his dark suit with a gold watch in his vest pocket, a Stetson hat tilted on the back of his head and handmade boots from a shop in Salinas, and Catherine was in her dress of emerald green velvet brocade with a stylish bonnet on her head. Ranchers had come from miles around to celebrate the first cattle shipments from the new railhead. The bull heads had been cooking underground since the night before and already the barroom downstairs was crowded with booted men.

They watched cattle being driven into the railroad corrals and, lifting their gaze past the corrals, they could see the clouds of dust rising across the river, where the *vaqueros* from Trescony's Rancho San Lucas were driving their herd, along with cattle from ranches in the Oasis country. Will Cleary was among them.

Jeremiah's oldest son was a tenant farmer on the Trescony grant with more than a thousand acres on shares, most of it prime farm land. He had moved there with his bride, Honora O'Keefe, two years earlier. But Jeremiah had been appalled when Will first told him what he was doing.

"You'll be a tenant? With a landlord?" Jeremiah said incredulously. "There's no need. You have your homestead, and you'll be owning more of your own land after a bit, when I'm gone."

"You don't understand, Dad," Will said, trying to placate his father. "It's not that way. This isn't Ireland. Mister Trescony is very fair. It's not a fixed rent. I'm to give him a quarter of the crop and a quarter of what I make on cattle. And I'm to have a house and barns."

It took a great deal more explaining for Will to make his father accept what he'd done. And to work out a business

371

arrangement for Will to use Jeremiah's equipment to get started. But Jeremiah's doubts about his twenty-eight-year-old son were soon assuaged. Will had rapidly turned a profit and was making a name for himself as a progressive farmer.

Jeremiah was proud of him, but couldn't be showing it, of course. He turned his attention back to the corrals where they were penning the bawling cattle from Wild Horse. The steers all looked fat, in good shape, far superior to those longhorns he'd once driven along the San Benito River. It had taken him years after Molly's death before he'd tried Herefords again. But he finally did and was glad he had. Today they were everywhere. Jeremiah took out his bandanna and mopped his brow. It was already hot this June morning. Good thing they were in the shade of the veranda of this new hotel.

"Look, Jerry, there's Buck and Kitty," Catherine said, pointing to riders driving the herd of cattle emerging from the cloud of dust on the Long Valley road. Cleary steers were mixed in with those of Joseph Wexler and other neighbors, and Buck O'Keefe was ramroding the drive. As the cattle made the turn into town, Jeremiah could also see Tim on horseback and then Seamus, back in the dust, riding drag. At sixteen, Seamus was a good cowboy, a top hand with the horses, he loved them so, but not quite right about other things. The terrible scarlet fever had left him with the mind of a ten-year-old.

With the bellowing steers, the shouting cowboys, the clash and clang of the rail cars being shoved into position at the chutes, the din was tremendous. Jeremiah watched Kitty in the midst of it on horseback by the stockyard gates. His beautiful daughter was checking brands for the quarter circle triangle, and cutting the Cleary steers into their pen, while her husband, Buck, kept count. Good man, that Buck, Jeremiah noted, and a wonder with Seamus. And if he wanted to allow his wife to ride astride and be a cowboy, that was his business.

Catherine wasn't so sure about the propriety of Kitty appearing in town in her split skirt, a Stetson on her head, and doing a man's work. But the young woman was certainly happy these days. Buck seemed to enjoy her help and took pride in his unorthodox wife. Catherine saw Kitty cut back a steer as deftly as any cowboy. It was hard to imagine this was the same person, dressed all in white lace, a wreath of silk flowers holding a veil on her golden head, who had come down the aisle of San Juan Mission on her father's arm just a year ago. Catherine sighed. Let Kitty enjoy her freedom now. She'll be cooped up in the house soon enough when the babies start coming.

When the festivities were over in the early afternoon, the Clearys boarded the train to the music of Souza's "Stars and Stripes Forever," played for the sixth time that day by the enthusiastic Knights of Pythias band. The train chugged away to the cheers and huzzahs from the crowd at track side. Catherine marveled at the speed, it was only last year they were in the wagon, hot and dusty, making this same trip to Soledad for supplies. Only this morning they'd eaten breakfast in their Long Valley home, and tonight they were to be guests at the Laurel Wreath Club's supper dance at Pacific Hall in Salinas. It had been nearly seven years since she'd been to Salinas, not since they'd recieved word of Jerry's death.

Catherine had wondered when Jeremiah told her about the trip to Salinas. They'd be staying at the Abbott House, he'd said, and to bring clothes for some social events. Would they finally be sharing a room again? Surely, he'd not publicly acknowledge their estrangement by booking separate rooms. Perhaps, Catherine hoped, if they shared a room once more, if they shared a bed, he'd hold her.

The train ground to a halt, brakes screeching and steam escaping. Catherine found herself looking down the main street of King's. There wasn't much to it. She could see buildings going up and hogs running loose. Jeremiah judged the wheat crop that surrounded the town to be nearly ready to harvest, full and heavy to his practiced eye. That King fellow would make his critics back down, he thought. The same as Will had done.

Jeremiah's glance fell on a newspaper left on a seat by a departed passenger, a copy of the new *Salinas Valley Settler*. The headline caught his eye. *Gold Bonanza in Los Burros. Town of Manchester Booms.* That was where Matthew had been. Jeremiah picked it up and began to read, *Manchester, the supply center of the Los Burros Mining District, now has 350 people, reports John Harbolt, who recently visited this editor. The boom was caused by the discovery, near the head of Alder Creek, of a large vein of gold-bearing quartz by Willie Cruikshank. This mine, known as The Last Chance, is estimated to contain some $3,000,000 worth of gold. However, the neighboring Tarantula mine, also owned by Cruikshank in partnership with Matthew Cleary, and a number of others, has been abandoned.*

There was more to the story, but Jeremiah tossed the paper aside. He sat looking out the window, watching the valley pass by, but not seeing it. Poor Matt. He lost out again. Jeremiah thought of his father's last words to him on that day long ago when the two of them left for America. "Matthew will need some looking after," he'd said. Well, God knows he'd tried.

When the train pulled into Salinas, they were met by the hotel coach from the Abbott House and were soon climbing the stairs from the lobby. Catherine anxiously followed the bellman and was relieved when he showed them into a single, spacious room on the second floor. Jeremiah excused himself for a business appointment and Catherine surveyed the luxury about her.

How grand, she thought, and never a moment in her life back in Ireland did she think that one day she might be in such a place. *Daft, I'd have been to be dreaming so.* She filled the huge bathtub and reveled in it, relaxing from the train trip and her anxieties, as she soaked. She laced up her corset, but it was just for fashion. She was still slim despite her fifty-four years. She slipped on her new damask-rose colored, velvet ball gown and adjusted the bodice, re-arranged her hair, and buttoned up her shoes. Catherine checked the finished result in the mirror and approved. If only Jeremiah would.

It was a wonderful party and the leaders of Salinas and their ladies made Catherine feel welcome. Animated conversation flowed all around her. Even Jeremiah was attentive, and this gave her hope, but they didn't dance. It was after midnight when they left the party and Jeremiah tucked a lap robe about her on the carriage ride back to the Abbott House. *Would it lead to anything else? Please, God, let him relent. Six years was so long.*

Now she lay in bed, wide awake, waiting for Jeremiah's return from downstairs, where he'd met some friends for a nightcap. She wondered anxiously if he would lay in bed beside her so she could, once again, go to sleep in his arms. Catherine felt a knot of expectation, a glow of hope, growing in her breast.

But it ebbed as the hours dragged by and Jeremiah didn't come. It was almost dawn when Catherine finally gave in to exhaustion. But she came quickly awake when she heard the door open softly, and smelled the aroma of tobacco smoke and brandy. He didn't turn on the gas light and she could hear him shrugging out of his clothes. Catherine felt the bed sag as he lay down. She held her breath.

Jeremiah turned his back to her and was soon softly snoring.

* * * * *

When the train stopped in San Lucas on their return home, Jeremiah escorted Catherine across the street, and while she shopped in Goldwater's store, he went to the post office.

"A letter for you from Ireland, Mister Cleary," the postmistress said. He sat down on the bench in front of the store to look it over. It was postmarked from Cork. Somebody had written it for Liam, or was it bad news about Liam? Finally, Jeremiah took a deep breath and tore it open.

Dear Uncle Jeremiah, it read. He ran his eye to the bottom of the letter. It was signed *Your nephew, Patrick Cleary.* He would be Liam's eldest son, about the same age as Jerry would have been.

He hurriedly read the letter. Not bad news. Good news. Wonderful news! Powerful news! Jeremiah could hardly believe it.

Liam owned the farm!

Liam Cleary was the owner of more than fourteen acres, the Cleary holding in Coolnagurrane, Skibbereen, Ireland.

How did that come about?

My father wants you to know that he has made the first payment to the Land Commission for purchase of our farm. This was made possible by passage of the Land Acts through the efforts of the Land League. The amount of our annual rent, which is thirty pounds, will be paid each year for seventeen years, that being the fair price of our holding. Terry and I have promised father that we will continue the payments if he is ever unable to do so. He asked me to tell you that the Cleary family now owns our own land.

The contents of the letter whirled around in his brain as he helped Catherine into the surrey. All the way up Long Valley to the ranch he mulled it over in his mind. Forty years of memories suddenly came flooding back, memories that Jeremiah had suppressed all this time. He walked the path from Skibbereen up to Coolnagurrane. He saw the furze in bloom, its yellow flower bursting against the green. He went past the Hurley cottage, still whole in his mind, although he knew it had been knocked. And there was the Cleary land, potatoes growing hale and hearty, the blooms lush, the cows cropping grass in the meadow, sheep grazing, pigs and chickens by the door of the whitewashed cottage, which gleamed in the sunlight, cleaned by the morning rain.

And now it belonged to Liam and to his sons. It was still Cleary land. And always would be.

Was it possible? Had Jerry really contributed to that? *Efforts of the Land League,* Patrick had written. The words of the letter cried out to him. He fingered it in his pocket.

The news story in *The Skibbereen Eagle* last year, a clipping which Catherine had left out for him to find, had said the same thing. *Land League Brings Reform.* Jerry had died in the service of the Land League. *Efforts of the Land League,* the words throbbed in his brain. Could it be that his son had died for a purpose, that his death had not been for a useless cause?

If Liam owned the Cleary land, then Jerry's death had real meaning. And, if Jerry died for a purpose, then Jeremiah had wronged Catherine all these years. He didn't know if she would ever forgive him. Or if he could forgive himself.

When they arrived home, Catherine immediately went to change and freshen up. She was taking the pins from her hair when she was startled by a knock on her bedroom door. "Yes?" she called.

"Catherine, I must be talking with you," Jeremiah said through the closed door. "Could you kindly be coming into the parlor?"

Curious, slightly apprehensive, Catherine entered the parlor and found Jeremiah sitting by the window, staring into the garden. He rose when she came in and stood beside her as she seated herself. Silently he handed her Patrick's letter, then sat across from her, watching anxiously as she read it. When she'd finished, Catherine looked up at him and met his eyes. What did he want from her?

"Sure now," she said in a flat voice, "and isn't that just grand."

"Aye, it's grand, Catherine," Jeremiah's words were so soft she could hardly hear him. He walked to the window and again stared out into the garden. He spoke with his back to her, as if he was talking to himself. "Liam owns the Cleary land through efforts of the Land League. Tenant farmers all over Ireland are now able to buy their holdings. Jerry didn't die in vain."

Jeremiah turned back to his wife. "My son was a hero. He died for a grand cause." His pleading eyes looked directly into hers.

"I've wronged you so, Catherine. These past six years since Jerry was killed, I wanted to love you, but I couldn't. I believed that your ideas had taken my son from me for a hopeless cause. I was wrong." Jeremiah's voice broke. "I can't be forgiving myself, Catherine, but could you find it in your heart to forgive me?"

She sat quietly. Her outward serenity hid a turmoil of conflicting emotions. Her heart had leapt at Jeremiah's words. Thank God, he had finally forgiven her. Yet she found herself unable to respond. The years of rejection had left scars that were too deep. She felt a surge of the hurt pride she had thought was long gone. At last she raised her eyes to him.

"I just don't know, Jerry. You'll have to give me some time to think."

She rose and with great dignity left the room. He sat for a time in the darkened parlor with his head in his hands wondering what he could do.

As the days went by, Jeremiah watched her more attentively than he had in years. He saw with new appreciation all the small things she did to make life secure and happy for the family. He found himself aware of her needs and even anticipating them in a way he never had before.

Gradually, in the warmth of his new attention, Catherine found the protective shell she had built around her feelings for Jeremiah starting to dissolve. She was touched by his sometimes clumsy efforts to make amends.

One rainy day she found him trying to restore order to his small, cramped and cluttered room off the kitchen. She stood in the doorway watching for a moment, then said softly, "Jerry, wouldn't it be easier if you just moved your things back into our room?"

He looked up at her and a slow, sweet smile began spreading across his face. He reached out and took her in his arms. "Ah, Cauth," he said, "Cauth darlin'!"

CHAPTER FIFTY-FIVE

WILL CLEARY WAS ABOARD the morning train northbound out of San Lucas. Dressed in a business suit, complete with high collar, tie and stickpin, a gold chain across his vest securing his pocket watch, he was feeling very good about himself. He was on his way to Salinas for an appointment at the bank and he had great expectations. Will had written an application for a loan, asking five thousand dollars to partially finance a new Holt harvester, the innovative combine manufactured in Stockton. The cost would be about seven thousand by the time it was delivered to San Lucas and assembled. This was a sizable investment in 1890, especially for a young man only thirty-one years of age.

But Will had talked it over with his father and Jeremiah had been encouraging. The harvester would require a team of twenty-six horses to pull it through the field, but that was no problem for the Clearys. It would be a huge advantage over a stationary machine.

"They'll work just fine in great, wide, flat fields such as your place, Will, but I don't think they'd work so well here in Long Valley," Jeremiah said. "We've too much rolling ground. But one day, you'll be seeing it, when they'll make them adjustable to pull along these hillsides. Until that day I'll be sticking to the old stationary Fairbanks-Morse."

Jeremiah thought a moment and then added, "You could do the harvesting for some of the Brandenstein tenants as well as for Tom Cross and other farmers on the Trescony. That way a Holt would pay for itself in no time."

Will was thinking of those things as the train sped down the valley. If it worked out as he planned, he'd be asking Mr. Trescony for a lease on more acreage. Will had managed to save some money in the five years that he'd been farming on the Trescony, and he'd never had to borrow any. But this was such a good investment he knew he'd have no trouble. He left the train and made his way to the bank, where, with great confidence, he took a chair across the desk from Charlie Wetzel, who was now president as well as chief lending officer for the Salinas City Bank.

The banker stared solemnly at Will's loan application sitting in front of him on the polished surface of his large mahogany desk. Wetzel picked up the paper and slowly shook his head. Finally he cleared his throat and said, "I'm sorry, Mister Cleary. Please don't take offense, but your youth is against you. I see on your application that you're only thirty-one. The directors don't visualize someone so young as a sound risk."

"But I've been farming on my own for five years now and you can see that I've accumulated some capital."

"Yes," the banker agreed, "but perhaps I should suggest that you use your own capital for any new equipment."

"I really want to conserve my capital for other investments," Will replied. "Certainly the new Holt combine is security enough for the loan."

"Well, under other circumstances, it might be considered so, Mister Cleary. But you must admit that these combines are revolutionary. Will they ever completely take the place of the established makes, the stationary thresher? We have our doubts. And we note that you are a tenant, not a landowner. We'd have no recourse."

"But I do own one hundred and sixty acres," Will protested.

"Yes, I see that you do. But that land is completely surrounded by your father's land and it has no right-of-way. Not very good security for the bank. I'm sorry, Mister Cleary. Perhaps your father would co-sign your note?"

Damned if he'd ask his father to co-sign, Will thought, as he rode the train back to San Lucas in an angry mood. When he stepped down from the train, instead of heading across the river to his own place, he rode his saddle horse up Long Valley, covering ground at a long trot, anxious to tell his father the result of his interview.

"The man's an ass," Jeremiah said when Will repeated Wetzel's remarks. "That bank was very progressive at one time, but they're getting fat and sassy and wouldn't be knowing the worth of a new idea if it jumped up and bit them."

"I don't want you to sign for me, Dad. I'll wait another year or so for the Holt and with decent crops I can pay cash."

"That's all well and good," Jeremiah said. "I'd sign for you in a tick, if you were wanting me to do it. But it's the attitude of that damn Wetzel and his bank that bothers me." Jeremiah was mad. He had no patience with such short-sighted fools. "I've heard there's talk of another bank forming in Salinas. I'll look into that myself."

A month later Jeremiah was celebrating with friends at the Abbott House bar, having just won the top awards at the Seventh District Fair held in Salinas. A Cleary mare with colt had taken first prize in the draft horse class and their Percheron stallion had been judged best of show. Tim had exhibited a team of gray buggy horses, which had been blue ribbon winners and crowd favorites. Only one incident had caused the Clearys some momentary distress.

Earlier that afternoon Jeremiah and Catherine had been sitting in their box by the arena watching the stock horse classes, in which Seamus was showing a well-reined Cleary filly, one the boy had trained himself. He worked the horse before the judges, circling her, backing her, galloping off and then bringing her up in front of the judges to a sliding stop, her hind legs under her. Just perfect.

Jeremiah smiled at the round of applause from spectators. Now they'll really see something, he told himself, as Seamus prepared to work a steer in the live part of the competition.

The filly faced the steer, head down, ears out, alert, ready to move. The steer turned to the left and she reacted, swinging her feet to cut off the animal. The steer came back the other way, and again the filly was right on top of him, turning him back. Seamus didn't use the reins, simply shifted his weight as the horse moved beneath him.

The steer darted to the left and suddenly cut back to the right. The filly swung left, then right, her nimble feet hardly touching the ground.

Then there was a gasp from the crowd.

Suddenly, Seamus was on the ground. The filly, riderless, empty saddle and all, was still working the steer, facing the animal, penning it in the corner. Seamus had trained this horse so well she'd gone out from under him on a turn. She'd moved so swiftly he'd lost his balance. The horse was disqualified because of Seamus' fall, but everyone could see that she was easily the best of the class.

But Seamus looked as if he was about to cry. Catherine started to rise from her seat in the box to go to him, but Jeremiah was already on his way, climbing the railing and stepping onto the track, where Seamus still sat on the ground, tears beginning to roll down his cheeks. Jeremiah put his arm around the boy and helped him to his feet. Seamus picked up his hat and sheepishly looked at his horse.

"There now, Son. There now, it's all right. Your horse did so well, you can be proud. Everyone knows you trained the best one in the class. Catch your horse, lad, and hear them clapping for you."

As Seamus approached the filly she stepped up to him and stood, eyes on him, ears cocked forward, waiting for him, and the audience gave them a standing ovation. Seamus tried to choke off his tears and his sniffles. He rubbed his nose with the back of his hand, swung up, and rode off.

Few among the spectators knew that this tall, handsome, nineteen-year-old cowboy was really just a ten-year-old boy inside. And it was all right for a ten-year-old to cry. So Seamus did, where no one could see him, as he loaded all the Cleary horses into the cattle car, and rode with them on back to San Lucas.

Jeremiah had several offers on the horse, but declined to sell. The fair had added more luster to the fame of Cleary horses, and he figured there'd be more demand than ever. Jeremiah lit up his pipe, well satisfied, and he knew that Seamus would soon forget his embarrassment. Ten-year-olds have a way of getting on with things.

The fine showing of Seamus' filly was still the main topic of conversation in the Abbott House bar that afternoon. "That reminded me of a time long ago," Charlie Levins was saying. "I was at a branding at your place and you were roping off that big sorrel with the blazed face, remember? There was some kind of a wreck, ropes got crossed or something, and you just stepped off onto the fence. That horse of yours was out there in the corral all by himself, just spinning to the right from the weight of the *romal* on his neck. Talk about well-reined horses!"

Jeremiah smiled. Oh yes, he remembered. That sorrel had been one of his favorites. Called him Blaze and hated to sell him. But he had needed the money to help buy another piece of land. Which prompted him to say, "Did you hear that farm property near Gonzales brought three hundred dollars an acre?"

Bill Martin nodded. "Yeah, but that was one-sixty of prime ground, and included a house, a barn, plenty of water and good fences. One of the Tavernettis bought it for four thousand, eight hundred, total."

"Cash or financed?" Jeremiah asked.

"I heard the bank next door gave the money at eight percent interest," Charlie Levins said.

"Eight percent?" Jeremiah questioned.

"High, isn't it?" Levins noted.

"That's about where they are just now," Martin explained.

"If they'll be after lending it at all," Jeremiah growled. "It's a wonder they lent the money, even with security such as that."

"Yeah, they're getting tighter and tighter," Levins agreed. "Don't tell me you're having trouble with the bank, Cleary?"

"Not I," Jeremiah answered. He took a draw on his pipe and knocked it out in his hand. "But it's things I'm hearing. When this country was new the bankers would take the risk along with a man if he had a good, sound idea. But not anymore. It's gilt-edged security they'll be wanting to lend a two-bit piece."

He went back to sipping his brandy as the talk continued about bankers and interest rates, and wages, which had gone back up to two dollars a day, about grain prices and cattle prices. When the conversation turned to politics, and Bill Martin said, "That damned Harrison is no better than Cleveland was — " Jeremiah excused himself. That was a never-ending argument and he had to dress for supper.

Catherine was dressed and ready when he entered the room. Jeremiah noted the stack of bundles and boxes in the corner, apparently sent over from Hales' Department Store, where Catherine had spent several hours shopping. He nodded his approval at the look of her midnight-blue gown and the delicate pearl choker that set off her hair and still soft skin.

The Clearys had just finished their meal and were drinking coffee, when a prosperous-looking man approached their table. He introduced himself as C.L. Menke, a Salinas businessman, and suggested that Jeremiah might like to join him and some friends for a nightcap back at the Abbott House. As soon as Jeremiah had seen Catherine to their room, promising he wouldn't be late, he returned downstairs to find three men waiting for him in the bar.

There were firm handshakes all around as Menke said, "Mister Cleary, meet John Alexander and Gene Palmtag," They all sat down, ordered drinks and took out cigars. Jeremiah waved away the offer and filled his pipe. Menke wasted no time in getting to the point. "Mister Cleary, my asso-

ciates and I are considering the establishment of a new bank
to serve this valley. We are looking for investors."

"Yes," Alexander injected. "We're interested in associating
ourselves with reputable people as stockholders and particularly desire representation on the board from the southern
part of our county. We know you by reputation and you'd be
very welcome should you consider investing with us."

"I see," Jeremiah replied, taking several puffs on his pipe.
"And when your bank is established, gentlemen, will you staff
it with men who aren't afraid of new machinery and new
ideas?"

"Of course, Mister Cleary," Gene Palmtag assured him with
no hesitation. "That is the motivation of those involved in
forming this new bank. You may depend upon it that our goal
will be to assist innovative methods of improving the economy
of our valley, particularly of agriculture."

Well, well now, Jeremiah thought to himself, word certainly
gets around fast. Only that afternoon he'd participated in a
discussion criticizing current banking policies and attitudes,
and here he was being approached by the obvious competition
of the established bank. He'd heard rumors, but was surprised
it had gone this far.

"When is all this happening, this new bank?" he asked.
"When must you be having an answer?"

"We have no intent to rush you, Mister Cleary. But we've
developed a prospectus you might find interesting. I'll mail it
to you," Menke said. "Next time you're in Salinas I could go
over it with you during lunch."

Jeremiah rose from the table, again shaking hands with the
three men. "Thank you, Mister Menke, I'll be doing that. Good
day, gentlemen."

As he lay in bed that night, his arm around the sleeping
Catherine, her head resting on his shoulder, he had to smile to
himself. *It's a bit smug, you are, Jerry Cleary, but you needn't
be thinking you're such a grand one. Still now, it's a long way
you've come when the bankers are looking up the likes of you.*

CHAPTER FIFTY-SIX

CATHERINE PUT THE CLIPPERS into the pocket of her garden-ing smock and let the afternoon breeze cool her. She stood in the shade of tall eucalyptus trees and from her rose garden could see all around the ranch—cattle grazing in the golden stubble, a pasture dotted with draft horses and a few saddle horses, a patch of green where Jeremiah was experimenting with irrigation, the neatly-kept fences, whitewashed barn and outbuildings, and the large equipment shed for the freight wagon, a surrey, the harvester and a variety of other farm implements.

She gathered up her roses and carried them into the empty kitchen where she arranged them in several vases to decorate the dining room. Where was Wah Tuh? She must confer with him about supper. It had to be something special because Will and Honora and their children would be coming. Would Wah Tuh let her help? He was very jealous of his kitchen. Good grief, thought Catherine. His kitchen? Whose kitchen was it, anyhow?

Jeremiah had brought the Chinese cook home from Salinas several years ago when the harvesting crews had grown so large, and there were three regular, year-around ranch hands to be fed. With Kitty and Buck living down at the Thompson place and Annie married to Charlie Phillips and in her own home in Bitter Water, there was more than Catherine could do, even with Peggy's help. Nor did she have Maria Salazar to call upon since Maria and Calistro had moved back to San Juan to be near her aging folks. Jeremiah had given them a thousand dollars when they left. Something no landlord in Ireland would ever do.

Jeremiah had insisted that all meals be prepared in the main kitchen and that all the men eat at the large family table. That's the way things were done at the Jeffersons when he'd first come to California and it had made a great impression on him. So Jeremiah had installed Wah Tuh in the *adobe* bunk house, and given him full reign in the kitchen. Now he'd hardly let Catherine do a thing. But he was an excellent cook and an amiable, good-hearted old tyrant.

Catherine was by the sink, just starting to pump water for her rose vases, when Wah Tuh came bustling into the kitchen. "No, no, Missy," he scolded, taking over at the pump handle. "Wah Tuh fix roses. You get rest." Catherine had to smile because the words came out *loses* and *lest. So, Catherine Hurley Cleary*, she said to herself, *were you ever thinking that one day you'd have your own cook and that he'd be bossing you around?* She reminded him about Will and his family coming for supper and made a hasty exit from the kitchen.

Will! She'd been thinking about him all day. Catherine sat in the parlor and picked up her needlepoint, but it didn't occupy her whole mind. As she stitched the pillow she was working on, she remembered the things she'd heard about Will at Wexler's branding last week.

* * * * *

"Goodness, Cauth, don't you worry about Will carrying all that money?"

"Money? What money, Lucille?"

Catherine and Lucille Wexler, along with several other women from the neighboring ranches, were preparing dinner to be served after Joseph Wexler's branding. They'd been talking about the new Alberto school on the Trescony grant that was named after old man Trescony, who'd left four acres of his land for that purpose. Catherine knew that Will had helped organize the other ranchers to get the new school district approved and had made a generous donation to help build the schoolhouse. That was before Will and his wife, Honora, even had children old enough to go to school. Now they had four, and Will was still serving on the school board. Mary and Nora were sweet little girls at six and seven, but Patrick and his little brother, Matthew, were absolute scamps. Honora dressed them up in Little Lord Fauntleroy outfits, which the boys hated and always managed to ruin the minute they jumped out of their father's surrey.

"Didn't you know, Cauth? Will does most of the banking for south county ranchers. He picks up money for the payrolls during harvest season," Lucille Wexler continued. "Every time he goes to Salinas, he comes back loaded with money, not just for his own crews, but for your husband's and most of the others."

Catherine discovered that Will was indeed taking the morning train to Salinas once a week, doing business at the bank for several of the ranchers, and returning on the evening train. Sometimes he carried several thousand dollars, much of it funds for others.

"Aren't you afraid someone will try to rob him?" Lucille asked. "Everyone knows he does this, and he's going home on that road from San Lucas after dark. But my Joe says that any robber knows Will carries a gun in his buggy."

Good grief, Catherine thought. Robbers, guns? Our Will in danger? Does Honora know? She's so calm about things. If she does worry, she'd never show it. But Catherine appreciated the stories about Will. About the poor families he'd helped, the money he'd loaned, about the times he'd sent hired men, or gone himself, when a farmer was too ill to do his chores, about the many acts of kindness Will did, sometimes without realizing it, and about the entertainments and socials he'd organized for the community, such as the Harvest Ball in San Lucas.

And then there was that incident of the terrible grain fire when Will was custom harvesting for Tom Cross. Everybody was talking about it when she was shopping in Goldwater's store in San Lucas. No one could say for sure how it started. It was in the middle of one of those fierce August heat spells that seared a person's lungs, made it difficult even to breathe, and the suns rays shimmered against the grain. Will himself was driving the twenty-six horse team pulling the new Holt combine, cutting a twenty-four foot swath through the grain, a thick, heavy-headed crop some three feet high. So maybe it was started by sparks from the gears or the wheels striking a rock.

Suddenly somebody yelled, "Fire."

The separator man scrambled to the ground and began to kick and stomp, and swing a sack. Will looked behind him and saw the gray smoke curling up from the windrow of chaff. It slowly moved into the stubble. There was no wind to fan it, so it seemed to smolder in place for a long moment, and then the red flames burst forth and began to lick at the grain on the uncut edge.

The horses smelled the smoke billowing up behind them and turned their heads, unable to see around the blinders, but frightened, and began to neigh, and rear up in their harness. The other men had climbed down from the harvester, and were slapping at the flames with sacks, but the fire gained momentum. It began to race through the grain toward the harvester.

Will yelled at the horses, and tried to put the team into a run, but the horses were unmanageable. He realized they'd never pull the combine from the path of the fire. He jumped down and hurriedly unhitched them, starting with the two leaders. Several of the five-man crew left the blaze and ran to help him. They quickly separated the six-horse spans, leading the frantic animals from the approaching flames and to the edge of the field safely out of the way.

But Will had to leave his new Holt combine in the field.

How on earth the fire missed the harvester, no one knew. But it did. There it was when the flames died down, sitting amid the blackened stubble, one side scorched, but otherwise unharmed. But Tom Cross' crop was totally destroyed.

"And do you know, Cauth," a woman told her. "That son of yours insisted on covering half of what Tom lost after the crop insurance. Said it must have been his fault because his combine caused the fire. Fires happen all the time. It wasn't his fault. He didn't have to do that. But he did. You can be so proud of him."

Catherine was proud of him and she knew Jeremiah was, though he'd never say so. Yes, Will certainly was becoming widely known and well thought of throughout south county. His farming practices were so successful that many others were following them. Where he'd once been the subject of criticism for his progressive methods, Will was now well respected. There was talk up and down the valley now about putting Will up for Monterey County supervisor. Catherine learned that a delegation had called upon him, including Andy Copley and J.A. Trescony, both former supervisors and men of importance in the valley, to encourage Will to run.

And that young editor of the new *Salinas Valley Settler,* Fred Godfrey, had written some flattering articles about Will Cleary. Godfrey and his wife had stopped off at the Long Valley ranch when they were driving around the countryside, getting acquainted with the area, and Catherine had invited them in for tea. Godfrey had wanted to interview Jeremiah about his irrigation project. But Jeremiah had declined and suggested that the newspaperman interview his son instead.

Will didn't even have to campaign, except for political cards in the *San Lucas Herald* and *The Settler* and some posters scattered around. When the votes were counted, Will had won by a landslide. He carried every precinct and San Lucas went for Will Cleary seventy-seven to three.

"I'd hate to find out who those three were," Will said with a big grin. "Might be my relatives."

At age thirty-five he became the youngest supervisor on the board. Jeremiah was proud of his son to the bursting point, but he'd die before he'd show it or mention it to anyone.

CHAPTER FIFTY-SEVEN

A<small>T SIXTY-THREE YEARS OF AGE,</small> Jeremiah Cleary still stood ramrod straight. His thick hair was completely gray, but his body had remained lean and muscular and he rode his horse with the same grace and ease as the young cowboys who worked on his ranch. Today Jeremiah was dressed in a crisp white shirt, his black string tie knotted just so after four attempts, his three-piece business suit impeccable, a gold watch chain draped across the front of his vest, and his derby squared on his head in a dignified set. He strode briskly along Main Street in Salinas. With the prospectus in hand for the new First National Bank of Salinas, he was fighting a sense of self-importance as he entered the office building to meet C.L. Menke for their luncheon appointment.

A few moments later Jeremiah and the banker were walking down Market Street toward the Harvest Grill, engaged in friendly conversation. Jeremiah never would have noticed the man washing the windows of the Lucky Shamrock Saloon if he hadn't had to jump aside to avoid being splashed by soapy water. Irritated, Jeremiah glanced at the swamper, who immediately turned away, toward the dim interior of the bar. Jeremiah stopped in front of the place. He was curious. There was something familiar about that man.

Uncertain what to do, Jeremiah stood for a second by the saloon door, then turned to Menke. "Please excuse me," he muttered, "I'll be right back."

Menke looked a little puzzled, but said, "Of course."

Jeremiah followed the swamper into the gloom and was immediately assailed by the odor of stale beer and tobacco smoke. When Jeremiah had adjusted his eyes to the light, he spotted the man in the furthest, darkest corner of the saloon, sitting slumped at a table, his head turned away.

Jeremiah walked over to the table. "Matt?" he asked. The man raised his bleary eyes. It was his brother. Slowly he stood up. "Aye, it's me, Jerry," he said. But he looked so old, so wrinkled and haggard. His tall frame was even thinner and he was slightly stooped. His Levis and flannel shirt were ragged.

"Matthew, my brother. What are you doing here?"

"I work here, " Matthew muttered, waving his hand at the nearby bucket and mop. "I clean up the place." He sank back into his chair.

Jeremiah sat down, reached out and laid his hand over Matthew's hand, trembling on the table top. "Matt, what's wrong? Are you sick?"

"Wrong? Nothing's wrong. I'm fine. And how's yourself?" he spoke with a hint of his old spirit. "Don't you be worrying about me." Matthew shook off Jeremiah's consoling hand. "You go on with your high and mighty friend." He nodded at the doorway where Menke was standing, looking somewhat impatient as he peered into the saloon.

Jeremiah saw the banker waiting for him. *Good Lord, what will he think? And here he is inviting me to join his bank. Will he still want me if he finds out this derelict is my brother?* Jeremiah looked back at Matthew. "I have a meeting. I'll be back in an hour and we'll talk. Stay right here. Wait for me."

"Why should I?"

"My God, man. I'm your brother. I haven't seen you for thirteen years. I want to talk with you."

Matthew gave his brother a long, steady look, then nodded. "I'll be here."

Menke was waiting for Jeremiah on the street. With a raised eyebrow, he inquired, "And who was that?"

They'd started to walk on together, but Jeremiah stopped, faced him and took a deep breath. He looked the banker straight in the eye, and replied, "He's my brother."

They went on to the restaurant without exchanging a word and sat at their table. Jeremiah wondered what Menke might say, but the banker didn't question him further. They ordered and when the waiter left, Menke pleasantly surprised him by restating the invitation for Jeremiah to become a charter stockholder and serve on the board of the new First National Bank of Salinas. Jeremiah thanked the banker, but said that there were a few points in the prospectus that he'd like to discuss. But it was difficult to keep his mind on Menke's explanations. He kept picturing Matthew, waiting for him back there in the saloon. It seemed to Jeremiah that it took forever to be served and that the meal took even longer to eat.

"Everything seems very satisfactory to me," he told Menke, trying not to sound too abrupt. "I'll stop in your office tomorrow morning with my answer. But you'll have to excuse me now." Jeremiah took out his watch and flipped open the case. Two hours had gone by. He hoped Matthew hadn't left. He snapped the case shut and hurried from the restaurant, replacing the watch in his vest as he went.

Matthew was sitting against the far wall of the Lucky Shamrock, a bottle of Old Overholt and two small glasses on the table in front of him. He filled both glasses as Jeremiah joined him.

"Will you be having one with me, Brother?" he asked, a challenge in his eye. Jeremiah returned the look and picked up the other glass. "*Slainte*," Matthew said as they clinked their glasses together.

"Now, Matt, tell me how things are with you." Jeremiah's concern was deep and caring.

"Fine, fine," Matthew said. Then he glanced around the dismal saloon. "Up and down, up and down," he amended. "What about you, Jerry? Sure and don't you look the prosperous one. That farming finally paying off?"

"Good years and bad years," Jeremiah answered.

Matthew nodded. "Mining was the same. I hit it big for a while, Jerry. We were following a grand vein of gold and my share was mounting up — " He stopped and let his voice trail off.

"Well then, why didn't you let me know? You could have come back for Connie, made a life for yourself."

"Let you know?" Matthew half rose from his seat and glared at his brother. "And wasn't it yourself that told me to stay away from you and your family?"

"I was provoked."

Matthew slowly sank back into his chair. "Aye, that was a damn fool thing I did, Jerry. But you don't have a forgiving bone in your body, either."

"Sure and it's me here now, isn't it?"

"Don't be doing me any favors with your high and mighty presence, Jerry Cleary. Who needs you?"

"And don't you be so goddammed touchy," Jeremiah retorted. "I'm your brother and I'm wanting to know about you."

Mollified for the moment, Matthew poured himself another shot and motioned toward Jeremiah, who shook his head, but picked up his half-full glass for another sip. Matthew studied his brother out of red-rimmed eyes, and then said. "Well, I returned to Los Burros and worked the Tarantula, the one I'd traded for with Willie Cruikshank, and it paid well for a while. I thought I'd finally made my big strike. But I couldn't go back to Long Valley." He looked sideways at Jeremiah. "So I went up to San Francisco to celebrate. I figured there was plenty more gold where that had come from, so I spent it." He gave Jeremiah a crooked grin. "There're a lot of good poker players in San Francisco," he said. "Right. Wine, women and song, as they say. Easy come, easy go." Matthew gave his brother a defiant grin and tossed off his whiskey.

"And then?" Jeremiah prodded.

"The damn vein gave out. It didn't even pay wages, so we closed her down. Shut her up. And right next to us was the claim I'd traded to Willie, the Last Chance, and he was taking out millions." Matthew gave a sardonic laugh. "Ain't that the luck of the Irish?"

"So what did you do?"

"Well, I went back into Monterey for a bit. Did some black-smithing. Went back to Los Burros and mucked around for a while, but nothing turned out — " The brothers sat in silence for a few moments and then Matthew filled his glass again and finally asked, "What about Connie? How is she, Jerry?"

"She's fine, Matt. Just fine. Grew into a beautiful woman, a grand person." Jeremiah said. "She's married."

"Aye. I know."

Jeremiah raised an inquiring eyebrow. Matthew sighed. "When I was in Monterey I was watching on the street as this fancy carriage went past. I thought I recognized Connie—but it had been so long — " He took a deep breath and continued. "Then I heard about the wedding, so I took a look in the mission church and a peek at the party after. Some celebration."

"Why didn't you make yourself known?" Jeremiah asked.

"Sure and wouldn't that have been something now? Me being introduced to that Baxter bunch? And this is Connie's father, is it? How nice! They'd have called off the wedding. No, Brother, you were more the one to be doing the honors, prancing up the aisle in your grand duds with my daughter on your arm like you were the bloody King of England." Again he gave the bitter laugh and then lapsed into silence.

Jeremiah didn't know how to reply without raising Matthew's ire all over again. So he sat quietly, too. Then his brother asked, "Have you seen Connie? Is he good to her? How is she?"

"Annie visited her at her home in San Francisco. Connie was fine. Annie said the house was huge, on the top of Nob Hill, with servants and all—just like you promised her."

"Only someone else gave it to her," Matthew muttered. "She probably doesn't even remember me. And who could be blaming her?" Matthew filled his glass. "Jerry," he asked. "Are you ever thinking of home?"

"Home?" Jeremiah asked.

"Aye, Skibbereen."

"Well now," Jeremiah answered, happy to have a new subject. "Things are just grand in Ireland. Liam owns the land."

"Owns the land? The Cleary holding?" Matthew was amazed. "And how could that be?"

"The bloody Brits finally passed some land reform acts, forced on them by an organization called the Land League," Jeremiah explained. "My Jerry was a hero in the cause of the Land League. Killed, he was, in defense of a cottage at Drimoleague back in eighteen-eighty."

"Ah, Jerry, I didn't know. He was a fine, bright lad, always had a bit of fun in him. I'm sorry."

"Well—Liam is buying the farm from the Land Commission, so much a year instead of paying rent," Jeremiah said. "I never thought the day would come that the Clearys would be owning their own land in Ireland."

"And you're owning your own land here in America." Matthew picked up the bottle of whiskey. "Well then, that calls for a drink. Would you be joining me?" Jeremiah accepted a bit more from the half-empty bottle and they raised their glasses. *"An Sciobairin!"* they cried in unison.

"Those were the days," Matthew said.

"My God, Matt, have you forgotten how we starved, how they made us grovel, tried to make us feel we were less than human?"

"I was thinking more of when we were lads, chasing the *colleens,* singing and dancing at the crossroads. I've forgotten the rest."

"Not me," Jeremiah said. "I've tried to forget, to put those awful, terrible days behind me, but always they're there, festering in the back of my mind." He sat in silence, thinking about Matthew, still seeing the fun, never the serious side of things, even now.

"And Jerry, remember when we were in line to get off the ship in Boston, the good old Sir Willard Pottinger, and they were asking us our birthdays? We had no papers and I wasn't knowing my birthday. Not for sure. So when you told him December twenty-fifth, I said, March seventeenth." Matthew laughed. "Sure, if it was good enough for St. Patrick, it was good enough for me."

"I don't want to be remembering that ship ever again, Matt. It was godawful."

"Come on, Jerry. Be thinking of the good times," Matthew said. "You always were the sobersides, with your nose in a book. But we did have some good times before the famine and, then again, there in Boston. Remember those *hooleys* up at John Hurley's place? All the *colleens* were giving you the eye. You could have had your pick."

But what Jeremiah remembered was keeping his eye on Matthew as he drank and danced the jigs and disappeared outside with the various girls. But he nodded amiably. "And that time in Panama," Matthew recalled with a laugh. "Oh, that was a grand town. And weren't we the ones to get a skinful that night?"

You did, Jeremiah thought. *But it was me who saved you from that whore and her thug when they were rolling you for your money. And carried you away from harm and watched over you until you sobered up. You have a selective memory, my brother.*

Jeremiah asked after a moment, "You could have stayed with me on the land, Matt. Any regrets?"

"Regrets? Of course not!" Matthew looked pensive. "Well now, maybe one or two. Lupe, for one. I really did love her. And Connie — " He looked directly at Jeremiah. "I loved that little girl and I did miss her. I wanted to come back to her." He shook his head sadly and Jeremiah saw tears gather in the corners of his brother's eyes. Matthew lifted the bottle of whiskey from the table and turned it around in his hands, holding it to the dim light, studying it. There was a great sadness in his voice. "It was that I loved this more."

Jeremiah reached for Matthew's hand. "Come home with me, Matt. Back to the ranch. You can live there."

Matthew snatched his hand back with a jerk and sat up straight in his chair. "I will not!" he exclaimed vehemently. "I'll take no man's charity. I make my own way."

Jeremiah glanced around the shabby saloon, appraising it. Matthew scowled. "I like it. I have a little room in back and I earn my keep. My money's my own, enough for this." He indicated the whiskey bottle. "And enough to eat. And if any man doesn't like it, to hell with him."

They talked all afternoon and Jeremiah noted that Matthew, who'd been steadily drinking the whole time, appeared to be no drunker than when he'd first found him. Finally, Jeremiah consulted his time piece and realized he was to meet Catherine at the Abbott House in a few minutes. He invited Matthew to join them for supper.

"And wouldn't that be a sight to behold? Me waltzing into the Abbot House?" Matthew laughed. "No, Jerry," he said. "I'm after thanking you. But that's not my part of town."

Jeremiah nodded. "Then we'll have dinner together tomorrow noon. I'll come by and meet you here."

"You could," Matthew said. "Maybe."

The next day, at twelve sharp, Jeremiah entered the Lucky Shamrock and eagerly searched the dark, dingy barroom for his brother. Matthew wasn't at the table in the back. He wasn't anywhere. Jeremiah stepped up to the bar. "That man I visited with here yesterday? The swamper that lives in the back?" Jeremiah asked the bartender. "Is he around?"

"Swamper?" the bartender asked, puzzled. "Nobody lives in the back. Oh, you mean that old drunk? I paid him a dollar for washing the windows and he left."

Jeremiah walked from the Lucky Shamrock with a heavy heart. He wondered if he'd ever see Matthew again. And although he searched for him each time he came to Salinas, he never did.

CHAPTER FIFTY-EIGHT

JEREMIAH POLITELY HELD THE CHAIR for Catherine and then seated himself next to Will at the head of the table. This was Will's night and the entire Cleary family had gathered to honor him.

Annie Phillips looked over at her father. This was a big moment for him, she knew, basking in Will's success. She was proud of her brother, too. But being eight months pregnant, and with a *deeshy* one—as Aunt Cauth would say—squirming by her side, Annie was worn out.

There'd been some critical looks cast her way when she entered the reception room at the Abbott house. There were those puritanical folks who thought it inappropriate for a woman to appear in public when pregnant. But Annie didn't want to miss Will's big moment and Charlie had agreed, allowing her to attend. It had been a great day, but now Annie was ready for it to end. She thought wistfully of that soft bed reserved for her upstairs.

Early that afternoon the family had taken up two rows of benches in the court house meeting room to witness the swearing-in ceremony. Will Cleary stood up before the presiding judge of the superior court of Monterey County and took the oath, pledging to serve the people of the county, the State of California, and the United States of America.

Then he took his seat at the table with the four other supervisors. Chairman Fields of Monterey shook his hand and welcomed Will Cleary to the board. He was now the sworn representative of south county, supervisor of the fourth district. Jeremiah shifted in his seat, struggling to conceal his pride, as he watched his son.

Since there wasn't any real business before the county board that day, this first meeting of January 1890, was mostly ceremonial, seating the newly-elected member, choosing a chairman, and getting organized. They allowed Will to make his first motion, the one to adjourn, and everybody had a good laugh.

· Then the photographer, an officious little man who took far too long getting just the right pose on the courthouse steps, held things up for almost an hour as he moved county officials this way and that, popping his head in and out of the black hood covering his camera.

Finally, it was time for the reception, and the supervisors gathered with their families and guests in the main room of the Abbott House. Visitors, all the people of Salinas and half the people of the county, it seemed, dropped in to meet Will Cleary. He was congratulated, his hand pumped, his wife, Honora, presented, his children admired, his views solicited. He took it all with a pleasant smile. He decided to enjoy the moment, but he knew it would pass. Just as soon as he took an unpopular stand on some issue, he told himself.

A short while later the Cleary family came together in the private dining room upstairs. Will finally stopped roaming around the room and took his place between Jeremiah and Honora, who kept her four children under control with a nod here and a frown there.

Jeremiah looked down at the end of the table where Kitty sat with Buck, five-year-old Bucky between them, and baby Julie, squirming on her lap. Jeremiah was always startled by his daughter's beauty, especially when she dressed up for special occasions, such as this. There was more than a hint of Molly in her that tugged his heart. He'd become used to seeing Kitty on a horse and admitted she'd been a good hand, but she was a homebody now, and seemed happy in motherhood.

Buck, now there was a fine son-in-law, Jeremiah thought. He managed the cattle operation for Cleary Ranches, and Seamus was his shadow. Buck was good to the boy. Jeremiah thanked God for leaving Seamus the ability to handle horses.

There was Tim, tall and lean, still unmarried at thirty-three. Amy Barnes had long ago rejected him and ranch life, and gone to live in the big city by the bay. But Tim had never quite gotten over her. He'd become almost a recluse socially. Jeremiah wondered if he'd ever marry now. Ah well, at least he was a successful rancher with his own homestead and farming a big piece of the Brandenstein's land near San Ardo.

Jeremiah gazed for a moment at Peggy, who looked exactly like Catherine—even sounded like her, except for Catherine's soft brogue—and Peggy's husband, Joe Carrigan, who ran the livery stable in San Lucas. Jeremiah liked his son-in-law's progressive thinking. Joe was planning to add a line of steam carriages to his livery business as soon as they were perfected. Jeremiah couldn't stand the idea of the damn things, but he knew they were coming. Either them or the gas buggies, he groused to himself.

Annie caught his eye and gave him a smile. He smiled back, but he noted how tired she looked. Never marry a clod buster, wouldn't she now? Our school teacher had settled in after all, wife of quiet, amiable Charlie Phillips, Bitter Water farmer and sheepman. Sheepman, it was. But, ah well, he was a fine man for all of that and a good husband to Annie.

Sitting next to his daughter was his niece, Connie Baxter, who had come down from San Francisco with her husband Christopher to honor Will. So much like her mother with her dark beauty and graceful bearing, Jeremiah thought, remembering Lupe Morales. But Annie had told him how badly Connie wanted a child and he saw how Connie spoiled Annie's children whenever she could.

His gaze fell on the black coat and white collar of his son, Danny, on leave from the seminary. Father Daniel Cleary, he'd soon be, and it was still a puzzle to Jeremiah. A handsome lad who always had his pick of the girls in San Jose, as well as those in Long Valley. But 'the calling' had come to him as he finished college at Santa Clara—and he had surprised his family when he told them he had chosen to serve God. Was it a way to atone for his unwitting part as a child in his mother's death?

Jeremiah wondered. Still they all knew Dan would be a good priest. And wouldn't Molly be proud and pleased. An American family we may be, Jeremiah thought, but there's a bit of the Irish tradition here. One for the church and one for the road, as the saying goes.

One for the road. That was his Jerry. Jeremiah felt that familiar clutch in his heart. If only Jerry were here to share this. His mind went back to the description he'd received long ago of the inscription on the Jerry's tombstone in Skibbereen—*Jeremiah Cleary Jr. 1861-1880. He died for Ireland*—Then, as if reading her husband's mind, Catherine turned to him, smiling lovingly.

Danny said grace, thanking the Lord for the bounty bestowed on this family, and Will, in response to raucous demands of "Speech, speech!" rose up from his chair, grinning proudly at everyone. He expressed his thanks for "the support of my wonderful parents and this entire family. I'll always be grateful that I'm a Cleary and I hope you'll always claim me."

The family cheered and applauded and Jeremiah thought his heart would burst with the joy and gratitude that he felt. *Our Will, my son, taking his place as an elected leader in the government of this nation. Oh sure, it's but a small bit of our American democracy, but it's the grass roots and that's where it all starts. And now a Cleary has a hand in it.*

He looked down that long table again, blinked back the tears that clouded his vision of these children whom Catherine had mothered, and their grandchildren, and he savored the thought. He reached under the table for Catherine's hand. "Cauth," he said, "Cauth darlin' — "

She looked up at him and saw the emotion on his face, his mouth curved in that old sweet smile. He looked, once more, around the table, then back to her. She smiled and nodded her understanding. To have arrived at this proud point in his life made all the hardships, adversities, and even tragedies, worth it. He could look back over his life and know that it was well lived. The proof was in front of him now, in his children, and in their children. And he couldn't leave them a better legacy than the land he had worked so hard to gain, the freedoms he'd found in it and the love he felt for it. If Jeremiah knew anything, he knew that.